T0210532

Lecture Notes in Computer Science 8850

Commenced Publication in 1973
Founding and Former Series Editors:
Gerhard Goos, Juris Hartmanis, and Jan van Leeuwen

More information about this series at http://www.springer.com/series/7409

Emile Aarts · Boris de Ruyter
Panos Markopoulos · Evert van Loenen
Reiner Wichert · Ben Schouten
Jacques Terken · Rob Van Kranenburg
Elke Den Ouden · Gregory O'Hare (Eds.)

Ambient Intelligence

European Conference, AmI 2014
Eindhoven, The Netherlands, November 11–13, 2014
Revised Selected Papers

 Springer

Editors

Emile Aarts
Technische Universiteit Eindhoven
Eindhoven
The Netherlands

Boris de Ruyter
Philips Research Europe
Eindhoven
The Netherlands

Panos Markopoulos
Technische Universiteit Eindhoven
Eindhoven
The Netherlands

Evert van Loenen
Philips Research
Eindhoven
The Netherlands

Reiner Wichert
Fraunhofer IGD
Darmstadt
Germany

Ben Schouten
Technische Universiteit Eindhoven
Eindhoven
The Netherlands

Jacques Terken
Technische Universiteit Eindhoven
Eindhoven
The Netherlands

Rob Van Kranenburg
Waag Society
Amsterdam
The Netherlands

Elke Den Ouden
Technische Universiteit Eindhoven
Eindhoven
The Netherlands

Gregory O'Hare
University College Dublin
Dublin 4
Ireland

ISSN 0302-9743
Lecture Notes in Computer Science
ISBN 978-3-319-14111-4
DOI 10.1007/978-3-319-14112-1

ISSN 1611-3349   (electronic)

ISBN 978-3-319-14112-1   (eBook)

Library of Congress Control Number: 2014958742

LNCS Sublibrary: SL3 – Information Systems and Applications, incl. Internet/Web, and HCI

Springer Cham Heidelberg New York Dordrecht London

Printed on acid-free paper

Springer International Publishing AG Switzerland is part of Springer Science+Business Media
(www.springer.com)

Preface

The annual Ambient Intelligence conference is the prime venue for research on ambient intelligence, with an international and interdisciplinary character. It brings together researchers from the fields of science, engineering, and, design working toward the vision of ambient intelligence.

Volume 8850 of Springer's LNCS series is the formal proceedings of the 11th event in the Ambient Intelligence series, an event that took place in Eindhoven, the place where the conference first started in 2003 as a European Symposium on Ambient Intelligence. The return of the conference to its birthplace is not a superficial coincidence. It reflects the need for this conference and the community of researchers it serves to define their own identity and direction for the future, and the realization that while much of the original ambitions for this research field have been realized a lot remains still to be done.

Since the emergence of ambient intelligence as a vision on consumer electronics, telecommunications, and computing technologies for the time frame 2010–2020 much has changed. The original conceptions of the field discussed, e.g., by Harwig and Aarts[1] still drive current developments." Researchers are still working towards embedding technology in the environment, supporting context awareness, personalization, and adaptivity of ambient intelligence technologies, and even adapting system behavior autonomously to meet user's needs. These ambitions take new meaning and a higher complexity nowadays as they pertain to more numerous, miniaturized, and complex devices than foreseen in the early days of the field. On the other hand, early scenarios of ambient intelligence, as for example those of the ISTAG advisory group which Europeans researched for more than a decade, are starting to reach the consumer market and to become a part of our daily lives. As ambient intelligence is applied in different application domains and new themes arise for the field, it became necessary to explore in-depth some of the most vibrant areas of research in ambient intelligence.

In 2014, the AmI conference was thus organized along a set of thematic tracks, which cover current areas of research in ambient intelligence. These tracks were led by each of the editors of this volume, who recruited specialized reviewers. Track chairs proposed rankings of articles which were merged in a process moderated by the program chairs of the conference. The tracks for AmI 2014 are the following:

- Ambient Assisted Living
- Internet of Things
- Ambient Play and Learning
- Smart Buildings and Cities
- Intelligent Driving
- Data Science

---

[1] Harwig, R., & Aarts, E. (2002). Ambient intelligence: invisible electronics emerging. In Interconnect Technology Conference, 2002. Proceedings of the IEEE 2002 International (pp. 3–5). IEEE.

- Smart Healthcare and Healing Environments
- Ambient Persuasion
- New and Emerging Themes

Full and short papers were reviewed in a single review process, where reviewers were advised to adjust their expectations on completeness of the work and the contribution expected from each paper to its length. Each paper was reviewed by at least two reviewers, and the median number of reviews was 3. On the basis of this review, a ranking was made and a selection of the papers suitable for inclusion in the proceedings and for presentation at the conference resulted in accepting 26 out of the 59 papers submitted (acceptance rate 46 %).

We hope that this collaborative effort has resulted in a rewarding volume that captures current trends and evolving themes in this field, and helps as a reference point for researchers, students, and industry.

We wish to thank all authors for contributing their work, and the reviewers for the effort they have put in the selection process and in providing feedback to help authors improve the presentation of their work.

October 2014
Emile Aarts
Boris de Ruyter
Panos Markopoulos
Evert van Loenen

Organization

Organizing Committee

General Chairs

Emile Aarts
Boris de Ruyter

Program Chairs

Panos Markopoulos
Evert van Loenen

Theme Chairs

Ambient Assisted Living	Reiner Wichert
Internet of Things	Rob van Kranenburg
Ambient Play and Learning	Ben Schouten
Smart Buildings and Cities	Elke den Ouden
Intelligent Driving	Jacques Terken
Data Science	Emile Aarts
Smart Healthcare and Healing Environments	Evert van Loenen
Ambient Persuasion	Panos Markopoulos
New and Emerging Themes	Gregory O'Hare

Review Committee

Kenro Aihara	National Institute of Informatics, Japan
Margherita Antona	ICS-FORTH, Greece
Carmelo Ardito	University of Bari, Italy
Juan Carlos Augusto	Middlesex University, UK
Matthias Baldau	FTW Telecommunications Research Center Vienna, Austria
Emilia Barakova	Einhoven University of Technology, The Netherlands
Ellis Bartholomeus	Ellisinwonderland, The Netherlands
Robbert Jan Beun	Utrecht University, The Netherlands
Rafael Bidarra	Delft University of Technology, The Netherlands
Lars Braubach	University of Hamburg, Germany

Pamela Briggs	Northumbria University, UK
Javier Caminero	Telefonica R&D, Spain
Charitos	National and Kapodistrian University of Athens, Greece
Yiqiang Chen	ICT/CAS, China
Wei Chen	Eindhoven University of Technology, The Netherlands
Adrian Cheok	Keio University, Japan
Stefano Chessa	University of Pisa, Italy
Mauro Dragone	University College Dublin, Ireland
Markus Endler	Pontifical Catholic University of Rio de Janeiro (PUC-Rio), Brazil
Babak A. Farshchian	SINTEF ICT, Norway
Peter Froehlich	FTW Telecommunications Research Center Vienna, Austria
Kaori Fujinami	Tokyo University of Agriculture and Technology, Japan
Francesco Furfari	CNR-ISTI, Italy
Sarah Gallacher	University College London, UK
Pedro Gamito	ULHT, Portugal
Matjaz Gams	Jožef Stefan Institute, Slovenia
Maria Ganzha	University of Gdańsk, Poland
Nikolaos Georgantas	Inria, France
Dimitris Grammenos	FORTH-ICS, Greece
Hans W. Guesgen	Massey University, New Zealand
Jaap Ham	Eindhoven University of Technology, The Netherlands
Weili Han	Fudan University, China
Otthein Herzog	TZI, Universität Bremen, Germany
Peizhao Hu	NICTA, Australia
Christine Julien	University of Texas at Austin, USA
Achilles Kameas	Hellenic Open University, Greece
Julia Kantorovitch	VTT Technical Research Centre of Finland, Finland
Maurits Kaptein	Eindhoven University of Technology, The Netherlands
Evangelos Karapanos	Madeira Interactive Technologies Institute, Portugal
Vassilis-Javed Khan	NHTV University of Applied Sciences, Academy for Digital Entertainment, The Netherlands
Vassilis Kostakos	University of Oulu, Finland
Matthias Kranz	Universität Passau, Germany
Andrew Kun	University of New Hampshire, USA
Joyca Lacroix	Philips Research, The Netherlands

Rosa Lanzilotti	University of Bari, Italy
David Lillis	University College Dublin, Ireland
Brian Lim	Fraunhofer Center for Sustainable Energy Systems, USA
Johan Lukkien	Eindhoven University of Technology, The Netherlands
Mitja Lustrek	Jožef Stefan Institute, Slovenia
Antonio Mana	University of Málaga, Spain
Bruce Mehler	MIT, USA
Alexander Meschtscherjakov	University of Salzburg, Austria
Florian Floyd Mueller	RMIT University, Australia
Mirco Musolesi	University of Birmingham, UK
John O'Donoghue	University College Cork, Ireland
Harri Oinas-Kukkonen	University of Oulu, Finland
Zoltan Papp	TNO, The Netherlands
Fabio Paterno	CNUCE-CNR, Italy
Bastian Pfleging	University of Stuttgart, Germany
Santi Phithakkitnukoon	The Open University, UK
Susanna Pirttikangas	University of Oulu, Finland
Aske Plaat	University of Leiden, The Netherlands
Andreas Riener	Johannes Kepler University Linz, Institute for Pervasive Computing, Austria
Natalia Romero	Technical University of Delft, The Netherlands
Alex Rosemann	Eindhoven University of Technology, The Netherlands
Marco Rozendaal	Technical University of Delft, The Netherlands
Sean Russell	University College Dublin, Ireland
Albert Salah	Boğaziçi University, Turkey
Moises Sanchez	University College Dublin, Ireland
Carmen Santoro	ISTI-CNR, Italy
Thomas Schlegel	TU Dresden, Germany
Ronald Schroeter	QUT – CARRS-Q, Australia
Antonio Skarmeta	University of Murcia, Spain
Iris Soute	Eindhoven University of Technology, The Netherlands
Anna Spagnolli	University of Padova, Italy
Kostas Stathis	Royal Holloway, University of London, UK
Teck-Hou Teng	Nanyang Technological University, Singapore
Oscar Tomico	Eindhoven University of Technology, The Netherlands
Manfred Tscheligi	University of Salzburg, Austria
Stefano Valtolina	Universitá degli Studi di Milano, Italy
Erik Van Der Spek	Eindhoven University of Technology, The Netherlands
Aart Van Halteren	Philips Research, The Netherlands

Contents

Analyzing Sounds of Home Environment for Device Recognition

Svilen Dimitrov, Jochen Britz[(✉)], Boris Brandherm,
and Jochen Frey

Deutsche Forschungszentrum für Künstliche Intelligenz, Saarbrücken, Germany
{Svilen.Dimitrov,Jochen.Britz,Boris.Brandherm,
Jochen.Frey}@dfki.de

Abstract. Home environments are one of the subjects of study regarding ambient intelligent systems for various purposes, including development of assistance systems for the elderly and energy consumption optimization. Sensing the environmental state via different sensors is the first and crucial component of every ambient intelligent system. In this work we investigate the use of environmental sounds for touch-free audio-based device recognition in a home environment. For this purpose, we analyzed sound characteristics of typical home appliances using different processing techniques. We are using the acquired knowledge to develop a flexible set of features, which can be set manually or determined automatically. To classify the device-specific acoustic fingerprints – consisting of a significant subset of our features – we use established supervised learning techniques, whereby we optimized the straightforward ones. After building a recognition basis for the recognition of fixed length sound buffers on demand, we implemented a live recognition mode for real-time environment monitoring, providing runtime setup adjustments. We then extended our work with the recognition of untrained, simultaneously working, known devices by mixing their records, utilizing semi-supervised learning. We then anticipated promising results in our evaluation in various aspects, including recognition rate, performance for the different combinations of features, as well as to study the reliability of an automatic mixing of trained data.

Keywords: Ambient Intelligence · Smart Home · Sound-based Device Recognition

1 Introduction

In our modern way of life we are surrounded by an increasing number of devices, which we use to perform a large variety of activities. Some of those activities are not always straightforward and we often need some assistance to perform them. To make this happen, one has to give some intelligence to the devices to make them able to understand our intentions and to fit into our needs. In other words: making those devices sensitive and responsive to our presence, instead of relying on us to learn how to operate them. Making the devices more sensitive to human actions is one of the goals

© Springer International Publishing Switzerland 2014
E. Aarts et al. (Eds.): AmI 2014, LNCS 8850, pp. 1–16, 2014.
DOI: 10.1007/978-3-319-14112-1_1

in the notion of activity recognition. This is the first step of designing a so called ambient intelligent system, which at first anticipates human actions with their purpose in a given environment, and then acts in an intelligent manner by predicting and assisting future actions. This should hold especially in the case, where humans are experiencing difficulties in performing those actions, but there are many further applications, such as optimizing electrical energy consumption.

In this work we study the sensing component of an ambient intelligent system. Such a component utilizes sensors and techniques to process their data in order to extract the desired information about the environment. Most studied techniques for this task, in respect to the human perception, are using visual and haptic sensors. Considering our perception, an additional way to sense the environment is by the perceived sounds. For this purpose, we introduce our Sound-based Device Recognition Framework – a fully developed system for device recognition based on analyzing environmental sounds. Our environment consists of a normal home. Its devices are commonly used for performing daily tasks, like the electrical toothbrush, the shaver, or the washing machine. Most of those devices create or disperse sounds, while being used to perform different activities. We study the most frequently used devices and the nature of the sounds, which accompany their usage. We then use this knowledge to transform those sounds to different acoustic representations in order to extract their most telling characteristics for the purpose of sound-based device fingerprinting. For the gathering of acoustic fingerprints we build a database, which is later used as a knowledgebase for further classification tasks. The latter are performed by trying out different machine learning algorithms and evaluating their performance in terms of complexity, recognition accuracy and adaptation capability. We then expand our work by adding further system capabilities, like live recognition using buffers of variable length and automatic mixing of different sounds for then the recognition of untrained combinations of known devices. Finally, we evaluate different aspects of the implemented recognition techniques in a smart home setup.

2   Related Work

Ambient intelligence has become a trending field in computer science as a natural consequence of high-instrumented environments, where each device is a target to embedding a microchip with increasing computational power. However, not all devices possess some sort of intelligence, nor do they need to. Furthermore, the so called intelligent devices are often not meant to be intelligent in a way besides accomplishing their function in a constant manner, regardless of environmental effects and regardless of potential improvement possibilities. From this standpoint, ambient intelligence is about to provide an intelligent interaction between different environmental parts, to integrate them in a holistic intelligent system, which automatically adapts to further environmental changes and incrementally increases the knowledge about the users [4, 22].

2.1 Sensor-Based Environment Monitoring

The first component of such a system is the environment-sensing component, which recognizes all types of activities, ranging from long to short term and from large-scale to small-scale activities. Video cameras are a popular choice for a sensor when it comes to recognizing user activities, because they can provide a detailed knowledge about the ongoing activities in a home environment. On the other hand, cameras have some fallacies such as being obtrusive for its inhabitants regarding their presence [2], and usually suffer from bad recognition in sub-optimal light conditions. In addition, cameras are expensive and require computationally intensive algorithms for recognition [11].

Another function of the environment-sensing component is to recognize the different parts of the environment itself. Those include different devices, which are commonly used for performing different activities, or those devices performing periodic miscellaneous tasks by themselves. Since we investigate the device recognition part, we first get familiar with activity recognition using sounds and translate their results into our case (see Section 2.2). Then we make a comparison with the current research progress the concrete case of device recognition, mostly using power-based sensors (see Section 2.3).

2.2 Sound-Based Activity Recognition

Another touch-free technique of recognition, regarding the human perception, is based on analyzing the audible sounds in a given environment. On the on hand, most of the sound-based recognizers are limited in recognizing human speech, together with some of its characteristics like speaker recognition and his emotional state in order to obtain detailed information about their subject of interest. On the other hand, there are very few studies, which aim to examine in an abstract way the daily human activities in a home environment according to their acoustic characteristics [9, 10, 12, 16, 18, 20, 21]. Despite their generalized way of analyzing sounds, they are all developed in a healthcare perspective and often make the implication that certain sound implies certain activity, which is not necessarily true. This slightly differs from our perspective of building up a set of audibly distinguishable entities, most of them being devices in an active state, without attempting to interpret their further meaning. Furthermore from a sound-processing standpoint, all of the mentioned studies use very similar techniques, which represent a small range of the available sound transformation techniques for recognition [15]. In this context, this study aims to integrate and evaluate also further recognition methods, based on refining and tuning of existing sound processing techniques and various machine learning algorithms, for the task of device recognition.

Among the most related works to our study, the most competing one has been done by Stäger et al. They have studied into detail different aspects of an activity recognition system, which we consider as important, too, like performing an optimization friendly installation [19] with carefully selected feature sets. However their biggest difference to our intended framework is that their recognition setup relies on wearable sensors, which is an uncomfortable way of sensing information. The second most competing work has been done by Istrate et al. [9]. They perform a large variety of sound processing techniques for their recognition, but in their tests they used data from multiple environments and trained the recognizer with 90% of it. In both points our work intends to do exactly the opposite. We first intend to create a personalized setup, and second to use less training data. Other interesting capabilities, which are out of the scope of this paper, but are implemented, include sound event detection and an attempt to recognize rare short-time events like glass breaking. The third related work collective also made an excellent job in placing multiple microphones and exploiting their installation, but we consider their setup as being too overwhelming for our purposes.

2.3   Power-Based Device Recognition

Usually device recognition stands for recognizing different devices according to their interface. For instance, a recognizer scans the environment using different communication protocols like WiFi or Bluetooth and relies on the devices to support those protocols. However, not all devices had to support such communication protocols. Another recent research trend is to recognize electrical devices via a series of methods like using energy monitoring sockets, power analyzer [1, 6], and electromagnetic interference [5]. The problem is that all of those devices have to be electrical and connected to the power supply. Nevertheless, not all of the devices are electrical, nor should they be. Examples include toilet flush or a toothbrush. Some toothbrushes are electrical but they rely on batteries for their function, which makes them "invisible" for the mentioned technologies in their acting time. A natural way of recognizing devices, according to the human sense would be by analyzing their sounds. This includes the case where someone is using them to perform some activities, as well as the case, where they perform some periodic miscellaneous tasks without being operated directly by humans.

3   Sound-Based Device Recognition

Figure 1 below illustrates our proposed process from an activity to its corresponding device recognition.

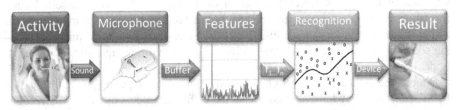

Fig. 1. Illustration of our process from an activity to the corresponding recognition

It starts with the environment (see Section 3.1) where some activity occurs (Section 3.2). Its sounds are captured by a microphone (see Section 3.3), and used to extract a desired set of features (see Section 3.4) to classify the devices (see Section 3.5). Furthermore we introduce sound mixing for recognizing untrained combination of devices (see Section 3.6). Finally we present how we cover the described process in a Sound-based Device Recognition Framework (see Section 3.7).

3.1   Environment

Since the main goal of this study is to provide device recognition in the smart home, the architecture, the implementation and the evaluations are centralized on this infra-structure. For the setup we have a home environment consisting of a single room (see Figure 2). For the sound monitoring a single microphone is used. We assume there is only one activity running at a time, with a single user that performs it. However as mentioned in the introduction, during certain activities, there may be multiple devices running at the same time, like shaving while showering. Activities consisting of sim-ultaneously occurring actions are called complex activities. Our goal is to recognize all used devices during such a complex activity.

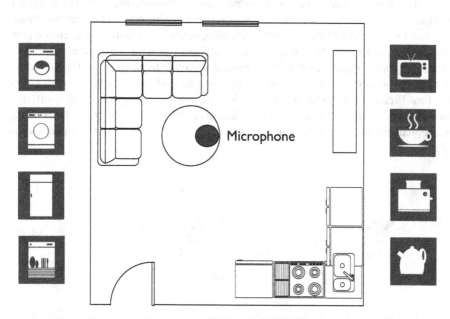

Fig. 2. Illustration of a one room home environment with its typical devices and their corre-sponding locations. The red dot represents a sample placement of the microphone. One should note that we are interested only in those devices that produce sound.

Compared to differently sensor equipped home environments our approach enables very simple and low cost installation. We eventually aim to optimize the sound pro-cessing and machine learning element components to complete the objective of creat-ing a personalized low-cost recognition system.

3.2   Activity and Device Types

In this section we define the activity types, which determines the different devices and their corresponding actions in a home environment. The latter are of interest in this paper, due to the various device types used to perform them. It has to be noted that some devices perform miscellaneous tasks on a periodical basis. Such a task may or may not be part of an activity. Thus we assume that all recorded sounds are caused by tasks that correspond to at least one activity type.

In our framework the activity type encapsulates all types of activities, which produce sounds for time intervals longer than our smallest recognition window of 0.1s. Since we are interested in recognizing the devices used in activities we introduce a device type for devices used to perform the according activity. As we mentioned, not all of the activities are performed by humans. For example, a heating element starts heating by itself, when the temperature falls beyond a given threshold. We define the state of the device as active, if it disperses sounds. According to the heater example, it is on standby or inactive while measuring the temperature and active while heating.

To enable deeper knowledge about the used devices the user can determine whether the activity is performed with an electrical device while training the recognizer. On this basis one can make statements in recognition whether the recorded activity is performed with an electrical device. For example if we have five activities like brushing teeth with an electrical toothbrush, cleaning using a vacuum cleaner, coffee making using a moka pot, showering and speaking, we can separate those activities into three categories – performed with an electrical device (first two), performed with a non-electrical device (second two) and the last one performed without any device at all (see Figure 3). So after the recognition request the recognizer assigns different probabilities for the occurrence of each activity, and by those probabilities, one can make statements as to which of the currently defined three activity categories this was.

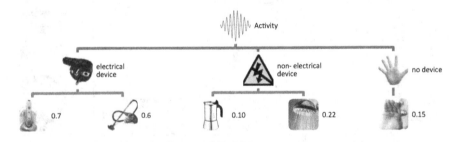

Fig. 3. This figure shows an example of deducting the sound source of an underlying activity

3.3   Sound Recording and Buffering

Besides setting up the hardware there is a need to setup the software and its recording parameters. While choosing flexible recording settings, one still has to convert those unified metrics for the later transformation, which always results in data loss. So instead of bothering with conversion, we fix the recording parameters to unified supported constants, which satisfy our needs. It has to be noted that we make no assumptions about the capabilities of the recording device and we aim to use a single generic sound recording device.

The sampling frequency of the recorded sound is set to the most common used 44100 Hz (also used in compact disks). It has been chosen because every hardware supports this rate. Not all of the microphones support stereo recording though, which might produce some deviations during the hardware setup as well, so the number of channels is reduced to one (mono recording). For the sound transformations it is useful to have high precision variables, so the bit depth is set to 32 bit signed integer per sample, which doubles the standard bit depth value of 16 and is uniformly supported as well.

To extract the spectrum of the audio signal we performed a Fast Fourier Transformation (FFT). To increase the spectral resolution we set the FFT buffer to 4096 samples. For record frames we have chosen a variable time length, which is at least twice the FFT buffer size. The latter is important considering our choice of Hamming window function, where window overlapping makes sense in order to avoid missing recording information. Furthermore, to standardize the test data we chose a record length of 10 seconds. After performing the FFT we cropped the frequency window between 80 Hz and 5000 Hz. This frequency range contains the most distinguishable features in the spectrum, according to our manual study and automated evaluation of different signals. Further reasoning for this choice is the unsteady behavior of the frequency response, which different microphones provide. To handle further disturbances in the frequency response of our chosen range we implemented various filters at spectrum level.

3.4   Feature Extraction

In order to make a decision which features we should select, we first studied the nature of the sounds produced by devices using speech and music analysis software (see Figure 4). The first notable difference from the mentioned domains was that our signals were most noise-like, similar to the environmental sounds studied by [3]. So we had to consider a specific feature choice, different from the one used by speech and music recognition fields.

For activities performed with electrical devices it is typical that most of the defining part of the sound comes from its electrical motor, which is the actual sound source. An interesting finding was that other activities performed with non-electrical devices, like showering, have similar spectrograms compared to electrical devices.

We present the features in the order of their addition to the framework over the implementation process, which was influenced by our perception of sound and the conclusion from the last subsection. For example, the first perceivable feature of a sound is its loudness, so we chose to start with it. Then, in a mathematical perspective, zero crossings are one of the most important characteristics of a function, together with its maximums and minimums. Subsequently, we implemented a set of 8 features, for the task of audio-based device fingerprinting.

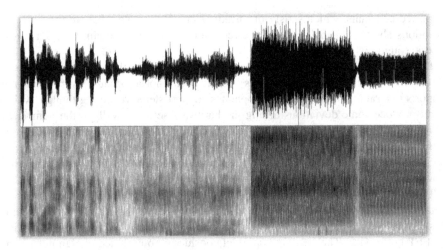

Fig. 4. Plot of 10 second recording of speech (first quarter), music (second quarter), epilator (third quarter) and hair trimmer (last quarter). Above we see the waveform of the recording and below its spectrogram between 80 Hz and 5000 Hz.

- **Loudness (LA)** is the average cumulative energy of the spectrum over the recognition interval. Note that this is a relative measure and is very dependent on filters and especially noise cancellation algorithms. Due to the nature of the feature it is also very important whether the activities occur at the same place, because the loudness is very dependent on their distance to the microphone.
- **Zero Crossing Rate (ZCR)** is the only feature derived from the time/amplitude domain (e.g., without processing the raw signal), after deciding to compute loudness after the filtering. To count zero crossings we check whether we have a zero crossing after each received sample.
- **Pitch (PA) and First Formant (FF)** is the pitch is also called fundamental frequency and represents the lowest frequency of a sound wave. It can be measured by looking at the global maximum in the spectrum, while the second global maximum after the pitch in the spectrum is the first formant.
- **Pitch Span (PS)** is a temporal feature, which refers to the span of values, which the pitch takes over time. For some devices, like a vacuum cleaner, the pitch is steady and does not vary over time, while for some other devices, like a toothbrush, the pitch varies over time. In some cases, pitch span refers to the distance between the pitch and the first formant over time, due to the ambiguity of automatic distinction between local maximums (see Figure 5).
- **Pitch Energy (PE)** is the amount of energy as part of the whole energy, which surrounds the pitch in a 10% rectangular window (e.g. the 10% of the signal around the pitch as middle point).
- **Spectral Flatness (SF)** is an important measure, which is very useful to distinguish meaningful sound from noise (see Figure 5).

- **Spectral Roll Off (SRO)** is the point where the spectral function falls down. It provides important information about the main energy concentration over the frequencies.

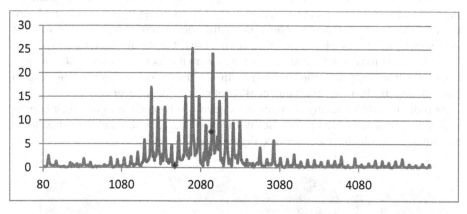

Fig. 5. Plot of spectrum of a hair trimmer illustrating that determination of the pitch and the first formant are a hard task. For the current snapshot the pitch would be calculated as 1975 Hz, while the first formant, would be 2234 Hz. One should note that over time those peaks switch, making the pitch vary between the mentioned two values, which is the way we compute the pitch span. Red points represent the beginning and the end of the interval for computing the pitch energy.

3.5   Device Classification

For a straightforward device classification we use the one-dimensional nearest neighbor algorithm. To enable fast runtime we use a single reference value. This reference value can be manually chosen either as the first, the last or the average of all features in the training set. The implemented algorithm provides a runtime with complexity in O(df) with number of devices (d) and number of enabled features (f).

To realize a more sophisticated solution, we use Infer.NET [14] as a state-of-the-art machine-learning library. Infer.NET implements the bayes point machine [8] in a standard supervised learning setting. The algorithms are trained via expectation propagation [13].

We also made a comparison between Infer.NET classifiers and our implementation of the multi-dimensional nearest neighbor for our test corpus with all selected features. Our results showed that for testing with single training, both recognizers achieved the same recognition accuracy. The drawback of Infer.NET was that it ran about 10 times slower, which is reasonable, considering the much larger number of computations it has to perform. However, with the increasing number of training data Infer.NET steadily increases its recognition rate, while our optimized implementation had a nearly constant recognition rate. Consequently, we anticipate a tradeoff between the runtime and the recognition rate, where one might choose the best option for the underlying setup.

3.6   Mixing

Mixing sounds is a novel approach in the field of sound-based activity recognition. It has been discussed in the field of music recognition for mixing different instruments in order to attempt their combined recognition [23]. However the technique used here is slightly different and avoids volume normalization, which is important for musical instruments, since they can play at different intensity, but mostly irrelevant for devices, which often have steady loudness. We are aware that defining which activities can occur simultaneously is a non-trivial task. In our framework we implemented up to three mixing mechanisms. Each mix consists of at most three records.

In order to test the mixing component we recorded two activities and their combination, and then we mixed automatically the recorded activities and compared them according to the obtained features (see Figure 6).

Fig. 6. Illustration of the comparison between automatically generated mix of records and a real mix according to their features

To test whether mixing works or not, we compared 6 records of tooth brushing and showering together with their automatic and real mixes to illustrate their similarity in terms of the first three implemented features (see Figure 7).

We obtained similar results when mixing other devices, except while mixing the record of a blender and a vacuum cleaner. This mixing shared almost the same feature values between the automatic mixing and real mixing, except their average pitch energy. For instance, in the mixed version the pitch of the blender was perceived to be stronger, so it dominated and produced similar values throughout the tests. While in the real mixes of both devices we measured an average pitch ranging between 586 Hz and 915 Hz with one occurrence of 1531 Hz. Such deviations can be explained by the occurrence of acoustic resonance, which can alter the pitch frequency. Another possible explanation is that the sum of the energies at some frequency bin might be the strongest energy in the mix and thus regarded as a pitch by the sound-processing unit.

3.7   Sound-Based Device Recognition Framework

We implemented a graphical user interface (GUI), which provides fast access to all functions and combinations of our sound-based device recognition framework. It is also important to visualize some of the sound derivations and to enable live tracking of relevant features.

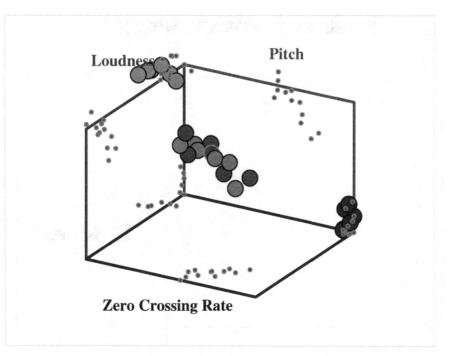

Fig. 7. Three-dimensional plot consisting of 6 experiment results with real (red) and automatic (green) mix of showering (blue) and tooth brushing (orange) according to the distribution over loudness, zero Crossing rate and Pitch

In the following, we introduce the architecture of our sound-based device recognition framework. Its main part is the developer GUI, which contains all of the functionality of the system, while there is also a client, which can connect with the main program to ask for recognition results (see Figure 8). An example of a client can be a smartphone, which can provide basic tasks like training the recognizer and requesting recognition, without providing the user with all possible configuration steps.

The developer GUI and the client application are both separated in two components, responsible for the sound processing and machine learning parts. From the user perspective, the user first creates records and then attempts to recognize them. Training the recognizer is realized by adding an activity with its corresponding device if it exists. A further way of increasing the knowledge of the recognizer is realized by providing a user feedback mechanism after presenting the recognition result. The last two properties are the basis of building an incremental learning system, which aims to make better recognitions over time in terms of a growing number of recognizable devices and recognition accuracy. The latter means that the system is capable to start from scratch after being installed in a personalized setup and rely on the user to build its knowledge. A further important capability is changing the settings during a live-recognition mode, which enables in depth control during the development process.

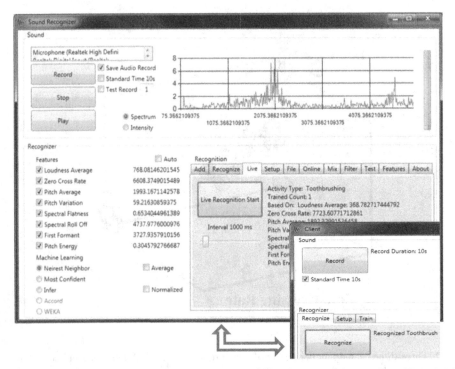

Fig. 8. Screenshot of our sound-based device recognition framework interacting with a simple client application to provide a mobile recognition service

4   Results

We ran an evaluation in a home environment with a static microphone setup and recorded 150 records to build up our test corpus. It consists of 25 classes problem, out of which 20 classes represent devices, 3 classes are mixes of two devices, and the other two classes are speaker and silence. We ran the implemented multi-dimensional nearest neighbor algorithm with single training for the task of recognizing 125 devices consisting of 5 occurrences from each of the 25 classes. We tested the power set of all features. This means, with our implemented 8 features we tested 255 combinations, excluding the empty set. The results of best and worst performing feature combinations together with the average recognition results are shown in Table 1.

With a single feature for recognition we obtained best results for LA, directly followed by ZCR and PA. They were also the first three implemented features. It is interesting, that the combination of those three was nowhere near to matching the performance of the winners in the next two categories.

Table 1. Best, worst and average true positive recognition rate for all different feature combinations of different set sizes. The results in brackets were up to 1 recognition close to the provided result.

Feature Count	Best Set	Result	Worst Set	Result	Average Result
1	LA, (ZCR, PA)	52%	FF	30.4%	44.6%
2	LA, SRO	81.6%	SRO, FF	49.6%	67.49%
3	LA, SF, FF	93.6%	PS, FF, PE (PS,SRO,PE)	62.4%	76.69%
4	LA,PA,SF,FF (LA,SF,SRO,FF)	97.6%	PS,SRO,FF,PE	64%	79.97%
5	LA,PA,SF,SRO,FF	97.6%	ZCR,PS,SF,SRO,FF PA,PS,SRO,FF,PE	68.8%	80.66%
6	LA,ZCR,PA,SF,SRO,FF LA,ZCR,SF,SRO,FF,PE LA,PA,SF,SRO,FF,PE	94.4%	ZCR,PA,PS,SF,SRO,FF,PE (ZCR,PA,PS,SRO,FF,PE) (ZCR,PA,PS,SF,SRO,FF)	72%	80.06%
7	LA,ZCR,PA,SF,SRO,FF,PE	93.6%	PA,PS,SF,SRO,FF,PE (ZCR,PA,PS,SRO,FF,PE)	74.4%	79%
8	All Features	77.6%	All Features	77.6%	77.6%
AVG		85.9%		62.4%	73.26%

For feature coupling, we anticipated also an interesting result having SRO in the best combination as well as in the worst combination. In addition, the FF is present in both, the best and the worst result sets. This is a clear evidence that the combination of features is crucial for the recognition process, rather than having one strong feature, supporting our claims in Section 2.2.

We can see also that LA performs well and could not be found in any of the worst results. This is due to the nature of the electrical devices to have a certain loudness level, especially, due to the fixed position of the microphone. It is important to note that most of the devices are used at fixed locations.

For best recognition set we identified two combinations, which beat the 97% rate and one not far behind – <LA,PA,SF,FF> (97.6%), <LA,PA,SF,SRO,FF> (97.6%), and <LA,SF,SRO,FF> (96.8%). We identified the reason for these exceptional good results being the sound processing setup for the environment, as well as most of the devices being tested throughout the development, thus enabling the precise extraction of their characteristics.

Our average results between 4 and 7 feature sizes was about 80%, which is also a same feature count, where the best results peaked. We tested our automatic feature selection algorithm and it chose a set of 6 features to obtain 91.2% recognition accuracy. Thus we conclude that the feature count range between 4 and 7 features is the best performing.

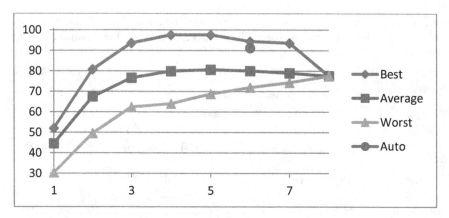

Fig. 9. A plot of best (blue) vs. average (green) vs. worst (red) results in terms of the different recognition rates (y-axis) according to the different feature set size (x-axis). The violet point represents the automatic feature selection, which selected 6 features and obtained 91.2% recognition accuracy.

Figure 9 shows a visualization of the results from Table 1. Both, the best and the average cases increase their accuracy for feature count up to 4 and 5, and from that point on there is a declining. Thus we observe that the increasing number of features doesn't necessarily mean better recognition, as mentioned in the introduction. However, more features should be implemented, since the worst-case recognition rate is increasing with the number of used features.

5   Conclusion

There are many contributions in the field of sound-based device recognition provided in this work. We have first shown that we can significantly reduce the complexity of a sound recognition system in a personalized home setup, as well as implement different ways to achieve this at both sound processing and machine learning levels. Our second contribution is in mixing automatically activities for their untrained recognition, where we obtained good results. We made also a detailed comparison between automatically mixed records of some activities and their real simultaneous occurrences.

We performed a manual study of specific characteristics of sounds produced by devices and made a full testing of all combinations of features to identify the best performing set. Most of those characteristics were not regarded by the majority of related works for the case of general activity recognition, since they are not applicable for speech recognition, which is their conventional research starting point. However, according to our evaluation, combinations of our chosen features are definitely important for classification of activities in a home environment. In addition, we implemented an automatic feature selection mechanism. Both, the chosen feature set for implementation, and their automatic selection for recognition, performed well in our evaluation. We adopted different machine learning techniques and optimized a couple of them for our purpose. We also introduced one of the first systems in the field of sound-based activity recognition, designed to learn over time using a feedback from the user and adapting its recognition settings, such as automatically choosing the best feature set.

References

1. Belley, C., Gaboury, S., Bouchard, B., Bouzouane, A.: Activity Recognition in Smart Homes Based on Electrical Devices Identification. In: Proceedings of the 6th International Conference on PErvasive Technologies Related to Assistive Environments, pp. 7:1–7:8. ACM, Island of Rhodes (2013)
2. Brey, P.: Freedom and Privacy in Ambient Intelligence. Ethics and Information Technology 7(3), 157–166 (2005)
3. Chu, S., Narayanan, S., Kuo, C.-C.: Environmental Sound Recognition With Time-Frequency Audio Features. IEEE Transactions on Audio, Speech, and Language Processing 17(6), 1142–1158 (2009)
4. Cook, D.J., Augusto, J.C., Jakkula, V.R.: Ambient Intelligence: Technologies, Applications, and Opportunities. Pervasive and Mobile Computing 5(4), 277–298 (2009)
5. Gupta, S., Reynolds, M.S., Patel, S.N.: ElectriSense: single-point sensing using EMI for electrical event detection and classification in the home. In: Proceedings of the 12th ACM International Conference on Ubiquitous Computing, pp. 139–148. ACM, New York (2010)
6. Hart, G.: Residential energy monitoring and computerized surveillance via utility power flows. Technology and Society Magazine 8(2), 12–16 (1989)
7. Hastie, T., Tibshirani, R., Friedman, J.: The elements of statistical learning (2nd ed.). Springer (2009)
8. Herbrich, R., Graepel, T., Campbell, C.: Bayes point machines. The Journal of Machine Learning Research 1, 245–279 (2001)
9. Istrate, D., Vacher, M., Serignat, J.-F.: Embedded Implementation of Distress Situation. Identification Through Sound Analysis. The. Journal on Information Technology in Healthcare 6(3), 204–211 (2008)
10. Karbasi, M., Ahadi, S., Bahmanian, M.: Environmental sound classification using spectral dynamic features. In: 8th International Conference on Information, Communications and Signal Processing, ICICS, Singapore, pp. 1–5 (December 13-16, 2011)
11. Ke, S.-R., Hwang, J.-N., Yoo, J.-H., Choi, K.-H.: A review on video-based human activity recognition. Computers 2(2), 88–131 (2013)
12. Lozano, H., Hernáez, I., Picón, A., Camarena, J., Navas, E.: Audio Classification Techniques in Home Environments for Elderly/Dependant People. In: Miesenberger, K., Klaus, J., Zagler, W., Karshmer, A. (eds.) ICCHP 2010, Part 1. LNCS, vol. 6179, pp. 320–323. Springer, Heidelberg (2010)
13. Minka, T.P.: Expectation Propagation for Approximate Bayesian Inference. In: Proceedings of the 17th Conference in Uncertainty in Artificial Intelligence, UAI 2001, pp. 362–369. Morgan Kaufmann Publishers Inc., San Francisco (2001)
14. Minka, T., Winn, J., Guiver, J., Knowles, D.: Infer.NET 2.5. Microsoft Research Cambridge (2012)
15. Müller, M., Ellis, D.P., Klapuri, A., Richard, G.: processing for music analysis. IEEE Journal on Selected Topics in Signal Processing 5(6), 1088–1110 (2011)

16. Sehili, M.A., Lecouteux, B., Vacher, M., Portet, F., Istrate, D., Dorizzi, B., Boudy, J.: Sound Environment Analysis in Smart Home. In: Paternò, F., de Ruyter, B., Markopoulos, P., Santoro, C., van Loenen, E., Luyten, K. (eds.) AmI 2012. LNCS, vol. 7683, pp. 208–223. Springer, Heidelberg (2012)
17. Stäger, M.: Low-Power Sound-Based User Activity Recognition. Swiss Federal Institute of Technology Zurich, Information Technology and Electrical Engineering. ETH Zürich, Zürich (2006)
18. Stager, M., Lukowicz, P., Troster, G.: Implementation and Evaluation of a Low-Power Sound-Based User Activity Recognition System. In: Proceedings of the Eighth International Symposium on Wearable Computers, pp. 138–141. IEEE Computer Society, Washington, DC (2004)
19. Stager, M., Lukowicz, P., Troster, G.: Power and accuracy trade-offs in sound-based context recognition systems. PerCom -. Pervasive and Mobile Computing 3(3), 300–327 (2007)
20. Temko, A., Malkin, R., Zieger, C., Macho, D., & Nadeu, C.: Acoustic Event Detection and Classification in Smart-Room Environments: Evaluation of CHIL Project Systems. Cough, 5–11 (2006)
21. Wang, J.-C., Lee, H.-P., Wang, J.-F., Lin, C.-B.: January 4). Robust Environmental Sound Recognition for Home Automation. IEEE Transactions on Automation Science and Engineering 5(1), 25–31 (2008)
22. Weber, W., Rabaey, J., Aarts, E.H.: Ambient Intelligence. Springer (March, 2005)
23. Wieczorkowska, A., Kolczyńska, E., Raś, Z.W.: Training of Classifiers for the Recognition of Musical Instrument Dominating in the Same-Pitch Mix. New Challenges in Applied Intelligence Technologies III(134), 213–222 (2008)

SALT: Source-Agnostic Localization Technique Based on Context Data from Binary Sensor Networks

Filippo Palumbo[1,2]($\boxtimes$) and Paolo Barsocchi[1]

[1] Information Science and Technologies Institute, National Research
Council of Italy, Pisa, Italy
{filippo.palumbo,paolo.barsocchi}@isti.cnr.it
[2] Department of Computer Science, University of Pisa, Pisa, Italy
palumbo@unipi.it

Abstract. Localization is a key component for many AAL systems, since the user position can be used for detecting user's activities and activating devices. While for outdoor scenarios Global Positioning System (GPS) constitutes a reliable and easily available technology, in indoor scenarios, in particular in real homes, GPS is largely unavailable. For this reason, several systems have been proposed for indoor localization. Recently, several algorithms fuse information coming from different sources in order to improve the overall accuracy in monitoring user activities. In this paper we propose a Source-Agnostic Localization Technique, called SALT, that fuses the information (coordinates) provided by a localization system with the information coming from the binary sensor network deployed within the environment. In order to evaluate the proposed framework, we tested our solution by using a previous developed heterogeneous localization systems presented at the international competition EvAAL 2013.

Keywords: Indoor Localization · Binary Sensor Network · Sensor Fusion · Ambient Assisted Living

1 Introduction

Localization of devices and people has been recognized as one of the main building block of context aware systems [1–3], which have one of their main application field in Ambient Assisted Living (AAL) applications. It is a key component of many AAL systems, since the user position can be used for detecting user's activities, activating devices, etc. While in outdoor scenarios Global Positioning System (GPS) constitutes a reliable and easily available technology, for indoor scenarios GPS is largely unavailable. For this reason, several systems have been proposed for indoor localization. These algorithms fuse information coming from different sources in order to improve the overall accuracy in monitoring user activities. In literature, each solution has advantages and shortcomings, which,

© Springer International Publishing Switzerland 2014
E. Aarts et al. (Eds.): AmI 2014, LNCS 8850, pp. 17–32, 2014.
DOI: 10.1007/978-3-319-14112-1_2

in most cases, can be summarized in a trade-off between precision and installation complexity (and thus costs). In practice, although indoor localization has been a research topic for several decades, there is still not a *de-facto* standard. Moreover, localization in AAL applications has specific requirements due to the fact that AAL systems must be deployed in real homes. In particular, localization system for AAL should be well hidden, easy to install and configure, and reliable. Most of them use range-based localization methods. These systems exploit measurements of physical quantities related to beacon packets exchanged between the mobile and the anchors (devices deployed in the environment whose position is a priori known). Radio signal quantities measured are typically the Received Signal Strength (RSS), the Angle Of Arrival (AOA), the Time Of Arrival (TOA), and the Time Difference Of Arrival (TDOA). Although AOA or TDOA can guarantee a high localization precision, they require dedicated hardware. This was a major drawback, in particular for AAL applications where low price and unobtrusive hardware are required.

In this paper we propose a framework overlay that, fusing the output of an underlying localization system with context information, improves their overall precision. Usually, the context information are sensor nodes with the most elementary sensing capabilities that provide just binary information (*binary sensors*). These binary information such as open/closed doors, on/off switches, or present/not-present in beds or chairs, can be used to infer that the user is in the room where the sensor is installed or, more precisely nearby it [4]. Thus, the combination of different sensor signals of different systems produces a more accurate and robust system solution. Information collected from binary sensor networks reduces uncertainty, improves accuracy, and increases tolerance to failures in estimating the location of observed user. By combining information from many different sources, it would be possible to reduce the uncertainty and ambiguity inherent in making decisions based only on a single information source. Furthermore, the proposed system is able to provide a rough localization information in absence of a dedicated subsystem with a room-level accuracy. When the proposed technique is used in absence of a dedicated localization system, using only the context data received from the binary sensor network, it is able to provide the position in terms of last room visited by the user. This is useful in the case of AAL scenarios involving the use of assistive robots [5]. When an alarm is raised due to, e.g., a fall detection or emergency call, the caregiver can pilot the robot in the last known room occupied by the user for a prompt reaction.

Recently, an international competition, called EvAAL (*Ev*aluating *AAL* Systems through Competitive Benchmarking), has been organized in order to evaluate and compare indoor localization systems for AAL solutions [6]. In particular, the last three years EvAAL focused on evaluate several localization systems not only from the point of view of position accuracy and system reliability, but also on compatibility with existing standard, deployment effort and user acceptance [6–8]. In this work, we use the datasets coming from the EvAAL's competitors in order to show both how their performance increases using the proposed Source-Agnostic

Localization Technique (SALT) based on the binary sensor network overlay and how our system would have performed as a stand-alone system. In this way, the proposed SALT overlay is totally transparent with respect to the underlying localization systems that could be based on several signal types (infrared, ultrasound, ultra-wideband, and radio frequency), signal metrics (AOA, TOA , TDOA, and RSS), and metric processing methods (triangulation and scene profiling).

The paper is organized as follows: Section 2 surveys related work into indoor localization area, Section 3 depicts the details of our solution, Section 4 provides both the description of the living lab hosting the EvAAL'13 competition, the binary sensor network on which leverages SALT, and the localization systems presented at EvAAL'13 that will be used to evaluate the proposed technique. Section 5 shows the performance of the proposed approach, while concluding remarks are presented in Section 6.

2   Related Work

In literature the indoor localization problem is solved by means of ad hoc solutions, among which one of the most promising is based on wearable technologies. Indoor localization systems can be classified based on the signal types and/or technologies (infrared, ultrasound, ultra wideband, RFID, packet radio), signal metrics (AOA angle of arrival, TOA time of arrival, TDOA time difference of arrival, and RSS received signal strength), and the metric processing methods (range-based and range free algorithms) [9]. Each solution has advantages and shortcomings, which, in most cases, can be summarized in a trade-off between several metrics (such as accuracy, installation complexity etc..). Data fusion techniques may be used to integrate the information obtained from different sensor sources [10–12] in order to reduce the localization error. In [10] the authors survey Bayesian filtering techniques for multi sensor fusion, arguing that probabilistic fusion methods are heavy in terms of computational load, requiring a centralized infrastructure to run the algorithms. A symbolic wireless localization device using a Bayesian network to infer the location of objects covered by IEEE 802.11 wireless network is developed in [13], where RSS received from different access points are quantified. Simple binary sensors in a Bayesian framework are also used in [14] to provide room-level location estimation and rudimentary activity recognition. In [15] a HMM (Hidden Markov Model) is used to stabilize a Bayesian-based location inference output in a WiFi-based localization system. In the domain of mobile robotics, RFID and Bayesian inference is used to perform obstacle detection, mitigating multipath effects [16,17]. A recursive Bayesian estimator, integrating WSN-based location data and kinematic information, is presented in [18]. Most of the works in literature employ Bayesian inference concepts in the design stage of the localization system and infrastructure.

Improvements in indoor positioning performance have the potential to create opportunities for businesses. However system performances greatly differ because both, the environments have a number of substantial dissimilarities and different technologies have a different performance. Our approach makes possible to improve the existing localization systems by adding a software overlay (that is sorce-agnostic) that receiving the information from the binary sensor network, usually deployed in smart environments, is able to reduce the overall localization error.

3   Source-Agnostic Localization Technique

The proposed solution aims both at providing a rough localization information in absence of a dedicated subsystem with a room-level accuracy, and at increasing the accuracy performance of an underlying localization system exploiting the context data provided by a home automation/monitoring sensor network typically deployed in a AAL smart environment. Several AAL projects [1] make use of this kind of sensor networks in order to help people in the automation of typical tasks [19] like switching on/off lights and HVAC systems [20] or to help remote caregivers in the activity monitoring of the assisted person [21]. Gathering the information about when and where a sensor or actuator is activated, we built a software overlay that can autonomously track the user movement in the house and, when a dedicated localization system is present, it can significantly enhance its accuracy.

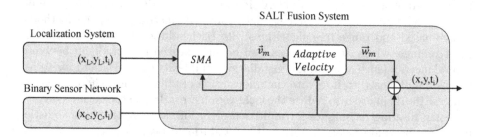

Fig. 1. The overall SALT fusion system

Figure 1 shows the overall SALT technique. For each sample provided by the localization subsystem (x_L, y_L, t_i) representing its output coordinates at time t_i, we built a geometric model of the trajectory that keeps track of the current position and of the velocity v_m calculated on previous samples received using a Simple Moving Average (SMA). When a context data (x_C, y_C, t_i) is received from the binary sensor network, the SALT overlay gives as output the coordinates of the corresponding activated sensor, since it represents a checkpoint of the user path. When no context data is received, we apply SALT on the data received from the localization system in order to fuse it with the information given by the binary sensor network in the previous steps.

---

[1] http://www.aal-europe.eu/

The basic assumption of the proposed fusing technique is that in the samples following the activation of a sensor, the position of the user is most likely in a neighbourhood of the position given by the previous contextual information. In order to take into account this *a priori* knowledge, when a new observation is received by the underlying localization system, we use the speed v_m to create a new vector $\boldsymbol{w}_m$ starting from the contextual data point and heading to the coordinates provided by the localization subsystem. The new estimated position (x, y, t) will be the head of $\boldsymbol{w}_m$ of size $w_m = v_m$. We iterate the process for each new context and localization data received adapting the parameter w_m to the new observations (*AdaptiveVelocity* block in Figure 1). The following equations represent analytically the position update process:

$$x(t_i) = x(t_{i-1}) + w_m cos(\alpha)\Delta t$$
$$y(t_i) = y(t_{i-1}) + w_m sin(\alpha)\Delta t$$

where α represents the angle between $\boldsymbol{w}_m$ and the map reference system.

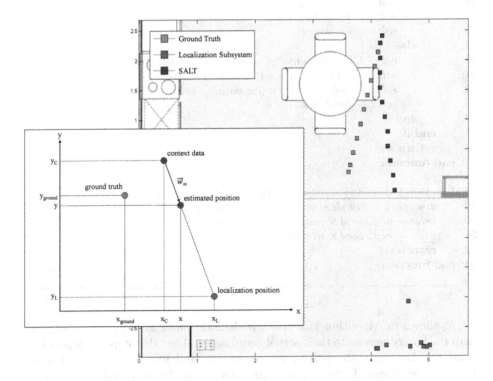

Fig. 2. Graphic representation of the SALT technique. In the box the coordinates of the actual position (ground truth), the context data, the localization system output, and the estimated position are shown.

Algorithm 1. Source-Agnostic Localization Technique

```
 1: procedure MAIN
 2:     (context_data, loc_data, salt) ← InitializeToNull()
 3:     InitializeMap()
 4:     while true do
 5:         (context_data, loc_data) ← GetData()
 6:         salt ← SaltFusion(context_data, loc_data)
 7:     end while
 8: end procedure

 9: function SALTFUSION(context_data, loc_data)
10:     if context_data ≠ null then
11:         salt.x ← context_data.x
12:         salt.y ← context_data.y
13:         salt.t ← context_data.t
14:     else if loc_data ≠ null then
15:         if salt = null then
16:             salt.x ← loc_data.x
17:             salt.y ← loc_data.y
18:             salt.t ← loc_data.t
19:         else
20:             vel ← ComputeVelocityComponents(loc_data, salt)
21:             salt.x ← salt.x + vel.x × (loc_data.t − salt.t)
22:             salt.y ← salt.y + vel.y × (loc_data.t − salt.t)
23:             salt.t ← loc_data.t
24:         end if
25:     end if
26:     return salt
27: end function

28: function COMPUTEVELOCITYCOMPONENTS(loc_data, salt)
29:     avg_speed = SimpleMovingAverage(loc_data)
30:     vel.x ← avg_speed × cos(alpha(loc_data, salt))
31:     vel.y ← avg_speed × sin(alpha(loc_data, salt))
32:     return vel
33: end function
```

As shown in Algorithm 1, a first initialization phase is required in order to map the binary sensors to their actual coordinates. After this step, the algorithm waits for data from the pervasive environment and iteratively calls the core function *SaltFusion()*. Here we can see that when the proposed technique is used in absence of a dedicated localization subsystem (*loc_data* equals null), it is able to provide the position (structure *salt* in the algorithm) of the last context data (structure *context_data* in the algorithm) received. We can associate the information of the last room visited by the user using the coordinates of the corresponding sensor activated. This is useful in the case of AAL scenarios involving the use of assistive robots [5]. When an alarm is raised due to, e.g., a fall detection or emergency call, the caregiver can pilot the robot in the last known room occupied by the user for a prompt reaction.

Figure 2 shows a graphic representation of the update process after a context data is received. It shows a typical case where the underlying system gives a wrong position due to some changes in the environment like a door opened/closed or a furniture moved from its usual position. Indeed multipath effects due to reflections and diffraction from doors or furniture affect localization systems based on radio signal propagation [22]. Using the proposed technique these outliers are mitigated, increasing the overall accuracy of the underlying localization system fused with the proposed overlay.

4   Experimental Setup

In order to test and validate the proposed fusion overlay, we used the datasets provided by EvAAL [2], an international competition on localization systems for Ambient Assisted Living (AAL) scenarios. The objective of this competition is to award the best indoor localization system from the point of view of AAL applications [6]. EVAAL aims at enabling the comparison of different AAL solutions, by establishing suitable benchmarks and evaluation metrics that will be progressively refined and improved with time. In particular, EvAAL focuses not only on comparison of hard data such as accuracy of positioning and system reliability, but also on soft data like compatibility with existing standards, deployment effort and user acceptance.

4.1   The Living Lab

The competition was hosted by the Smart Home Living Lab, at the Technical University of Madrid[3] in Spain. The Living Lab is an open space environment of about 100 m^2 composed by a kitchen, a dining room, a bedroom, a bathroom, and a porch as shown in Figure 3. The Living Lab is equipped with domotic equipment, which includes configurable switches, lights, movement sensors, as well as electronic kitchen appliances. Hence the localization systems can exploit the information produced by these devices as consequence of the movements and actions of the actor. In the next subsection the description of the domestic equipment (i.e. binary sensor network) that we will leverage in this work will be given.

The fundamental studies of target tracking often focus on networks composed of sensor nodes with the most elementary sensing capabilities that provide just binary information about the target, indicating whether it is present or absent in the sensing range of a node. These so-called binary sensor networks constitute the simplest type of sensor networks that can be used for target tracking. In the

---

[2] http://evaal.aaloa.org
[3] http://smarthouse.lst.tfo.upm.es/

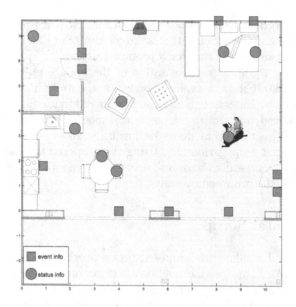

Fig. 3. The map of the Living Lab and the coordinates of the binary sensor network deployed in the Living Lab. Squares represent sensors giving information only when an event is raised, circles represent sensors giving information about their status.

Living Lab there are many simple binary sensors. These sensors have different properties which, when exploited, can reveal a surprising amount of information. Figure 3 shows the deployment of the binary sensors that the proposed source-agnostic localization technique exploits. The devices drawn with squares in Figure 3 are the following:

- Magnetic contact sensor: The Jung magnetic contact FUS4410WW are installed in the living lab. In particular, in the entrance door, in the living room door, in the bathroom door, and in the kitchen door.
- Switches: They are Jung KNX push-button modules F30, that generate the events when pressed.
- Liquid level sensor: This sensor has been used to understand when the user presses the button to drain the water closet. Indeed, it is able to detect the level of the liquid that flows.
- Electrical usage sensor: This sensor has been used to verify if the oven is turned on or not.

The binary information produced by these sensors are processed by the SALT system only when an event occurs i.e if the switches are pressed (on or off), or if the doors change their state (opened or closed). The devices drawn with circles in Figure 3 are the following:

- Electronic stationary bicycle with embedded computer and activity monitor: The output of this device is if the bicycle is running or not.

- Chair presence sensors: It is a force-sensing resistor that consists in a conductive polymer, which changes resistance in a predictable manner following application of force to its surface. This sensor has been used to verify if a user is in the chair or in the armchair.
- Bed presence sensors: The force-sensing resistor has been used to very the presence of a user on the bed.
- Flood sensor: This sensor has been used in the bathroom to verify if a user takes a shower.

In this case, the binary information is held by the SALT system until the status changes i.e when the user sits down on a chair the status is held until the user stands up.

4.2   Competitors and Technologies

In this section the competing localization systems chosen as test for the SALT technique are presented. In particular we selected the systems presented in 2013 edition since they are based on an heterogeneous technologies. Six teams were accepted to the 2013 indoor localization competition, the description of their systems is as follows:

AmbiTrack [23] – It is a marker-free camera-based localization and tracking system, i.e., it does not require the users to carry any tag with them in order to perform localization. This system also exploits the binary information coming from the switches and from the bicycle of the living lab.

LOCOSmotion [24] – This system is an indoor person tracking system that uses Wireless LAN fingerprinting and accelerometer-based dead-reckoning. Also this system exploits the binary information coming from the switches and from the bicycle of the living lab to infer the user position.

FEMTO-ST [25] – The systems is based on an hierarchical positioning algorithm which manages a multi-positioning system composed of a GPS positioning system, a Wi-Fi based fingerprinting and trilateration system, and a marker analysis system.

IPNLas [26] – The system uses an application for mobile phones (Android OS) that evaluating the RSS from the access points in the environment is able to localize the mobile pone inside buildings.

MagSys [27] – This system is based on the principle of resonant magnetic coupling, which means that it uses an oscillating magnetic field as the physical medium for localization. Thus, the mobile generate a magnetic field that periodically expands and contracts and the anchors evaluating this magnetic field. Furthermore the system includes additional acceleration and gyroscope sensors which are used as input to a filter stabilizing the location estimate.

RealTrack [28] – The mobile hand-held units periodically enter into active state and initiate the time-of-flight (ToF) ranging. Access points measure the RSS of the incoming radio signal. ToF and RSS data is processed by the server using a particle filter within localization algorithms. The structure of the building, air pressure value and the inertial measurement unit data are also taken into consideration by the system.

5   Performance Evaluation

In this section we first explain the tests made in the living lab followed by the performance analysis of the proposed technique applied to the systems competing in EvAAL 2013. During the tests, an actor wears the equipment the competitors

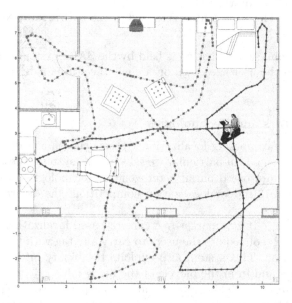

Fig. 4. The three different paths: path 1 (green line), path 2 (red line), and path 3 (blue line)

requires to carry (if any) and moves along a set of predefined paths (the chosen paths are represented in Figure 4). In this scenario, the actor has to be located while moving in the living lab along predefined paths. The expected output of the localization systems is the stream of his actual positions (in bi-dimensional coordinates) and the respective timestamps. During this phase, only the person to be localized is inside the Living Lab. Each localization system is requested to produce localization data with a frequency of 1 sample every half a second. The path includes 3 waiting points, where the actor has to stay still in the same position for 5 seconds. The reference localization system is used to compare the localization data generated by the competitors with the ground truth. The reference consists in a set of pre-defined paths the actor has to follow with a predefined speed. The Living Lab's floor was covered with marks (with different colors to distinguish the right and left foot) that indicate each single step the actor has to follow. Moreover, the actor was synchronized by a digital metronome that indicates the right cadence (one beep for each step), guaranteeing the repeatability of the test.

The performance of the proposed SALT system are given in terms of increase in *accuracy* of the competitors localization systems when the SALT overlay is

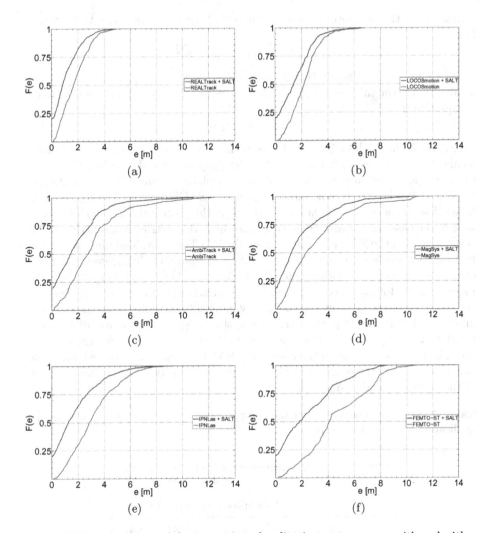

Fig. 5. CDFs comparison of the competitors localization systems error with and without the application of the SALT overlay

applied. The accuracy is the classical measurement for goodness of a localization system, it is based on samples of the distance between the point where the system thinks the user is and the point where the user really is. During the tests, the actor puts his feet on the marks at exactly the one-second times that are chimed by a loudspeaker: in those instants the reference point is the midpoint between the marks on which the feet are. The positions in intermediate instants are linearly interpolated from those points.

We define the error ϵ (equation 1) as the euclidean distance (in two dimensions) between the real point where the actor is (x_r, y_r) and the 2-D coordinates estimated by the competing system with or without the proposed SALT overlay (x, y).

$$\epsilon = \sqrt{(x_r - x)^2 + (y_r - y)^2} \tag{1}$$

The Cumulative Distribution Function (CDF) of ϵ is the probability that the localization error takes a value less than or equal to e meters and it is defined in equation 2.

$$F(e) = P(\epsilon \leq e) \tag{2}$$

Figure 5 shows the CDFs of the localization error ϵ using the EvAAL 2013 localization systems, with and without the proposed SALT overlay. Figure 5a shows the localization performance of the first place ranking of the competition, the REALTrack system, with and without the SALT overlay. The figure highlights that the accuracy increases by exploiting the proposed SALT technique: in 75% of the cases the localization error with the SALT overlay is lower than 1.7m compared with the 2.5m of error without the SALT overlay. The same trend can be seen for the other five competitors (subfigures from 5b to 5f). However, for two of the competitor, LOCOSmotion (Figure 5b) and AmbiTrack (Figure 5c), the increase in performance is not as evident as in other competitors. This because the two competitors already use the binary information coming from the switches and from the bicycle. In particular, these systems exploit the binary information to infer the user position at that time, but in the aftermath these information are not taken into account as in the case of the SALT system. From these results, we can conclude that the proposed SALT system significantly improves the accuracy of the localization systems.

Table 1. Accuracy comparison of the competitors localization systems without the application of the SALT overlay

	without SALT		
	1-Quantile	2-Quantile	3-Quantile
REALTrack	0.8840	1.6483	**2.4834**
LOCOSmotion	1.3728	2.1758	**2.8201**
AmbiTrack	1.5283	2.7590	**3.8603**
Magsys	1.1769	2.2986	**4.1779**
IPNLas	1.7295	2.8531	**4.1862**
FEMTO-ST / HMPS	2.8728	4.0774	**6.7843**

Tables 1 and 2 show in details the performance achieved by the localization systems we took into consideration compared with the application of the SALT overlay. The last column in 2 is the improvement when the third quartile is considered between using SALT or not. REALTrack, Magsys, IPNLas and

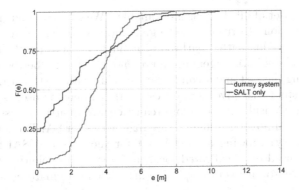

Fig. 6. The resulting CDFs for the SALT algorithm using only the binary sensor network and for the dummy localization system used as a comparison

FEMTO-ST systems improve their accuracy of about 30%, 33%, 36%, and 41%, respectively. While the systems that already used some binary information (i.e. LOCOSmotion and AmbiTrack) improve their accuracy of about 13% and 24% respectively. Moreover, from these results we can also conclude that, although the binary information reduces the localization error, the choice and the design of a localization algorithm is the most important issue. In fact, the ranking in terms of accuracy remains unchanged (see Table 2) except for the IPNLas and Magsys systems that, increasing the accuracy of about 36% and 33% respectively, would have had a better score.

Table 2. Accuracy comparison of the competitors localization systems with the application of the SALT overlay

	with SALT			
	1-Quantile	2-Quantile	3-Quantile	
REALTrack	0.2558	0.8162	**1.7322**	**+30.25%**
LOCOSmotion	0.3638	1.3957	**2.4318**	**+13.77%**
IPNLas	0.2976	1.2567	**2.6625**	**+36.40%**
Magsys	0.3212	1.2067	**2.7839**	**+33.37%**
AmbiTrack	0.3316	1.4387	**2.9170**	**+24.44%**
FEMTO-ST / HMPS	0.3885	1.8091	**3.9887**	**+41.21%**

Descrivere performance come stand alone system usando come confronto un dummy system che dice solo il centro della stanza In order to also show how the SALT overlay performs in absence of an underlying localization system, we run out algorithm on the three paths using only the sensors actually activated by the actor (a small subset of all the sensors available). We compared our results with a dummy localization algorithm able to give information on the room occupied by the actor during his paths: bathroom, main room, and porch. In Figure 6 the resulting CDFs of both system are represented showing a better outcome for SALT considering the first and second quartile. This is due to the intrinsic nature of the SALT system that gives a good estimation when the user is nearby the activated sensor. Considering the more realistic third quartile measure, the two systems performs almost the same (4 and 4.26 meters for SALT and the dummy system respectively) showing a good result for the proposed SALT technique since it doesn't need of a dedicated localization system exploiting the already present binary sensor network, typically installed in a smart house for AAL scenarios.

6   Conclusion and Future Work

In this paper we propose a Source-Agnostic Localization Technique (SALT) that fuses the information provided by a localization system already present a smart home with the information provided by the binary sensor network deployed in the environment. In order to evaluate and to show the full transparency of the proposed solution, we tested it by using the localization systems presented at the EvAAL 20013 international competition. On average, we measured an increasing of accuracy of about 30% from the performance experienced by the localization systems that don't use the context information, while the accuracy of the localization systems that exploit the information provided by the switches and by the bicycle in the living lab is, on average, about 20%.

In future work we plan to investigate how the performance changes according with the number of binary sensors deployed in the environment and the possibility to apply artificial intelligence techniques in order to deal with more than one user moving in the house.

Acknowledgments. This work was supported by the EU Commission in the framework of the GiraffPlus FP7 project (Contract no. 288173).

References

1. Want, R., Hopper, A., Falcao, V., Gibbons, J.: The active badge location system. ACM Transactions on Information Systems (TOIS) **10**(1), 91–102 (1992)
2. Abowd, G.D., Atkeson, C.G., Hong, J., Long, S., Kooper, R., Pinkerton, M.: Cyberguide: A mobile context-aware tour guide. Wireless Networks **3**(5), 421–433 (1997)
3. Cheverst, K., Davies, N., Mitchell, K., Friday, A., Efstratiou, C.: Developing a context-aware electronic tourist guide: some issues and experiences. In: Proceedings of the SIGCHI Conference on Human Factors in Computing Systems, pp. 17–24. ACM (2000)
4. Barsocchi, P., Chessa, S., Ferro, E., Furfari, F., Potorti, F.: Context driven enhancement of rss-based localization systems. In: 2011 IEEE Symposium on Computers and Communications (ISCC), pp. 463–468. IEEE (2011)

5. Coradeschi, S., Cesta, A., Cortellessa, G., Coraci, L., Gonzalez, J., Karlsson, L., Furfari, F., Loutfi, A., Orlandini, A., Palumbo, F., et al.: Giraffplus: Combining social interaction and long term monitoring for promoting independent living. In: 2013 The 6th International Conference on Human System Interaction (HSI), pp. 578–585. IEEE (2013)
6. Barsocchi, P., Chessa, S., Furfari, F., Potorti, F.: Evaluating ambient assisted living solutions: The localization competition. IEEE Pervasive Computing 12(4), 72–79 (2013)
7. Salvi, D., Barsocchi, P., Arredondo, M.T., Ramos, J.P.L.: EvAAL, evaluating aal systems through competitive benchmarking, the experience of the 1st competition. In: Chessa, S., Knauth, S. (eds.) EvAAL 2011. CCIS, vol. 309, pp. 14–25. Springer, Heidelberg (2012)
8. Álvarez-García, J.A., Barsocchi, P., Chessa, S., Salvi, D.: Evaluation of localization and activity recognition systems for ambient assisted living: The experience of the 2012 evaal competition. Journal of Ambient Intelligence and Smart Environments 5(1), 119–132 (2013)
9. Ruiz, A.R.J., Granja, F.S., Prieto Honorato, J.C., Rosas, J.I.G.: Accurate pedestrian indoor navigation by tightly coupling foot-mounted imu and rfid measurements. IEEE Transactions on Instrumentation and Measurement 61(1), 178–189 (2012)
10. Teixeira, T., Dublon, G., Savvides, A.: A survey of human-sensing: Methods for detecting presence, count, location, track, and identity. ACM Computing Surveys 5 (2010)
11. Nakamura, E.F., Loureiro, A.A., Frery, A.C.: Information fusion for wireless sensor networks: Methods, models, and classifications. ACM Computing Surveys (CSUR) 39(3), 9 (2007)
12. Wymeersch, H., Lien, J., Win, M.Z.: Cooperative localization in wireless networks. Proceedings of the IEEE 97(2), 427–450 (2009)
13. Castro, P., Chiu, P., Kremenek, T., Muntz, R.: A probabilistic room location service for wireless networked environments. In: Abowd, G.D., Brumitt, B., Shafer, S. (eds.) Ubicomp 2001. LNCS, vol. 2201, pp. 18–34. Springer, Heidelberg (2001)
14. Wilson, D.H., Atkeson, C.G.: Simultaneous tracking and activity recognition (star) using many anonymous, binary sensors. In: Gellersen, H.-W., Want, R., Schmidt, A. (eds.) PERVASIVE 2005. LNCS, vol. 3468, pp. 62–79. Springer, Heidelberg (2005)
15. Ladd, A.M., Bekris, K.E., Rudys, A.P., Wallach, D.S., Kavraki, L.E.: On the feasibility of using wireless ethernet for indoor localization. IEEE Transactions on Robotics and Automation 20(3), 555–559 (2004)
16. Joho, D., Plagemann, C., Burgard, W.: Modeling rfid signal strength and tag detection for localization and mapping. In: IEEE International Conference on Robotics and Automation, ICRA 2009, pp. 3160–3165. IEEE (2009)
17. Jia, S., Sheng, J., Takase, K.: Improvement of performance of localization id tag using multi-antenna rfid system. In: SICE Annual Conference, pp. 1715–1718. IEEE (2008)
18. Klingbeil, L., Wark, T.: A wireless sensor network for real-time indoor localisation and motion monitoring. In: International Conference on Information Processing in Sensor Networks, IPSN 2008, pp. 39–50. IEEE (2008)
19. Aarts, E., Wichert, R.: Ambient intelligence. Springer (2009)
20. Ding, D., Cooper, R.A., Pasquina, P.F., Fici-Pasquina, L.: Sensor technology for smart homes. Maturitas 69(2), 131–136 (2011)

21. Palumbo, F., Ullberg, J., Štimec, A., Furfari, F., Karlsson, L., Coradeschi, S.: Sensor network infrastructure for a home care monitoring system. Sensors **14**(3), 3833–3860 (2014)

22. Gomez, J., Tayebi, A., Saez de Adana, F.M., Gutierrez, O.: Localization approach based on ray-tracing including the effect of human shadowing. Progress In Electromagnetics Research Letters **15**, 1–11 (2010)

23. Braun, A., Dutz, T.: AmbiTrack - marker-free indoor localization and tracking of multiple users in smart environments with a camera-based approach. In: Botía, J.A., Álvarez-García, J.A., Fujinami, K., Barsocchi, P., Riedel, T. (eds.) EvAAL 2013. CCIS, vol. 386, pp. 83–93. Springer, Heidelberg (2013)

24. Fet, N., Handte, M., Wagner, S., Marrón, P.J.: Enhancements to the locosmotion person tracking system. In: Botía, J.A., Álvarez-García, J.A., Fujinami, K., Barsocchi, P., Riedel, T. (eds.) EvAAL 2013. CCIS, vol. 386, pp. 72–82. Springer, Heidelberg (2013)

25. Salem, A., Canalda, P., Spies, F.: A gps/wi-fi/marker analysis based simultaneous and hierarchical multi-positioning system. In: Botía, J.A., Álvarez-García, J.A., Fujinami, K., Barsocchi, P., Riedel, T. (eds.) EvAAL 2013. CCIS, vol. 386, pp. 106–116. Springer, Heidelberg (2013)

26. Quintas, J., Cunha, A., Serra, P., Pereira, A., Marques, B., Dias, J.: Indoor localization and tracking using 802.11 networks and smartphones. In: Botía, J.A., Álvarez-García, J.A., Fujinami, K., Barsocchi, P., Riedel, T. (eds.) EvAAL 2013. CCIS, vol. 386, pp. 117–127. Springer, Heidelberg (2013)

27. Pirkl, G., Lukowicz, P.: Indoor localization based on resonant oscillating magnetic fields for aal applications. In: Botía, J.A., Álvarez-García, J.A., Fujinami, K., Barsocchi, P., Riedel, T. (eds.) EvAAL 2013. CCIS, vol. 386, pp. 128–140. Springer, Heidelberg (2013)

28. Moschevikin, A., Galov, A., Soloviev, A., Mikov, A., Volkov, A., Reginya, S.: Realtrac technology overview. In: Botía, J.A., Álvarez-García, J.A., Fujinami, K., Barsocchi, P., Riedel, T. (eds.) EvAAL 2013. CCIS, vol. 386, pp. 60–71. Springer, Heidelberg (2013)

Detecting Walking in Synchrony Through Smartphone Accelerometer and Wi-Fi Traces

Enrique Garcia-Ceja[1,2], Venet Osmani[1]([✉]), Alban Maxhuni[1],
and Oscar Mayora[1]

[1] CREATE-NET, Via alla Cascata 56D, Trento, Italia
A00927248@itesm.mx,{venet.osmani,alban.maxhuni,
oscar.mayora}@create-net.org
[2] Tecnológico de Monterrey, Campus Monterrey,
Av. Eugenio Garza Sada 2501 Sur, Monterrey, N.L., México

Abstract. Social interactions play an important role in the overall well-being. Current practice of monitoring social interactions through questionnaires and surveys is inadequate due to recall bias, memory dependence and high end-user effort. However, sensing capabilities of smart-phones can play a significant role in automatic detection of social interactions. In this paper, we describe our method of detecting interactions between people, specifically focusing on interactions that occur in synchrony, such as walking. Walking together between subjects is an important aspect of social activity and thus can be used to provide a better insight into social interaction patterns. For this work, we rely on sampling smartphone accelerometer and Wi-Fi sensors only. We analyse Wi-Fi and accelerometer data separately and combine them to detect walking in synchrony. The results show that from seven days of monitoring using seven subjects in real-life setting, we achieve 99% accuracy, 77.2% precision and 90.2% recall detection rates when combining both modalities.

Keywords: Social interactions · Accelerometer · Wi-fi · Ambient intelligence · Health and wellbeing

1 Introduction

Interaction between people is one of the basic human activities and it impacts a number of life aspects, including wellbeing. The association between wellbeing and human interaction, specifically social interaction has been well established. Subjects with low quantity of social relationships are typically less healthy, psychologically and physically, manifesting higher risks for a wide range of conditions – from psychiatric disorders to accidents and even mortality [1], while individuals who maintain a certain level of social engagements are shown to be more successful in coping with stress [2]. Several studies have demonstrated that the amount of social activity is negatively correlated with depressive behavior while socialization can help in alleviating depressive symptoms [3,4].

© Springer International Publishing Switzerland 2014
E. Aarts et al. (Eds.): AmI 2014, LNCS 8850, pp. 33–46, 2014.
DOI: 10.1007/978-3-319-14112-1_3

The current practice of using surveys, diaries and self reporting methods to record social interactions has several drawbacks such as recall bias, memory dependence, and high end-user effort for continuous long term monitoring [5]. Also, many serious mental illness (SMI) require lifelong management and individuals need to constantly look for signs that might indicate relapse [6], which is infeasible with manual methods. The use of technology can alleviate many of these problems, specifically, wearable devices with embedded sensors, which can continuously record data in an unobtrusive manner.

Miniaturization of sensors makes it possible to collect different types of data. It is common to have wearable devices with several embedded sensors like accelerometers, gyroscopes, Bluetooth and Wi-Fi, to name a few. In recent years, several research works have taken advantage of those sensors to infer different aspects of the user's context, including physical activities, location and proximity to other users. For example, the accelerometer sensor has been used to recognize physical activities, including walking, running and sleeping [7,8]. It has been shown that it is also possible to recognize social actions like drinking, laughing, speaking, with a single accelerometer [9]. Another important aspect for context aware systems is *location*. The Bluetooth and Magnetometer sensors have been used to locate a user in indoor environments where GPS usually fails [10–13]. The Wi-Fi sensor has also been used to classify proximity between mobile devices [14], which is important to identify social structures and relationships [15–17].

However, the majority of these works have focused on detecting activities that pertain to individual users; that is, establishing statistical models of activities and using sensor data to classify these activities. One issue with this approach is that it is difficult to generalize models across diverse population, since it is challenging to obtain vast set of diverse training data. In contrast, our work focuses on understanding synchrony of activities between people, and we are particularly interested in detecting synchrony of activities when people are in proximity. For this work, we focus on detecting walking activity synchrony using accelerometer data and Wi-Fi traces collected using smartphones worn by subjects in an everyday setting. Our main motivation in detecting walking in synchrony between subjects, is that walking together (going to lunch for example) is an important aspect of the overall social interaction, which has been studied in our previous work [18–20].

In this work we first used the accelerometer and Wi-Fi data independently to detect walking in synchrony. Then we evaluated performance of our method when combining both modalities. Using both sources of information helped to increase the overall accuracy of detecting joint walking activity.

This paper is organized as follows: Section 2 will present related work in this area. In Section 3 we will describe the methodology which includes: data collection details, pre-processing, accelerometer data analysis and Wi-Fi data analysis. Section 4 presents the experiments and results and finally, in Section 5 we draw the main conclusions.

2   Related Work

The use of sensors to infer user context and interactions has gained a lot of interest in recent years. For example, in [21], the authors used Wi-Fi signal strengths to infer the location of a client and to classify whether or not the client is in motion. To perform the inference, they used Hidden Markov Models (HMMs). They achieved an accuracy of 87% for the motion classification and a median error of 1.5 meters for the location inference. Welbourne et al. [22] also used Wi-Fi signals to infer the user's place but they also added more sensors like accelerometers and barometric pressure sensors in order to highlight significant places based on the activity that occurs there. The aforementioned works perform the inferences in a user-centric manner, i.e., they do not take into account interactions between users. In [23] they started to explore the use of sensor data from mobile phones to discover the relationships between users. The information they collected includes call logs, Bluetooth proximity devices, cell tower ids, application usage and phone status. In their study, 100 subjects participated in the data collection process over a period ranging from 2 to 7 months and they were able to infer friendship relationships with over 90% accuracy.

Another work that takes into account relations between users is the one of Vu et al. [24]. They used Wi-Fi and Bluetooth data to predict what persons a user will meet, predict future location and stay duration at that location. Sekara & Lehmann [25] demonstrated that weak links obtained from Bluetooth signal strength data have a lower probability of being observed at later times and thus, a lower probability of sharing an online friendship. Carreras et al. [26] used Wi-Fi RSSI to detect proximity between users without the need of any external infrastructure since they introduced a duty-cycle method. This method consists of allowing the devices to alternatively act as Portable Hot Spot (PHS) and client mode.

Social Network Analysis (SNA) visualizations and methods have been used to extract friendship relationships from sensor data. Oloritun et al. [15], predicted friendship ties based on duration of interactions from smartphones data by modeling them as undirected weighted graphs where the weight represents the duration of the interaction. Their results suggest that there is a significant correlation between close friendship and interactions in weekend nights. Another method from SNA is Link Prediction, which consists of predicting future or missing links in a network. Yang et al. [27] used Link Prediction with human mobility information in order to predict future proximity topologies.

In this work we focus on the problem of inferring walking interactions between users. Several of the mentioned works relay on the assumption that two persons interact if they are close to each other, however this may not be the case. It is more likely that any two given persons are interacting if they are walking together than if they are just close to each other so our results may benefit other works that use interaction information to infer higher order social relationships. To the best of our knowledge there are no works that attempt to classify joint walking interactions *between users* by using just accelerometer data or by combining acceleration and Wi-Fi sensors. One of the advantages of using these type of sensors is that they are non-visual and non-auditory thus, they mitigate privacy concerns and do not interfere with the individual's daily routines [18].

Table 1 shows a summary of related work classified by the different data sources used and by type. User-centric type means that the work does not take into account the interaction between users but is oriented towards single user i.e., it focuses on context details rather than higher-level interactions. Multi-user means that the work does take into account several users and their possible interactions but does not infer social relationships. This work lies between user-centric and social inference (i.e., multi-user) because it does take into account the interaction between users but it does not try to infer social structures and higher-level relations.

Table 1. Classification of different related works according to data source and type

Work	Data sources	Type
Krumm & Horvitz [21]	Wi-Fi	user-centric
Welbourne et al. [22]	Wi-Fi, accelerometers,pressure sensors	user-centric
Carreras et al. [26]	Wi-Fi	multi-user
This work	Accelerometer,Wi-Fi	multi-user
Eagle & Pentland [23]	Bluetooth,call logs,cell towers,application usage,phone status	social inference
Eagle et al. [28]	call logs, cell towers,Bluetooth	social inference
Vu et al.[29]	Bluetooth,Wi-Fi	social inference
Vu et al. [24]	Bluetooth, Wi-Fi	social inference
Sekara & Lehmann [25]	Bluetooth	social inference
Lerman et al. [17]	Digg,Twitter	social inference
Carrasco et al. [30]	Simulated Wi-Fi	social inference
Oloritun et al. [15]	Bluetooth	social inference
Yang et al. [27]	different datasets	social inference
Yu et al. [16]	Bluetooth,location,voice calls,text messages	social inference
Stopczynski et al. [31]	Questionnaires,Facebook,Phone sensors	social inferecne

3 Methodology

In this section we describe the details of the data collection process, pre-processing steps and finally the accelerometer and Wi-Fi data analysis.

3.1 Data Collection

The data was collected continuously using two smartphones running Android OS. An application was developed to collect accelerometer and Wi-Fi data from the smartphones' sensors. The sampling rate for the accelerometer sensor was set at 5Hz. This sensor returns the acceleration for each of the x,y and z axes along with a timestamp. The application continually scans Wi-Fi Access Points and stores their Basic Service Set Identifier (BSSID), which is a unique address that identifies each Access Point through MAC address.

The data was collected with 7 subjects in 7 different days during working hours (approx. between 9 a.m and 6 p.m). The experiment was carried out in an office environment where most of the time the users are working on a computer. For each day, one of the smartphones was carried by a *control user* and the other phone was given to a *test user*. There was 1 *control user* and 6 *test users* (one test user collected data for two different days). Three of the *test users* were unknown to the *control user* and the other three *test users* work in the same office as the *control user*. The *control user* took note of the start and end time of each of the walking interactions, i.e., when both users walked together while going for coffee, lunch and other joint walking activities, such as going home. The users were free to use their phone in any way they wanted; that is, there were no restrictions put on the users to carry the phone in a specific manner or at a specific position of the body.

3.2 Pre-processing

An initial examination of raw accelerometer data revealed substantial noise, as expected. Hence, the raw accelerometer data was smoothed with an average filter of length 3:

$$v_s(t) = \frac{1}{n} \sum_{i=t-n}^{t-1} v(i) \tag{1}$$

where v is the original vector, v_s is the smoothed vector and n is the window length. This filter was applied to each of the 3 acceleration axes. Then, in order to take into account the overall movement of the smartphone the magnitude of the acceleration was computed as follows:

$$M(t) = \sqrt{a_x(t)^2 + a_y(t)^2 + a_z(t)^2}, \tag{2}$$

where $a_x(t)$, $a_y(t)$ and $a_z(t)$ are the accelerations at time t for each of the axes. Since each user has its own way of moving (some users tend to move more than others), the magnitude M was standardized ($\mu = 0$ and $\sigma = 1$) relative to each user.

3.3   Acceleration Analysis

The next step was to synchronize in time the data of both users because the application on each phone was not started exactly at the same time and we also needed to take into account the small variations of the internal clocks of the phones. To accomplish this, we divided the time into slots of ten seconds each and computed the mean magnitude for each of the slots such that the data for both users lied in a common time scale. Figure 1 shows the magnitudes for the control user and one of the test users.

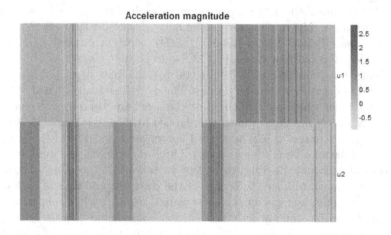

Fig. 1. Heat map of the acceleration magnitudes of the control user and one of the test users. u1 is the control user and u2 represents the test user. The x axis represents time.

Since we are interested in significant changes of acceleration between both users that occur almost at the same time, we now compute the magnitude difference for each user as follows:

$$D(t) = |M(t) - M(t-1)| \qquad (3)$$

Figure 2 shows the result of applying this filter. Now we can see that the magnitude changes are emphasised. We can also see that the red lines are fragmented but we want to arrange them into blocks so it is easier to detect when both users are moving at the same time. To 'group' the fragmented lines into blocks we applied the following filter:

$$V(t) = \Theta \left(\sum_{i=t-(n-1)}^{t-1} |D(i) - D(i+1)| - \varepsilon \right) \qquad (4)$$

where Θ is the Heaviside function, ε is a threshold (set to 1) and n is the window size which was set to 10. Figure 3 shows the result after applying this

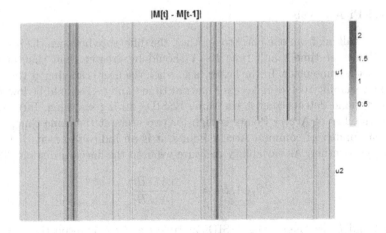

Fig. 2. Heat map of the magnitude differences for each user. u1 is the control user and u2 represents the test user. The x axis represents time.

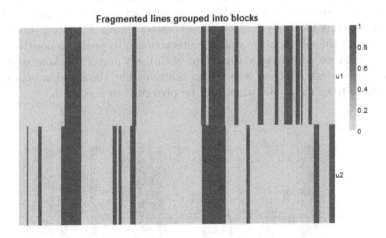

Fig. 3. Resulting blocks after grouping fragmented lines. u1 is the control user and u2 represents the test user. The x axis represents time.

filter. Now we can see more clearly, when both users were moving at the same time by looking at the intersection of the blocks.

Once we have found the resulting blocks we predict a positive walking interaction if the time slot is within a block and $V(t)_{u1} == 1$ and $V(t)_{u2} == 1$ where $V(t)_{u1}$ and $V(t)_{u2}$ are the resulting vectors after applying Eq.(4) for the *control user* and the *test user*, respectively.

3.4   Wi-Fi Analysis

If a user is walking from one place to another, the difference between the in-range Access Points at time t and time $t-1$ should be greater than that of user staying at the same place. In the latter case, when the user is staying at the same place the variability between Access Points at time t and $t-1$ should be low since the smartphone detects almost the same BSSIDs during scanning. Intuitively, if the variability of Access Points is high for two users at the same time, while sharing a number of common Access Points, it is an indication that they may be walking together. As variability measure we used the Jaccard distance [32]:

$$D_j(A, B) = 1 - \frac{|A \cap B|}{|A \cup B|} \tag{5}$$

where A and B are the sets of BSSIDs at time t and $t-1$, respectively. In the extreme case, when the smartphone detects the same Access Points over time, i.e., the user is not moving, the variability will be 0. On the other hand, if the Access Points at time t are completely different from those at time $t-1$ the variability will be 1. Figure 4 shows the Wi-Fi BSSIDs variance for both users over time. We can see that the variance tends to increase within the red blocks (when the user is moving based on accelerometer data). The green horizontal lines represent the self reported walking interactions. To predict a positive walking interaction we added the variances of both users and if this sum is greater than a given threshold, then it is set as positive. The threshold selection was done using a ROC curve [33] which will be presented in Section 4.

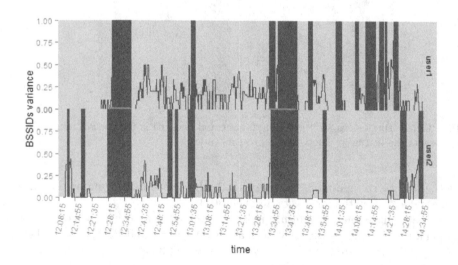

Fig. 4. BSSIDs variance over time. user1 is the control user and user2 represents the test user. The green lines show the self reported walking interactions.

Fig. 5. Predictions when using just accelerometer data for all subjects. Red lines represent negative predictions and Green lines represent positive predictions (walking together).

4   Experiments and Results

In this Section we present the results of the walking interactions detection when using: 1) Accelerometer data; 2) Wi-Fi data; and 3) Accelerometer data combined with Wi-Fi data. We performed the recognition between the control user and each test user (7 trials in total).

Figure 5 shows the resulting predictions when using just accelerometer for 7 different days (quantified confusion matrix is shown in Figure 7). Red lines represent negative predictions and Green lines represent positive predictions (walking together). It can be seen that the classes are unbalanced, i.e., most of the time slots are negatives (97.2%). The overall accuracy of the predictions was 0.984; but given the unbalanced nature of data we also present specificity, sensitivity (also known as *recall*), positive predictive value (PPV) (also known as *precision*) and negative predictive value (NPV). These measures are summarized in Table 2. All metrics are greater than 0.9, except the PPV which was 0.657. The PPV was low because there were many false positives (See Figure 5). The false positives are due to the fact that users were moving or walking at the same time even though they were not in proximity to each other.

Table 2. Results with accelerometer data

Accuracy	Sensitivity	Specificity	PPV	NPV
0.984	0.902	0.986	0.657	0.997

Now we evaluate the predictions by using just Wi-Fi data. Figure 6 shows the resulting ROC curve[1] for different threshold values of the BSSIDs variance computed with Eq.(5). This plot represents the trade off between sensitivity and specificity for different threshold values. We can see that a good threshold value is around 0.424 since it produces a combination of sensitivity and 1 - specificity that is close to the upper left corner. The diagonal represents a random classification so, a value below the diagonal means that the classifier for that specific threshold performed worse than a random guess. The resulting Area Under the Curve was 0.95 and it represents the probability that a classifier will rank a randomly chosen

---

[1] The ROC curves were produced with the ROCR package [34].

positive instance higher than a randomly chosen negative one. Based on the ROC curve it seems that using just acceleration is better than using just Wi-Fi data. This is because there is no threshold value in the ROC curve that produces a combination of both sensitivity and specificity that are greater or equal to the ones obtained when using accelerometer data.

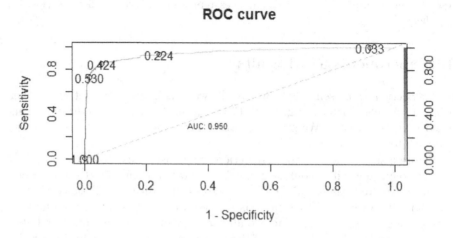

Fig. 6. Resulting ROC curve for different threshold values of the BSSIDs variance

Finally, we performed the prediction by combining both, accelerometer and Wi-Fi data. Many of the false positives are there because the users may be walking at the same time even though they are in different places. We used Eq.(5) to compute the distance between the control user and the test user at any given time slot. If the distance between the users is 1 it means that they are in different places so the prediction can be corrected. Table 3 shows the results when combining both sources of information.

Table 3. Results with accelerometer and Wi-Fi data

Accuracy	Sensitivity	Specificity	PPV	NPV
0.990	0.902	0.992	0.772	0.997

We can see that the accuracy and specificity increased; the sensitivity and NPV remained the same and the PPV had a significant improvement (from 0.657 to 0.772). Figure 7 shows the resulting confusion matrices when using just accelerometer data and when using accelerometer with Wi-Fi data. We can see that the second column of the matrices remained the same. The first columns of the matrices had a significant change because the false positives where reduced considerably by ruling out detected interactions from accelerometer data that were not real because the users were in different places.

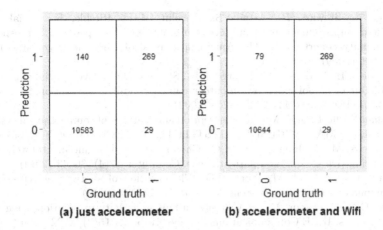

Fig. 7. Confusion matrices when a) using just accelerometer data and b) combining accelerometer and Wi-Fi. 1 means a walking interaction and 0 no interaction.

5 Conclusions and Future Work

In this work we showed how accelerometer and Wi-Fi data collected from smartphones can be used to classify walking in synchrony between users. First, we used accelerometer data and Wi-Fi data independently. Our results suggest that using just an accelerometer gives better results than using just Wi-Fi. Then, we combined both sensors and the overall accuracy increased because when adding Wi-Fi it was possible to reduce the false positives due to the fact that the persons may be walking at the same time but in different places. Our experiments were tested in an office environment and these results are indicative of performance of our method. We plan to extend this work to a larger sample of subjects and investigate other types of interactions in synchrony, including commuting interactions such as being in the same car, bus or train.

Acknowledgments. Enrique Garcia-Ceja would like to thank Consejo Nacional de Ciencia y Tecnología (CONACYT) and the AAAmI research group at Tecnológico de Monterrey for the financial support in his PhD. studies. This work was supported by EIT ICT Labs, Social Gym project.

References

1. James, S.H., Karl, R., Debra, U.: Social relationships and health. Science **241**(4865), 540–545 (1988)
2. Sheldon, C., Thomas, A.W.: Stress, social support, and the buffering hypothesis. Psychological Bulletin **98**(2), 310–357 (1985)

3. Isaac, V., Stewart, R., Artero, S., Ancelin, M.-L., Ritchie, K.: Social activity and improvement in depressive symptoms in older people: A prospective community cohort study. The American Journal of Geriatric Psychiatry **17**(8), 688–696 (2009)
4. Bosworth, H.B., Hays, J.C., George, L.K., Steffens, D.C.: Psychosocial and clinical predictors of unipolar depression outcome in older adults. International Journal of Geriatric Psychiatry **17**(3), 238–246 (2002)
5. Nathan Norfleet Eagle. Machine perception and learning of complex social systems. PhD thesis, MASSACHUSETTS INSTITUTE OF TECHNOLOGY (2005)
6. Matthews, M., Abdullah, S., Gay, G., Choudhury, T.: Tracking mental well-being: Balancing rich sensing and patient needs. Computer **47**(4), 36–43 (2014)
7. Edmond, M., David, M., Noel, E.O.: Classification of sporting activities using smartphone accelerometers. Sensors **13**(4), 5317–5337 (2013)
8. Lara, O.D., Labrador, M.A.: A survey on human activity recognition using wearable sensors. IEEE Communications Surveys Tutorials **15**(3), 1192–1209 (2013)
9. Hayley, H., Gwenn, E., Jeroen, K.: Classifying social actions with a single accelerometer. In: Proceedings of the 2013 ACM International Joint Conference on Pervasive and Ubiquitous Computing, UbiComp 2013, pp. 207–210. ACM, New York (2013)
10. Aparicio, S., Perez, J., Bernardos, AM., Casar, J.R.: A fusion method based on bluetooth and wlan technologies for indoor location. In: Multisensor Fusion and Integration for Intelligent Systems, MFI 2008, pp. 487–491 (August 2008)
11. Carlos E.G., José C.C., Ramon F.B.: Bluetooth-wifi based combined positioning algorithm, implementation and experimental evaluation. Procedia Technology 7, 37–45 (2013), 3rd Iberoamerican Conference on Electronics Engineering and Computer Science, CIIECC 2013
12. Jaewoo, C., Matt, D., Chris, S., Ig-Jae, K., Pedram, R., Micaela, W.: Indoor location sensing using geo-magnetism. In: Proceedings of the 9th International Conference on Mobile Systems, Applications, and Services, MobiSys 2011, pp. 141–154. ACM, New York (2011)
13. Carlos, E.G., José, C.C. Ramon, B.: Location identification using a magnetic-field-based FFT signature. Procedia Computer Science 19, 533–539 (2013), The 4th International Conference on Ambient Systems, Networks and Technologies (ANT 2013), the 3rd International Conference on Sustainable Energy Information Technology (SEIT 2013)
14. Alessandro, C., Matteo, P., Carlo, B., Fabio, L., Massimo, V.: Proximity classification for mobile devices using wi-fi environment similarity. In: Proceedings of the first ACM International Workshop on Mobile Entity Localization and Tracking in GPS-less Environments, pp. 43–48. ACM (2008)
15. Rahman, O.O., Anmol, M., Alex, P., Inas, K.: Identifying close friendships in a sensed social network. Procedia - Social and Behavioral Sciences 79(0), 18–26 (2013), 9th Conference on Applications of Social Network Analysis (ASNA)
16. Zhiwen, Y., Zhou, X., Zhang, D., Schiele, G., Becker, C.: Understanding social relationship evolution by using real-world sensing data. World Wide Web **16**(5–6), 749–762 (2013)

17. Kristina, L., Suradej, I., Jeon-Hyung, K., Rumi, G.: Using proximity to predict activity in social networks. In: Proceedings of the 21st International Conference Companion on World Wide Web, WWW 2012 Companion, pp. 555–556. ACM, New York (2012)
18. Matic, A., Osmani, V., Mayora, O.: Trade-offs in monitoring social interactions. IEEE Communications Magazine 51(7), 114–121 (2013)
19. Matic, A., Osmani, V., Mayora, O.: Speech activity detection using accelerometer. In: 2012 Annual International Conference of the IEEE Engineering in Medicine and Biology Society (EMBC), pp. 2112–2115 (August 2012)
20. Matic, A., Osmani, V., Mayora-Ibarra, O.: Analysis of social interactions through mobile phones. Mobile Networks and Applications 17(6), 808–819 (2012)
21. Krumm, J., Horvitz, E.: LOCADIO: inferring motion and location from wi-fi signal strengths. In: The First Annual International Conference on Mobile and Ubiquitous Systems: Networking and Services, MOBIQUITOUS 2004, pp. 4–13 (August 2004)
22. Welbourne, E., Lester, J., LaMarca, A., Borriello, G.: Mobile context inference using low-cost sensors. In: Strang, T., Linnhoff-Popien, C. (eds.) LoCA 2005. LNCS, vol. 3479, pp. 254–263. Springer, Heidelberg (2005)
23. Nathan, E., Alex(Sandy), P.: Reality mining: Sensing complex social systems. Personal Ubiquitous Comput. 10(4), 255–268 (2006)
24. Vu, L., Do, Q., Nahrstedt, K.: Jyotish: A novel framework for constructing predictive model of people movement from joint wifi/bluetooth trace, pp. 54–62 (March 2011)
25. Sekara, V., Lehmann, S.: The strength of friendship ties in proximity sensor data. PLoS ONE 9(7), 1–8 (2014)
26. Carreras, I., Matic, A., Saar, P., Osmani, V.: Comm2sense: Detecting proximity through smartphones. In: 2012 IEEE International Conference on Pervasive Computing and Communications Workshops (PERCOM Workshops), pp. 253–258 (March 2012)
27. Yang, Y., Chawla, N.V., Basu, P., Prabhala, B., La Porta, T.: Link prediction in human mobility networks. In: 2013 IEEE/ACM International Conference on Advances in Social Networks Analysis and Mining (ASONAM), pp. 380–387 (August 2013)
28. Eagle, N., Alex (Sandy), P., David, L.: Inferring friendship network structure by using mobile phone data. Proceedings of the National Academy of Sciences 106(36), 15274–15278 (2009)
29. Long, V., Klara, N., Samuel, R., Indranil, G.: Joint bluetooth/wifi scanning framework for characterizing and leveraging people movement in university campus. In: Proceedings of the 13th ACM International Conference on Modeling, Analysis, and Simulation of Wireless and Mobile Systems, MSWIM 2010, pp. 257–265. ACM, New York (2010)
30. Carrasco-Jiménez, J.C., Celaya-Padilla, J.M., Montes, G., Brena, R.F., Iglesias, S.: Social interaction discovery: a simulated multiagent approach. In: Carrasco-Ochoa, J.A., Martínez-Trinidad, J.F., Rodríguez, J.S., di Baja, G.S. (eds.) MCPR 2012. LNCS, vol. 7914, pp. 294–303. Springer, Heidelberg (2013)

31. Stopczynski, A., Sekara, V., Sapiezynski, P., Cuttone, A., Mette, M.M., Jakob, E., Sune, L.: Measuring large-scale social networks with high resolution. PLoS ONE **9**(4), 1–24 (2014)
32. Jaccard, P.: Nouvelles recherches sur la distribution florale. Bull. Soc. Vaud. Sci. Nat. (1908)
33. Metz, C.E.: Basic principles of ROC analysis. Seminars in Nuclear Medicine **8**(4), 283–298 (1978)
34. Sing, T., Sander, O., Beerenwinkel, N., Lengauer, T.: ROCR: visualizing classifier performance in R. Bioinformatics **21**(20), 3940–3941 (2005)

SIMDOMO: A Tool for Long-Term Simulations of Ambient-Assisted Living

Massimo Zancanaro[1(✉)], Michele Marchesoni[1], and Giampaolo Armellin[2]

[1] Fondazione Bruno Kessler, Trento, Italy
{zancana,marchesoni}@springer.com
[2] Centro Ricerche GPI, Trento, Italy
giampaolo.armellin@cr-gpi.it

Abstract. In this paper, we introduce SIMDOMO, a tool to simulate human activities in virtual sensorized houses. The purpose of the tool is to facilitate the generation of large amount of data for the design and evaluation of ambient-assisted living applications. Specifically, for experimenting with visualizations of home activities over long periods (years or decades); for training and testing algorithms to recognize changes of behaviors or anomalies that would be difficult to observe in real settings or in lab; testing infrastructures for robustness and scaling; as well as, for assessing business models. SIMDOMO allows defining "human behaviors" in terms of temporally anchored activities: these behaviors can then be automatically replicated introducing small random variations to make the data more varied. The time of the simulation can be accelerated by several factors allowing the generation of decades of simulated life in few hours. We believe that this tool addresses an urgent need in the field of Ambient-Assisted Living.

1 Introduction

Ambient Assisted Living [4] is a research area aimed at investigate technologies for supporting elderly and people with special needs in their daily lives in order to allow them to live longer in their own homes. Data and information quality in this domain is a pressing issue [3]. A variety of middleware architectures are available today that allow experimenting in real homes. Yet, real case studies are often impractical or even impossible. For example, testing the possibility of detecting long-term cognitive decline or assessing the usability of a visualization tool for monitoring hundreds of houses simultaneously would require collecting large amounts of data for long-term periods. Similarly, business decision-makers may need the evaluation of *what-if* scenarios (for example, the assessment of the cost-quality of sensors to use in the environment) that would require repetition of studies with different type of equipment.

Some of the data and information quality issues may be tackled by means of reliable models bootstrapped from small datasets (as suggested for example by Wan and colleagues [5]). Another approach is to simulate data provision in a fast and reliable way. Simulations are long known to be a useful tool to validate ideas, concepts and technologies in situations for which practical experimentation is difficult or impossible [2].

© Springer International Publishing Switzerland 2014
E. Aarts et al. (Eds.): AmI 2014, LNCS 8850, pp. 47–50, 2014.
DOI: 10.1007/978-3-319-14112-1_4

Simulations are not much used in Ambient Assisted Living research although there are some notable exceptions. For example, Autexier and colleagues [1] propose a virtual reality environment to simulate the deployment of assisting technologies in homes. Yet, this approach is mainly aimed at envisioning the impact of the deployment of a given technology and it does not directly addresses the issue of data and information quality as discussed above. In this paper, we describe SIMDOMO, a simulator of domestic sensorized environments aimed at generating large amount of data from simple descriptions of human behaviors.

2   Design Goals

In designing SIMDOMO, our main goal was to provide a tool that may support non-technical people (specifically, nurses, expert in gerontology, social services operators, and so on) in describing "typical" and "atypical" lifestyle in terms of codified behaviors and subsequently to be able to generate large amount of data simulating those behaviors. Specifically, our goals were the following: (i) testing infrastructures of data collection and analysis for what concerns efficiency, robustness, reliability; (ii) develop and test stochastic algorithm for pattern recognition from sensors' data; (iii) assess visualization from large amounts of sensors data, specifically for what concerns long time intervals; (iv) validate *what-if* scenarios to assess business cases.

3   SIMDOMO: Simulation of Domestic Sensorized Environment

SIMDOMO is a Java application that replicates defined behaviors in sensorized settings with accelerated time and provides the effects of those behaviors to external applications (for visualization, modelling or other uses).

```
0.     Repeat every day
1.     Gets out of the bed [7am-8am]
2.     Is in the corridor [10mins later]
3.     Is in the bathroom [1mins later]
4.     Is in the corridor [10-15mins later]
5.     Is in the kitchen [1min later]
6.     Is in the living room [10am-12pm]
7.     Is in the corridor [1 min before]
8.     Is in the kitchen [12.30pm-14pm]
9.     Is in the corridor [1 min before]
10.    ...
```

Fig. 1. An example of a codified behavior (a temporal sequence of actions)

A "behavior" is a sequence of actions performed by simulated occupants of a domestic setting. The sequence is defined in terms of temporal constraints which are either "absolute" (for example, an action occurs between 8.30am and 8.35am every day) or "relative" (for example, an action occurs 10 minutes after the previous one). This approach allows to easily defining relatively complex behaviors in operational terms so that domain expert rather than simulation experts may define them. Although this approach may be weaker than the definition of abstract models of behavior, it better suits the goal of the tool, which is generating large amount of data about coded behavior in order to use this data for testing visualization tools or infer stochastic modelling rather than study the accuracy of the behavior defined. Fig. 1 provides an example of a behavior defined as a temporal sequence of movements and the simple action "*getting out of the bed*": the script describes a part of "typical day" of a person in a house. It is worth noting that the temporal specification (both absolute and relative) can be specified as interval: upon execution the system will randomly select a specific time in that interval and, in this way, each repetition may be slightly different. The example describes a behavior repeated every day. Using this approach, it is easy to merge this "typical behavior" with another behavior describing an exception (such as an emergency or skipping breakfast): a different behavior may be defined as occurring on a specific day, for example, on 1 June. Similarly, it is possible to define a set of behaviors that model a progression toward a less sustainable life style as a sequence of behaviors that span several months of year. For example, the behavior in Fig. 1 can be repeated every day from January to March and be replaced by other behaviors (describing a progressive late wake up in the morning, for example) in the subsequent months.

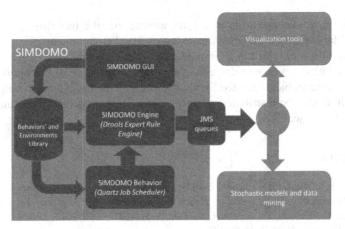

Fig. 2. SIMDOMO general architecture

The *SIMDOMO* architecture is displayed in Fig. 2. It is composed by three main modules: the *SIMDOMO Behavior* module that schedules the execution of the actions, the *SIMDOMO Engine* module that instantiates the execution of the actions in the defined environment and finally the *SIMDOMO GUI* that supports the definition of behaviors, environments and sensors (not yet realized). The *SIMDOMO Behavior* module reads a definition of a behavior and execute it by allowing some variations (so that each replication is not exactly the same of all the other replications). This module does not check for consistency of the behavior nor for the definition of the action but it just schedule and activate the actions according to the temporal constraints. When the temporal reference is an interval (as in the steps 1,4,6 and 8 in Fig. 1) the scheduler simply choose a random time in that interval. In this way, the execution of a given behavior may slightly change every repetition. The core of this module is an instance of Quartz[1], a very efficient open source job scheduler. The *SIMDOMO Engine* module receives the notifications of an action and simulate its execution in the environment: it uses a description of the environment and the sensors to simulate the effects (in terms of sensors' activations). This module uses JBoss Drools Expert[2], an open source rule engine to map actions' execution to sensors' readings (basically, each sensor is modelled as a group of Expert rules and the execution of an action consists on the activation of the corresponding rules). In this way, the same behavior may generate different data in different environments (which means that different rules are used). Finally, the (simulated) sensors' readings are made available through a JMS[3] queue to external services. The services may read all the data or subscribe to a subset of sensors.

In initial tests, SIMDOMO was able to generate data from simple behaviors (similar to the one described in in Fig. 1) with hundreds of simultaneous replications and by the speed of time increased by a factor of one thousand using a standard desktop computer.

4   Conclusion and Further Work

In this paper, we discussed the initial implementation of a tool that support the generation of data of long-term behaviors in a sensorized environments.

Although the tool is still in an initial stage of development, we believe that the ideas presented here can boost a discussion about the importance of this approach for the design of future ambient-assisted living.   At present, the tool is in a pre-alpha version and it will shortly be distributed as open source. This work has been funded by the SUITECASE project.

References

1. Autexier, S., Hutter, D., Stahl, C.: An Implementation, Execution and Simulation Platform for Processes in Heterogeneous Smart Environments. In: Augusto, J.C., Wichert, R., Collier, R., Keyson, D., Salah, A.A., Tan, A.-H. (eds.) AmI 2013. LNCS, vol. 8309, pp. 3–18. Springer, Heidelberg (2013)
2. Banks, J.: Handbook of Computer Simulation. Principles, Methodology, Advances, Applications and Practice. John Wiley and Sons (1998)
3. McNaull, J., Augusto, J.C., Mulvenna, M., McCullagh, P.: Data and Information Quality Issues in Ambient Assisted Living Systems. ACM J. Data Inform. Quality **4**, 1 (2012)
4. Sun, H., Florio, V.D., Gui, N., Blondia, C.: Promises and challenges of ambient assisted living systems. In: Proceedings of the 6th IEEE International Conference on Information Technology (2009)
5. Wan, J., O'Grady, M.J., O'Hare, G.M.: Bootstrapping Activity Modeling for Ambient Assisted Living. In: Zeng, D., Yang, C.C., Tseng, V.S., Xing, C., Chen, H., Wang, F.-Y., Zheng, X. (eds.) ICSH 2013. LNCS, vol. 8040, pp. 96–106. Springer, Heidelberg (2013)

---

[1] http://quartz-scheduler.org/

[2] http://www.drools.org/

[3] http://docs.oracle.com/javaee/6/tutorial/doc/bncdq.html

Recognition of Bed Postures Using Mutual Capacitance Sensing

Silvia Rus[1]([✉]), Tobias Grosse-Puppendahl[1], and Arjan Kuijper[1,2]

[1] Fraunhofer IGD, Fraunhoferstr. 5, 64283 Darmstadt, Germany
{silvia.rus,tobias.grosse-puppendahl,arjan.kuijper}@igd.fraunhofer.de
[2] Technische Universität Darmstadt, Hochschulstr. 10, 64289 Darmstadt, Germany
arjan.kuijper@gris.tu-darmstadt.de

Abstract. In recent years, mutual capacitive sensing made significant advances in the field of gathering implicit contextual data. These systems find broad usage in pervasive activity-recognition systems, installed stationary or made portable. In the domain of context recognition new ways of interaction with the environment opened up since conductive objects can be detected under certain conditions at distances up to 50 cm.

This paper investigates an approach to recognize bed postures using mutual capacitance sensing. The overall goal is to develop a technological concept that can be applied to recognize bed postures of patients in elderly homes. The use of this contextual data may lead to many desired benefits in elderly care e.g. the better prevention of decubitus ulcer, a condition caused by prolonged pressure on the skin resulting in injuries to skin and underlying tissues. For this, we propose a low-cost grid of crossed wires of 48 measurement points placed between the mattress and the bed sheet. The experimental results analyze a set of five lying positions. We achieved for all tested individuals an accuracy of 80.76% and for several individuals of the same bodysize an accuracy of 93.8%.

Keywords: Activity recognition · Capacitive sensing · Ambient assisted living

1 Introduction

A specifically demanding use case, addressed in this paper, is the decubitus ulcer prevention, called also bedsore or pressure sore prevention. The last name describes the process best, since the decubitus ulcer develops on skin which is exposed to too much pressure for a prolonged time. The presented system is of a preventive nature intended to alarm the caretaker to look after the bedridden person and change its position every one to two hours [12]. This paper envisages a system which might be used at home or in hospitals, where responsible personnel is on-site to react to the alarm of the system. The system would monitor the bed posture changes of the bedridden person. The information of how long a person has been lying in a certain position can help the caregiver to decide which action

© Springer International Publishing Switzerland 2014
E. Aarts et al. (Eds.): AmI 2014, LNCS 8850, pp. 51–66, 2014.
DOI: 10.1007/978-3-319-14112-1_5

to take. For example the bedridden person has been positioned during sleep to one lateral side. When the bedridden person changes the position on her own the caregiver can know how the person moved through sleep and avoid placing her back to the previous posture. This prevents that specific body parts will be exposed to higher pressure over longer time, which may harm the bedridden person.

In order to realize a system that detects bed postures, multiple approaches have been already developed applying different sensing modalities. For example, it is common to use capacitive pressure sensing or camera-based visual data. However, previous approaches require expensive hardware and are often not easy to deploy. Therefore, we propose an extremely easy to deploy and inexpensive to produce bed sheet. It is comparable to a large capacitive touch-screen and uses standard affordable hardware components. We propose to use capacitive sensing in shunt mode to achieve the goal. In capacitive sensing, the use of shunt mode [15] allows for a high number of measurements which have positive influence on the recognition performance. Therefore, a grid of wire electrodes is placed on top of the mattress and measures the proximity to body parts. Applying shunt mode requires a distinct transmitter and receiver electrode. In the following Section 2, this sensing principle is explained in more detail and approaches to detect bed postures using different sensing methods are presented. The hardware setup and the processing software are presented in Section 3, while the bed posture recognizing software, the effectuated experiments and the achieved results are presented in Section 5. Finally, the conclusion and the future work are addressed in Section 6.

2   Related Work

2.1   Capacitive Sensing

Through touch screens the capacitive sensing technology has entered every-day usage. Various layers of transparent nanowires are placed on top of each other creating intersections between them. As a conductive object enters the sensing area, the mutual capacitance at the intersection is measured [1]. A capacitance sensor detects a change in capacitance once a conductive object touches it or gets into the sensing area. Before capacitive sensing spread into the domain of human-computer interfaces, it was already widespread in industry like the measurement of liquid levels, humidity and material composition [13].

In capacitive sensing three measurement modes can be differentiated. These are the *loading mode*, the *transmit mode* and the *shunt mode*, shown in Figure 1. In *loading mode* the displacement current in the transmitting electrode is measured. The displacement current is induced by a grounded object moving and changing the electric field. The advantage of this mode is the possibility of easy shielding the electrode against the influence of surrounding existing electric potentials [5]. This is the mode meant when generally talking about capacitive sensing. In *shunt mode*, a capacitance is measured by introducing a grounded

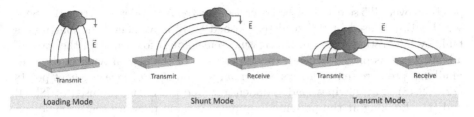

Fig. 1. Three different capacitive measurement modes identified by Smith et al. [15], [5]

object in the electric field between the transmitting and the receiving electrode and measuring the displacement current in the receiving electrode. If a higher precision is needed multiple transmitters and receivers can be used. This can be regarded as an advantage to loading mode which requires one sensor per measurement. The number of possible measurements in shunt mode is n = (number of transmitters * number of receivers). The third mode is the *transmit mode*. Here, the object introduced in the electric field between the transmitter and receiver is not grounded and needs to be strongly coupled to the transmitter.

From the three capacitive sensing modes, we use the shunt modeto build the system for the bed posture detection.This mode is very similar to the ones used in modern capacitive touch-screens. The bed basically represents a big touch-screen with crossed wires which allow for sensing the mutual capacitance between the wires' intersections.

2.2   Bed Posture Recognition

Lots of research has been done to investigate the way people sleep. Besides capturing the vital signs of a person, the lying position is also a good metric for investigating possible sleeping disorders. Different approaches exist to detect this characteristics of sleep using different sensing measures like acceleration, visual data, temperature, pressure, capacitance and combinations of these.

The pressure on the vertebral spine during sleep is an important indicator for the quality of sleep. This is what the authors of [7] achieved by differentiating if a person is lying or sitting upright in the bed using capacitive sensors. Therefore, they placed six electrodes underneath the mattress of a bed. When a person lies down it activates a pattern of these electrodes. The algorithm can detect the person's bedding posture. Multiple approaches for detecting bed postures exist which apply resistive and capacitive pressure sensors. For example Liu et al. [9], [10] use a high density sensor bed sheet for monitoring the patients' rehabilitation exercises. It is composed of three layers where the top textile layer is coated with 64 conductive lines, the middle layer is eTextile material and the bottom textile layer is also coated with 128 conductive lines, perpendicular to the first layer. At each intersection of the conductive lines a pressure sensor node is formed, giving a total of 8192 pressure sensors. The mean of the achieved precision over all 5 selected on-bed exercises is 83%. An Under Mattress Bed Sensor (UMBS) is used in [18] to detect in-bed body movement. The mattress is built by integrating a grid of 24 pressure sensors in a foam mat in the form of a band which is placed beneath the upper torso of the person lying in the bed. Similarly, pressure sensor arrays with a varying number of measurement points (72, 132,48), form (stripes, pads), dimensions and placement are used by [8], [4] and [11]. Looking at the presented approaches using pressure sensors, one can observe that the detected positions are very different between the various deployments. A direct comparison between the high density sensor bed sheet with 8192 pressure sensor nodes and the pressure sensor matrix with 72 pressure sensors cannot be directly performed, even if the detected positions overlap. The reason is that since for the high density sensor bed sheet only the precision is given, while and for the pressure sensor matrix the accuracy is given. The pressure sensor matrix and the FlexiForce pressure sensor bands have detected comparable positions and have achieved accuracies of 84% and 87%. The number of deployed sensor nodes is slightly higher for the system with the higher accuracy. Thus, no direct connection can be drawn between the number of measuring points and the achieved accuracy. A very high accuracy range of 94% - 100% is achieved with the pressure sensitive mattress. This is due to the fact that its classifier only differentiates between lying and sitting positions.

Different camera systems are used to acquire the visual data. In [3] a 3D Time of Flight (ToF) camera, in [21] a common digital camera and in [14] a depth camera is used. These are designed mainly as fall-detection systems but can also identify a lying posture. Accelerometers are used to detect bed postures like lateral left and right, supine and ventral. They are attached to the body on the sternum and on the right thigh [20] or worn at the dominant wrist [2].

The techniques presented above can be used independently to detect the bed posture, but systems using them in a combination also exist, e.g. visual and capacitive sensing data[16], acceleration and capacitive sensing data [6] or even a combination of temperature, light, tilt and acceleration [17].

3   Prototype

In the following we present our smart bed sheet and describe the different components used to realize it. First, we present a system overview in Section 3.1 and describe the applied evaluation boards in detail, the electrode grid and the sensors at the receiver side. We conclude by describing the firmware on the OpenCapSense evaluation boards in Section 3.2.

3.1   Hardware Components of Smart Bed Sheet

Figure 2 chematically depicts the three main components of the smart bed sheet. These are the wired grid with the sensing unit, the evaluation boards to which the grid is connected and the PC with the visualization implementation in MATLAB. The two boards are named after their function. Hence, the Tx Board is

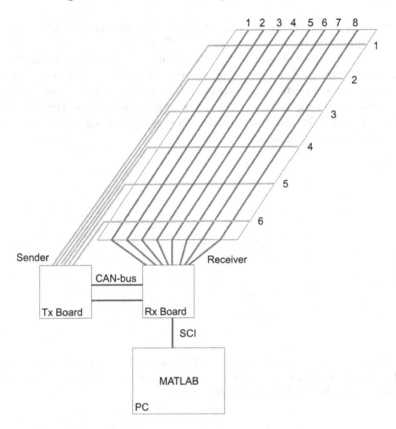

Fig. 2. Schematic overview of setup. Two OpenCapSense evaluation boards connected by a CAN-bus interface for synchronization. The transmitting board sends out the signal through the electrodes while the receiving board RxBoard collects the data, processes it and sends it to the PC to be analyzed by MATLAB.

used for transmitting the signal and the Rx Board is used to process the received information. It then sends the calculated value to the PC using a USB connection. A Matlab program receives the data and performs digital signal processing and classification.

OpenCapSense is a capacitive sensing toolkit presented in [5] to enable the easy development of capacitive systems. The toolkit has been published as an open-source project and is inspired by the CapToolKit [19]. Besides loading mode, it also supports shunt mode which has been used for the measurements performed in this.

Besides a powerful floating point microntroller, OpenCapSense has eight capacitive sensing channels. They can be used for either transmitting or receiving a signal through an elecotrde. It is possible to build sensing arrays by connecting multiple evaluation boards CAN-bus and synchronize them. The board has a connection to the PC, which serves as the 5V power supply. Moreover, messages are passed to the computer through the onboard serial-to-USB interface. All these connection interfaces are shown in Figure 4.

The board interfaces might be used as both input or output ports. In order to connect sensors in shunt mode or loading mode, the interfaces need to be set up to be output ports. The board offers to functionality to generate signal using a pulse-width-modulation. This allows for adjusting the frequency of the transmitted signal. In our final bedsheet we generated signals on six output ports, oscillating at a frequency 7.3 KHz.

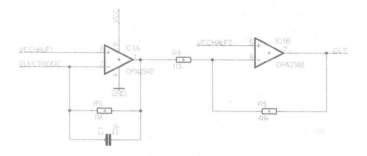

Fig. 3. Each receiving electrode is connected to a sensor with a transimpedance amplifier. The sensor amplifies the incoming displacement current from a transmitting electrode and amplifies it for further processing.

On the receiver side, dedicated hardware has been developed to evaluate the received signals. The transmitted signals are received by an amplifier configuration displayed in Figure 3. The circuit is built of two stages, a transimpedance amplifier with a low pass filter, followed by an inverting amplifier with a gain of 4 (G = 40k/10k). The circuit of the low pass filter is built by adding a capacitor across the feedback resistor of the operational amplifier. The output voltage is passed to the ADC on the OpenCapSense board. This design is inspired by Smith et al. [15].

3.2   Data Processing

The role of the transmitting board is to alternate the output sender pins on which the rectangular signal is sent. The transmitting board TxBoard starts its operation by setting the sending frequency and initializing the CAN-bus interface, the SCI interface and the output pins. It listens for messages on the CAN bus, which indicate to start sending on a certain output pin. Starting the transmission a square signal at 7.3 kHz is sent. The receiving board subsequently transmits through the CAN-bus the next output pin on which it expects the transmitter board to send the signal.

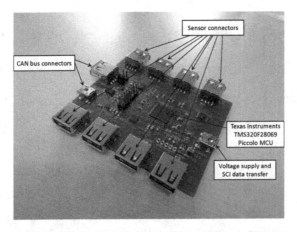

Fig. 4. Interfaces of OpenCapSense evaluation board

On the other end, the receiver switches through all its receiving ports and then sends the next expected sender on the CAN-bus. For each measurement at the receiver a window of 1024 values (the size of the ADC buffer) is collected at once. Ten of these windows are collected per receiver.

As shown in Figure 5, the original signal is windowed and the magnitude of the Fourier Transform is calculated. The peaks of the magnitude are added up. For different frequencies of the sent rectangular signal, the peaks of the amplitude are placed differently. This way, operating the system using FDMA (Frequency Division Multiple Access) would be possible by adding up the peaks in intervals which are specific for the expected frequency. This calculated value represents the sensed value transmitted to the PC through the SCI interface, together with the according sender and receiver information.

Concluding, one can say that for each sender the sum of maxima of the magnitude of the Fourier Transform is calculated and the mean is built over a number of w windows. This mean value is sent to the PC, where the MATLAB script described in Section 4 further processes it.

4   Implementation

In this section we describe how the received values are further processed using MATLAB. We will start by describing the calibration of the system, then a few processing steps of the normalized values and will finish by describing the choice of features.

The sensed values are continuously received at the serial port using MATLAB, which has real-time read capacity of the serial port. For a single measurement point, in this case sender 3, receiver 5, the raw data while a person was lying down is displayed in Figure 4. In this figure, a person sits down on two crossed wires. First, the sensed value is at about 3100 while at measurement point 15 the sensed value rises about 1500 reaching the sensed value of 4500.

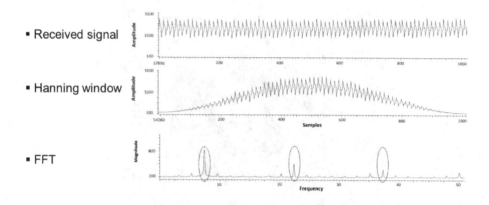

• Received signal

• Hanning window

• FFT

Fig. 5. The received signal is windowed, a Fourier Transform is applied on the signal and in the resulting magnitude of the FFT, the amplitudes are added up resulting the sensed value

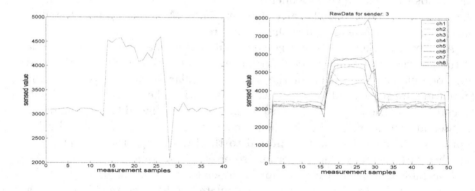

Fig. 6. Visualization of measured raw data of a single measurement point (sender 3, receiver 5) and of all eight receivers of sender 3

This steep rise is due to the fact that a person was lying down on this sensor node. In Figure 4, the sensed values for all receivers of sender 3 are displayed. Between measurement points 15 and 31 a person was lying down in this area whereas all other measurement points were taken while the bed was empty. We can see that even in the empty state not all receivers are at the same value. Furthermore, the difference between the empty bed values and the person lying values is different, e.g. for receiver 3 (ch3) the difference is around 4500 while for receiver 5 (ch5) the difference is around 3000. This leads to the conclusion that an equalization of the sensing range, a normalization, needs to be done in order to be able to compare the sensor values. For this, the system needs to be calibrated. This is done by detecting the sensed values of the empty bed and the

Table 1. Sensing range first calibration

Sender \ Receiver	1	2	3	4	5	6	7	8
1	5705	2842	4502	4953	4866	4426	2988	5444
2	5710	2873	4509	4925	4835	4464	2984	5410
3	3896	1762	3128	3404	3283	3111	2049	3693
4	6427	3921	4943	5493	5479	5201	4067	5954
5	3632	2103	2763	3153	3091	2917	2166	3188
6	5540	2323	3617	4740	5100	4711	2557	5103

Table 2. Sensing range first calibration

Sender \ Receiver	1	2	3	4	5	6	7	8
1	5018	2180	3011	3634	3737	3418	2289	4910
2	5040	2194	2968	3623	3755	3441	2250	4908
3	3438	1177	2076	2523	2621	2453	1481	3367
4	4756	2696	3425	4020	3826	3624	2867	5058
5	3127	1677	2229	2705	2594	2510	1851	3242
6	5090	2703	3686	4474	4329	4025	2727	5593

Table 3. Variation of the sensing range between two calibrations

Sender \ Receiver	1	2	3	4	5	6	7	8
1	687	662	1491	1319	1129	1008	699	534
2	670	679	1541	1302	1080	1023	734	502
3	458	585	1052	881	662	658	568	326
4	1671	1225	1518	1473	1653	1577	1200	896
5	505	426	534	448	497	407	315	-54
6	450	-380	-69	266	771	686	-170	-490

values for the same object for all sensor nodes. For two of these measurements we have calculated the sensing range. The results are shown in Tables 1 and 2. Table 3 shows the difference between the sensing range of the two calibrations. We observe that some sensing range extend and some get smaller, being different each time.

Next, after receiving the sensed values through the serial port, these are normalized using the sensing range determined by the calibration. Once the normalization is done, the square root is applied on the data to boost smaller signals in order to enhance detecting smaller objects. In the left image of Figure 4 we show the normalized 6x8 data and in the right image the square rooted and twice interpolated data. We used a cubic interpolation.

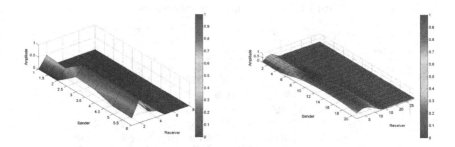

Fig. 7. 6x8 Normalized data and interpolated data

4.1   Features of Bed Postures

To detect bed postures, we thought of treating the matrix with the sensor values as an image. From this image we extract features like the mean and the center of gravity. The center of gravity is computed as the maxima of the average of the row and the average of the column. To further granulate the results, the image is divided into 8 sections like shown in Figure 8. We decided to use eight sections by looking at the resulting interpolated image and trying to find matching features for the image. The right image of Figure 8 is formed by creating a grayscale image of the left image and displaying it in 2D, proportional to a 6x8 matrix. The colored dots represent the center of gravity calculated for each section, while the bigger yellow dot is the computed center of gravity of the whole image. Finally, next to the eight means and eight centers of gravity (8 pairs of row and column coordinates), the overall mean and center of gravity have been used as features, resulting in 27 features collected for each image.

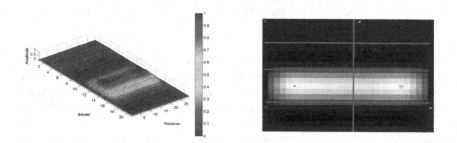

Fig. 8. Visualization of normalized values and view of sections with overlaid center of gravity per section and whole image

5   Experiment

In this section, we present our experiment, the setup and the evaluation criteria.

5.1   Setup

The goal of the experimental setup is to evaluate postures that are typical for the elderly or persons who are bound to the bed. A possible use-case for recognizing these postures is to support a caregivers in rebedding patients. This is especially useful when persons sometimes have active and inactive phases. For example in active phases, rebedding can be avoided, while on the other hand, inactive phases may lead the caregiver to change the patient's bedding postures more frequently. However, there are numerous other application scenarios like the *quantified self* trend. This could allow persons to capture their own sleeping behaviours and make inferences about improvements in the living environment.

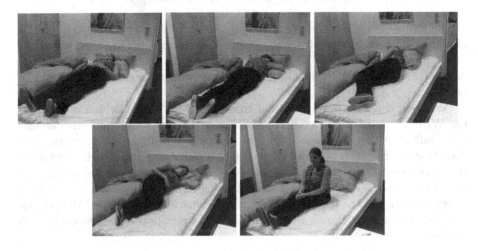

Fig. 9. Common bedding postures used for the experiments

The use-cases mentioned above induced as to apply our smart bed sheet on classifying discrete user postures. Therefore, the bed sheet was placed on an ordinary bed with a length of 2.0 m and a width of 0.8 m, as depicted in Figure 9. The bed sheet provides 48 measurement points, with eight horizontal and six vertical wires, a part of which is shown in Figure 10. In our first stage of the experiment, we asked 14 persons to lie on the bed with previously defined postures. The test persons were only instructed by few words, allowing them to carry out the postures as variable as possible.

5.2   Feature Extraction and Classification

The recorded test set included the following postures: Sitting on the bed, lying on either the right and left side, lying on the stomach or back. As noise or movements in the region around the bed might lead to problems, we also recorded a number of instances for an empty bed. Based on the data measured on the 48

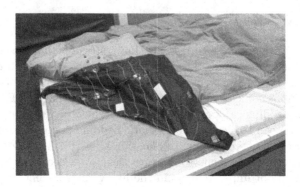

Fig. 10. Prototype bed sheet with wired grid

measurement points, we extracted a number of features, which were explained in the previous section 4.1. The features included the center of gravity and the mean sensor value, each calculated for eight uniform sub-regions and the overall bed.

We applied a J48-trained decision tree for our evaluation, which is based on the WEKA framework[1]. Decision trees enable a quick evaluation on how features influence the classifier's decisions and which features are important for classification. For each posture, we recorded a set of 45 images each of 48 measurement points, displayed and extracted the features form each of them. The test persons carried out each posture, allowing them to vary between different interpretations for the specific posture. For evaluation, we assigned the recordings for each test person to two dedicated sets and applied a cross evaluation on them.

5.3   Results

After carrying out the first experiments, we quickly realized the person's weight and height had much more influence on the classification performance than expected. It is very difficult to have a good recognition performance for persons with very different body sizes. The difference in sensor measurements of a heavy person (80 kg) compared to a small person (60 kg) for the same posture is depicted in Figure 11. Such examples show that features which are invariant to body-size are very hard to find when the sensing area is a rather limiting factor. Investigating translation-invariant features was not necessary since the bed's area was quite small and minor body translations did not have a big effect on the recognition performance.

Including all body sizes, we achieved a very poor recognition performance of 80.76% overall accuracy for 14 test persons. Based on these observations, we decided to limit our next experiment on a set of eight persons who are in

---

[1] http://www.cs.waikato.ac.nz/ml/weka (date accessed: 2014-08-21)

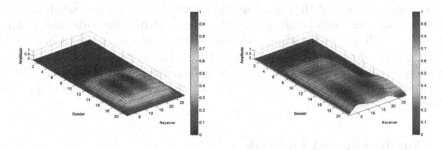

Fig. 11. Images of two persons with different weight sitting on the bed

the interval between 80-95 kg. This lead to an improved performance of 93.8% overall accuracy. It can be concluded that our feature set, as well as the whole setup, depends strongly on body height and weight. In the future, the design of features which are more invariant to such circumstances is therefore a very important prospect to us. The two resulting confusion matrices for both sets are depicted in Figure 12. .

Limited data set (≥ 80kg)						Overall data set						← classified as
a	b	c	d	e	f	a	b	c	d	e	f	
357	0	0	0	0	3	**568**	0	16	45	1	0	a = sitting
0	**327**	0	33	0	0	0	**530**	2	57	2	0	b = side right
0	0	**316**	44	0	0	0	0	**585**	0	45	0	c = side left
0	1	0	**359**	0	0	45	123	156	**306**	0	0	d = stomach
1	0	48	4	**307**	0	0	9	170	17	**434**	0	e = back
0	0	0	0	0	**360**	0	0	0	0	0	**630**	f = empty

Fig. 12. The classification performance depends highly on the person's body height and weight. Separating the test sets into persons with similar body properties, e.g. separating the persons by weight, leads to a much better performance in the data sets.

Also, the resulting decision trees in the set with small persons were significantly smaller, having a depth of five levels, than the ones generated with the overall test set, resulting in depths of seven or more levels. The trees show that center-of-gravity features (COG) contribute significantly to the classification. With regard to the bed sheet's different sections, features from the sections in the middle of the bed are used more often in classification. On the other hand, sections representing data from the test persons' heads and feet are included less often in the decision trees. The reason can be seen in the inhomogeneous weight distribution on the mattress. The proximity to body parts has less influence on a mutual capacitance measurement than the deformation of the underlying mattress, caused by large weight on the measurement point. As expected, the mean features are used to decide between classes like *lying on stomach* and *lying on back*, where the weight in the corresponding regions is significantly different.

We can conclude that the classification performance currently depends highly on the test persons' body height and weight. The small bed size makes it hard for developers to design features that are invariant to these properties. Compared to the regions around a person's head and feet, the regions in the middle are more important for classification. Increasing the number of measurement points in the bed sheet's center region can lead to a better recognition performance in the future.

6   Conclusion and Outlook

In this paper we realized a prototypical bed sheet which can recognize bed postures and pressure points which can be applied for decubitus ulcer prevention in hospitals or at home. In contrast to previous work, the bed sheet is very easy to realize and to handle. It uses simple conductive wires which are inexpensive and can be replaced without great effort. The prototype is composed of a wire electrode grid connected in capacitive shunt mode, where senders are placed horizontally to the bed posture and receivers are placed longitudinal to the bed. Measuring the mutual capacitance between these electrodes allows for detecting the presence of human body parts. These electrodes are connected to two OpenCapSense evaluation boards. The data is treated like an image of 48 pixels. It is normalized, interpolated and features like the mean and the center of gravity are calculated for different regions of the image. The evaluation with 14 participants resulted in a overall accuracy of 80.76% while the accuracy of a subset of taller test persons weighting between 80-95 kg resulted in an accuracy of 93.8%.

There are various areas in which the smart bed sheet can be improved for future iterations. One of the challenges is the design of features which are more invariant to body height and weight. Furthermore, the influence of the calibration on the sensitivity of the bed sheet has to be investigated in order to detect smaller body parts like hands and feet. This could be achieved by improving the setup of the electrode grid. We could also investigate if for a small household the bed sheet could be able to identify persons just by lying down on the bed. In any case, our goal is to realize bed posture recognition using capacitive sensing in order to support the prevention of decubitus ulcer.

References

1. Barrett, G., Omote, R.: Projected-capacitive touch technology. Information Display **26**(3), 16–21 (2010)
2. Borazio, M., Blanke, U., Van Laerhoven, K.: Characterizing sleeping trends from postures. In: 2010 International Symposium on Wearable Computers (ISWC), pp. 1–2. IEEE (2010)

3. Diraco, G., Leone, A., Siciliano, P.: Human posture recognition with a time-of-flight 3d sensor for in-home applications. Expert Systems with Applications (2012)
4. Foubert, N., McKee, A., Goubran, R., Knoefel, F.: Lying and sitting posture recognition and transition detection using a pressure sensor array. In: 2012 IEEE International Symposium on Medical Measurements and Applications Proceedings (MeMeA), pp. 1–6 (2012)
5. Grosse-Puppendahl, T., Berghoefer, Y., Braun, A., Wimmer, R., Kuijper, A.: Opencapsense: A rapid prototyping toolkit for pervasive interaction using capacitive sensing. In: 2013 IEEE International Conference on Pervasive Computing and Communications (PerCom), pp. 152–159 (2013)
6. Grosse-Puppendahl, T., Berlin, E., Borazio, M.: Enhancing accelerometer-based activity recognition with capacitive proximity sensing. In: Paternò, F., de Ruyter, B., Markopoulos, P., Santoro, C., van Loenen, E., Luyten, K. (eds.) AmI 2012. LNCS, vol. 7683, pp. 17–32. Springer, Heidelberg (2012)
7. Hamisu, P., Braun, A.: Analyse des schlafverhaltens durch kapazitive sensorarrays zur ermittlung der wirbelsäulenbelastung. Ambient Assisted Living-AAL (2010)
8. Hsia, C., Liou, K.J., Aung, A.P.W., Foo, V., Huang, W., Biswas, J.: Analysis and comparison of sleeping posture classification methods using pressure sensitive bed system. In: Annual International Conference of the IEEE Engineering in Medicine and Biology Society, EMBC 2009, pp. 6131–6134 (2009)
9. Liu, J.J., Huang, M.C., Xu, W., Alshurafa, N., Sarrafzadeh, M.: On-bed monitoring for range of motion exercises with a pressure sensitive bedsheet. In: 2013 IEEE International Conference on Body Sensor Networks (BSN), pp. 1–6. IEEE (2013)
10. Liu, J.J., Xu, W., Huang, M.C., Alshurafa, N., Sarrafzadeh, M., Raut, N., Yadegar, B.: A dense pressure sensitive bedsheet design for unobtrusive sleep posture monitoring. In: IEEE International Conference on Pervasive Computing and Communications (PerCom), vol. 18, p. 22 (2013)
11. Ni, H., Abdulrazak, B., Zhang, D., Wu, S.: Unobtrusive sleep posture detection for elder-care in smart home. In: Lee, Y., Bien, Z.Z., Mokhtari, M., Kim, J.T., Park, M., Kim, J., Lee, H., Khalil, I. (eds.) ICOST 2010. LNCS, vol. 6159, pp. 67–75. Springer, Heidelberg (2010)
12. für Innovationen im Gesundheitswesen und angewandte Pflegeforschung e.V., I.: Dekubitus - immer noch ein problem in der pflege (2003–2013). http://www.dekubitus.de/dekubitusprophylaxe-lagerungstechniken.htm (October 31, 2013)
13. Pratt, S.: Ask the application engineer 35 (2006)
14. Shotton, J., Sharp, T., Kipman, A., Fitzgibbon, A., Finocchio, M., Blake, A., Cook, M., Moore, R.: Real-time human pose recognition in parts from single depth images. Communications of the ACM 56(1), 116–124 (2013)
15. Smith, J.R.: Electric field imaging. Ph.D. thesis (1999)
16. Teske, P.: Ein Multisensor-System zur Sturzerkennung. Master's thesis, HAW Hamburg, Berliner Tor 5, 20099 Hamburg (2012)
17. Van Laerhoven, K., Borazio, M., Kilian, D., Schiele, B.: Sustained logging and discrimination of sleep postures with low-level, wrist-worn sensors. In: Proceedings of the 12th International Symposium on Wearable Computers (ISWC 2008), pp. 69–77. IEEE Press (2008)

18. Walsh, L., McLoone, S.: Non-contact under-mattress sleep monitoring. Journal of Ambient Intelligence and Smart Environments **6**(4), 385–401 (2014)
19. Wimmer, R., Kranz, M., Boring, S., Schmidt, A.: A Capacitive Sensing Toolkit for Pervasive Activity Detection and Recognition. In: IEEE International Conference on Pervasive Computing and Communications (PerCom 2007). IEEE Computer Society (2007)
20. Wrzus, C., Brandmaier, A.M., Von Oertzen, T., Müller, V., Wagner, G.G., Riediger, M.: A new approach for assessing sleep duration and postures from ambulatory accelerometry. PloS one **7**(10), e48089 (2012)
21. Yu, M., Naqvi, S., Wang, L., Chambers, J., et al.: Posture recognition based fall detection system for monitoring an elderly person in a smart home environment (2012)

SoPresent: An Awareness System
for Connecting Remote Households

Pavan Dadlani[1], Tommaso Gritti[1], Caifeng Shan[1],
Boris de Ruyter[1], and Panos Markopoulos[2(✉)]

[1] Philips Research, High Tech Campus 34, 5656AE Eindhoven, The Netherlands
{Pavan.Dadlani,Tommaso.gritti,Caifeng.Shan,
Boris.de.ruyter}@philips.com
[2] Department of Industrial Design, Eindhoven University of Technology,
Den Dolech 2, 5600MB Eindhoven, The Netherlands
P.Markopoulos@tue.nl

1   Introduction

Families and friends are often separated by distance making it difficult for them to stay in touch with each other. A prolific number of popular communication technologies and social are testimony how important informal and social communication with friends and family can be, and how this can drive industrial and business developments. Despite the abundance of communication technologies and media, separation of friends and families often leads to unmet communication needs [12] and even to social isolation, when families are separated and particularly with regards to elderly living alone. This has motivated a considerable number of explorations into how context sensing and Internet connectivity could support families to stay aware of each other.

Some well-known early attempts to apply context sensing technology for supporting awareness between friends and family, particularly focusing on elderly users are the Digital Family Portrait system [14] and the Diarist [10]. The Digital Family Portrait used sensors to collect information regarding the activities of an elder at home which were displayed as an abstract graphical pattern at a remote household of their son or daughter. The Diarist was a similar set up, proposed by [10], where the instantaneous information regarding the whereabouts and activities of the elder was supported by more detailed narratives regarding the activities of the day as interpreted by the sensing environment at the home of the elder. Such early attempts focused on demonstrating the value of context sensing as part of a connectedness oriented communication application, demonstrating affective benefits like increased social connectedness, lower feelings of anxiety, etc. Notably, the applications mentioned are fundamentally asymmetrical with one communication party (the elder in these cases) being the one observed and their remote son or daughter playing the role of the observer, who might be expected to provide help and emotional support if needed, but who receives with low effort some reassurance and awareness of the situation of their parent.

This asymmetry can have considerable implications regarding how such communication systems are experienced or used. It creates obvious privacy concerns, where

© Springer International Publishing Switzerland 2014
E. Aarts et al. (Eds.): AmI 2014, LNCS 8850, pp. 67–79, 2014.
DOI: 10.1007/978-3-319-14112-1_6

one party is presumed to be willing to share information about their daily life activities as they happen: that is, the typical step for most social communication applications and social media of composing a message and posting it has been replaced by an automated capture and continuous flow of information to the connected party. Of course, such disclosure and loss of privacy may be compensated in certain contexts by the affective benefits these systems provide, e.g., feeling safe that someone is watching, feeling connected, reduced anxiety, etc. as found in the field studies where such systems were evaluated [10, 2, 8]. However, there are also cases where potential users expressed concerns regarding their privacy or where they developed ways to circumvent the system from monitoring them and 'fool' the system in order that it would not disclose actual details of their activities. The problem with asymmetrical information flows is a general concern for systems connecting groups of people, leading researchers to stipulate that systems should minimize asymmetry of information between data owners to data users [9], by decreasing the flow of information from data owners to users and increasing information flow from users to owners. This principle, originally expressed in the context of information systems, would favor more symmetrical set-ups where bi-directional communication is enabled, as for example in [2], but also where the overall set-up is symmetric in its information capture and display capabilities.

The pursuit of symmetry between users of groupware systems has been research that characterizes the last two decades of work in the field of CSCW. Technical characteristics of the systems may need to be overcome to allow symmetrical access to information, symmetrical presentation of users, applying principles such as What You See is What I See (WYSIWIS). The symmetry regarding the information about ourselves that we don't mind others to know and the information that we would like to see about others, is a typically voiced requirement of users; see for example [6] and [8].

However, a careful review of reports on deployments of such systems has shown that despite the sustained attempts by researchers who create and design related systems, almost all empirical studies to date report asymmetries emerging during actual use [16]. This asymmetry is perhaps not surprising, as even with a level playing field technically, people will have differing needs, different opportunities for participation and desired levels of social interaction.

An alternative perspective is to enable people to apply social norms, by allowing them to perceive socially meaningful cues regarding each other's activity; this pertains to the notion of social translucence which was originally introduced as a framework for guiding the design of groupware systems [4]. In that work Erickson and Kellog comment on how in daily encounters in the physical world we adjust our behavior to visible and meaningful social cues from others: we might hold a door open for the person following us even if we do not know them, because we know they see us and we are accountable to them for letting the door close in their face or not. In their turn they might speed up seeing us hold the door as a matter of courtesy because they note we are in a hurry. This interplay of visibility and accountability is enabled by the fact that we see each other and we let social norms play out and drive our behavior.

With regards to context aware systems supporting social connectedness between remote individuals, social translucence amounts to enabling the observed party to know when he or she is being observed [11]. The very visibility of this information renders the observer accountable towards the observed, which then allows them to adjust their behaviour to protect each other's privacy, to be polite in initiating and closing interactions, to enable behaviours relating to saving face and plausible deniability where further interaction is not desirable [15].

The framework of Social Translucence has guided the design of several internet based applications. Here we describe the design, implementation and initial evaluation of SoPresent, a socially translucent system to support awareness of whereabouts of a remote friend or family member.

2   Design of SoPresent System

An analysis of user needs based on interviews, focus groups and cultural probes was conducted focusing on cross generational communication and particularly empty nesters: parents whose children reach adulthood and leave the family nest and who attempt to substitute physical proximity with communication media. This study reported in [1] concluded that:

- Phones and direct communication are difficult to set-up given varying availability of the two parties and are often cut short; there is an opportunity for sustained, lightweight and peripheral communication.
- There is a danger for the system to be perceived as excessive and controlling; however, a communication system should enable the two parties to stay involved with each other.
- Sharing experiences as they occur is preferred than reporting the daily life activities the other party is engaged in.
- The user research focused on an initial attempt to provide symmetry regarding the awareness of connected parties focused on detecting similarity between activities at the two locations.
- Objectively collected information regarding the well-being of the other party can provide reassurance regarding their well-being over and above messages/explicit communication.
- Informal, lightweight and regular interactions, like greetings, are valued and provide a personal touch to information collected through context sensing.

A first system supporting symmetrical communication was based on similarity matching: a context sensing system was constructed based on audio and video scene analysis that notifies the two parties when they engage in similar activities. While an empirical study showed that this functionality was very much valued and led to an increased level of social connectedness experienced, it also suffered from some limitations. Sensing and classifying user activities reliably in different contexts is very hard and could lead to missing such events or providing false notifications. Further, when people are in different time zones as it is quite common for the user scenario considered here, the chances of them engaging in similar activities (e.g., cooking dinner, watching TV, etc.) are diminished. A second iteration of this system was decided would notify the two parties of the presence of the other and give an indication of their activity, as a way to enhance feelings of social presence and social connectedness.

Rather than instrumenting the environment with a variety of sensors, as for example in the Digital Family Portrait system and the Diarist system discussed earlier, here we opt for a single dedicated device, e.g., placed in a living room that will capture contextual information, interpret it and render it on a similar remote device. We decided to create a device that would capture activity at one environment using video and audio, and would analyse captured signals to extract meaningful social cues regarding the activity at that location. Led lights on the device would be used to display the social cues extracted at the remote location. The advantage of embedding all functionality in one device pertains to the ease of installation and the flexibility it provides to users regarding the placement in the home. The functionality implemented relies on audio and video scene analysis algorithms to capture presence and activity, together with computational intelligence for interpreting contextual data.

Contrary to a video media space where raw video and audio signals are transmitted, this approach allows us to deal separately with the communication of awareness information and the communication of information regarding what an observer can see of the observed. More specifically, two versions of the systems were created: one where the presence and activity of the other party is displayed to the remote participant, without letting the observed know whether anyone can see this information. This unidirectional flow of information is completely symmetrical: both parties see the same about each other.

The second version of the system requires the observer to actively invoke the device to present information about the observed. By tapping on the device the display is lit up to represent the presence or not of the remote person (and their relative position compared to the remote device). However, this tapping causes the remote device to also light up showing to the observed that someone is watching them or requested information about them. In this way the watcher becomes accountable through a socially translucent system to the watched.

3   Implementation

We set out to implement the concept as a stand-alone communication device based on audio and video scene analysis. The device captures presence and activity information from one site and renders this through colored lighting on a connected device at a remote location. Based on the design concept and the user context analysis the following technical requirements were identified:

- The device should be capable of observing a complete room, from a single point of view.
- The device should be reachable for the user rather than, say, ceiling mounted, to allow user interactions, e.g., tapping.

- There are no stringent requirements on maximum distortions of captured images.
- The integration of such sensor in a consumer device should be feasible, without a development of special lenses or mirrors, and at low cost.
- The total weight of the device should be limited, possibly below 1 Kg, to allow for a device to be easily moved within the home.

An indoor scenario implies the presence of close-by objects. Multiple camera systems typically produce strong artefacts for objects that are closer than the working distance for which they have been designed (typical values for the minimum working distance are in the range of one or more meters). This property, together with the greater cost of the hardware needed to combine multiple camera streams, excluded any design involving multiple cameras.

Furthermore, the application scenario requires analysis of the behavior of users in a room. Systems based on one single rotating camera are not suitable, presenting strong artefacts for any moving objects. Mechanically moving parts is also not preferable for systems which should not undergo constant maintenance, since they are more likely to be subject to failure. Excluding systems based on multiple cameras and a single rotating camera, the only remaining option consists of a catadioptric system: a system combining a camera together with a mirror.

Below are some of the important parameters of the prototype:

- **Mirror.** The relevant feature of the mirror is the maximum surface angle: a very large angle allows viewing a greater vertical area in the mirrored view, at the cost of much larger distortion, and lower resolution. We opted for a relatively shallow maximum angle of 35°, given the fact that we are combining a mirrored view and a direct view.
- **Camera.** With regards to the camera, the most important property is the maximum resolution. We selected a 3 Megapixels sensor capable of acquiring high level of details. At that resolution, a maximum frame rate of 11 fps was possible hardware components available at the time. This relatively high resolution is advantageous for detecing activity in large environments. In applications scenarios in smaller spaces, the same camera can be used in lower resolution, with scaling performed in hardware. At lower resolution the frame rate can be substantially higher, allowing the detection of more fluid motion.
- **Lens.** The lens is a fundamental component of the system. The lens focal length in combination with the sensor size, determines the total angle of view, which directly affects the portion of the captured image that can be seen under direct view and mirrored view. Another important property is the minimum focusing distance; depending on whether it is necessary to capture sharp images of a user interacting with the device, this property should be considered. In our set-up, we set the manual focus at a middle distance range, and opt for a small aperture to maximize the available depth of field. The maximum aperture, while affecting the sensitivity in low light is not very relevant in our prototype, since a large depth of field is needed to acquire sharp images in a large distance range. Furthermore, in order to keep diffraction artefacts to the minimum, systems adopting wide lenses should opt for a small aperture, unless extremely high quality lenses are used. In an application with the necessity of working in low light, this property should be carefully considered.

- **Mirror-camera distance.** Similar to the lens' focal length, the distance between the camera and the lens affects the portion of the image that is captured directly or after being reflected by the mirror. In our prototype, this distance is set to approximately 3.5 cm.

The product design of the device needed to ensure that it blends in a home environment, but at the same time making sure it is inviting for users to interact with. Below we list some of the main design requirements.

- The device should arouse curiosity in the user to interact with it. We see a trend in the consumer electronics industry that peculiar shapes and colors that are out of the ordinary attract users more. This is one of the reasons why we moved away from just augmenting an existing consumer electronic device a previous research has done, e.g., augmented electronic photo frames.
- The device should not be too bulky to be able to move it around the home.
- The device should use an ambient display to render colored auras to render awareness information.
- The device should allow for explicit interaction to support two modalities: requesting information from the observed party and sending a token or message to the remote party.

Figure 1 shows some of the initial design rendering options of the SoPresent device.

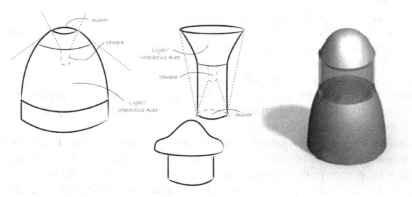

Fig. 1. Two alternative designs for the device and 3D rendering of the selected model

A typical use of this device involves detecting the particular region in the environment in which people are active. It is possible to achieve good detections without the need of a rectified image by using a combination of motion detection, background segmentation and color analysis.

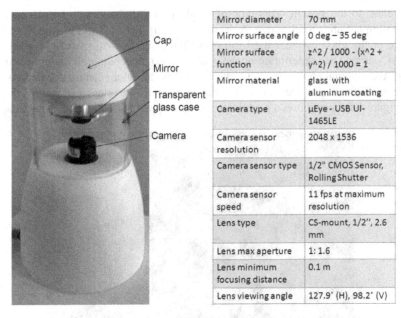

Mirror diameter	70 mm
Mirror surface angle	0 deg – 35 deg
Mirror surface function	$z^2 / 1000 - (x^2 + y^2) / 1000 = 1$
Mirror material	glass with aluminum coating
Camera type	μEye - USB UI-1465LE
Camera sensor resolution	2048 x 1536
Camera sensor type	1/2" CMOS Sensor, Rolling Shutter
Camera sensor speed	11 fps at maximum resolution
Lens type	CS-mount, 1/2", 2.6 mm
Lens max aperture	1: 1.6
Lens minimum focusing distance	0.1 m
Lens viewing angle	127.9° (H), 98.2° (V)

Fig. 2. Final prototype of the SoPresent device with device specifications

Fig. 3. Images acquired with the described prototype system. At the center of the image the lens is visible, surrounded by the cylinder supporting the device. The mirror is easily movable, and allows it to be placed so that its center is not coinciding with the center of the image. In this case, for example, the mirror is lowered to allow for a larger field of view in the portion of the room which is larger, corresponding to the top region of the image.

A raw image captured with the device is displayed in Figure 4. As it can be seen, quite some details are visible both far and close to the device, while at the same time a large part of the ceiling is captured. The advantage of this configuration is clear when observing Figure 5, in which the device is able to capture the face and hands of a person close to the system. This type of result allows the device to be placed quite freely within a home environment. A drawback of this device worth mentioning is the presence of the glass cylinder used to protect the camera-mirror pairas, scratches on the glass surface can deteriorate image quality. Also, depending on the optical properties of the material chosen for the transparent cylinder, glare can appear under some lighting conditions. Anti-reflective coating applied to the glass can help reducing glare. Figure 6 further shows a superimposed unwrapped mesh and a rectified image.

Fig. 4. Images captured with the device, showing a user positioned at close distance to the device. Both hands and face are visible, while at the same time the full body can still be observed.

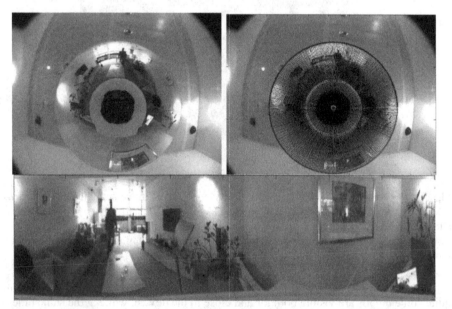

Fig. 5. Original image, unwrapping mesh superimposed to the image, and rectified image of the central ring. Note that only the central part of the image is rectified in these examples.

3.1   Implementation of Similarity Matching

The SoPresent device captures presence and activity information from one site and renders this (through color lighting) on a connected device at a remote location. The vision system can detect a user's proximity, and the angle relative to the device (0-360 degrees). Currently three proximity levels are considered: *far*, *close*, and *middle*, thus the camera view is divided into corresponding areas. To describe the angle, a reference axis is defined. The size of each area and the reference axis can be adjusted via a program interface; otherwise, default settings are used.

Under the assumption that the user will enter/leave the room in the "far" area (e.g., the doors are in the "far" area), motion detection and background subtraction algorithms run to detect foreground objects in the "far" area. Once the user enters the camera view, he or she will be detected and the system state will be set as "user entered". The system then keeps tracking the user and estimates his or her proximity and angle relative to the device. If no user is detected and the user was detected in the "far" area in a previous frame, a counter is started. For the next-coming frames, if the user is detected, the counter will be reset to zero; otherwise, the counter keeps increasing. If the counter is larger than a predefined threshold, the user is regarded as left (i.e., not present); the system state will be set as "user left". The system can further detect the activity level based on motion, or if a new object comes into view, detect its color (RGB value) and send to the remote side.

If both connected devices detect similar contextual situations, e.g. both users are at the same angle and/or proximity with respect to their device, or if similar moving objects at each remote location are of the same color, or if similar activity levels are detected, then the devices will glow in a particular pattern to make their users aware that there is a similar situation happening at the moment.

Fig. 6. Installation of SoPresent at two different rooms in a home simulation laboratory. Each device displays the presence of the remote party and reacts to the proximal observer's presence.

4   Qualitative Evaluation

A qualitative study was conducted with target users among empty nesters and their children (N=5): three participants were children who moved out of home, one participant was an empty nester, and one participant who has senior parents being empty nesters and has children herself to take care of.

Participants were invited to a home simulation laboratory where the SoPresent device was demonstrated showing how it uses audio and video scene analysis to capture the context of its surroundings and displays awareness information to a similar remote device, while also allowing to explicitly sending messages by tapping or caressing the device. The study was based on interviews probing participants for their feedback on the following topics: 1) concept of caressing the device to send a message, 2) tapping the device to request detail information about the remote party (e.g. activity level) and the related social translucence concepts, 3) sharing presence information, 4) privacy concerns, in particular for having a camera in their living room, and 5) testing the concept of matching contextual similarity.

All participants use either phone calls and texting to keep in touch with their remote family members, and some even use Skype to stay in touch. Although, nobody expressed any concern with current methods of communication, they immediately see the value of being able to exchange lightweight messages via the SoPresent device. Messages like "I'm thinking about you", "good morning", etc. are examples of fragile tokens that participants valued to share with their remote significant other. The SoPresent device allows users to send colors to the remote device by placing a colored object near their device which is then picked up by the camera and that color would be rendered on the remote device. Subjects were interested in using the color language to exchange lightweight information between remote significant others. It would however require them to establish a color coding mechanism, e.g. red mean 'call me', blue means "I'm thinking about you", etc. In fact, one of the subjects exchange phone 'tinkles' with their significant other, i.e. send a missed call just to say that they are thinking about them.

Presence information was the second valued piece of awareness information that participants appreciated. On the other hand, activity levels in the remote environment captured by the audio and video signals were less valued, in particular by the older participants. However, there was a preference for requesting activity information from the observed rather than getting it constantly through the device, while the observed can accept or reject the request, and accordingly share contextual information to the remote party.

Three participants (the youngest children) immediately valued the concept of matching contextual similarity, e.g. both parties sitting on the couch and/or watching TV. The serendipitous moments would trigger further interaction with the remote party (e.g. calls or texting).

Privacy was not seen as an issue by the participants. Although all do not want to invade the privacy of the remote party, being able to request for the information first such that users have control on what and when is shared, was highly preferred for the awareness of activity levels. In particular with using a camera to capture contextual information, participants did not express any concern with having such a device to capture information as long as no raw images or videos were being sent to the remote party, but rather abstract and high level contextual information or for exchanging lightweight messages.

5   Discussion

A variety of systems supporting context sensing in a living environment have been created and evaluated through experiments and field trials. We have argued that in many ways the asymmetry of these earlier systems renders them to some extent monitoring technologies to support independent living rather than communication media.

The concepts of symmetry and social translucence which are well understood in the domain of computer supported cooperative work have guided the design of a few systems, most notably awareness cues provided to members of online communities [5]. Also, [15] adopted the framework of social translucence to provide availability cues to people interacting with instant messaging applications. The aim there was to make communication smoother and to make it easier for communicating parties to evaluate the availability of the other. However these ideas have not yet been explored in the domain of Ambient Intelligence. In this paper, we have discussed how these concepts can be used to guide the design of ambient intelligence systems designed to support connectedness.

Home media spaces, or in other words permanent video links connecting households can be a straightforward alternative way to connect remote family members. However, such systems are typically perceived as more privacy intrusive and do not necessarily support social translucence. While in physical proximity people are aware when they are being observed, this does not necessarily hold in video based communications. The implementation of SoPresent shows how extracting information from sensors (even if in this case cameras were used), allows one to quite accurately manage requirements on symmetry and translucence.

Social translucence provides a powerful conceptual framework for designing communication media that is usefully applied in the domain of ambient intelligence. This conceptual framework guides designers beyond considerations of usability and fit to context, to reason regarding how ambient intelligence can mediate social interactions. There are few other frameworks that have been proposed to play this role. Iachello and Abowds' [7] howed how the concept of Data Proportionality deriving from principles for fair information practices can guide the design of context aware systems. This framework however does not provide guidance regarding the social interaction issues that are more relevant in communication media.

[3] describes the device of PeP a perception pillar, a device which uses motion sensors and microphones to detect user activity and LED's to display it, which can potentially support a similar scenario to SoPresent. PeP was designed with different aims in mind, specifically as a way to make perception of information visible to the user. The notion of Perceptual Crossing they describe has several analogies to the concept of Social Translucence but given its focus on perception and cognition rather than social

interaction is silent regarding to why and how cues about an agent's perceptive abilities influence how humans experience interaction with the system.

Romero et [13] discuss how common ground theory provides an alternative framework to guide designers of Ambient Intelligence systems supporting communication scenarios as discussed here. Applied to the SoPresent system it can be seen how the visibility of remote agents and their ability to perceive one's activity creates common ground, i.e. knowledge that is known to be shared amongt agents. However, common ground is better able to guide the design of explicit interactions where the user intentionally 'grounds' elements of information and indicates they become shared knowledge rather than how accountability emerges out of non-intentional back ground interactions as in the case of social translucence.

6   Conclusion

We have presented the design and evaluation of SoPresent a device that encapsualates context sensing and display capabilities to support tele-presence scenarios. The device itself presents an advance over earlier systems which relied on instrumentation on the environment and was to designed to respect social norms regarding social interaction and privacy. As such it presents an interesting design case for guiding the design of ambient intelligence systems based on the notion and conceptual framework of social translucence, which originates from the domain of computer supported cooperative work. The device was evaluated positively by users, and further field testing would help uncover how this device can be embedded in the daily living and communication patterns of its users. As a design case, the research presented has illustrated how the Social Translucence provides a much needed handle on social interaction issues relevant for ambient intelligence systems.

References

1. Dadlani, P., Markopoulos, P., van Bel, D., Smolders, K., Pijl, M., de Ruyter, B., Aarts, E.: Similarity awareness: Using context sensing to support connectedness in intra-family Communication. Journal of Ambient Intelligence and Smart Environments - Design and Deployment of Intelligent Environments 5(5), 425–441 (2013)
2. Dadlani, P., Markopoulos, P., Sinitsyn, A., Aarts, E.: Supporting peace of mind and independent living with the Aurama awareness system. JAISE 3(1), 37–50 (2011)
3. Deckers, E., Wensveen, S., Ahn, R.,Overbeeke, K.: Designing for perceptual crossing to improve user involvement. In: CHI 2011, pp. 1929–1938. ACM (2011)
4. Erickson, T., Kellogg, W.A.: Social translucence: an approach to designing systems that support social processes. ACM TOCHI 7(1), 59–83 (2000)
5. Erickson, T., Kellogg, W.A.: Social translucence: using minimalist visualisations of social activity to support collective interaction. In: Designing Information Spaces: The Social Navigation Approach, pp. 17–41. Springer, London (2003)
6. Friedman, B., Kahn Jr., P., Hagman, J.: Seeverson, R: The Watcher and the Watched: Social Judgements About Privacy in a Public Place. Human-Computer Interaction 21, 235–272 (2006)

7. Iachello, G., Abowd, G.D.: Privacy and proportionality: adapting legal evaluation techniques to inform design in ubiquitous computing. In: Proceedings of the SIGCHI conference on Human factors in computing systems, pp. 91–100. ACM (April 2005)

8. Khan, V.J., Markopoulos, P.: Busy families' awareness needs. International Journal of Human-Computer Studies **67**(2), 139–153 (2009)

9. Jiang, X., Hong, J.I., Landay, J.A.: Approximate information flows: Socially-based modeling of privacy in ubiquitous computing. In: Borriello, G., Holmquist, L.E. (eds.) UbiComp 2002. LNCS, vol. 2498, pp. 176–193. Springer, Heidelberg (2002)

10. Metaxas, G., Metin, B., Schneider, J., Markopoulos, P., de Ruyter, B.: Daily Activities Diarist: Supporting Aging in Place with Semantically Enriched Narratives. In: Baranauskas, C., Abascal, J., Barbosa, S.D.J. (eds.) INTERACT 2007. LNCS, vol. 4663, pp. 390–403. Springer, Heidelberg (2007)

11. Metaxas, G., Markopoulos, P., Aarts, E.H.: Modelling social translucency in mediated environments. Universal Access in the Information Society **11**(3), 311–321 (2012)

12. Romero, J., van Baren, J., Markopoulos, P., de Ruyter, B., IJsselsteijn, W.A.: Addressing Interpersonal Communication Needs through Ubiquitous Connectivity: Home and Away. In: Aarts, E., Collier, R.W., van Loenen, E., de Ruyter, B. (eds.) EUSAI 2003. LNCS, vol. 2875, pp. 419–429. Springer, Heidelberg (2003)

13. Romero, N., Markopoulos, P.: Grounding Privacy with Awareness: A Social Approach to Describe Privacy Related Issues in Awareness Systems. In: Awareness Systems, pp. 207–229. Springer, London (2009)

14. Rowan, J., Mynatt, E.D.: Digital family portrait field trial: Support for aging in place. In: SIGCHI Conference on Human Factors in Computing Systems, pp. 521–530. ACM (2005)

15. Szóstek, A.M., Markopoulos, P., Eggen, B.: Attaining mutual awareness of the availability status. Journal of Communications Research **2** (2011)

16. Voida, A., Voida, S., Greenberg, S., He, H.A.: Asymmetry in media spaces. In: CSCW 2008, pp. 313–322. ACM (2008)

Multi-tenancy Aware Ambient Assisted Living Platforms in the Cloud

Carsten Stocklöw[1]($\boxtimes$), Alejandro M. Medrano Gil[2], Alvaro Fides Valero[3],
Michele Girolami[4,5], and Stefano Lenzi[4]

[1] Fraunhofer Institute for Computer Graphics Research,
Fraunhoferstr. 5, 64283 Darmstadt, Germany
carsten.stockloew@igd.fraunhofer.de
[2] Life Supporting Technologies at Universidad Politécnica de Madrid,
Avd. Complutense, 28040 Madrid, Spain
amedrano@lst.tfo.upm.es
[3] ITACA at Universidad Politécnica de Valencia,
Edificio 8G Camino de Vera s/n, 46022 Valencia, Spain
alfiva@itaca.upv.es
[4] ISTI-CNR, 56124 Pisa, Italy
{michele.girolami,stefano.lenzi}@isti.cnr.it
[5] Department of Computer Science, University of Pisa, 56124 Pisa, Italy

Abstract. Over the last years, Ambient Assisted Living (AAL) technologies have seen a remarkable grow up. Although this field has been researched for many years and different projects have investigated and proposed AAL platforms with a rich set of functionality, the current market situation still favors isolated solutions. A possible reason is that those platforms are too complex to be easily setup and maintained. Also, resource sharing is possible between services, but not between platforms. A promising alternative is provided by the cloud computing approach which integrates common services in a shared way.

Thus, we propose to use an AAL platform as Platform-as-a-Service in the cloud to offer all functionalities of AAL platforms to services in the cloud while being able to connect to platforms running in each home. We discuss different aspects of this approach and propose a simple verification scenario. An exemplary adoption is discussed for the platform universAAL.

Keywords: AAL Platform · Cloud Computing · Smart Environments

1 Introduction and Motivation

The requirements analysis in various EU projects on platforms and services for Ambient Assisted Living (AAL) scenarios have shown that such platforms must provide a rich set of functionalities to fulfill its demands as the needs of the target focus groups - mainly elderlies or differently abled persons - are very diverse. Increasing the capabilities of a platform typically also increases

© Springer International Publishing Switzerland 2014
E. Aarts et al. (Eds.): AmI 2014, LNCS 8850, pp. 80–95, 2014.
DOI: 10.1007/978-3-319-14112-1_7

its complexity for aspects like interoperability and configurability, as well as its demands on the underlying infrastructure like processing power and memory consumption.

Especially for facilities with multiple end users like elderly care centers with different homes for the assisted persons the complexity can be an issue and a reason to decide for *isolated solutions*. These solutions provide support for specific purposes for which the anticipated requirements are often restricted to the targeted aims and its affect are restricted to the local closed space where the end user is living. Although the current market situation favors isolated solutions over open and interoperable AAL platforms, the advantages of these platforms have been often discussed in various projects, e.g. the avoidance of vendor lock-in, the extendibility, the orchestration of services and reasoning on context data, and the sharing of resources and infrastructure.

However, even with AAL platforms the so-called AAL Spaces (distinct physical spaces with a network of AAL-aware nodes), like the homes, are still isolated and resources are not shared between different homes. This results in high demands on the overall performance and an increased effort that is needed for setup and maintenance of the complete system.

A promising alternative is provided by the *cloud computing* approach which centers certain functionalities in an external node or network. The cloud can be either offered over the Internet or be realized as a private cloud that runs directly at the organization; it benefits, for example, from pooling effect to optimize the usage of resources. Using the cloud for individual services is an obvious choice but then this service may not benefit from the capabilities of an AAL platform; it is only an isolated extension.

Therefore, we propose to use the AAL platform itself as the cloud. This way, all the functionalities of the platform are available in the form of cloud services. Then, such services will be available to other ones in a seamless way. The decision of having a service running in the home AAL Space or in the cloud is left to the deployer. Resources can be shared between homes and the effort for setup and maintenance is reduced as only the one cloud needs to be adapted instead of multiple homes.

However, the main challenge of this approach is the so-called *multi-tenancy* - the ability to handle different clients, or tenants (in our example, a home would be a tenant).

We will investigate the possibility of having an AAL platform in the cloud and discuss required adaptations to the platform and the services. Additionally, we propose a *simple verification scenario* to test our approach.

This paper is structured as follows: section 2 reviews related work. Section 3 describes the main characteristics of AAL platforms as we will use this general view in the following discussions. Section 4 details on multi-tenancy and the possibility of using an AAL platform in the cloud. Section 5 discusses an exemplary adoption of our approach with the AAL platform universAAL and section 6 concludes.

2   State of the Art

As cloud computing is a promising approach, many separated services have been ported to the cloud. This includes services from the AAL domain, especially services for data storage: Zheng et al. [1] have designed a cloud storage platform with semantic query technology for the use by mobile devices and Doukas et al. [2] uses the cloud to store patients health care records and medical images. Koufi et al. [3] introduces access from an Android device to emergency medical services running in the cloud.

Regarding the usage of AAL platforms in the cloud, Corredor et al. [4] describe the Knowledge-Aware and Service-Oriented (KASO) Middleware to connect small devices over a lightweight middleware with a service cloud. However, the multi-tenancy aspect was not considered.

Multi-tenancy is naturally an aspect for platforms that are designed for the cloud, but are not equipped with advanced functionality for smart environments. Google App Engine [5] uses namespaces to differentiate between different tenants. All the API calls that are provided by the cloud will make use of that namespace; calling external services without handling multi-tenancy by the application can result in data leaks. Amdatu[1] enhances the OSGi-platform with multi-tenancy capabilities. A special BundleActivator needs to be defined by each application; this activator is used to create separate instances for tenants.

The last two platforms use a different instance for each tenant, thus effectively running in level two SaaS maturity level (see section 4.1).

So far, it was not investigated to have a complex AAL platform running in the cloud that is capable of handling multi-tenancy where tenants may be other instances of the AAL platform.

3   The AAL Platform

In this section we briefly describe the functionalities and communication capabilities of a generic AAL platform. This will serve as a base for the following discussions about the transfer of an AAL platform to the cloud.

3.1   Terminology

Following the terminology from universAAL, an *AAL Space* is defined as a distinct physical space where people may need assistance, such as the home, a hospital, the airport terminal or a public space. Inside every space, a number of AAL-aware nodes provide AAL services to humans or to other AAL-aware nodes. An *AAL-aware node* is a physical device (tablet, smart phone, notebook or workstation) that is equipped with the the necessary software to interact with other nodes.

---

[1] http://www.amdatu.org

3.2   Functionality

Over the last decade many AAL related projects have been funded by the EU commision, among them we cite PERSONA [14], SOPRANO [6] and the recent universAAL [7] project. Such projects have defined and refined over the years a rich set of capabilities that a generic AAL platform must take into account:

- context management: storage of context data, distribution of changes of the contextual state, reasoning on context data to infer higher-level data from low-level data;
- service management: execution of services, brokerage between service providers and service consumers, orchestration of services;
- UI management: support for multimodal interaction with adaptivity and adaptability;
- Remote interoperability: integration of external services like webservices or RESTful services, connection between different networks of AAL-aware nodes forming AAL spaces that logically represent distinct physical spaces.

Additionally, an AAL platform must provide for security, reliability, configurability, personalization, and are often realized as distributed systems with a middleware layer that hides distribution and heterogeneity. These features go beyond what is typically offered by classical home automation systems.

Apart from the functionality provided by the platform, new features can be added with applications (or services). Those services may have different levels of access to the underlying platform, e.g. to read/write files, open sockets, access databases, etc. It is the responsibility of the AAL platform to ensure that only those operations that are approved by an administrator can be performed.

3.3   Communication Patterns

In an AAL space, nodes can communicate with each other; the communication patterns that we will consider for this work are as follows:

- call-based communication: the service provider (service callee) registers, at some service registry, its service profiles that describe the services it provides. The service consumers (service callers) can discover and invoke such services;
- event-based communication: the context consumer (context subscriber) subscribes for certain context data. It will be notified asynchronously as soon as the the context provider (context publisher) publishes matching context data. The event-based communication fulfills the publish-subscribe communication pattern.

Service calls and context events are the messages that are exchanged among components. Furthermore, the platform performs a brokerage between service provider and consumer, and between context publisher and subscriber.

We distinguish between three different layers of connectivity:

1. connector layer: establishes a connection between different AAL-aware nodes forming a network of nodes. Possible protocols are, for example, TCP, reliable multicast (e.g. JGroups), Advanced Message Queuing Protocol, or Message Queue Telemetry Transport.

2. brokerage layer: works on top of the connector layer and realizes the mentioned communication patterns of call-based or event-based communication.
3. gateway layer: works on top of the brokerage layer and connects different networks of AAL-aware nodes.

4   AAL platform in the Cloud

4.1   Discussion on SaaS Maturity Model

The Everything-as-a-Service model of cloud computing defines three different levels of abstraction (see Fig. 1): Infrastructure-as-a-Service (IaaS), Platform-as-a-Service (PaaS), and Software-as-a-Service (SaaS). Depending on the concrete implementation some AAL platforms may not allow to have different versions or implementations of the same software. In that case, the platform and all of its services should be considered a SaaS and thus, the platform may be needed to be instantiated multiple times which results in increased resource requirements. It is also possible that the AAL platform in the cloud can be considered a PaaS and all of its services a SaaS.

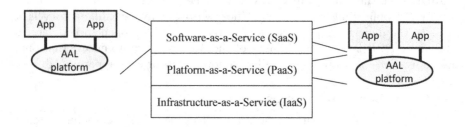

Fig. 1. Everything-as-a-Service: cloud-computing architecture and its association with AAL platforms and AAL services; AAL platform can be either part of SaaS (left) or PaaS (right)

The key difference for services running in the cloud or outside the cloud is the capability to be able to handle multi-tenancy with each AAL Space representing a tenant. When running in a separated AAL Space like the home, a service may need to handle different users of that space, but it does not need to be aware of different spaces. On the other hand, when a service is running in the cloud then multiple spaces can connect to that service and it must be assured that information of one space is not leaking into another space.

Microsoft has defined a maturity model for SaaS[2] with four levels of maturity (see Fig 2). Forrester has also defined a maturity model for SaaS[3] with six levels

---

[2] http://msdn.microsoft.com/en-us/library/aa479069.aspx
[3] https://www.forrester.com/Forresters+SaaS+Maturity+Model/fulltext/-/
   E-RES46817

of maturity. However, this model can be almost mapped to the four levels of the model from Microsoft with some levels being refined and described in more detail. For the following discussions we consider only the model from Microsoft.

- level 1: ad hoc/custom: each tenant has access to its own version of the software. Each instance of the software is independent form other instances;
- level 2: configurable: all tenants have access to a separate instance of the software, but the code of that software is the same for all tenants and configurable to be able to work tenant-specific;
- level 3: configurable, multi-tenant-efficient: all tenants have access to the same instance of the software that needs to be able to distinguish between different tenants;
- level 4: scalable, configurable, multi-tenant-efficient: adds a load balancer to increase the scalability by having a certain number of tenants for each instance.

The four levels of maturity form a continuum with the first level having *isolated* code and data, and the fourth level having *shared* code and data. Generally speaking, the higher the sharing of code and data is, the higher is the risk that information from one tenant is leaking into the space of another tenant. However, isolation typically imposes a high demand on memory and processing power.

One challenge is to determine whether the AAL platform can be considered a PaaS with the services running as SaaS or the AAL platform together with all its services should be considered a SaaS. This depends very much on the concrete realization of the AAL platform and the brokerage and communication between different services in the cloud. If the AAL platform is running as a SaaS, it needs to be started for every instance of the services or even every tenant which results in high requirements to the infrastructure in the cloud, especially to memory consumption and processing power. Also, the profiling and configuration of the services is an important aspect to consider; common configuration parameters need to be adapted for all instances which requires appropriate configuration tools.

The first level supports different code and data for each tenant. Having different code has a high demand on maintenance as bug fixes may be applied to multiple versions of the software. Additionally, resources cannot be shared between different instances of the software. If the AAL platform does not allow having the same service started with different implementations then it might be needed to run the platform and the services as SaaS. In our case, we have the same code but want to scale for high number of tenants which makes this level unattractive.

The second level works with the same code that is configurable to be able to handle the needs of different tenants. Still, the requirements to the infrastructure can be very high. It may not be possible for the AAL platform to run as a PaaS as the platform may not support the creation and management of different instances of the same service.

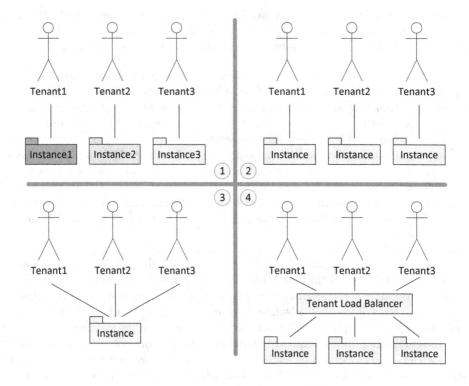

Fig. 2. SaaS maturity model

The third level only runs one instance of each service. The AAL platform can run as a PaaS, but the services themselves need to be able to handle multiple tenants. In this case, security is partially delegated to the service.

The fourth level adds a load balancer for scaling up to very high numbers of tenants. Each instance can be considered a setting as in level three with the load balancer distributing the tenants between the different instances. The distribution can typically be done according to the authentication during connection establishment. Having multiple instances again increases the effort of configuration, but may be needed to allow scalability.

4.2   Considerations for Multi-networks: Defining the Scope of Messages

A network of AAL-aware nodes can generally be connected to an arbitrary number of distinct networks which, in turn, can have connections to other networks, thus building a network of networks. As shown in Fig. 3 the red network could be an AAL Space in the home that is connected to a network n1 in the cloud. This network n1 can have connections to the networks n2 and n3, e.g. to provide

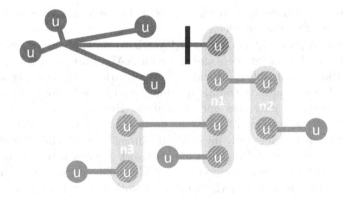

Fig. 3. Considerations for multi-networks: AAL aware nodes are marked with u; the red network (top left) is an AAL Space for a tenant; gray blocks n1, n2, and n3 denote different networks that may also have tenants connected

additional services that a service in n1 needs to fulfill its purpose. Therefore, it is a possibility to add additional information to each service call or context event that identifies the *target* so that the target service or node can be addressed directly. However, this complicates the definition of the call/event and is dependent on the concrete setup. Each service in the home (or the broker in the home) would need to be configured with the actual setup of networks which makes the deployment more complicated and error-prone.

In some cases we can know about the actual setup, especially when using a private cloud with the cloud being, e.g. in the elderly care center in which the home is. When the cloud is public we cannot know and we cannot verify the actual setting. A provider of the cloud may decide to add additional networks to provide additional functionality to its clients without the need to re-configure each home AAL Space.

Therefore, we can simplify the communication by omitting any information about the target; the home AAL Space only has one connection and is only aware of this one cloud network. This boundary is indicated by a black line in Fig. 3. However, on the cloud side, we still need to have the information about the *source* to associate responses to the correct tenant. If the communication flow is initiated in the cloud it is needed to have information about the concrete tenant(s) to adress. Thus, we define the *scope* of a message as the set of remote AAL networks that are involved in the communication flow. This has the advantage that services running outside the cloud do not need to be able to handle multiple tenants; the scope is only used in the cloud.

4.3   Selecting a Layer of Connectivity

As mentioned in the generic description of AAL platforms in section 3, we distinguish between connector layer, broker layer, and gateway layer. The connection between an AAL Space and the cloud can be realized in connector and gateway layer because the broker layer works on top of the connector layer and uses the network provided by the connector.

The main purpose of the connector layer is to provide connectivity at the network level and transfer messages between AAL-aware nodes, e.g. using a reliable multicast protocol. It provides the foundation for the brokerage layer which then defines common communication patterns and allows the exchange of messages between providers and consumers. However, the connector layer is not aware of the content of messages or the representation of data that is sent. Therefore, it provides only limited capabilities for a filtering of messages to separate the local network from the cloud network as not every message should be exchanged between these two networks. Additionally, it must be ensured that data is not leaking from one AAL Space into another AAL Space.

These features could probably be added to the connector layer, but then these adaptations need to be ported to other connectors as well. When switching to a different connector the effort for adaptions might be a considerable aspect.

The gateway, on the other hand, works on top of the brokerage layer and is aware of the representation of the data. It provides an additional layer on top of the local network to allow the formation of multi-networks that can communicate with each other. Thus, the gateway seems to be a more promising approach.

4.4   Communication Between Cloud Services

If the AAL platform is running in the cloud, we can make use of all the functionalities that the platform provides, i.e. multiple services can be started and communicate with each other. In that case each service needs to be aware of multi-tenancy and needs to forward the scope to the next service so that a communication flow that involves multiple services can be associated with the correct source AAL Space to avoid leaking.

Fig. 4 shows an example of a communication flow: a service in the red AAL Space (App1) calls a cloud service (App2, e.g. an Agenda service). App2 needs access to a database that is provided by a second cloud service (App3, CHE - terminology taken from project universAAL). Neither the calling of App3 nor any calls that App3 would make must leak into the second AAL Space.

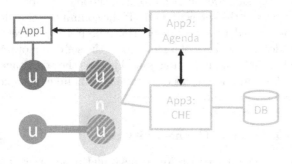

Fig. 4. Communication flow between services running in the cloud

There are different ways to avoid leaks, i.e. multiple instances of a service could be started with each instance being clearly associated with a specific scope but this would correspond to level two maturity level. Another possibility would be to handle messages consecutively. A service can only handle a message if the previous message is fully processed. The broker can ensure that a service can only invoke other services or send context events with the scope that it was called with. However, a consecutive processing could have a serious impact on the overall performance compared to a parallel processing.

According to our assumptions for services running in the platform, the services can have a wide range of security restrictions. A service can also be allowed to perform certain operations like access to databases, sockets, or files. Therefore the platform cannot fully guarantee that services are isolated and that data is not leaking from one AAL Space into another. Security can be - to a certain degree - delegated to the application level. The handling of multiple tenants should be supported by the platform and the interfaces should make this handling as easy as possible for services. For our approach, the only thing that needs to be done by the services is the forwarding of the scope from one message to the next.

4.5 Definition of a Simple Verification Scenario

With the discussions and considerations in the previous sections we can define a simple scenario to verify our approach and generally, AAL platforms running in the cloud. This scenario is shown in Fig. 5.

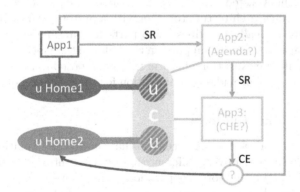

Fig. 5. Simple verification scenario; SR: service request; CE: context event

The gray box in the middle denotes the AAL platform in the cloud. Home1 and Home2 are two separate AAL Spaces. The communication flow is as follows: App1 calls App2, App2 calls App3, and App3 sends an event that is received by App1. As the communication is initiated by Home1 no message should be received by the second AAL Space Home2. This is indicated by a red arrow in the picture.

As a concrete example, App2 could be an agenda service and App3 could be a service that provides a generic access to a database in which the agenda data is stored. When an agenda item changes, a context event is issued and App1 is notified about this change.

5   Realization

To verify our concept, we discuss the application of the concept to the AAL platform universAAL (version 3.1) that can run as a PaaS in the cloud for level three SaaS maturity.

5.1   The universAAL Project

Over the years, many projects on platform for AAL systems have been funded by the EU. Those projects have all investigated a different approach and have had a different set of functionalities, i.e. Amigo [8], GENESYS [9], MPOWER[10], OASIS [11], PERSONA [12], and SOPRANO [6]. In FP7, Call 4, only one platform project was funded that should not create a new platform; instead, this project should investigate existing approaches and consolidate them into a platform that converges the most promising aspects of existing platforms. The overall goal was, to "make it technically feasible and economically viable to conceive, design and deploy innovative new AAL services".

The universAAL platform(UNIVERsal open platform and reference Specification for Ambient Assisted Living) [7] has created, amongst others, a reference model and a reference architecture together with a prototypical implementation. The architecture basically describes three parts for runtime support, development support, and community support. In the following, we focus on the runtime support, especially the execution platform that is supposed to run in the home of an assisted person and provides the foundation for the execution of applications.

5.2   The Execution Platform

The requirements analysis for AAL scenarios has shown that a platform for AAL needs to provide support in very different aspects, i.e. context management, service management, UI framework, cooperation with remote services etc. This has led to a sophisticated architecture with a rich set of functionalities. Additionally, the analysis has shown the potential of using semantic descriptions for services, context, and UI handling, thus building on open standards like RDF[4] and OWL[5].

The important parts for our work are the middleware with its communication brokers, and the remote capabilities, i.e. the AAL Space gateway that is designed to connect two AAL Spaces with each other; and the remote API that can use protocols like SOAP or REST to achieve interoperability even if the AAL platform is not running in the home.

---

[4] Resource Description Framework.
[5] Web Ontology Language.

5.3   Communication Channels

The communication between components is achieved by three buses:

1. the context bus is an event-based bus that notifies subscribers about a change in context data by sending a context event from the publisher to the subscriber;
2. the UI bus is a call-based bus that is specialized on interaction with end users; it sends a UI request from the UI caller to a UI handler which responds with a UI response;
3. the service bus is a call-based bus that allows to call a certain functionality.

The service bus does not handle only one message. The service caller sends a service *request* to the bus. At this time it is not known if there is a service available or even more than one service. The bus performs a brokerage, finds matching service callees and sends service *calls* to those callees. Return values are provided by a service response.

Thus, we have the following kinds of bus messages: context event, service request, service call, service response, UI request, and UI response. All of these messages can be assigned a scope. In the following sections we focus on the service bus and the context bus as the UI bus is similar to the service bus.

5.4   Usage of AAL Space Gateway

The AAL Space Gateway is a component that connects two universAAL networks to exchange bus messages. The two networks each have its own set of buses and perform a brokerage between provider and consumer. To exchange messages, we basically have two options:

1. Remote brokerage: all messages (service requests and context events) are sent over the gateway to the remote universAAL network and are evaluated on the remote site.
2. Local brokerage: local proxies are created for remote functionality, i.e. each remote service provider and context consumer registers with its profile or subscription in the local network. Only if the local brokerage finds a match, the message is sent to the remote site. This method requires a tracking mechanism for the middleware to be notified when a new service registers to a bus so that the proxy can be created in the connected network.

Option 1 has a higher demand on network bandwidth between the two gateways whereas option 2 has a higher demand on management of the proxies. A mixed model is possible to decide for each connection or even for certain services which option to take. However, in the current implementation the local brokerage is implemented.

When a message is received by the cloud gateway a scope is added to the message, with the scope being the ID of the AAL Space of the sender. This scope is forwarded to all messages along the communication flow. When a message is received by the cloud gateway from within the cloud, the scope is removed and the message is forwarded to the respective tenant AAL Space.

The AAL Space Gateway supports the incorporation of filter, or operations, to be checked for each creation of a proxy or even for each message that is sent or received. These operations can be used to enhance privacy, security, and efficiency by restricting the set of services that are made available on the remote site. For the use of operations, see also section 5.6.

5.5   Verification of the Simple Scenario

To verify out approach we discuss the realization according to the simple scenario defined in section 4.5. The two AAL Spaces Home1 and Home2, and the cloud (C) are separate networks of AAL aware nodes. Those networks consist of at least one node running the universAAL platform, but a network can also consist of more than one node. The connection between the two homes and the cloud is realized by the AAL Space Gateway - each home has a gateway and the cloud has a gateway. During initialization a proxy is created in the homes for each service running in the cloud and the ID of each home AAL Space is provided to the cloud gateway. This AAL Space ID serves as scope of the messages in the cloud.

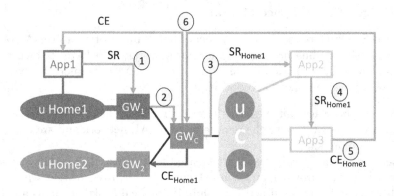

Fig. 6. Simple verification scenario in universAAL; SR: service request; CE: context event; SRx: service request related to tenant x; CEx: context event related to tenant x

The communication flow is as follows:

1. App1 sends a service request to the bus which sends a service call to the proxy created by GW_1 (and maybe other service callees in Home1). Neither the service request nor the service call need to have a scope; Home1 is not aware of multi-tenancy. GW_1 may apply some filtering to determine whether the call can be sent to the cloud gateway GW_c
2. GW_1 sends the service call to the gateway of the cloud

3. GW_c adds the scope and sends the service call to the desired app - App2
4. App2 needs the functionality of another app to fulfil its purpose and sends a service request/call to App3 and forwards the scope in that request/call
5. App3 sends a context event. This event is only related to Home1 and should not leak into Home2. App3 forwards the scope in the context event.
6. GW_c receives the context event. From the scope it knows that the communication comes from Home1. As the context event comes from Home1, GW_c forwards the event to Home1 but not to Home2. This forwarding rule will preserve the privacy among different spaces. GW_1 receives the event (without scope) and it forwards the event in Home1 to App1 that is the recipient.

5.6   Security Considerations

It is assumed that basic security is already provided by the AAL platform, e.g. the encryption of data during transmission. Additional security considerations for the multi-tenancy aspect and AAL platform in the cloud are as follows.

The AAL Space gateway can perform a filtering of messages and these filters can be configured for the gateway component on both sides of the communication - the home AAL Space and the cloud. The filter can determine whether a proxy needs to be created in the remote site for service providers and context consumers, and whether a service call or context event needs to be sent or considered when received.

Additionally, the bus could perform a filtering. For example, the bus could block all messages without a scope as this message might come from a component that is not aware of multi-tenancy. The bus could also allow only messages to be sent from a component with a certain scope if this component has received a message with the same scope before (within a certain time frame). This filtering should be optional and configurable.

6   Discussion and Conclusions

Although the advantages of AAL platforms have been discussed in many projects, they have not yet found their way to the market. A possible reason for such barrier is the complexity for the deployment and the maintenance of the AAL platform in different kind of locations (such as home, hospital, office). In this paper, we have proposed the use of the cloud computing in order to move some of the functionality provided by an AAL platform to the cloud. The solution we have proposed has some advantages and implications for the stakeholders in the AAL application domain.

By carefully choosing the default behaviour of the components in a tenant-aware scenario, already developed applications don't need adaptation in order for them to be integrated in the system. Default behaviour is assuming the components are non-tenant-aware: each message is treated as if they are meant for all scopes. Having these applications broadcasting all their messages means that the application will be able to interact with any cloud service regardless of the nature of the remote service (under consideration of security aspects). On top of the default behaviour tenant-aware applications can make use of the default behaviour or block it by defining a specific set of scopes for each message. This simple API extension to develop tenant-aware applications means that developers familiar with the AAL platform are not required to train on new infrastructures or advanced concepts to be able to develop these applications.

Using this simple concept, tenant-aware applications are able not only to track where the messages are generated, and interact exlusively with that space, but they can also implement tenant to tenant communication, circumventing the premise of "no message going to the cloud should leak to other spaces". By delegating part of the security to the applications, these have more power and can overcome the rigidity of the adaptation of the platform to the cloud. Having this freedom, service providers and software designers are free to design any service they need despite the complexity.

In this scenario developers and deployers are expected to have very distinct skills. Through the simple API developers are freed from most deployment details; equally deployers are not required to know implementation details. Applications can be deployed arbitrarily in tenant-only, tenant-cloud, or cloud-cloud setups. Deployers will have to configure the connections (Gateways) and the security required by each.

An important and interesting cloud service for the platform is one which is able to relay installation and configuration commands. Through this service the burden of installation and maintenance can be centralized as a cloud service, thus optimizing the resources required for the increasingly complex system.

Given all these beneifts, the expected impact for service providers using the proposed solution is an increase in efficiency managing human and machine resources; resources can be shared between different AAL Spaces. Overall, service costs could be reduced. Pervasive services that not only work at home but are able to extend through the cloud, unrestricting the AAL space from the physical person, now including the virtual representation of the user over the cloud.

A large scale evaluation of this approach is currently being performed within the project ReAAL [13] that aims at offering the services of the universAAL platform to at least 5000 users.

Acknowledgments. This work was partly supported by European Commission under CIP ICT PSP project ReAAL (grant agreement 325189).

References

1. Zheng, W., Xu, P., Huang, X., Wu, N.: Design a cloud storage platform for pervasive computing environments. Cluster Computing **13**(2), 141–151 (2010)
2. Doukas, C., Pliakas, T., Maglogiannis, I.: Mobile healthcare information management utilizing cloud computing and android os. In: 2010 Annual International Conference of the IEEE Engineering in Medicine and Biology Society (EMBC), pp. 1037–1040 (August 2010)

3. Koufi, V., Malamateniou, F., Vassilacopoulos, G., Prentza, A.: An android-enabled mobile framework for ubiquitous access to cloud emergency medical services. In: 2012 Second Symposium on Network Cloud Computing and Applications (NCCA), pp. 95–101 (December 2012)
4. Corredor, I., Martnez, J.F., Familiar, M.S.: Bringing pervasive embedded networks to the service cloud: A lightweight middleware approach. Journal of Systems Architecture **57**(10), 916–933 (2011). Emerging Applications of Embedded Systems Research
5. Prodan, R., Sperk, M., Ostermann, S.: Evaluating high-performance computing on google app engine. IEEE Software **29**(2), 52–58 (2012)
6. Klein, M., Schmidt, A., Lauer, R.: Ontology-centred design of an ambient middleware for assisted living: The case of soprano. Towards Ambient Intelligence: Methods for Cooperating Ensembles in Ubiquitous Environments (AIMCU), 30th Annual German Conference on Artificial Intelligence (KI 2007), Osnabrück (September 2007)
7. Hanke, S., Mayer, C., Hoeftberger, O., Boos, H., Wichert, R., Tazari, M.-R., Wolf, P., Furfari, F.: universaal an open and consolidated aal platform. In: Wichert, R., Eberhardt, B. (eds.) Ambient Assisted Living. Non-series, vol. 63, pp. 127–140. Springer, Heidelberg (2011)
8. Schmalenstroeer, J., Leutnant, V., Haeb-Umbach, R.: Amigo context management service with applications in ambient communication scenarios. In: 2007 Revised Papers Constructing Ambient Intelligence - Am I 2007 Workshops Darmstadt, Germany, pp. 397–402 (November 7–10, 2007)
9. Obermaisser, R.H.: GENESYS: A Candidate for an ARTEMIS Cross-Domain Reference Architecture for Embedded Systems. SVH
10. Mikalsen, M., Hanke, S., Fuxreiter, T., Walderhaug, S., Wienhofen, L.W.M.: Interoperability services in the mpower ambient assisted living platform. In: MIE, pp. 366–370 (2009)
11. Pioggia, G., Ricci, G., Bonfiglio, S., Bekiaris, E., Siciliano, G., De Rossi, D.: An ontology-driven multisensorial platform to enable unobtrusive human monitoring and independent living. In: Ninth International Conference on Intelligent Systems Design and Applications, ISDA 2009, pp. 620–623 (November 2009)
12. Fabbricatore, C., Zucker, M., Ziganki, S., Karduck, A.: Towards an unified architecture for smart home and ambient assisted living solutions: A focus on elderly people. In: 2011 Proceedings of the 5th IEEE International Conference on Digital Ecosystems and Technologies Conference (DEST), pp. 305–311 (May 2011)
13. ReAAL project: make it ReAAL (2013–2016). http://www.cip-reaal.eu

Monitoring Patients' Lifestyle with a Smartphone and Other Devices Placed Freely on the Body

Mitja Luštrek$^{(\boxtimes)}$, Božidara Cvetković, and Vito Janko

Department of Intelligent Systems, Jožef Stefan Institute, Ljubljana, Slovenia
{mitja.lustrek,boza.cvetkovic,vito.janko}@ijs.si

Abstract. Monitoring patients' lifestyle can result in an improved treatment, but it is often not critical enough to warrant dedicated sensors. However, many consumer devices, such as smartphones, contain inertial sensors, which can be used for such monitoring. We propose an approach to activity recognition and human energy-expenditure estimation for diabetes patients that uses a phone and an accelerometer-equipped heart-rate monitor. The approach detects which of the two devices is carried or worn, the orientation of the phone and its location on the body, and adapts the monitoring accordingly. By using this approach, the accuracy of the activity recognition was increased by up to 20 percentage points compared to disregarding the orientation and location of the phone, while the error of the energy-expenditure estimation was decreased.

Keywords: Activity recognition · Energy expenditure estimation · Smartphone · Heart-rate monitor · Accelerometer · Location · Orientation · Diabetes

1 Introduction

Monitoring patients' lifestyle can often allow physicians to better advise on disease management and to verify the compliance with the prescribed treatment. Our work is motivated by diabetes treatment, where the information about the patients' activities and physical exertion is quite useful, but not critical enough to warrant dedicated sensors. Fortunately the number of consumer devices that contain inertial sensors is increasing, providing opportunity for lifestyle monitoring without dedicated sensors. The prime example of such a device is the smartphone, while others include heart-rate monitors and activity-monitoring wristbands. However, monitoring activities with such devices is challenging because the users can freely choose which devices to carry at any given time, and they can be carried in various orientations and locations.

Activity recognition is probably the most mature area of lifestyle monitoring, and while it is often done with smartphones, the issue of varying orientation and location is rarely addressed. Thiemjarus [1] normalized the orientation of the phone, increasing the accuracy by 16 percentage points. Martín et al. [2] detected the location of the phone and used different activity-recognition models for different locations, increasing the accuracy by 4–10 percentage points. A few researchers also measured physical exertion or human energy expenditure with smartphones [3], but without addressing the varying orientation and location.

© Springer International Publishing Switzerland 2014
E. Aarts et al. (Eds.): AmI 2014, LNCS 8850, pp. 96–99, 2014.
DOI: 10.1007/978-3-319-14112-1_8

In this paper we present an activity-recognition and energy-expenditure-estimation approach using a smartphone and an accelerometer-equipped heart-rate monitor. It automatically adapts to whichever of the two devices is on the user's body, and both normalizes the orientation of the phone and detects its location.

2   The Proposed Activity-Monitoring Approach

The proposed approach can use any number of sensing devices carried or worn by the user, but in our experiments we used two: a smartphone, which could be placed in any orientation in the breast or trousers pocket or in a bag, and an accelerometer-equipped heart-rate monitor worn on the chest. The activity-monitoring pipeline is shown in Fig. 1. First, we detect whether each of the two devices is present on the user's body. Second, if the phone is present, we detect walking in an orientation- and location-independent fashion. When a 10-second period of walking is detected, we use it to normalize the orientation and detect the location of the phone. When the phone is not carried, the information on the orientation and location is reset until the next period of walking. Third, we invoke the activity-recognition model appropriate for the current device configuration, which uses features based on the acceleration data from one or both devices. And fourth, we invoke the appropriate energy-estimation model, which uses the recognized activity, acceleration features and the heart rate if available.

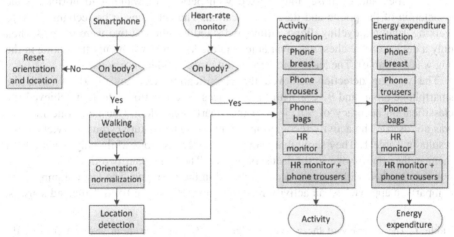

Fig. 1. The activity-monitoring pipeline

The smartphone is considered **present** on the user's body unless the screen is on, indicating that the phone is in use, there is an ongoing call, or the phone is completely still. The heart-rate monitor can self-report whether it is being worn.

The **normalization of the orientation** is based on the assumption that the average acceleration during walking corresponds to the Earth's gravity. We compute a quaternion matrix representing the rotation between the average orientation of the smartphone during 10 seconds of walking, and the preferred orientation corresponding to the phone's longest side being perfectly aligned with the gravity [4]. This matrix is then applied to acceleration data to normalize it in real time.

The **walking detection, location detection** and **activity recognition** are done in essentially the same way, using machine learning. First, the stream of acceleration data is segmented into 2-second windows. Then, a number of features are computed for each window, forming a feature vector. The feature vectors computed from training data are fed into a machine-learning algorithm, which outputs a classification model for one of the three tasks. When new data are obtained, the same features are computed and fed into the model, which outputs the activity or location. The Random Forest algorithm as implemented in the Weka suite [5] was used to train all the classification models, since it outperformed other tested algorithms. The **energy-expenditure estimation** is done similarly as the previous three tasks, except that the window length is 10 seconds and regression models are used instead of classification. The Support Vector Regression algorithm from Weka was used to train the models.

3   Experimental Evaluation

The proposed activity-monitoring approach was evaluated on recordings of 10 volunteers wearing the heart-rate monitor and simultaneously carrying smartphones in all the locations in various orientations. They performed a scenario consisting of everyday activities and exercise, interspersed with periods of walking to normalize the orientation of the phone and detect its location. The activities to be recognized were walking, running, cycling, lying, sitting and standing (the last two were merged when only a device on the chest was available, and the last three when only the phone in the bag was available). The leave-one-person-out cross-validation was used.

The walking detection achieved the classification accuracy of 91.1% with the smartphone alone and 92.2% with both devices. The location detection achieved the classification accuracy of 90.3% with the smartphone alone (the heart-rate monitor was not used). The activity recognition and energy expenditure estimation yielded the results in Table 1. They show that using two devices is worthwhile only when one of them is the smartphone in the trousers pocket. The redundant two-device configurations are marked with a star and not included in the averages. The last column shows comparison approaches: an activity-recognition system using fixed dedicated sensors,

Table 1. The accuracy of the activity recognition [%], and the mean absolute error of the energy expenditure estimation [MET, 1 MET is the energy expended at rest]

| | | Heart-rate monitor | Smartphone | | | | Comp. |
			Breast	Trousers	Bags	Average	
Activity recognition	One device	81.7	87.9	78.9	79.5	82.1	83.7
	Two devices		83.8*	92.7	60.9*	92.7	92.8
Energy expenditure est.	One device	0.74	0.87	0.92	1.15	0.92	1.00
	Two devices		0.76*	0.72	0.87*	0.72	

trained and tested on a similar dataset as ours, and a state-of-the-art consumer device for energy-expenditure estimation (www.bodymedia.com). Our approach performed similarly to the first despite not using fixed sensors, and better than the second.

To evaluate the gains from the orientation normalization and location detection, we tested the activity monitoring with each of these features turned on or off. Table 2 shows the gains in activity recognition are substantial, while the gains in energy-expenditure estimation are modest and only present if both features are turned on.

Table 2. The accuracy [%] of the activity recognition and the mean absolute error of the energy expenditure estimation [MET] with/without orientation normalization and location detection

	Activity recognition	Energy expenditure est.
Without orientation, without location	63.4	0.98
With orientation, without location	68.7	1.17
Without orientation, with location	74.7	1.04
With orientation, with location	83.6	0.92

4   Conclusion

We presented an approach to activity-monitoring of diabetes patients with a smartphone and an accelerometer-equipped heart-rate monitor that can detect whether and how the devices are worn or carried, and adapt the monitoring accordingly. This increased the accuracy of the activity recognition by 20 percentage points and modestly lowered the error of the energy-expenditure estimation. We plan to upgrade the activity recognition with higher-level activities (e.g., work, leisure, eating). Afterwards, the approach will be tested on diabetes patients, whose data is currently being collected. We also plan to apply it to other domains, both in medicine and sports.

References

1. Thiemjarus, S.: A Device-Orientation Independent Method for Activity Recognition. In: International Conference on Body Sensor Networks, pp. 19–23. IEEE, New York (2010)
2. Martín, H., Bernardos, A.M., Iglesias, J., Casar, J.R.: Activity Logging Using Lightweight Classification Techniques in Mobile Devices. Pers. Ubiquit. Comput. **17**, 675–695 (2013)
3. Cvetković, B., Kaluža, B., Milić, R., Luštrek, M.: Towards Human Energy Expenditure Estimation Using Smart Phone Inertial Sensors. In: Augusto, J.C., Wichert, R., Collier, R., Keyson, D., Salah, A.A., Tan, A.-H. (eds.) AmI 2013. LNCS, vol. 8309, pp. 94–108. Springer, Heidelberg (2013)
4. Tundo, M.D., Lemaire, E., Baddour, N.: Correcting Smartphone Orientation for Accelerometer-based Analysis. In: MeMeA, pp. 58–62. IEEE, New York (2013)
5. Hall, M., Eibe, F., Holmes, G., Pfahringer, B., Reutemann, P., Witten, I.H.: The WEKA Data Mining Software: An Update. ACM SIGKDD Explorations **11**(1), 10–18 (2009)
6. Kozina, S., Gjoreski, H., Gams, M., Luštrek, M.: Three-layer Activity Recognition Combining Domain Knowledge and Meta-classification. J. Med. Biol. Eng. **33**(4), 406–414 (2013)

Tell Me What to Eat – Design and Evaluation of a Mobile Companion Helping Children and Their Parents to Plan Nutrition Intake

Runhua Xu[1], Irena Pletikosa Cvijikj[1], Tobias Kowatsch[2(✉)],
Florian Michahelles[1], Dirk Büchter[3], Björn Brogle[3], Anneco Dintheer[3],
Dagmar I'Allemand[3], and Wolfgang Maass[4]

[1] ETH Zurich, Zurich, Switzerland
{rxu,ipletikosa,fmichahelles}@ethz.ch
[2] University of St.Gallen, St.Gallen, Switzerland
tobias.kowatsch@unisg.ch
[3] Children's Hospital of Eastern Switzerland, St.Gallen, Switzerland
{dirk.buechter,bjoern.brogle,anneco.dintheer-tervelde,
dagmar.lallemand}@kispisg.ch
[4] Saarland University, Saarbrücken, Germany
wolfgang.maass@iss.uni-saarland.de

Abstract. Obesity is a global issue and has a direct impact on the public and private healthcare system. In this paper we describe the design and evaluation of a novel mobile health application that supports obese children and their parents to improve their nutrition intake. First results from quantitative app usage logs, questionnaires and interviews indicate that the mobile health app provides relevant information to attain a balanced nutrition. A discussion of the results and an outline of future work conclude this paper.

Keywords: Children · Parents · Overweight · Obesity · Mobile App · Healthcare

1 Introduction

Obesity is a global issue and has a direct impact on public and private healthcare system [1]. In Switzerland, prevalence of overweight and obesity in childhood has stabilized over the last ten years but 20% of children remain overweight and urgent efforts are needed to control the epidemic [2]. Implications of these observations are not only psychological and physiological drawbacks for those being affected but it has also serious effects on the public and private healthcare sector by increasing costs due to overweight- and obesity-related comorbidities and a lack of health supply [3]. In Switzerland, for example, obesity-linked disease costs have more than doubled from 2.600 Mio USD in 2001 to 5.800 Mio USD in 2006 [4], which equals to almost 10% of all health expenses in Switzerland (according to the Swiss Statistical Office).

In order to address these issues, multi-professional programs with physical activity, nutritional and behavioral interventions have been proposed [5]. Such programs were

© Springer International Publishing Switzerland 2014
E. Aarts et al. (Eds.): AmI 2014, LNCS 8850, pp. 100–113, 2014.
DOI: 10.1007/978-3-319-14112-1_9

shown to have positive effects on therapy outcomes [6]. However, due to limited personal and financial resources, only a small percentage of children affected can participate in such programs. In Switzerland, for example, this is less than one percent of overweight children [3].

Information technology has the potential to improve outcomes of health interventions and to significantly reduce costs [7, 8]. Therefore, we propose to address the problem by a novel mobile app that accompanies obese children and their parents during everyday situations, namely planning of their nutrition intake.

The contributions of this paper are as follows: In the next section, we provide some examples from related work that leverages IT to improve people's health condition. Based on major shortcomings of these research endeavors, we then describe the design process of the mobile health app. This process included not only computer scientists and information systems researcher but also several physicians, nutrition experts, obese children and their parents. We proceed with the description of a pilot study, in which the mobile health app was assessed, and present the results. Finally, the discussion and future work shed light on how to further validate, revise and improve the proposed mobile health app.

2   Related Work

2.1   Health Applications

In this section we present various examples of health applications that have the potential to support health-promoting behavior in teenagers (for a comprehensive list of prototypes and preliminary studies on IT-supported obesity interventions see [9]). For instance, Huston [10] is a mobile app that fetches users' physical activity data from a pedometer and demonstrates it on a mobile phone. UbiFit Gardens [11] links a user's daily step count to the emotional state of a garden shown on the screen of her/his mobile phone. Fish'n'Steps [12], a social computer game that translates a player's daily foot step count to the growth and facial expression of a fish, reveals the effectiveness of using games and emotional design to improve users' attitudes towards physical activities.

In addition to encouraging people to do more physical exercises, other apps aim at helping people to optimize their nutrition intake. For example, HyperFit [13] is an Internet service for personal management of nutrition and exercise. It monitors users' diet and exercise behavior through logging and barcode scanning tools. PmEB [14] is another app that enables people to log their food intake and physical activity everyday. Calorie consumption and expenditure is calculated so that users can self-monitor their calorie balance in real time. Regarding the design of recipe recommendation apps, Harvey et al. [15] revealed that healthiness, preference on specific ingredients, and preparing time have been found to be relevant to users. Wu [16] shows that compatibility, perceived usefulness and perceived ease of use have strong influence on people's acceptance on mobile applications in the healthcare domain. According to design styles, Khan [17] shows that parents prefer straightforward design while children and teenagers prefer gamification and social interaction.

2.2 Shortcomings of IT Interventions for Childhood Obesity

Although there are already many applications available to help people form a healthier lifestyle, at least four shortcomings can be observed. First, Kowatsch et al. [9] conducted a systematic review of 17 research papers and 13 commercial applications and found out that the majority of these applications did not consider a multi-professional approach as recommended and, in most cases, they did not evaluate evidence-based effects on health outcomes. Furthermore, applications reviewed [ibid.] had not been co-designed and evaluated by therapists, children, their parents and IT experts together. In addition, only few IT-supported health interventions are tailored to children and adolescents with their individual needs and requirements (e.g. weightdog.me or kurbo.com). Moreover and with a particular focus on diet behavior the following can be observed: Although people's preference on specific ingredients is one of the most important factors in recipe recommendation, current applications have not taken it into account. Finally and most important, the applicability of a mobile app in the day to day life of the patient and his family together with side effects regarding dieting or excessive IT use were not documented for most applications.

Consequently, our research aims to address these shortcomings and thus, we decided to develop a novel mobile health app. As a first step, we focused on diet-related services as described in the remainder of this paper (complementary services are developed and described in [9] and [18]).

3   Design Process

3.1   Research Setting

Teenagers with overweight or obesity, defined as body mass index above percentile 90 of reference data [2], were recruited from patients in an outpatient pediatric department to co-design the mobile health app in workshops, by questionnaires, interviews and practical everyday use as mentioned below. The patients were participating in a multiprofessional obesity program. The local ethics committee approved the design process and pilot test of the mobile health app. Informed consent was obtained both from patients and parents.

3.2   Concept of the Mobile Health App

To determine the app's services, a situation-based design approach was adopted [19, 20]. Through interviews and workshops with obese children, their parents and physicians, several requirements with a focus on diet behavior were identified: First, the app should recommend recipes based on ingredients available at home, prioritize desired ingredients of the patients, and foster a diverse meal plan based on the consumption history of previously chosen ingredients. Second, as the users navigate through the recommendations and make their choices, they should receive direct feedback on recipes and ingredients with regard to healthiness. Finally, the app should also help physicians trace and evaluate children's therapy compliance.

To avoid dieting and to ensure an adequate balanced composition of the proposed recipes, 50 recipes were selected by a nutrition expert from a cooking book [21] that is not only widely used in the national primary education but also a standard book in almost every household of the targeted patients and their families. Quality of recipes and quantity of nutrients are in accordance with recommendations of the Swiss Society for Nutrition (www.sge-ssn.ch). The most important messages include a diversified choice out of each main nutrient group with an adequate portion size. These recipes and their corresponding ingredients were saved locally in the app. Detailed information about how to cook the recipes was described in a cookbook with which the patients and their parents were supplied together with a mobile device running the app.

3.3   Services of the Mobile Health App

The mobile health app was realized on an Android-based tablet PC and is used together with a cooking book [21] as shown in Fig. 1.

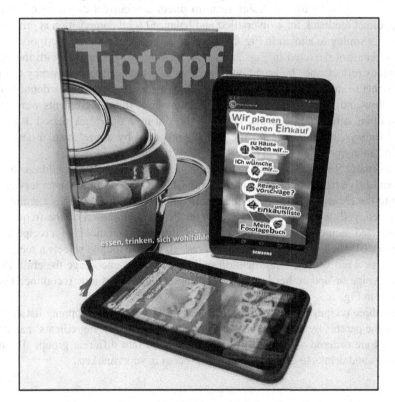

Fig. 1. Overview of the mobile health app with five diet-related services

The app consists of five diet-related services as shown on the main screen of the mobile health app in Fig. 1. These servicers are:

1. Available Ingredients service ("At home, we have ...") designed for parents

2. Desired Ingredients service ("I would like ...") designed for patients

3. Recipe List service ("Recipe recommendations?") designed for patients

4. Shopping List service ("Our shopping list") designed for parents

5. Photo Documentation service ("My photo diary") designed for patients

The Available Ingredients service helps parents log the available ingredients at home. By entering the name and quantity of ingredients, a list of available ingredients can be created and stored in a local database on a mobile device. In addition, ingredients can also be modified and deleted with the help of the same service.

Similarly, children can add and modify their desired ingredients with the help of the Desired Ingredients service. The only difference to the Available Ingredients service lies in the fact that a direct feedback is provided, which was perceived as an important design choice by the design team to direct and correct diet-related behavior. That is, direct feedback for a diversified and balanced food composition is provided in a form of a smiley as shown in Fig. 2a together with a brief textual description similar to the screenshot depicted in Fig. 2c in case the smiley was tapped with the finger. This smiley reflects the "balanced nutrition", namely the adequate frequency of intake with respect to nutrient content of this ingredient (refer to algorithm in detail below). Red, yellow and green smileys stand for the number of times ingredients were selected (too often, often and adequate, respectively) during a one-week period. By touching the smileys, the rationale for the color is provided by a brief textual description from an "anonymous" nutrition expert as shown in Fig. 2c.

Furthermore, Fig. 2b illustrates the Recipe List service used by children to select three out of five recommended recipes. Similar to the Desired Ingredients service with regard to the choice of a direct feedback rationale, each recipe also has a smiley with color green, yellow or red that serves as a feedback, again based on the frequency of prior selected recipes in the past week. The picture and ingredients of a recipe will be demonstrated when a "Details" button is pressed. In case a child selects a recipe with a yellow or a red smiley, a notification will be pop up to encourage the child to take another recipe or update her list of desired ingredients to get new recommendations, as shown in Fig. 2c.

Once three recipes are selected in the Recipe List service, a shopping list is generated for the parents by the Shopping List service (see Fig. 2d). Ingredients' names and quantities are ordered alphabetically and categorized into different groups like meat, vegetables and drinks to ease the shopping process in supermarkets.

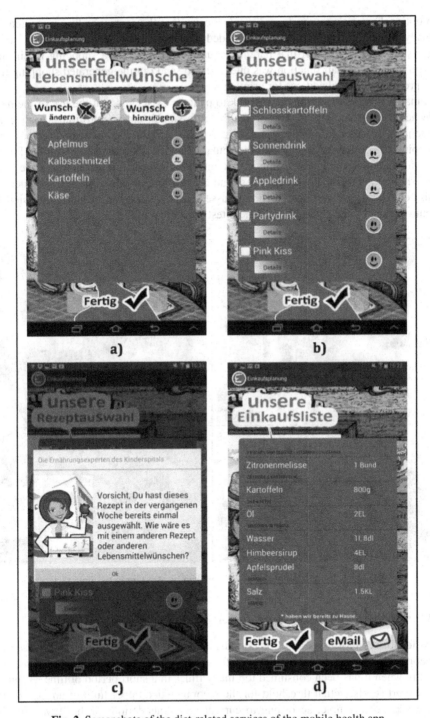

Fig. 2. Screenshots of the diet-related services of the mobile health app

An optional asterisk nearby ingredients indicates that the corresponding ingredient is already available at home, i.e. it was added to the list of available ingredients in a prior step. Due to the fact that parents requested a paper-based shopping list in the design phase, an email function was integrated to send out the generated shopping list to a pre-defined email address for printing.

Finally, it was crucial that a feedback to patients exists and that the use of the mobile health app is supervised by a health professional, e.g. a nutritionist, online or personally. In order to monitor patients' compliance to the recommended recipes and shopping list in their everyday life, the actual behavior is documented with the Photo Documentation service. For example, patients were asked to take photos of the purchased ingredients, the cooking process and the resulting meals as pieces of evidence. This behavioral data was shared and discussed with a supervising health professional. Pictures taken by the children in the field test are shown in Fig. 3.

Fig. 3. Pictures as pieces of evidence taken by children in the field test

3.4   Feedback and Recommendation Algorithm

Two feedback algorithms, one for ingredients and another for recipes, were used to generate the smileys. An ingredient in the 50 selected recipes was defined as unhealthy when it has been consumed too many times in a short period of time. A nutrition expert set the actual threshold for the recommended upper limit of an ingredient per week. For example, according to current recommendations on healthy nutrition (www.sge-ssn.ch), the threshold value for beef was set to four, which means it was better not to eat beef more than four times per week.

Whenever a recipe was selected with the help of the Recipe List service, the current timestamp would be compared with the *start_time* of all of the ingredients in that recipe. If the time difference was smaller than seven days, the *current_consumption* value of that ingredient would be increased by one. Then the feedback point of each ingredient was calculated from dividing its *current_consumption* value by the corresponding threshold value. This point was represented by a smiley as an intuitive feedback for the teenagers. High (> 0.7) and low (< 0.3) feedback points were represented by red and green smileys, respectively. Feedback points in between were represented by yellow smileys. Contrasting with that, if the time difference was larger than seven days, *start_time* of the ingredient would be replaced by the current timestamp and its *current_consumption* value would be set to one. Meanwhile, its feedback point was calculated based on the same strategy as described above.

Similarly, the feedback algorithm for recipes was also based on the consumption history of each recipe in the past week. A green or yellow smiley feedback was set to a recipe if it was consumed for up to once per week. In contrast, if a recipe was selected more than twice per week, it would be assigned a high feedback score.

The recommendation algorithm includes three factors: (1) current available ingredients at home, (2) current desired ingredients of the patients, and (3) current consumption history of all the ingredients. As parents stated that they needed healthy recipes that could reuse the available ingredients to the greatest extent, the healthiness of each recipe was calculated by using Eq.1:

$$\text{Healthiness} = \rho1 \cdot |\text{REP} \cap \text{AVB}| + \rho2 \cdot |\text{REP} \cap \text{DSR}| + \rho3 \cdot (\text{fb} - 10) \qquad (1)$$

The set REP represents all the ingredients in a recipe. The sets AVB and DSR reflect all the available and desired ingredients. The term |REP ∩ AVB| represents the number of elements in the intersection of REP and AVB. The weights $\rho1$, $\rho2$ and $\rho3$ were set to 3, 1, and 0.5 respectively in the mobile health app. These weights were selected empirically to make sure that factor (1) and (3) have a stronger influence than factor (2) on ordering all the 50 recipes. The parameter fb in the equation is set to 10, 5 or 0 for green, yellow and red smileys. Thus, the last polynomial serves as a punishment if an ingredient has been consumed more than 30% of its threshold value.

Before entering the Recipe List service, the value of "balanced nutrition" of each recipe is calculated first. All the recipes would then be ordered from the highest value of "balanced nutrition" to the lowest. Finally, the top five ranked recipes are shown in the recipe selection view (see Fig. 2b).

3.5   Data Collection

A logging mechanism was implemented for quantitative analysis of the screen time consumed: when a button of the mobile health app was pressed, a log entry in JSON format would be sent to the backend database by an HTTP Request. Such an entry includes user id, button name, current timestamp, and action related information such as editing an available ingredient or selecting three recipes. Color of smileys for recipes and desired ingredients would also be transferred to the backend when their corresponding services were used.

In addition to the log data, questionnaires were designed to get children and their parents' direct feedback on the design and functionalities of the mobile health app. Here, patients evaluated different aspects of the app on six-point Likert-scales ranging from strongly disagree (1) to strongly agree (6). An even number of the Likert-scale anchors was used to address common answer patterns (in particular, with regard to the neutral "neither" anchor if five or seven-point Likert scales would have been used) that were already observed by our health professionals in prior studies with the target group of this mobile health app.

4   Evaluation

4.1   Design of the Pilot Field Study

In order to test the mobile health app in a pilot study, the physician responsible invited several patients between age 11 and 14 who already participated in an individual obesity therapy in the outpatient department of the children's hospital. Second, a consultation with patients and parents was conducted to inform them about the objective of the study and the usage of the mobile health app. Then, a tablet PC with the app pre-installed, the cooking book and a monetary compensation were provided so that the family was able to buy the ingredients of the selected recipes. Patients and their parents were then asked to use the app at least once for meal planning, preparation and documentation purposes at home. For this task, they were given three weeks on average. Finally, patients, parents and physicians discussed the results during the second consultation in which the app-related questionnaires were filled out, too.

The primary research questions regarding the current work were:

1. Which sort of content provided by the mobile health app is perceived as useful information for selecting recipes?

2. Which sort of content provided by the mobile health app actually influences the decision on selecting recipes?

Whereas the first question is formulated from a more general third-person point of view, the second question addresses rather the individual perspective of the patients with regard to the actual decision-making situation. Answers to these questions would not only reveal first evidence on the utility of the mobile health app but they would also help the design team to further improve it.

4.2   Participants of the Study

Overall, six male children each with one parent participated during the first consultation and four male children with one parent during the second consultation between April and June 2013. The dropout of two families was not related to the study but rather to limited time resources of the patients and their parents. The average age of the four resulting patients was 12.8 (SD = 2.6).

4.3   Results of the Study

On average, 3.75 (SD=2.22) usage sessions with a length of 13 minutes (SD=4) were identified through the backend data log. Furthermore, the patients took 12.3 photos (SD=6.95) on average. Examples of these photos are depicted in Fig. 3. The descriptive statistics and details with regard to the two primary research questions are shown in Table 1.

Further empirical results of this study with a focus on other theoretical constructs such as perceived usefulness, perceived ease of use, perceived enjoyment (of the overall mobile health app to improve health behavior) or the potential of the mobile health app to improve shared understanding and cross-understanding among patient and therapist with regard to obesity therapy are published in [9] and [22].

Table 1. Descriptive statistics of the pilot study (N=4). Note: answers were anchored on six-point Likert scales ranging from strongly disagree (1) to strongly agree (6).

What content provides useful information for selecting recipes:		
Content	**Mean**	**Std. Dev.**
Order of recipe recommendations	3.50	1.30
Color of the smiley feedbacks	5.75	0.50
Image of a recipe	4.00	0.00
Ingredients of a recipe	4.50	1.00
What content has influenced my decision on selecting recipes:		
Content	**Mean**	**Std. Dev.**
Order of recipe recommendations	3.00	1.41
Color of the smiley feedbacks	4.50	1.29
Image of a recipe	4.00	1.41
Ingredients of a recipe	4.50	1.00
Estimated cooking time	4.25	0.50

Four patients selected 27 recipes during the field test. Recipes located in the first place, however, were selected only twice. Recipes located in other places were selected almost evenly, with seven times for the second and fifth place, six times for the third place and five times for the fourth place. Regarding the direct feedback via smileys and a brief textual description by the "anonymous" nutrition expert, patients found that the color of smileys was helpful in providing them with useful information for recipe selection, followed by the ingredients of recipes and the image of recipes.

When asked what influenced their decisions on choosing a particular recipe, children selected the color of smileys and ingredients of a recipe as the most influential aspects. From all the sessions except those identified as testing, only one recipe with yellow smiley was presented to a user, and it was not selected. All the other recipes were presented with green smileys.

The limited number of presented yellow and red smileys could be explained by the limited app usage per week, as well as the effectiveness of the recommendation algorithm.

With regard to the recipe recommendations, the algorithm performed in accordance with the recommendations of a nutrition expert. However, based on the qualitative feedback, almost all patients and their parents disliked the limited number of recipes for selection and the restriction that exactly three recipes should be selected each time, which was actually intended by the design team to reduce not only the complexity of the mobile health app but also of the tasks and homework of patients (and their parents) within obesity interventions in general.

5   Discussion and Conclusions

We presented the design and evaluation of a mobile health app that aims to help obese children and their parents to plan their daily nutrition intake. The smiley feedback was regarded important for providing valuable information and helping children to make decisions on recipe selection. The prototype's feedback and recommendation algorithm helped obese children to eat more diversified and healthier food due to the fact that none of the participants had selected a single recipe twice in a week. This is important in so far as overweight people tend to have a very limited choice of food [23]. It can also be concluded that those children were highly motivated because they used the prototype several times although they were requested to use it only once in the field test period.

Furthermore, an excessive use of the mobile health app was not observed. Together with the flexible advice on balanced meals and the supervision by a nutritionist or a physician this mobile health app may contribute to avoid potential side effects as media abuse or eating disorders.

From a therapist's point of view, the feedback loops on nutrition behavior and the photo documentation were important not only for the patient and his family to increase awareness on their lifestyle but also for the therapist to recognize, how recommendations were implemented at home.

Having more flexibility to select from all available recipes (in addition to the preselected three) was given the highest importance during the final qualitative feedback round. This must be taken into account when designing a mobile companion for high user involvement.

Based on the original design, recipes were ranked based on how well their ingredients match the current available and desired ingredients and how frequently their ingredients were consumed in the past week. Therefore, recipes with higher rank not only mean that they are healthier and cater better to the personal desire but also mean they bring financial advantages since they can reuse the available ingredients to the largest extent. Rationally, among all the five recommended recipes, the first one should be selected most frequently whilst the fifth one should be the least preferred.

Thus, reordering all the recommended recipes might help people make more "nutritional balanced" decisions. This strategy could be applied to other mobile apps that provide users with several options to select from (e.g. with regard to physical activities).

Overall, we could learn from this research that mobile health apps (1) enrich therapist-patient communication and relationship by incorporating advice through feedbacks, (2) help families to jointly engage not only in the decision process of selecting food and recipes but also in meal preparation and enhancing eating habits, and (3) have the potential to give more patients access to therapy programs through their scalability.

6   Future Work

As next steps, we plan to improve the mobile health app by removing current restrictions on recipe selection. In addition to nutrition intake planning, also patients' physical activities, relaxation and emotional self-regulation capabilities will be measured and integrated into IT-supported obesity interventions [9, 18]. An evaluation of these services, including their effects on therapy outcomes such as the body mass index is in progress [24-26]. Finally, the app should be also released in the app-store allowing an even broader evaluation with a larger population of users in the wild [27].

Acknowledgement. This work was part-funded by the Swiss National Science Foundation (SNF), Project 135552. The study was approved by the local ethical committee of St. Gallen, Switzerland, no. EKSG 10/118.

References

1. WHO: Obesity and overweight, Fact sheet N 311. 6.10.14 (2014). http://www.who.int/mediacentre/factsheets/fs311/en/
2. Murer, S.B., Saarsalu, S., Zimmermann, M.B., Aeberli, I.: Pediatric adiposity stabilized in Switzerland between 1999 and 2012. European Journal of Nutrition **53**, 865–875 (2014)
3. Hänggli, B., Laimbacher, J., Gutzwiller, F., Fäh, D.: Adipositastherapie bei Kindern und Jugendlichen in der Schweiz: Wo liegen die Hürden. Schweizerische Ärztezeitung **89**, 277–281 (2008)
4. Schneider, H., Venetz, W., Berardo, C.G.: Overweight and obesity in Switzerland - Part 1: Cost burden of adult obesity in 2007. Bundesamt für Gesundheit (BAG) (2009)
5. Sempach, R., Farpour-Lambert, N., L'Allemand, D., Laimbacher, J.: Therapie des adipösen Kindes und Jugendlichen: Vorschläge für multi-professionelle Therpieprogramme. Paediatrica **18**, 33–37 (2007)
6. Ho, M., Garnett, S.P., Baur, L., Burrows, T., Stewart, L., Neve, M., Collins, C.: Effectiveness of Lifestyle Interventions in Child Obesity: Systematic Review With Meta-analysis. Pediatrics **130**, e1647–e1671 (2012)
7. Spring, B., Duncan, J.M., Janke, E.A., Kozak, A.T., McFadden, H.G., DeMott, A., Pictor, A., Epstein, L.H., Siddique, J., Pellegrini, C.A., Buscemi, J., Hede-ker, D.: Integrating

Technology Into Standard Weight Loss Treatment: A Randomized Controlled Trial. JAMA Internal Medicine **173**, 105–111 (2013)

8. Agarwal, R., Gao, G.G., DesRoches, C., Jha, A.K.: The Digital Transformation of Healthcare: Current Status and the Road Ahead. Information Systems Research **21**, 796–809 (2010)

9. Kowatsch, T., Maass, W., Pletikosa Cvijikj, I., Büchter, D., Brogle, B., Dintheer, A., Wiegand, D., Durrer, D., Xu, R., Schutz, Y., l'Allemand-Jander, D.: Design of a Health Information System Enhancing the Performance of Obesity Expert and Children Teams. In: 22nd European Conference on Information Systems (ECIS), Tel Aviv, Israel (2014)

10. Consolvo, S., Everitt, K., Smith, I., Landay, J.A.: Design Requirements for Technologies that Encourage Physical Activity. In: Conference on Human Factors in Computing Systems (CHI 2006), pp. 457–466. Montréal, Québec, Canada (2006)

11. Consolvo, S., McDonald, D.W., Landay, J.A.: Theory-driven design strategies for technologies that support behavior change in everyday life. In: Olsen, D.R.J., Arthur, R.B., Hinckley, K., Morris, M.R., Hudson, S., Greenberg, S. (eds.) Proceedings of the 27th international conference on Human factors in computing systems, pp. 405–414. ACM, New York, NY, USA (2009)

12. Lin, J.J., Mamykina, L., Lindtner, S., Delajoux, G., Strub, H.B.: Fish'n'Steps: Encouraging Physical Activity with an Interactive Computer Game. In: Dourish, P., Friday, A. (eds.) International Conference on Ubiquitous Computing, Ubicomp 2006, pp. 261–278. Springer, Berlin, Germany (2006)

13. Jarvinen, P., Jarvinen, T.H., Lahteenmaki, L., Sodergard, C.: HyperFit: Hybrid media in personal nutrition and exercise management. In: 2nd International Conference on Pervasive Computing Technologies for Healthcare, pp. 222–226. IEEE (2008)

14. Tsai, C.C., Lee, G., Raab, F., Norman, G.J., Sohn, T., Griswold, W.G., Patrick, K.: Usability and feasibility of PmEB: a mobile phone application for monitoring real time caloric balance. Mobile Networks and Applications **12**, 173–184 (2007)

15. Harvey, M., Ludwig, B., Elsweiler, D.: Learning user tastes: a first step to generating healthy meal plans? Workshop on Recommendation Technologies for Lifestyle Change 2012. In: conjunction with the 6th ACM conference on Recommender Systems (RecSys 2012). ACM, Dublin, Ireland (2012)

16. Wu, J.H., Wang, S.C., Lin, L.M.: Mobile computing acceptance factors in the healthcare industry: a structural equation model. International Journal of Medical Informatics **76**, 66–77 (2007)

17. Khan, D.U., Ananthanarayan, S., Le, A.T., Schaefbauer, C.L., Siek, K.A.: Designing mobile snack application for low socioeconomic status families. In: Bardram, J., Mihailidis, A., Tentori, M. (eds.) 6th International Conference on Pervasive Computing Technologies for Healthcare (PervasiveHealth), pp. 57–64 (2012)

18. Pletikosa Cvijikj, I., Kowatsch, T., Büchter, D., Brogle, B., Dintheer, A., Wiegand, D., Durrer, D., Xu, R., l'Allemand, D., Schutz, Y., Maass, W.: Health Information System for Obesity Prevention and Treatment of Children and Adolescents. In: 22nd European Conference on Information Systems (ECIS), Tel Aviv, Israel (2014)

19. Carroll, J.M.: Making use: scenario-based design of human–computer interactions. MIT Press, Cambridge, MA (2000)

20. Janzen, S., Kowatsch, T., Maass, W.: A Methodology for Content-Centered Design of Ambient Environments. In: Winter, R., Zhao, J., Aier, S. (eds.) DESRIST 2010. LNCS, vol. 6105, pp. 210–225. Springer, Heidelberg (2010)

21. Affolter, U., Jaun Urech, M., Keller, M., Schmid, U.: Tiptopf - essen, trinken, sich wohlfühlen. Schulverlag plus, Bern, Schweiz (2012)

22. Kowatsch, T., Büchter, D., Pletikosa Cvijikj, I., Xu, R., Brogle, B., Dintheer, A., Wiegand, D., l'Allemand, D., Maass, W.: Design and Preliminary Evaluation of a Mobile Application for Obesity Experts and Children Teams. Poster. 7th Fribourg Obesity Research Conference (FORC-2013) – Pathways from Dieting to Weight Regain, to Obesity & to Metabolic Syndrome, Fribourg, Switzerland (2013)
23. Toselli, S., Argnani, L., Canducci, E., Ricci, E., Gualdi-Russo, E.: Food habits and nutritional status of adolescents in Emilia-Romagna. Italy. Nutrición Hospitalaria **25**, 613–621 (2010)
24. Büchter, D., Kowatsch, T., Pletikosa Cvijikj, I., Schutz, Y., l'Allemand, D., Maass, W., Laimbacher, J.: A Longitudinal Study Assessing an IT-supported Neurological Feedback in Obesity Intervention for Children and Adolescents' Emotional Self Control (Poster). Annual Congress of the foederatio Paedo medicorum helveticorum (fPmh), Basel, Switzerland (2014)
25. Büchter, D., Kowatsch, T., Pletikosa Cvijikj, I., Schutz, Y., l'Allemand, D., Maass, W., Laimbacher, J.: A Longitudinal Study Assessing an IT-supported Neurological Feedback in Obesity Intervention for Children and Adolescent Emotional Self Control. Swiss Medical Weekly **144**, 21 (2014)
26. Büchter, D., Kowatsch, T., Brogle, B., Dintheer, A., Wiegand, D.: Pletikosa Cvijikj, I., Maass, W., l'Allemand, D., Laimbacher, J.: Home Support of Obese Children and Adolescents by Means of Health Information Technology System: A Pilot Study for a Psychosomatic Therapy Concept. Swiss Medical Weekly **144**, 17 (2014)
27. Chamberlain, A., Crabtree, A., Rodden, T., Jones, M., Rogers, Y.: Research in the wild: Understanding 'in the wild' approaches to design and development. Designing Interactive Systems Conference (DIS 2012), pp. 795–796. ACM, Newcastle, UK (2012)

The Impact of the Environment on the Experience of Hospitalized Stroke Patients – An Exploratory Study

Elke Daemen[1], Evert van Loenen[1,2(✉)], and Roel Cuppen[1]

[1] Philips Research, Eindhoven, The Netherlands
[2] Eindhoven University of Technology, Eindhoven, The Netherlands
{elke.daemen,evert.van.loenen,roel.cuppen}@philips.com,
e.j.v.loenen@tue.nl

Abstract. The aim of this study is to understand neurology patients, family and caregivers experiences of in-patient care environments and to investigate the aspects of the healing process that can be supported by the environment. Our goal is to identify the role the environment plays during the process of being treated for and recovering from a stroke. The stroke patient's description of experiences during hospitalization will help researchers, medical professionals and architects in adjusting the environment according to their specific needs. A set of research methods was used to capture the experience, changing the role of researcher as an observer to a participatory approach, integrating the caregivers as creators of the research data [1], [2]. These methods included: shadowing, observation and interviewing, allowing nurses to describe their experiences and to obtain a voice in decision making. We built insights from healing environment literature combined with own field studies. Specific environmental needs identified include: dosing stimulus load, having social support, having access to single patient rooms, balancing clinical and personal environments, having a clear structure of the day, undisturbed sleeping and the need for information.

Keywords: Healing environments · Stroke · Contextual research

1 Introduction

The aim of this study is to understand experiences of neurology patients, family and caregivers in in-patient care environments and to investigate the aspects of the healing process that can be supported by the environment.

The awareness of the impact of the environment on recovery processes varied significantly in the course of history. Thousands of years ago, Greek temples were designed to surround patients with nature, music, and art to restore harmony and promote healing. The temples were built in locations of great beauty so patients could enjoy the views, could drink pure water and were placed in raised positions where they could enjoy cooling breezes of fresh air. In these days healthcare intervention did not yet exist, and patients could only eat good food, rest, sleep and gain spiritual strength from the Gods to get better [3]. Since that time, healthcare services have evolved, albeit linked to care that was directly related to injury, such as changing

© Springer International Publishing Switzerland 2014
E. Aarts et al. (Eds.): AmI 2014, LNCS 8850, pp. 114–124, 2014.
DOI: 10.1007/978-3-319-14112-1_10

bandages and delivering drugs. From the mid-19th century onwards, hospital building design evolved away from creating temples of healing towards being primarily concerned with function [3]. The English nurse Florence Nightingale was aware that much of disability and deleterious effects of severe illness came not from the primary disease or initial injury, but from the effects of being bedridden and confined in unsanitary conditions. She was the first to promote a holistic approach for a faster and better healing of patients by means of fresh air, cleanliness, attractive environments and communication. The effects of her improvements on patient's outcomes were reflected in the mortality figures for 1855, which fell from 42.7 deaths per 100 to 2 per 1000 within months of Nightingale's changes [4]. Since Nightingale, an immense progress in medical science has been made. More and more illnesses can be successfully treated, and, in the meanwhile, hospitals expanded to large commercial and specialized institutes focusing on infection control and investing in new technologies. This resulted in the creation of facilities that are functionally very effective but that are not necessarily suited to the psychological and emotional needs of patients and their family [5].

In the technically advanced and specialized hospitals patients and family find the sheer amount of advanced medical equipment, procedures and routines intimidating and disturbing. Confrontation with co-patients in bad conditions induces increased levels of anxiety in patients and their family. In addition in current healthcare settings, staff such as nurses and doctors has limited time for social interaction with patients to sooth them and to explain cure and care procedures thoroughly. Therefore encounters with healthcare situations are generally characterized by fear, anxiety and uncertainty [6]. These feelings are expected to increase stress, which in addition may hinder the patient's healing process by negatively affecting sleep, pain perception, and depression [7]–[9].

1.1   Healing Environments

The hospital building in which patients receive healthcare services is inherently part of their experience [10]. Well-designed facilities may increase positive feelings which could be beneficial for the patients' health and well-being. Since the 1970s consumers began to choose hospitals based on esthetic appeal, therefore various architecture and design communities started to work on how to create an environment in which the patients feel at ease and the staff can work pleasantly and without having stress [11]. As a result over the past decade, numerous guidelines on building hospitals that are not only effective but also provide a place to heal have been developed. The definition of a healing environment was born: a physical setting and supportive culture that nurtures the physical, intellectual, social and spiritual wellbeing of patients, families, and staff and helps them to cope with the stress of illness and hospitalization.

There is evidence suggesting that while people are in a hospital, the more they stay connected to the natural world - to sunlight, the rhythms of nature and pleasant views - the better their chances are for a speedy recovery [8]. From literature we know that according to [9], [12], [13], access to (rendered) nature views, including the presence of indoor plants, helps to increase the tolerance for pain and to reduce the use of pain medication. Also, contact with nature has, to a certain extent, a positive effect on short-term recovery from stress and mental fatigue [9], [13] and can accelerate the physical recovery from illness [14]. Not only nature views, but also exposure to daylight is found to be an important factor in the recovery process. Patients exposed to sufficient daylight are less stressed and appear to need less pain medication [15]. Bright (artificial) daylight exposure during day-time and avoidance of too much light exposure during night-time helps patients to sleep better at night [16] and to feel more energized during the day [17].

Especially a deep restorative and undisturbed sleep is of high importance for a fast recovery process in patients. Hospitalized patients often suffer from poor sleep and diminished circadian rhythms [18] [19] [20] [21] [22] [23]. According to [20] [24] poor sleep increases stress and since stress has adverse effects on recovery, sleeping problems are nowadays considered to be a major issue to be addressed in both small and large hospitals. Van de Glind et al. referred to a study that compared noise and quality of sleep [27]. In this study, the Pittsburgh Sleep Quality Index was filled in by 150 patients on 26 wards with different ward layout (single, double and multi bedded rooms). They concluded that factors that affect sleep quality were: patients staying in a different environment than normal, noise, footsteps, pain and being woken by nurses during the night for medical check-ups, and interestingly, not the fact that patient were nursed in a single, double or multi bedded room [27].

Lately, a great number of hospitals have chosen to provide more single bedded rooms to patients because there is growing confidence and evidence that these rooms have a positive effect on patients. Private patient rooms have become the industry standard in the United States because they better facilitate patient care and management, afford greater therapeutic benefits for patients and may reduce the rate of hospital-acquired infections, although conflicting results have been found [28] [27] [6]. According to a comparison study of satisfaction rates, hospitals with more single rooms had higher patient satisfaction rates [27], [29].

When patients are admitted to a hospital they spend most of their time in a patient room and although the term healing environment already exists for a long time, even today, most hospital patient rooms remain highly institutionalized environments that confine patients to an artificial and unfamiliar environment. For example patient rooms often have windows facing walls that block natural light from coming into the patient room. In short, the impact of the quality of the hospital environment is instrumental for the recovery process of patients.

In our research, the focus is on the department of the hospital in which stroke patients are hospitalized. So far little attention has been paid to research on the experience of hospitalized stroke from the patient's point of view. Stroke patient's descriptions of their experiences during hospitalization will help researchers, medical professionals and architects in adjusting the environment according to their specific needs. Furthermore the findings may assist in altering the environment to improve the stroke patient's recovery and in helping them to adapt to their deficit.

2   The Study and Method

The aim of this study therefore is to understand neurology patients, family and care-givers experiences of in-patient care environments and to investigate the aspects of the healing process that can be supported by the environment. Our goal is to identify the role the environment plays during the process of being treated for and recovering from a stroke.

2.1   Methodology

In-depth clinical ethnography with thick description of sensations and responses of stroke victims and their caregivers provides a meaningful method of studying the stroke experience. By definition, the aim of this tick description is to accumulate very dense, rich, specific information from observations and interviews [28]. Within the literature of the experience design community, there are numerous micro-methods documented by various practitioners under the collective banner of "field studies" [25]. The two methods that are most prevalent and most representative of these field studies are Contextual Inquiry and Participant Observation [26]. Participant observation serves almost as a blanket method covering all aspects of contextual research: interviewing, [29] observing, cultural material review, etc. Contextual inquiry is a field research method used in user-centered design. It is also often associated with participatory design methods.

2.2   Set-Up of the Study

A set of research techniques has been used to capture the experience, transitioning the role of researcher as an observer to a participatory approach with integration of the caregivers as creators of the research data [1], [2]. These techniques included: shadowing, observation and interviewing, allowing nurses to describe their experiences and to obtain a voice in decision-making.

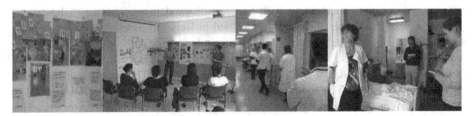

Fig. 1. Doing contextual research

Every field study started with a guided tour. This is not just an introduction to the different spaces, but also an introduction of the workflow and the experiences of stakeholders in the environments. The guided tour was given by a ward manager or similar, with a broad overview of the department. The tour was preceded by a briefing and a short explanation of the intended objectives to the clinical staff in charge.

Next we started with shadowing patients and care givers. The goal of shadowing is to understand the care experience from the perspective of a particular person in a particular role by observing the stakeholders' activities, movements, interactions with others, interactions with different equipment, and interaction with the environment. A researcher follows a pre-determined stakeholder while documenting the experience. The researcher tries to stay in the background with the aim to understand the actions and interactions of the participating stakeholder. Sometimes a researcher may ask the stakeholder to speak out loud as he or she goes through the experience, in order to explain what is happening. In this way, we gain a better feeling of the stakeholder's mindset and of the process.

In addition we carried out observations in different care environments, and had rapid consultations with different stakeholders that were present in these environments. These informal encounters enrich and verify the findings from the shadowing activity. The objective was to understand the activities in the spaces as they happen, including interactions with individuals and equipment. In this way we got an understanding of the main spatial issues and the interaction between the involved stakeholders in the space.

We also conducted semi-structured one-on-one (or paired) interviews with patients and family separately, and with staff and specialists. The goal of the interviews was to get a better understanding of the experience of the key stakeholders within the selected spaces, and to get insight into the person's mindset, motivations, needs, and emotions. In this ways we also got an insight into relevant activities and experiences that cannot be observed on site, such as family life at home, and looking for information.

During the visit we documented all the findings and continuously analyzed the data. At the end of each visit we had a draft experience flow ready to use in the next step: the multi stakeholder session. This is an interactive session facilitated by the research team, with the staff and specialist stakeholders. The objective of the multi stakeholder session is to validate and improve the draft patient experience flow.

2.3   Participants

We carried out contextual research in two neurology departments of two hospitals: one located in the Netherlands and one located in Belgium. One hospital was a general hospital with 405 beds serving a diverse population. The hospital is located in the center of the town and is easily accessible. The neurology department is situated in the new part of the hospital and opened its doors in 2008. The department has a capacity of 30 beds, one TIA room for day-care and a community room. The hospital is dedicated to people centric patient care, as defined in the Planetree model. The Planetree model of care is a holistic approach to healthcare, promoting mental, emotional, spiritual, social, and physical healing.

The second hospital is an academic hospital. The hospital has more than 1000 beds for acute care and extensive services for ambulatory diagnosis, treatment and care. Patients come to the hospital for all kinds of treatments ranging from basic to highly specialized. Patient care, teaching, scientific research and providing services to the population are the main tasks of the hospital. The neurology department was built in the late seventies. It has a stroke unit with 4 beds and the ward has a capacity of 26 beds.

3   Findings

Stroke patients suffer from brain trauma after having experienced a stroke and as a consequence in general have deteriorated skills. Neurology patients typically have a longer stay in the hospital (from several days to three weeks) in comparison with patients that are hospitalized on other wards, such as oncology and cardiology wards. A stroke patient goes through a number of 'phases' in his experience, usually marked by an event or a stay in a particular environment. Patients enter through the Emergency Room (ER), next they go to the Stroke Unit where they are monitored up to 72 hours, then they go to the neurology ward and finally they go to a rehabilitation center, elderly home or home. When patients have a stroke they experience a lot of fear and they feel like their world is falling apart. One occupational therapist expressed it like this: "Stroke is a very emotional experience. You were a perfectly capable person and you suddenly lose it." One of the patients, who is a Software engineer explained having a stroke like this: "When there is something wrong with the operating system of your body, it's serious. When you have a stroke, suddenly your entire view on life changes. I have a mortgage, and a young daughter".

Stroke patients have sustained permanent or non-permanent brain damage, which affects the way they behave and respond to their environment. Often the environment is not reassuring and makes patients and family even more fearful. One patient mentioned it like this: "When I came out of the elevator into the hallway, I was shocked to see all the rehab aids in the neurology department. I realized the situation was serious". Other patients can't remember what has happened to them in particular moments during their hospital stay: "I can't remember anything from the ER and my first day here. It's a scary idea to be missing part of your memory". In the ER the patients focus is on themselves, not on the environment or what is happening around them. Some patients do not consciously experience the ER due to CVA symptoms.

Our research identified several environmental needs, which will be discussed in the next section.

3.1   Dosing Stimulus Load

It was found important to take into account the number of stimuli provided in the room and the stimulus sensitivity of the patients occupying the room. Apathetic patients need more stimulation, aggressive or vivacious patients need less stimulation. The number of stimuli is determined by the number of objects in a room, color use and the congruence between different interior design features [6]. Stroke patients have a low threshold for stimuli. Frontal lobe damage will cause strong stimulus bound behavior. Patients with frontal lobe damage cannot shut out e.g., noises and light and may respond aggressively. Stimuli, such as light, noise, nurses running around and family visiting, in the neurology department are irregularly dosed. The amount and intensity of stimuli that a patient can handle in this environment depends a lot on the condition and phase of rehabilitation of the patient. Patients in the beginning of their rehabilitation process can often handle fewer stimuli, as one patient indicated: "I felt restless in the stroke unit." Nurses know that the amount of stimuli is often too high as a nurse indicated: "Patients say it is all ok, but it is not ok that it is so busy in the stroke unit. This is just not good for patients." Often family members are not aware and they decorate the room with cards and drawings, while patients can't handle this, as a nurse indicated: "It is nice that patients get lots of cards from family, but sometimes it's too much stimulus for them. So I take some away." Too many stimuli can lead to aggression and restlessness. Neurologists and doctors we interviewed are aware of the effects of stimulus on sleep quality and impairment, but other than using this information to diagnose or judge the progression of the patient's healing process, they are not personally involved in controlling or changing them.

Typically patients who just had a stroke are in need of a low stimulus environment. Often the need for low stimulus (low glare from daylight, ambient and task lights) is in conflict with the clinical schedule which requires certain lighting conditions such as for nurses charting the readings on paper (next to patient), nurses reading documents during transfer and nurses collecting blood samples or giving medication. On the other hand, a high stimulus environment can help patients recover by providing stimulating of the brain. Therefor personalizing the sensory load for individual patients in the neurology department could be very beneficial to patients. Currently there is a very irregular dosage of stimuli regardless of patient condition, which is tiring and distracting during therapy. For some patients, challenging them with stimuli is a good training, but it is again important to judge the patient's limits.

Stimulus levels are also irregularly dosed over the day. There is a difference between morning and afternoon activities. During the morning there is a very high stimulus load due to the clustering of various clinical and auxiliary activities (daily personal care, therapy, doctor's visit, cleaning, etc.). The morning is found by many patients to be straining due to the amount of activity and people present in the rooms at once, as one of the patients expressed: "It's too busy in the morning. There are three people in my room at once!" This is in contrast with the afternoon where boredom is often an issue certainly for patients who are getting better and have been in the hospital for a long time. This boredom can affect the patient's perception of pain.

3.2 Having Social Support

Social support has been described as emotional, informational and tangible support and is normally received from people in a social network and the family [8]. While being in a hospital social contacts are limited. This is unfortunate, because the need for social support increases when an individual is hospitalized. What we learned is that social contact with family and nurses is valued by patients, to prevent boredom and to give a feeling of contact with the outside world. They look forward to seeing family members and friends, to share their accomplishments or fears and to feel supported and loved. For patients it is therefore important that visitors make time for the patient, but visitors often experience a hospital setting as a sterile environment and therefore don't like to stay long in the hospital or even don't visit the patient, as one of the neurologists expressed: "The focus of the rooms is on medium care and not on going home. For example, there is not a lot of space for family in the patient rooms." The social contact with family and nurses is also high stimulus so it is important to be able to judge the patient's limits. This poses a dilemma: patients don't want to ask visitors to leave, although they are feeling exhausted. Patients will sometimes signal a nurse that they are too tired and the nurse will ask visitors to leave, but often patients don't dare to say this because they are afraid of the reaction of family members.

3.3   Single versus Multi Patient Rooms

Both of the hospitals we visited have a mix of single and multi-patient rooms. Depending on a patient's behavior, needs and severity of illness, nurses will decide where to put the patient: a single or multi patient room. A lot of patients, especially those with cognitive handicap are not consciousness of time, miss structure during their stay in hospital. A multi patient room could be beneficial for these patients as a nurse indicated: "Confused patients benefit from seeing the rhythm of activities of surrounding patients." The allocation could also depend on the visiting family (e.g. loud, visiting many times). There are benefits to both single patient rooms (quiet, privacy) and multi-patient rooms (social contact, structure, safety). Sharing a space can be difficult for some patients. The young patients typically appreciated a single patient room, because they find it more peaceful and private. Elderly patients often found a single patient room unpleasant because they miss the social contact with other patients and often feel isolated as a nurse indicated:" A lot of older patients enjoy the social contact in a multiple patient room." They may also associate the move with punishment for poor behavior or as an indication that their condition is worsening or they are being moved to a room in which they will die.

3.4   Balance Between Clinical and Personal Environment

The right balance between a clinical environment and a personal environment needs to be achieved for all stakeholders in the neurology department. Currently family members decorate room to make it more personal. On the other hand the patient rooms need to facilitate an optimal working environment for the hospital staff.

3.5   Providing Structure of the Day

A clear structure to the day is important for stroke patients to decrease risk of disorientation and confusion as one therapist stated: "Patients with a cognitive handicap often miss a consciousness of time – we try to give them a clear structure." Structure is also very important for patients in order to achieve a healthy sleeping pattern, to better handle rehabilitation therapy, and to consolidate their memories. A lot of patients, especially those with cognitive handicap miss a consciousness of time. For these patients everything must be structured and predictable. They do not easily accept changes. Also, memory was found to often be a problem for the patients. In the rehab center a diary is used to make it easier to recall what a patient has done during the day. It is difficult to stick to a strict day structure for the nursing staff, due to the unpredictable nature of care. For very structured patients this can be especially disconcerting.

3.6   Undisturbed Sleeping

What we learned during the study was that often the emotional impact of a stroke influences their wellbeing and ability to sleep, as a nurse indicated:" When patients can relieve their worries by talking with me, they can sleep better at night." Patients often feel ashamed to talk about their worries: "I didn't tell the nurse I was worried and that I couldn't sleep. They don't need to know that." It is very important for patients to sleep well in order to avoid confusing and disorientation, to better handle rehabilitation therapies, and to consolidate their memories. Efforts are made to activate patients during the day to stimulate a healthy sleeping pattern. Not only psychological problems influence the quality of sleep but also physical problems (e.g. pain), and environmental issues (e.g. noise) as one patient indicated: "You are in the room with a stranger, so it's always different then sleeping at home." Early in the morning the level of flexibility and improvisation nurses can work with is especially visible. Staff must wake patients for medication and care yet tries to be flexible with regards to the order of waking patients so they can sleep as long as possible. However, nurses think the falling asleep experience is more crucial than the wakeup experience. At night, care activities continue as normal. However, the lighting in patient rooms has not been optimized to allow for the nurse to do her job without disturbing the patient or surrounding patients from their sleep.

3.7   Need for Information

Patients expressed a need for information as one patient indicated: "In the hospital you don't know anything. For me information can be reassuring." Getting no or insufficient information can cause an insecure and unsettling feeling, while too much information can be frightening as a neurologist indicated: "Too much information about treatments can scare people. We tested this by giving more or less detailed information. Patients who got more detailed information were more scared." Also information should be given in such a way that patients understand and will remember it. Providing the patient information in a personalized way could therefore be very beneficial to the patient. Issues do arise in the case of patients with cognitive problems. Some have trouble understanding and remembering information given to them by the doctor. Also in the case of the discharge conversation patients can experience information overload. Although nurses try to talk slow and calm and pause to give patients the opportunity to ask questions, patients can't handle the amount of information provided to them. Having family present can support the patient. Sometimes nurses can support by repeating information to the patient. It is also important to prepare patient and family for the period after leaving the hospital. It is very taxing for family members or the partner when a patient returns home and needs to be cared for. This is facilitated by involving the family where possible in therapy and care and by setting expectations.

4   Conclusion

This research aims at identifying issues and needs of patients and staff on in-patient stroke departments, with an emphasis on the environments these stakeholders find themselves in during the post event recovery process. During their stay, neurology patients go through different phases (e.g. ER, stroke unit, general ward). We built insights from healing environment literature combined with field studies. It is important to find a balance between the insights from healing environments literature and the insights from the field studies, because the target group is complex, as patients can suffer from a range of different disabilities (e.g. neglect, limited eyesight). We found that the requirements for the environment differ significantly for these different phases. The environmental needs identified include: dosing stimulus load, having social support, having access to single and multi-patient rooms, balancing a clinical and personal environment, providing structure of the day, undisturbed sleeping and access to information. These may assist in altering the environment to improve the stroke patient's recovery and in helping them to adapt to their deficits.

Acknowledgements. We thank all patients, medical staff, researchers and designers that have contributed to defining and validating the issues, concepts, and solutions proposed in this work. Special thanks go out to Sachin Behere and Joanna Facey for participating in the study.

References

1. Goodman, E., Kuniavsky, M., Moed, A.: Observing the User Experience, p. 585. Elsevier Inc. (2012)
2. Martin, B., Hanington, B.: Universal Methods of Design. Rockport Publishers (2012)
3. Biley, F.C.: Hospitals: healing environments? Complement. Ther. Nurs. Midwifery 2(4), 110–115 (1996)
4. Dossey, B.: Florence Nightingale: Mystic, Visionary, Healer. Springhouse Corp, Springhouse (2000)
5. Ulrich, R.S.: Effects of Interior Design on Wellness: theory and recent scientific research. J. Healthc. Inter. Des. 3(1), 97–109 (1991)
6. Dijkstra, K.: Understanding healing environments: effects of physical environmental stimuli on patients, thesis, University of Twente (2009)
7. Becker, G., Kaufman, S.R.: Managing an uncertain illness trajectory in old age: patients' and physicians' views of stroke. Med. Anthropol. Q. 9(2), 165–187 (1995)
8. Ulrich, R.S., Zimring, C.: A review of the research literature on evidence-based healthcare design. HERD 1(3), 1–75 (2008)
9. Ulrich, R., Quan, X., Health Systems and Design, College of Architecture, Texas: The Role of the Physical Environment in the Hospital of the 21st Century: A Once-in-a-Lifetime Opportunity (September 2004)

10. Arneill, A.B., Devlin, A.S.: Perceived Quality of Care: the Influence of the Waiting Room Environment. J. Environ. Psychol. **22**(4), 345–360 (2002)
11. Altimier, L.B.: Healing environments: for patients and providers. Newborn Infant Nurs. Rev. **4**(2), 89–92 (2004)
12. Grinde, B., Patil, G.G.: Biophilia: does visual contact with nature impact on health and well-being? Int. J. Environ. Res. Public Health **6**(9), 2332–2343 (2009)
13. Ulrich, R.S.: View Through Surgery Window May Influence Recovery from surgery. Science **224**(21), 420–421 (1984)
14. Velarde, M.D., Fry, G., Tveit, M.: Health effects of viewing landscapes – Landscape types in environmental psychology. Urban For. Urban Green **6**(4), 199–212 (2007)
15. Walch, J.M., Rabin, B.S., Day, R., Williams, J.N., Choi, K., Kang, J.D.: The effect of sunlight on postoperative analgesic medication use: a prospective study of patients undergoing spinal surgery. Psychosom. Med. **67**(1), 156–163 (2005)
16. Wakamura, T., Tokura, H.: Influence of bright light during daytime on sleep parameters in hospitalized elderly patients. J. Physiol. Anthropol. Appl. Human Sci. **20**(6), 345–351 (2001)
17. Bringslimark, T., Hartig, T., Patil, G.G.: The psychological benefits of indoor plants: A critical review of the experimental literature. J. Environ. Psychol. **29**(4), 422–433 (2009)
18. Tranmer, J.E., Minard, J., Fox, L.A., Rebelo, L.: The sleep experience of medical and surgical patients. Clinical Nursing Research **12**(2), 159–173 (2003)
19. Southwell, M.T., Wistow, G.: Sleep in hospitals at night—Are patients' needs being met? Journal of Advanced Nursing **21**(6), 1101–1109 (1995)
20. Novaes, M., Aronovich, A., Ferraz, M.B., Knobel, E.: Stressors in ICU: Patients' evaluation. Intensive Care Medicine **23**(12), 1282–1285 (1997)
21. Dogan, O., Ertekin, S., Dogan, S.: Sleep quality in hospitalized patients. Journal of Clinical Nursing **14**(1), 107–113 (2005)
22. Kuivalainen, L.R.A., Isola, A., Meriläinen, P.: Sleep disturbances affecting hospital patients. Hoitotiede **10**(3), 134–143 (1998)
23. Shafiq, M., Salahuddin, F.F., Siddiqi, M., Shah, Z., Ali, R., Siwani, R.A., et al.: Sleep deprivation and its associated factors among general ward patients at a tertiary care hospital in Pakistan. Journal of the Pakistan Medical Association **56**(12), 614–617 (2006)
24. Topf, M., Thompson, S.: Interactive relationships between hospital patients' noise induced stress and other stress with sleep. Heart and Lung **30**(4), 237–243 (2001)
25. Potts, L., Bartocci, G.: Experience Design. In: Proceedings of the 27th ACM International Conference on Design of Communication, SIGDOC 2009, pp. 17–22 (2009)
26. Spinuzzi, C.: The methodology of participatory design. Technical Communication **52**(2), 163–174 (2005)
27. van de Glind, I., de Roode, S., Goossensen, A.: Do patients in hospitals benefit from single rooms? A literature review. Health Policy **84**(2–3), 153–161 (2007)
28. Chaudhury, H., Mahmood, A., Valente, M.: Nurses' perception of single-occupancy versus multioccupancy rooms in acute care environments: an exploratory comparative assessment. Appl. Nurs. Res. **19**(3), 118–125 (2006)
29. van de Glind, I., van Dulmen, S., Goossensen, A.: Physician-patient communication in single-bedded versus four-bedded hospital rooms. Patient Educ. Couns. **73**(2), 215–219 (2008)
30. Doolittle, N.D.: Stroke Recovery: Review of the literature and suggestions for future research. J. Neurosci. Nurs. **20**(3), 169–173 (1988)
31. Doolittle, N.D.: Clinical Ethnography of Lacunar Stroke: Implications for Acute Care. J. Neurosci. Nurs. **23**(4), 235–240 (1991)

An Investigation into Perception-Altering Lighting Concepts for Supporting Game Designers in Setting Certain Atmospheres Within a Videogame Environment

Hendrik Johannes Nieuwdorp[✉], Martin Beresford, and Vassilis-Javed Khan

Academy for Digital Entertainment, NHTV University of Applied Sciences,
Breda, The Netherlands
H.J.Nieuwdorp@gmail.com,
{Beresford.M,Khan.J}@NHTV.nl

Abstract. Lighting in video games is used to set moods and atmosphere, or can serve as a gameplay tool. This paper examines the effects lighting concepts can have on a virtual game environment on the players' navigation within the game. Previously known lighting concepts were tested in a virtual environment to determine if they have a similar effect on the perception of the presented virtual space as they do in real life, as well as the effect they have on the navigational behavior of players. In a game-experiment with 50 male participants we show that the previously known lighting concepts apply to the virtual environment in a similar manner as they do in real life, although the effects on the navigational behavior of the participants remain inconclusive.

Keywords: Virtual lighting · Perception of atmosphere · Game design

1 Introduction

Light has a profound effect on all aspects of human perception and behavior. Beyond the utilitarian aspects of light it has been shown that light affects several non-utilitarian aspects as well. For example, it has been shown that it can impact the perceived atmosphere of a certain environment (Custers et al., 2010).

Perception of a certain environment and the role of light has been studied from early on. Flynn's (1973) research resulted in a series of lighting concepts that may be used to alter the perception of a space through the usage of light. The research had a group of 96 participants examine a space at the General Electric Lighting Institute in Cleveland. The subjects were divided into 12 groups, and each group was subjected to different lighting setups. The setups varied usage between overhead downlighting, peripheral wall-lighting and combinations thereof in the space at different intensity levels and patterns. The participants were asked to describe the space according to a set of descriptors, which were grouped into five factors (or "categories of impression"), namely *Evaluative, Perceptual Clarity, Spatial Complexity, Spaciousness* and *Formality.* It was found that the different lighting setups induced some consistent and 'shared impressions' for the users, and thus could be used to create lighting setups

© Springer International Publishing Switzerland 2014
E. Aarts et al. (Eds.): AmI 2014, LNCS 8850, pp. 125–139, 2014.
DOI: 10.1007/978-3-319-14112-1_11

that have a predictable psychological effect on the space's occupants. The result of this research was a compiled set of five types of lighting concepts: *Visual Clarity, Spaciousness, Preference, Relaxation & Privacy*.

Visual Clarity, refers to how well an observer can perceive the scene in terms of architectural elements and objects, as well as the occupants within the space. In short, it deals with the degree of difficulty the observer has to 'read' the scene. Are the shapes in the scene easy to identify, or does the observer have to make an effort to do so, if he or she can identify them at all? This type of lighting is usually applied to work and meeting spaces.

Spaciousness, which refers to the user's perception of the spatial volume of the scene. Is the scene large and spacious, or is it small and cramped? This type of lighting is usually applied to areas where a large group of people gather or pass through.

Preference, which refers to the user's general evaluation of the space. In general, does the observer like or dislike the space? This type of lighting is usually applied to spaces where people reside over a longer period of time, rather than passing through.

Relaxation, also referred to in Steffy (2008) as *Tranquility*, which deals with the degree in which the observer feels at ease and relaxed. Does the space appear tranquil and calming, or does it unnerve the observer, making him or her feel tense? This type of lighting is generally applied to casual spaces such as lounges and restaurants.

Privacy, which refers to the observer's sense of feeling exposed. Does the space appear to be secluded and private, or does the space feel exposed and public? An example of this could be an actor on a stage (Public) versus a couple sharing an intimate dinner in a secluded nave at a restaurant (Private).

Going beyond the real world, light has been modeled and simulated in the virtual one. Lighting in video games plays an important role as apart from allowing the player to actually see the game environment and interact with it, it can be used to set certain moods. For instance, a generally dark lighting setup can be used to make a scene feel more mysterious or threatening, while a well-lit scene can set a calm and open, relaxing mood. In addition, lighting can be an important part of the gameplay and visual style of the game. It can also be used to focus attention and guide people towards a specific location through use of contrast in brightness (Ginthner, 2002).

Some research has been conducted on the subject of navigation of a virtual space, though this research did not look into lighting in particular. Vembar et al. (2004) looked into the effects visual cues had on the behavior of people in a virtual maze, with regards to navigation. They supplied three different cues; namely a 2D map, a '2D Map with a directionally ambiguous cue' and a '2D Map with a directional cue'. The research showed that from these cues, the directional cue had the most effect on decreasing the time it took the participant to reach the end goal, namely the center of the maze.

Conroy (2001) looked into using a virtual environment to help the study of how and why people move through a space based on spatial layout, and to see if movement in a virtual environment is analogous to movement in real life environments. This research showed that a virtual environment may be used to gather data about the most likely behavior of people with regard to movement through a similar real life space.

This research paper intends to partially complement the aforementioned research studies by looking at the effects of lighting patterns in particular. No prior research could be found as to whether or not Flynn's (1973) concepts also apply to a virtual game environment and its users, the players. This knowledge gap, raises several questions. If Flynn's concepts apply to a virtual environment, can these concepts also be used to influence player behavior? For instance, could a certain lighting style have an attracting effect on the general player base, or perhaps a repelling effect? Moreover, could this potentially be used by lighting and game designers to subconsciously influence the players into behaving in a certain, predictable way?

This paper presents a research study, in an attempt to look into whether Flynn's concepts apply in a similar manner to a virtual game environment as they do in real life, and whether they have an influence on the navigation of players through the virtual environment.

The contributions of this research, should these concepts apply to a virtual space in a similar manner as they do in real life, can be twofold:

1) Lighting designers can use the concepts to help them in the lighting design process for a given space, based on the needs of the project, as the lighting concepts provide a predictable result on the player's perception of a certain space.

2) Depending on the type of game, these lighting concepts could be used to manipulate the behavior of the player in a predictable way. This could benefit the design process as it would give the designers an additional tool to guide players in a certain direction, should the appropriate lighting concept be applied to the game environment or a section thereof. We also hypothesize that the lighting concepts may be divided into two groups, namely positive and negative, where the positive set of concepts would have an attracting effect on the player and a repelling effect for the negative set of concepts. For example, from the 'Spaciousness' concept, the 'Spacious' setup would have an attracting effect, and the 'Cramped' setup would have a repelling effect.

We hypothesize that the aforementioned lighting setups (Flynn, 1973) have an influence on the navigation of players in the game. Although it would follow that these lighting setups need to also apply to the game environment in the same way that they do in real life. It will thus be necessary to also prove or disprove that they do, leading to the two hypotheses that are the base for this research project:

Hypothesis A: The lighting setups as described by Flynn (1973) apply to the virtual environment in a similar manner as they do in real life. By "apply" we more specifically mean whether respondents recognize the positive and negative "connotations" in the lighting conditions

Hypothesis B: The lighting setups as described by Flynn (1973) have an influence on the navigation of players in the virtual environment, i.e. do respondents have a preference for positive or negative lighting conditions while navigating in a virtual environment?

These hypotheses are not interdependent since if in a virtual environment the effects of lighting differ from the real world, the effect on player behavior might still be consistent within games. In that case the first hypothesis would not be true, nevertheless lighting can very well be used to direct behavior.

This research study wants to contribute by investigating whether a well-known set of lighting concepts could potentially be used by game designers for creating certain moods in game scenes. Moreover, if proven that there is a link between the concepts and within-game navigation game designers would have a resourceful option in subconsciously guiding gamers in certain parts of the game.

2   Methodology

To properly determine what effects Flynn's (1973) lighting concepts have on the navigation of players in the virtual environment, the research also sought to determine if these concepts apply to the virtual environment in a similar manner as they do in real life. We conducted an experiment with 50 male gamers aged 18 to 26 years old. All of the participants were students at our university specializing in game development studies. This ensured that all participants were experienced with visual processing and navigating a virtual environment in the manner in which the experiment was held, in order to remove any influence these factors might have had on the results. Furthermore, the variables for this experiment were limited to the location and intensity of the luminance in the rooms, not including light color or surface materials on the room's geometry.

It should also be noted that, according to Vogels (2008), "...some researchers found interaction effects between luminance level, color temperature, color rendering, age and gender on people's mood...". As such, the research was conducted with only males, to exclude any possible influence that gender may or may not have had on the results. Their ages ranged between 18 and 25. All participants were also required to sign a participation agreement and were told that they could refer to the supplied instruction sheet at any time during the experiment, should any questions arise. It should also be noted that all participants received an anonymous participant ID number, which was generated at random.

This research project looks into the more specific categories of: *visual clarity, spaciousness, relaxation* and *privacy*. We feel that *preference* to a large extent overlaps with the four aforementioned categories. In addition, the tested concepts apply directly to games, as they can be used to set a certain mood and atmosphere, whereas preference covers a more general concept rather than a specific mood or setting.

2.1   Setting

Access to the same physical room for the duration of the entire experiment proved to be impossible, and as such, it was conducted in three separate rooms, where lighting conditions were kept as similar as possible. The rooms both featured mainly overhead downlighting and some sunlight coming in through windows. Each participant would be seated behind the same laptop computer, and the screen was placed for all participants in the same distance and angle, to ensure proper contrast.

2.2   Process

Participants were asked to navigate through a simple virtual environment, which was custom built in Epic Games' Unreal Development Kit, June 2013 Version. A player could only move in a closed building without being able to interact with any element in it. The environment featured no characters or props ('set dressing') to avoid any influence their placement might have had on the players. In terms of architecture, it was created to resemble a circular, symmetrical space, to remove the influence the architecture could have had on the navigational behavior of the player, thus narrowing down the number of influencing factors on the experiment.

The experiment itself consisted out of two phases; a blind and a directed, which took each participant approximately ten minutes to complete in total. Although participants first completed the blind test, we find that it is more convenient to present the directed test and then describe the blind test. Note that these phases relate to the two hypotheses; the blind test sought to address Hypothesis B, whereas the directed test sought to address Hypothesis A.

The directed test asked participants to navigate the virtual environment based on instructive tip given upon reaching the center of the particular room they occupied. The tips were displayed in the center of the participant's view. The screenshot below, from the virtual environment we developed, shows an example thereof (Figure 1).

Fig. 1. An example screenshot of a tip presented to the player during the directed test

Each participant then freely chose a path based on the given instruction. The participant had always only two choices: either left or right. The same room would appear twice in the experiment, only to have its instructions reversed, to ensure the validity of the data. For example, a participant first receives the test for 'Spaciousness', in which the instruction would be to 'take the most spacious path'. When this participant receives the test for 'Spaciousness' the second time, the reverse instruction is given, and the participant is asked to 'take the most cramped path'. The way in which the paths are lit determines which path is correct and which is incorrect. The screenshots below show an example of the 'Spaciousness' rooms (Figure 2); note how the alignment of the setups (Spacious / Cramped) is switched in the second image, relative to the room's geometry.

It should also be noted that this 'alignment switch' does not occur necessarily, but is randomized based on the experiment variant the participant is subjected to. In these examples, the correct path would be on the right hand side in both cases.

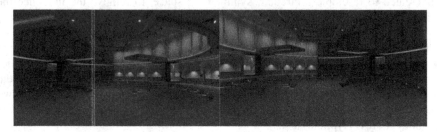

Fig. 2. An example of the same lighting concept as presented to the player, only the alignment of the two settings has been reversed for illustration purposes

Once a participant chose a certain path, the way behind would be blocked. This was done to prevent the participant navigating in the reverse direction (i.e. navigating back to a previously visited room). The participant would then continue down a corridor, that would lead to the next room and thus to the next setting.

This process would repeat until the participant had seen all settings twice. It should also be noted that the order in which these settings were presented to the participant would differ from variant to variant. This means that a given participant would be assigned to a variant of the experiment, in which the order in which settings would be presented to the participant would differ from variant to variant. In total, there were six variants (Figures 3 to 6), to which each participant was assigned at random, to a maximum of 10 participants per variant. This random assignment was generated using the random function in Microsoft Excel and was updated each time a new participant was registered into the spread sheet. In addition, to avoid having all 'correct' answers on one side, the room's geometry and lighting setup would be reversed along the Y axis, also at random. By randomizing the order and alignment of the rooms and thus settings, compensation was sought for influences that could not be controlled, such as mood, time of day, weariness and personality of the participant.

Note that during the entire experiment, the participants were provided with a printed-out reference sheet, which explained the controls for navigating the environment, as well as having a description of each term used to describe a lighting setting, to avoid confusion.

As aforementioned, participants completed the directed test after having completed the blind test. The blind test had participants navigate the virtual environment without any instructions or on-screen tips other than indicated on the printed reference sheet they initially got. By placing this test before the directed test, participants would not be 'primed' or biased with certain knowledge (e.g. Setting X could be identified as either Y or Z) that might influence their decision making process. The goal was to have the participants base their decision on intuition, in order to see if the entire pool of them would have a tendency to move towards a particular setting. It was hypothesized that they would prefer to move through a space that featured a 'positive' lighting setup, such as 'Spacious' versus 'Cramped'. Each participant moved through each setting once. Note that the attributes of 'positive' and 'negative' as described in table 1 are not part of Flynn's (1973) original work, nor part of Steffy's (2008) description of Flynn's work.

All data was collected automatically through a backend-logging system that was built into the virtual environment, which was invisible to the participants.

Table 1. Overview of Lighting Concepts & Settings and their positive or negative attribute

Concept	Setting	Positive / Negative
Visual Clarity	Visually Clear	Positive
	Visually Hazy	Negative
Spaciousness	Spacious	Positive
	Cramped	Negative
Tranquility	Tranquil	Positive
	Tense	Negative
Privacy	Secluded	Positive
	Public	Negative

Fig. 3. Example screenshot of the Visual Clarity setup. Visually Clear (left) vs. Visually Hazy (right).

Fig. 4. Example screenshot of the Spaciousness setup. Spacious (left) vs. Cramped (right).

Fig. 5. Example screenshot of the Tranquility setup. Tranquil (left) vs. Tense (right).

Fig. 6. Example screenshot of the Privacy setup. Secluded (left) vs. Public (right).

3 Results

3.1 Experiment Phase A, Directed Test Results

The results for both experiment phases feature four categories of lighting settings, where the upper setting would be a positive setting ,and the lower setting a negative setting (Table 2, 3).

Table 2. Results for Experiment A, directed test

Category	Setting	Times chosen correctly	Percentage
Visual Clarity	Visually Clear	50 out of 50	100%
	Visually Hazy	47 out of 50	94%
Spaciousness	Spacious	38 out of 50	76%
	Cramped	42 out of 50	84%
Tranquility	Tranquil	37 out of 50	74%
	Tense	33 out of 50	66%
Privacy	Secluded	14 out of 50	28%
	Public	9 out of 50	18%

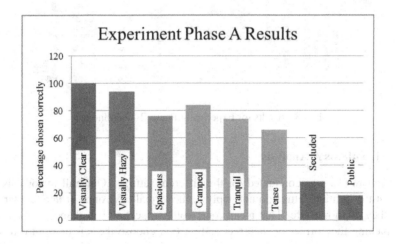

Fig. 7. Results for Experiment Phase A, the directed test

3.2   Experiment Phase B, Blind Test Results

Table 3. Results for Experiment B, blind test

Category	Setting	Times chosen	Percentage
Visual Clarity	Visually Clear	31 out of 50	62%
	Visually Hazy	19 out of 50	38%
Spaciousness	Spacious	28 out of 50	56%
	Cramped	22 out of 50	44%
Tranquility	Tranquil	21 out of 50	42%
	Tense	29 out of 50	58%
Privacy	Secluded	27 out of 50	54%
	Public	23 out of 50	46%

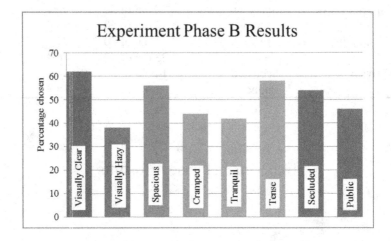

Fig. 8. Results for Experiment Phase B, the blind test

3.3   Hypothesis A Analysis

A Chi-square test was conducted for the different settings. Our null hypothesis (H0) state that the lighting setups do not apply to the virtual environment in a similar manner as they do in real life. That means one would expect a 50% chance of the participants picking the correct or incorrect setting (i.e. choose the left or right direction), resulting in an expected value of 25 in each category. The settings are each treated individually and the p value was set at .05.

The notation for the results would be:

$$\chi^2(1, N=25) = y , p<0.05$$

< y > stands for the resulting Chi-square value for that particular setting.

In Table 4, A stands for Accepted, and R stands for Rejected, with regards to the Null Hypothesis. Note that each setting was presented twice, meaning the participants had a total of two instances where they could choose the correct path, according to the instructions given. This results in the following:

Table 4. Data for analysis of Hypothesis A

	Observed frequency	Expected frequency	χ^2 result	H0 (A/R)
Visually Clear	50	25	25	R
Visually Hazy	47	25	19.36	R
Spacious	38	25	6.76	R
Cramped	42	25	11.56	R
Tranquil	37	25	5.76	R
Tense	33	25	2.56	A
Secluded	14	25	4.84	R
Public	9	25	10.24	R

When examining Table 4, there are three conclusions that can be drawn:

1.) All settings save for Tense have passed the Chi-square test, as such, their null hypotheses can be rejected.

2.) The settings for the Privacy category have an extremely low rate in which they are chosen by the participants, for both settings. This is the exact opposite of what was expected. This will be discussed in the Discussion section.

3.) The setting Tense from the category Tranquility seems to be on the borderline of being accepted, this will also be discussed in the Discussion section.

3.4   Hypothesis B Analysis

For the data regarding Hypothesis B, a similar approach was taken as with Hypothesis A. In this case, the H0 would be that Flynn's lighting settings have no influence on the navigation of the participant through the virtual environment. As such, the expected frequency of times in which the participant would choose a particular setting over another (i.e. choose the left or right direction), without being directed to choose a specific setting, was 25 out of 50.

Each setting was treated individually with a Chi-square test to either accept or reject the H0, with 1 degree of freedom and a P value of .05. The annotation for these results would be the same as it was with Hypothesis B.

In Table 5, A stands for Accepted, and R stands for Rejected, with regards to the Null Hypothesis. Note that in this case, the participants could only choose a particular setting over the other once, resulting in all settings having a combined maximum value of 50. As such, the final Chi-Result is calculated by adding the resulting chi-squared values of each category together. This resulted in the following:

Table 5. Data for analysis of Hypothesis B

	Observed frequency	Expected frequency	Combined χ^2 Result (y)	H0 (A/R)
Visually Clear	31	25	2.88	A
Visually Hazy	19	25		
Spacious	28	25	0.72	A
Cramped	22	25		
Tranquil	21	25	1.28	A
Tense	29	25		
Secluded	27	25	0.32	A
Public	23	25		

From Table 5, it is concluded that the H0 cannot be rejected, and the settings have no proven influence on the navigation of the player, as the variance in observed values vs. the expected values could be attributed to chance.

4   Discussion

Experiment Phase B (the blind test), which aimed at proving or disproving the hypothesis that Flynn's (1973) lighting concepts have an influence on navigation yielded inconclusive results. There are some factors that could explain these results.

First and foremost, the participants were only asked to choose between paths during the blind test once. By having a second cycle through the same rooms, as was done with the directed test, the results could have yielded a more accurate outcome. The results now could also be attributed to random chance, rather than a conscious decision made by the participant, when choosing a path.

Furthermore, both experiments have a certain limitation. The manner in which the lighting setups were interpreted and operationally defined was based on Steffy's book (2002). As there is only one interpretation what the lighting setups in the virtual scene should look like, that might be an inherent weakness and a point for future research. Our proposal for future research would be that multiple people, preferably with a visual arts background, come to an agreement of the virtual lighting setups according to Flynn's concepts.

Furthermore, this study utilized a single virtual environment. Further research could benefit from having participants navigate a series of different environments, to determine to what extent the environment itself influences the results.

Experiment Phase A (directed test), which aimed at proving or disproving the hypothesis that Flynn's lighting concepts apply to the virtual environment in a similar manner as they do in real life, was not without shortcomings either. Aside from the interpretation factor, the wording in the instructions could also have had an influence on the results. However, an attempt was made to compensate for any misunderstanding the participants might have experienced when given instructions by having a printed-out reference sheet present during the experiment, it turned out that it was used rarely. Each participant was asked to inspect the sheet before starting the study.

Moreover, certain terms and their respective settings are very much open to the interpretation of the participant. For example, the term spacious would indicate a large space. The settings that were intended to represent spacious and cramped could very easily be mixed up by the participant. In this example, a participant could see a brightly lit space as cramped as he or she can see the actual confines of the space, thus giving the room a finite and quantifiable size. A more dimly lit space could then be experienced as spacious as the participant either has a hard time detecting these confines, or could not detect the confines at all, possibly making the scene seem infinite in size. Another participant could interpret this the other way around, which would match the intended association as proposed by Flynn. In this study, well over half of the participants chose the correct paths, though the argument presented above is still valid.

Along this line of thought, the category Privacy, which dealt with the settings Secluded and Public, could be even more open to interpretation, based on the personality and experience of any particular participant. One could argue that by being placed in an environment where the lighting is focused mainly upon the person's area, leaving the peripheral areas to be (relatively) unlit, this person might feel as being 'in the spotlight' and thus experience the space as more public. Alternatively, this person might also have a severely limited view of his or her surroundings, or none at all, condensing the perceived space down to only the user's immediate area, making it seem like he or she is alone in this space, and thus feeling more secluded. This setting also has the issue that one individual might prefer a public space to a private space, swapping the given attributes of positive and negative around, whereas the opposite might be true for another person also.

Furthermore, this category of Privacy yielded the exact opposite results, when compared to what was expected; both settings scored quite low in the directed test, making it seem like the sample population would swap the two settings with each other, making the Public setting adhere to the guidelines for the Secluded setting, and vice versa. In this particular instance, the flaw most likely lay with the wording of the instructions rather than the participant's interpretation of the guidelines for each particular setting within this category. A clearer description rather than 'public' or 'secluded' would perhaps have yielded better results.

The same could be said for the category Tranquility, although the results in this category where less extreme as they were with the category Privacy.

The category Visual Clarity seems to have been abundantly clear to all participants, as this category had a near perfect score for the directed test, across all participants.

The experiment itself took approximately 10 minutes per participant to complete, which would seem to indicate that a longer test, or multiple cycles per participant, could improve the ecological validity of the results since longer play time would match the typical game play of console games.

Another factor that could be improved in this study is the way in which the participants were exposed to the environment. The screen of the laptop computer was adjusted manually for each participant, in order to have roughly the same contrast for each participant, due to LCD screen viewing angles. A brace or support for the participant's head, along with a funnel system could have greatly assisted this process, and improved the accuracy of the results, as it would then be certain that each participant has been exposed to the same contrast on the screen. Alternatively, by using a head mounted display this problem could be solved as well. It could be argued that usage of such a device would also increase the degree of perceived immersion felt by the participant during the experiment, which could also have an influence on the final perception of the lighting setups.

Lastly, to eliminate any gender bias, this study only included males. Due to both time constraints and convenience, the study could not be repeated with females only, to determine whether or not there would be an influence of gender on the results. That might be another point for future research.

5   Conclusion

In a study with 50 male participants navigating through a virtual game environment we examined whether the lighting concepts proposed by Flynn (1973) could be replicated. The interest of the study lies in that game designers can further exploit those concepts to create appropriate moods in certain parts of the game.

We actually were able to show that the lighting concepts do apply to a virtual (game) environment in a similar manner as in real life. This gives lighting designers for these types of environments a set of guidelines that may help improve and speed up the design process, which would hopefully result in higher quality environments and visualizations.

In the same study we also wanted to find out whether the lighting concepts would also lead gamers to choose a specific route in the game. This hypothesis was inconclusive based on our dataset and further research into this particular subject would be prudent, as there were certain limitations in our study.

The experiment was limited to only factor in the luminance location and intensity, based on Flynn's (1973) work, in order to have as little independent variables as possible, and thus a more reliable result. Future research could benefit from factoring in color, material finishes and gender.

Acknowledgements. This paper is a reworked piece from a paper written and submitted by H.J. Nieuwdorp as part of the requirements for the Bachelor's Degree in Game Architecture and Design at the NHTV University of Applied Sciences in Breda, The Netherlands.

First and foremost, credit and thanks should be given to both Mr. Flynn and Mr. Steffy, as without their work this study could not have taken place.
Furthermore, credit and thanks should be given to the following people:

- Kevin Bansberg, for creating a script that made data collection significantly easier and faster, which was a part of the logic system behind the experiment virtual environment.
- Bart Wagemans, for proofreading both the original paper, as well as beta testing the experiment before the participants came in.
- Twan de Graaf, for proofreading the original paper.
- Rachel van der Meer, for practical assistance.
- All participants for the experiment.
- Epic Games, for providing their game development kit, the Unreal Development Kit, for free on their website.

References

1. Conroy, R.: Spatial navigation in immersive virtual environments (Doctoral dissertation, University College London) (2001)
2. Custers, P.J.M., de Kort, Y.A.W., IJsselsteijn, W.A., de Kruiff, M.E.: Lighting in retail environments: Atmosphere perception in the real world. Lighting Research and Technology **42**(3), 331–343 (2010)
3. Flynn, J.E., Spencer, T.J., Martyniuk, O., Hendrick, C.: Interim study of procedures for investigating the effect of light on impression and behavior. Journal of the Illuminating Engineering Society **3**(1), 87–94 (1973)
4. Ginthner, D.: Lighting: Its Effect on People and Spaces. Informe Design, Web (2002)
5. Steffy, G.: *Architectural lighting design*. John Wiley & Sons (2002)
6. Vembar, D., Iyengar, N., Duchowski, A., Clark, K., Hewitt, J., Pauls, K.: Effect of visual cues on human performance in navigating through a virtual maze. In: Eurographics Symposium on Virtual Environments (June, 2004)
7. Vogels, I.: Atmosphere metrics. In: Probing Experience, pp. 25–41. Springer Netherlands

Ambient Influence for Promoting Balanced Participation in Group Brainstorming

Gianluca Schiavo[1,2]($\boxtimes$), Eleonora Mencarini[1,2], Alessandro Cappelletti[2], Oliviero Stock[2], and Massimo Zancanaro[2]

[1] University of Trento, Trento, Italy
[2] FBK-irst, Povo, Trento, Italy
{gschiavo,mencarini,cappelle,stock,zancana}@fbk.eu

Abstract. In this paper we present an ambient persuasive system designed to promote balanced participation during group brainstorming. The system gets information from participants' attention behavior during a brainstorming session and provides visual messages for facilitating balanced participation. In the present study, we investigated the effect that using subtle visual animations and explaining to the users the meaning of the subtle message had on influencing group behavior. Objective measures from data acquired through depth sensors, and subjective responses to questionnaires on usefulness and perceived influence of the technology intervention were collected. The results suggest that the ambient system is better accepted when the persuasive message is expressed in a subtle manner and an explanation of the system's persuasive strategy is provided.

Keywords: Ambient Influence · Peripheral Displays · Ambient Persuasive Systems · Shared Displays · Group Conversation

1 Introduction

In the domain of HCI and Ambient Intelligence, many different attempts have been made to influence group conversations by providing real-time feedback on the social dynamics. Ambient and peripheral technology have been proposed for visualize ephemeral aspects of co-located group activities (for example, time spent talking [1], patterns of turn-taking [2], attention received by other members [3]) with the aim of enhancing group interactions and favoring a more balanced participation. A balanced participation might indeed be considered a desired behavior in some collaborative activities, such as group brainstorming. Among the others, research in the area of smart meeting systems provides a number of examples of technologies that support participants in meetings by automatically analyzing their group behavior [4]. Besides using graphical and explicit feedback, recently also subtle and indirect modalities have been investigated. For example, Rogers et al. [5] explored the use of ambient displays to nudge behavioral change in people using subtle and abstract modalities of feedback. Studies have shown that subtle dynamic feedback presented implicitly (e.g. through simple animations presented at the periphery of user's attention) can foster

© Springer International Publishing Switzerland 2014
E. Aarts et al. (Eds.): AmI 2014, LNCS 8850, pp. 140–144, 2014.
DOI: 10.1007/978-3-319-14112-1_12

members experience and affect group behavior in a similar manner to more explicit strategies (e.g. using text, graphs and real-time statistics).

In this paper, we present the deployment of an ambient system aimed at facilitating balanced conversation in groups of four people. The system is an augmented small round table that monitors the group social dynamic through Kinect sensors [3]. Specifically, the system estimates the attention directed by each person to the other participants tracking their head orientation. Using this information, the system proactively sends peripheral messages to the group, with the aim of influencing the participants' behavior toward a more equal distribution of interventions.

During the deployment of such technology, we compared two strategies for influencing group social dynamics, namely using overt, language-based messages and a more subtle style of intervention presented by means of peripheral visual animations [3]. In this study, we investigated the effect that different strategies enacted by the system had on influencing group behavior and on participants' opinions. Moreover, in order to evaluate the effect of being aware of the function of the subtle messages, the system was presented to the participants with or without a preliminary explanation of the peripheral animation.

2   Study and Data Analysis

Twelve groups of 4 participants, a total of 48 people, participated in the study. An equal number of groups (4 groups) were randomly assigned to each condition: the subtle with explanation [S+], the subtle without explanation [S-] and the overt [O] condition. The participants were employees at a research center and were asked to brainstorm ideas on how to improve their workplace canteen service for 15 minutes. After the brainstorming session, they were asked to fill an individual questionnaire about their experience, the perceived disturbance of the system and the perceived cohesiveness of the group (a scale adapted form the Price and Muller Work Group Cohesion Index). The Attrakdiff questionnaire [6] was administered for assessing pragmatic, hedonic and appealing attributes of the technology, and a short personality inventory (BFI-10) [7] was used for investigating personality traits that may influence the user experience with the ambient system.

2.1   Behavioral Cues Analysis

We attempted to objectively estimate the equality of the distribution of attention at the group level by defining an equity index based on the Gini coefficient; a similar approach was previously used for measuring participation equality in group conversations using speaking time [1] and visual attention [2, 3]. Therefore, we calculated a balancing index, representing to what extent the amount of attention received by each participant was equally distributed in a range between 0 (unequal distribution) and 1 (equal distribution). For the S+ and the O conditions, the values are almost stable with an average value of .74 (SD= .14) and .84 (SD= .06) respectively. The overall average of the balancing index for the S- condition is .54 (SD= .19). In analyzing balancing index by quartiles, a significant difference occurred between the three conditions for the second quartile, corresponding to the 50% of the session time (Kruskal-Wallis test: H= 6.04, p<.05). Mann-Whitney tests (with Bonferroni correction) showed that conditions O and S- were significantly different (z = -2.3, p<.01), suggesting that attention in groups in the over condition were more balanced compared to the subtle condition without explanation after about 7 minutes of using the system. In the S+ condition, the pattern of values for the balancing index was more similar to the O condition than the S- condition, even though there were no statistically significant differences.

2.2   Questionnaire Results

Table 1 shows the result from the questionnaire. Regarding the perceived usefulness of the system, an ANOVA indicates a statistically significant difference in the scores for the three conditions. Post-hoc pairwise comparisons (Tukey's HSD correction) showed that participants in O perceived the system as more useful compared to S- (p<.01), but no differences were observed with respect to S+. Consistently with the pattern of the balancing index, participants in the overt condition reported that the system had a stronger influence compared to participants in the other two conditions (p<.05). Although, participants found the displays more distracting in the overt condition compared to the subtle conditions (p<.05). Finally, Group Cohesion Index was slightly lower in the subtle condition without explanation (p<.05).

Attrakdiff Results. Regarding the scores of the Attrakdiff questionnaire, we observed statistical significant differences in the "pragmatic" and in the "appeal" scales (Table 1). Post-hoc pairwise comparisons (Tukey's HSD correction) showed that:

- In the subtle condition without explanation, the system was perceived as less pragmatic compared to the other conditions (S- *vs* O: p<.01; S- *vs* S+ p<.05), suggesting that the users perceived the system as useless and/or meaningless;
- In the subtle condition with explanation, the system was considered more appealing than in the other two conditions (S+ *vs* S-: p<.01; S+ *vs* O: p<.05).

Personality Questionnaires. In the overt condition, extraversion scores negatively correlated with opinions regarding usefulness and perceived influence power (Pearson's r = -.691, p<.01 for "*I found the information displayed useful*", and r = -.521, p<.01 for "*I think the system had an influence on the discussion*"). In the subtle conditions, the conscientiousness trait (the tendency to show self-discipline) negatively correlated with scores on "*I think the system had an influence on the discussion*" (S+: r = -.685, p<.01; S-: r = -.521, p<.01). These results suggest that the overt system was mostly opposed by participants with high extraversion scores, while the subtle version was considered less effective for people with high score on consciousness.

Table 1. Responses (means and standard deviations) to the questionnaire. Items are on a 5-point Likert scale, while Attrakdiff scales are based on 7-point scale items. $N=48$

Items	[S+] Subtle with explanation	[S-] Subtle w/o explanation	Overt [O]	F values	p values
I found the information displayed useful	2.19 (*0.91*)	1.62 (*0.81*)	2.56 (*0.81*)	$F_{2,45}$= 4.99	**p < .01**
I think the system had an influence on the discussion	2.06 (*0.85*)	2.00 (*1.15*)	3.06 (*1.12*)	$F_{2,45}$= 5.13	**p < .01**
I think the system had a negative / positive influence	3.50 (*0.51*)	3.13 (*0.34*)	3.25 (*0.78*)	$F_{2,45}$= 1.78	p > .05
I was distracted by the displays	1.69 (*0.87*)	1.94 (*1.12*)	2.75 (*1.12*)	$F_{2,45}$= 4.50	**p < .05**
I was distracted by the Kinect	1.00 (*0*)	1.31 (*0.88*)	1.31 (*0.60*)	$F_{2,45}$= 1.38	p > .05
Cohesion	4.42 (*0.47*)	4.05 (*0.50*)	4.48 (*0.46*)	$F_{2,45}$= 3.86	**p < .05**
Pragmatic Scale	3.29 (*0.80*)	2.54 (*0.95*)	3.61 (*0.89*)	$F_{2,45}$= 6.69	**p < .01**
Hedonic Scale	3.81 (*0.69*)	3.83 (*0.89*)	3.35 (*0.77*)	$F_{2,45}$= 1.91	p > .05
Appeal Scale	4.33 (*0.76*)	3.59 (*0.64*)	3.68 (*0.54*)	$F_{2,45}$= 5.98	**p < .01**

3   Discussion and Conclusion

This paper discusses the effect of an ambient persuasive system that acts as an automatic facilitator by supporting the flow of communication during a group brainstorming. We investigated the effect of using different strategies (overt or subtle directives), and the effect of explaining to the users the system's behavior. Although a deeper evaluation needs to be performed, the results suggest that peripheral subtle messages are better accepted than overt directives, and they are not less effective provided that the participants understand their meaning. Moreover, personality traits seem to affect the way participants perceived the persuasive system. If confirmed, these findings have useful implication for the design of persuasive ambient systems aimed at improving brainstorming sessions.

Acknowledgments. The work reported in this paper is part of the PerTe project, partially funded by TrentoRise. We would like to thank all participants that took part in the study and Nadia Mana for her assistance with the experiment.

References

1. DiMicco, J.M., Hollenbach, K.J., Pandolfo, A., Bender, W.: The impact of increased awareness while face-to-face. Human Computer Interaction **22**, 47–96 (2007)
2. Terken, J., Sturm, J.: Multimodal support for social dynamics in co-located meetings. Personal and Ubiquitous Computing. **14**, 703–714 (2010)

3. Schiavo, G., Cappelletti, A., Mencarini, E., Stock, O., Zancanaro, M.: Overt or Subtle? Supporting Group Conversations with Automatically Targeted Directives. In: Proc. of the 19th Int. Conf. on Intelligent User Interfaces. pp. 225–234. ACM, New York, USA (2014)
4. Nijholt, A., op den Akker, R., Heylen, D.: Meetings and meeting modeling in smart environments. AI & Society **20**, 202–220 (2006)
5. Rogers, Y., Hazlewood, W.R., Marshall, P., Dalton, N., Hertrich, S.: Ambient influence: can twinkly lights lure and abstract representations trigger behavioral change?. In: Proc. of the 12th Int. Conf. on Ubiquitous Computing. ACM, New York, USA (2010)
6. Hassenzahl, M.: The Effect of Perceived Hedonic Quality on Product Appealingness. International Journal of Human-Computer Interaction. **13**, 481–499 (2001)
7. Rammstedt, B., John, O.P.: Measuring personality in one minute or less: A 10-item short version of the Big Five Inventory in English and German. Journal of Research in Personality. **41**, 203–212 (2007)

Steering Gameplay Behavior
in the Interactive Tag Playground

Robby van Delden[1], Alejandro Moreno[1], Ronald Poppe[2],
Dennis Reidsma[1]([⊠]), and Dirk Heylen[1]

[1] Human Media Interaction, University of Twente, PO Box 217,
7500 AE Enschede, The Netherlands
{r.w.vandelden,a.m.morenocelleri,d.reidsma,d.k.j.heylen}@utwente.nl
[2] Interaction Technology Group, Utrecht University, Princetonplein 5,
3584 CC Utrecht, The Netherlands
r.w.poppe@uu.nl

Abstract. This paper deals with steering player behavior in the Interactive Tag Playground (ITP). The ITP, an ambient environment instrumented with contact-free sensor technology and ambient display
capabilities, enhances the traditional game of tag by determining when
a valid tag has been made and visualising the current tagger. We present
three modifications of the ITP that aim to steer the gameplay actions
of the players. The modifications are intended to influence who will be
chased next by the tagger; to make good players easier to tag and less
skilled players harder to tag; and to influence the locations visited by
the players. We report on a user study showing that two of the three
modifications have a significant effect on the behavior of players in the
ITP and discuss opportunities for future research that follow from this
study.

1 Introduction

Digital and mixed reality games allow for interventions in the game state, game
difficulty, or game behavior. Technology can be used to steer the physical behavior of players, which in turn can impact the experience. Personalized adaptation
of the interventions allows people with different skills to play together, increasing
fairness and engagement in a fun and challenging experience [1,3].

This paper deals with steering player behavior in the Interactive Tag Playground (ITP). The ITP enhances the traditional game of tag. It is a large interactive ambient installation equipped with technology to create a playful experience
that stimulates physical and social interaction. In our ITP, players are automatically tracked and a circle is projected around them on the floor. The color of
the circle represents the role of the player as a *runner* (blue) or a *tagger* (red).
A tagger can tag a runner by letting their circles touch. If this happens, the
colors of the circles switch.

This publication was supported by the Dutch national program COMMIT.

E. Aarts et al. (Eds.): AmI 2014, LNCS 8850, pp. 145–157, 2014.
DOI: 10.1007/978-3-319-14112-1_13

Playing tag can be fun and exhausting, and entails a lot of physical as well as social activity. In our playground we find that player behavior in the game of tag is very well defined according to players' roles. In play sessions with non-instrumented tag, we have also observed people getting bored and disengaged. This happened for example because they were less skilled and therefore had to be tagger for prolonged periods of time, or because they were running from a tagger who was not skilled enough, offering too little challenge. In the Interactive Tag Playground we try to implement subtle interventions that can steer player behavior into different patterns while keeping the engagement high and the game experience intact. If selected well, such interventions could help balance the game, re-engage players that are less involved, get players to move more and to interact more socially [9].

For this study we focus on steering specific gameplay actions of players through three superficial modifications of the game. We explore if it is possible to (1) directly steer the tagger's choice of whom to chase next by pointing an arrow to one runner, (2) balance the time that each player is a tagger by changing the size of each player's circle based on the time they have been a tagger so far, and (3) get players to move around to specific locations on the playing field by placing power-ups that can be picked up. In the long run, automatic measurements and interpretations of player behavior will help deploy such interactive elements in our ambient play environment at the right moment, to steer player behavior in desired patterns.

In order to test the effectiveness of the three modifications introduced to the ITP, we performed a user study with eight groups of four participants playing four different versions of the tag game. Three versions constitute the three modifications (arrow pointing at one runner, adaptive circle size, and power-ups in the playing field); the fourth version is the standard ITP tag game without modifications, used as a baseline for assessing player behavior. We use the automatic measurements of positions from the tracking and the roles logged by the ITP to investigate whether the player behavior changed in the expected ways.

The remainder of the paper is structured as follows. The next section discusses related work on steering behavior in interactive art installations and embodied games. Then, after briefly introducing our ITP, we explain in detail how we steer players' behavior for this study, and formulate hypotheses concerning the effect of these interventions. In Section 4 we present the setup of our user study, followed by the results and observations from the play sessions in Section 5. The paper finishes with a conclusion and a discussion of where we want to go next with our research on play in the ITP.

2 Steering Behavior in Embodied Games

In the last two decades a large amount of research has addressed (ambient) technologies influencing behavior and/or persuading people into behavior change [5]. Most studies investigate the system as a whole. Instead, Hamari et al. advise to look into the single relevant individual constructs and their effects. We follow this advise and separately look into the different types of affordances.

In related work on interactive art installations and embodied games, we can distinguish between two types of behavior steering. One type aims to get people to initiate interaction with the interactive environment: an *invitation to play* [2,6]. Quite a few of those installations solicit specific behavior from the user by making that behavior the main or only means of interaction with the system. Examples are installations in which people form rings around a fountain to make the water respond [12] or in which people are invited to follow projected footsteps, interactively tracing a path on the floor [11]. The other type aims to solicit behaviors in the context of another activity to achieve additional goals. For instance, Landry et al. discuss an interactive playground that can indirectly control the tempo with which an embodied game is played [8]. We are interested in the second type. This distinction is similar to the different combinations of duration and type of behavior emphasized in Fogg's 'Behavior Wizard' grid for persuasive technology, a tool that acknowledges the importance of matching psychology to target behavior [4]. They suggest that new behavior that happens only once (e.g. someone making a movement to start interaction) versus an increase of behavior that has happened before (e.g. tagging someone more often), will require a different approach.

Another way the gameplay can be steered is adaptive balancing between players by assigning a handicap and by using dynamic difficulty adjustments to manipulate the status of the player and the placement and supply of items [7,10]. Balancing between players can help in letting people from different age groups and with different skills play together in an pleasurable experience [1]. It can also help in triggering the correct amount of challenge and increase the amount of movement [3]. In our current exploration to steer the gameplay we use a simple adaptive method, changing the size of the circles based on the time someone has been a tagger so far.

3   The Interactive Tag Playground

Our ITP is a large space where people can move freely, instrumented with ambient display capabilities and contact-free sensing technology. We project circles around the players' positions and their color indicates whether they are *tagger* (red) or *runner* (blue). Players can tag each other by letting their circles touch, upon which a bass drum sound is played. As often used in normal tag there is a *cooldown* period after a tagger tagged someone. In this period the tagger is not allowed to tag back the previous tagger. To visualize this we make the circle of the previous tagger semi-transparant during this two second period. To make it clear to the players that their circle moves with them, we also project a small trail behind the players.

At the start of the game one player is automatically assigned to be the tagger. In case a tagger disappears from the game (or from the tracking) for two seconds we re-assign another person to be the tagger. In the visualization we use pulsating circles, circles that grow and shrink a little in periods of four seconds. Each player has a random offset in this pulsation, creating a lively scene with different sized shapes even when people were standing still.

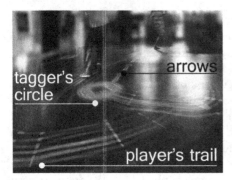

Fig. 1. Visualization (left) of the arrows and (right) the adaptive circles

The playground uses the depth-channel of 4 Kinects for tracking players. The Kinects are mounted to the ceiling and spread about 4 meters from each other at an approximate height of 5.3 meters. Two wide-angle projectors are also mounted to the ceiling and display the visualizations on the floor. One PC is connected to the 4 Kinects and is equipped with our tracking system to send the position of the players to another PC. The second PC uses this information to run the game implemented in Unity and display it with two the projectors.

The playing field that is covered with the projectors is approximately 6 by 7 meters. We use a black linoleum floor to project the neon-styled visualizations on (see Figure 1 and 2). The environment is darkened using curtains to improve the visualizations. We don't use any color information of the Kinect but only use the infrared based depth channels.

3.1 Steering Behavior Through Gameplay Elements

In our current interactive tag game we implement three different gameplay elements to influence the behavior of players. In this study we look whether our implementation was successful in achieving the targeted changes. We tried to influence gameplay in three ways: use arrows to suggest someone to be tagged, adaptive circle sizes in order to change the amount of time someone is a tagger, and power-ups to make players move more to certain positions. These three elements will be explained in further detail below.

Arrows. In playing tag one of the main choices to be made is whom to tag. In the 'arrow' version of the game, we try to influence that choice. To this end we use arrows pointing towards a random player, see Figure 1. Every time a player is tagged the arrows will point to another random player again. The only difference when someone with the arrow is tagged instead of someone else, is a slight change in the sound that is played. No further restrictions or changes follow from the assignment of the arrow.

We expect that these arrows will influence the decision of the tagger on whom to tag. This should lead to runners being tagged more often when they have an arrow pointing at them. Therefore, for the arrow condition we hypothesize:

Hypothesis 1. *A person with an arrow pointing at him/her are tagged more.*

Adaptive Circles. The adaptive circles are used to balance out the time players have the tagger role. This is achieved by adjusting the size of the circles of both taggers and runners. For instance, by making a tagger's circle bigger, it becomes easier for him to tag others. The size of the circle of all players is adjusted solely based on the time they have been taggers. When a player has been a tagger for more than the average amount of time, $\frac{gameTime}{\#players}$, then (a) when he is a tagger, his circle grows and (b) when he is a runner, his circle shrinks. The rationale behind this is that players that have been taggers for prolonged periods of time are either having difficulties tagging others or avoiding being tagged. This adaptation makes it easier for them to tag other players, and harder for other players to tag them. On the other hand, when a player's tag time is below the average, then (a) when he is a tagger, his circle shrinks and (b) when he is a runner, his circle grows. This is the opposite case as before, where we want to make it harder for this player to tag others and make it easier for others to tag him.

The formula for the circle adaptation is applied to every player in each frame, and is defined as:

$$addedSize = prevAddedSize + (\frac{timeBeingATagger}{gameTime} - \frac{1}{players}) * K \qquad (1)$$

where K is a constant that was empirically set to suit a 2 minute game, and the *prevAddedSize* variable is the size of the circle in the previous frame. To prevent the circles from getting too big or too small, predefined values where set to limit the minimum and maximum sizes. When a player switches roles, there is a small time window in which their circles quickly reset to their normal size before starting to shrink or grow.

We expect that this adaptive size will lead to a more balanced game in terms of the duration each player is a tagger. The differences between the duration of people being a tagger during one session should thus go down in the adaptive version of the game. Therefore, for the adaptive circle condition we hypothesize:

Hypothesis 2. *The variation, per group, in the duration of each player being a tagger, is lower for the adaptive game than for the standard game.*

Power-Ups. With power-ups we try to influence which locations the players visit during the game, steering players towards specific locations in the playing field. In previous work we have seen that runners often move near the border of the playground and the taggers move near the center. In our ITP we distributed power-ups outside these standard positions, power-ups for runners are in the

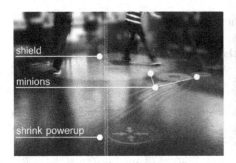

Fig. 2. Visualizations (left) of the *shrink* power-up and, the *minions* and the *shield* in use and (right) someone trying to collect a *shield* power-up

center and power-ups for the taggers are at the edges of the playground, see Figure 5. Power-ups were intended for either the tagger or the runner, the power-ups for the runners can't be gathered by taggers and vice versa. This way, it should be possible to steer players away from their normal playing strategy with respect to locations visited.

We implemented four types of power-ups. For the tagger there is a *grow* power-up and a *minions* power-up. The grow power-up increases the player's circle size and the minions power-up adds three small balls that rotate around the circle that can be used to tag someone with as well. For the runners there is a *shrink* power-up and a *shield* power-up. The shrink power-up shrinks the size of the circle. The shield power-up will create a 'force field' around the player, that slows down the speed with which the circles follow the real world location of the players in that force field. Both make it harder to get tagged. Both the runners and the taggers have one power-up that directly influences their size and one power-up that influences an area outside their circles.

All power-ups that are collected last for 25 seconds. Upon collection, the power-up disappears; every 10 seconds a new one appears that can be gathered. When a power-up is collected an accompanying sound is played. For the sake of experimental control, there are 8 positions at which the power-ups appear. Four around the center for the runners and four spread around the sides of the playground for the taggers (see Figure 5 in Section 5).

We expect that people will gather the power-ups and be in those (unusual) locations more often than in the normal condition. We therefore hypothesize:

Hypothesis 3a. *Locations visited by the runners change structurally in the power-ups game, runners will be near the middle of the playing field more often.*

Hypothesis 3b. *Locations visited by the taggers change structurally in the power-ups game, taggers will be near the edges of the playing field more often.*

4   User Study

With the ITP we investigated the effects of the previously described elements. We created four versions of the ITP, one for each game element and one without these game elements. We used a within-subject design: for each modified version of the game, we compared the measurements from players playing that version to the measurements from the same players playing the standard game as baseline.

4.1 Participants

In total 32 participants participated (27 male, 5 female), divided in eight groups of four participants playing the four versions of the game. Participants were mostly university students aged between 18-30 years. Some of the participants had participated in a previous user study involving the adaptive circle version of the ITP.

4.2 Procedure

Participants were asked to read and sign an informed consent form. The consent form also contained the explanation of the game, including a description of the power-ups. It also explained that four different types of versions of the ITP would be played, one with arrows, one with power-ups and two with just circles. We briefly explained the game and procedure of the user test. Each version was played for two minutes resulting in eight minutes of play in total. The order in which the games were played was semi-randomized. In each game the first player recognized by the tracking system was selected as the tagger. Players were given time to rest between each game session. Once they all agreed they were ready, the next session was started.

During the game two of our researchers were sitting directly outside the playground to start the game, observe the gameplay, check the tracker, and when necessary respond to questions about the playground.

After all the games were finished there was time for a group discussion of about 5 minutes. We asked questions like *'With a few keywords, how would you describe the experience of the playground?', 'Which different versions did you recognize, in which order and how do you think these versions work?', 'Which version did you like most?'* The entire session including filling in the consent form and discussion took around 30 minutes.

5   Results and Discussion

Before presenting the results for the three hypotheses, we will first present some qualitative observations and findings from the group discussions. We will then look into the quantitative results of the three targeted effects for each intervention separately. We will also discuss the implications of the results per element, taking into account the observations and findings from the discussions where relevant.

5.1   Group Discussion and Observations

Concerning the technical setup, there was a noticeable lag between the movements of the players and their circles following their movement, due to tracking and communication delays. When we asked the players about it, some found it irritating but most thought it made the game more interesting. You had to incorporate a different strategy, predicting the movement of the players, their circles and then trying to cut them off. As one group put it *'Is it a bug or a feature? [..] At the start it is frustrating, later on it became a part of the game'*. As for the tracking accuracy, in most locations players could stand shoulder to shoulder and still be recognized correctly by the system. Nonetheless, at some games players were switched when they were close to each other and made quick turns. At some other occasions, the tagger was reassigned to another player when a tagger was not recognized for some time by the tracker. We have observed around 10 of these glitches over all sessions. This led to discussion in the group and laughter as well as frustration.

When we asked players which game they liked most, 71% preferred the one with power-ups, 21% liked the one with adaptive circles and 8% the normal one. We also asked players to state some keywords describing the playground. Recurring responses were: *'sweaty, hot, tiring, exhausting, good exercise, interesting, cool, fun* and *innovative'*. This shows that players were having physical exercise and that they enjoyed it. Another clear sign of the performed activity was the visible sweat, red faces and the heavy breathing. Overall players were extremely positive about the mix of physical activity and technological enhancement.

Observations regarding the arrows. In all sessions, players noticed early on that they could tag anyone and not just the player that was being pointed at. This could be recognized by their chasing behavior and by remarks made during the game. We observed that the one initially being chased, seemingly often the one with an arrow pointing at them, was not always the one getting tagged eventually.

Observations regarding the adaptive circles. Certain players tried to make their circles grow with their movements. For instance, one tried to make a gesture with his hands and another tried to stand still. Most players recognized that the circles were growing or shrinking. However, most players thought it was related to the speed of running. Most of the people preferring the adaptive circles were from a group with an injured and a less skilled tagger in their midst, represented as session 8 in Table 2, but in this study we were not explicitly looking into how balancing might influence the game experience.

Observations regarding the power-ups. We heard and saw players exploring the effects of the power-ups, they were engaged in this exploration and discussed their findings with others. Therefore, we now think that by occasionally

Table 1. Table showing the percentages of players tagging someone who has been assigned an arrow in the arrow game version

Group	1	2	3	4	5	6	7	8	avg
%	46.2	50.0	37.5	50.0	50.0	40.0	50.0	23.1	43.35
# tags	13	18	8	10	12	15	8	13	12.1
# arrow tags	6	9	3	5	6	6	4	3	5.3

adding new kinds of power-ups over time, we might regain engagement of players that were less involved and increase social interaction. During the games there were at least two players explicitly hiding the power-up from the tagger by standing on top of it, making it almost invisible as their circle covered the power-up.

5.2   The Effect of Arrows

To investigate the effect the arrows had on the behavior of players, we logged which players were tagged in each game and whether they had an arrow pointing to them. With this we looked at Hypothesis 1.

Over the eight sessions, 43.3% of the players tagged were players that had arrows pointing towards them, see Table 1. The percentages of being tagged with an arrow, $D(8)=.257$, p=n.s., did not deviate significantly from normal. A two-tailed one sample t-test comparing to chance-level (0.33) does show a significant effect ($p < 0.05$) in the expected direction of people being tagged more often when an arrow is pointed at them. In our experiments pointing an arrow at someone in the ITP increased the chance of getting someone tagged more often.

Therefore, arrows might be used to make people more physically active and interact with each other more. For instance, it could be used to engage people that were less active in the game by pointing the arrow to them, or it could encourage people to walk more by assigning an arrow to someone further away. In addition, this offers another potential way of balancing the game, by pointing arrows at the players that had the lowest amount of tag time.

5.3   The Effect of Adaptive Circles

During the games we logged which player was the tagger, to investigate the effect of the adaptive circles (see Table 2). With this we looked at Hypothesis 2.

The standard deviations for the adaptive, $D(8) = 0.959, p = 0.803$, and for the baseline condition, $D(8) = 0.972, p = 0.910$, did not deviate significantly from the normal distribution. A two-tailed paired sample t-test comparing the standard deviations of the normal and adaptive sessions, showed a significant effect ($p < 0.05$), in the direction of the expected decrease for the adaptive version. This significant decrease shows we can balance the game: adaptive circle sizes lead to less variation in the duration of each player being a tagger. We strongly believe that balancing helps in making the game suitable for differently skilled players.

Table 2. Table showing the percentage of being a tagger per player for each session (s#), and the standard deviation in the session. On the left the adaptive condition, on the right the baseline unmodified game. Played with four players, the baseline percentage of being a tagger during this game is 25%. We highlighted the players being taggers the **longest** and the *shortest* percentage of the game.

s	std	players			
s1	13.3	29.7	**38.8**	*7.10*	24.3
s2	1.62	**27.0**	24.7	*23.1*	25.2
s3	8.81	*14.8*	21.9	**35.5**	27.8
s4	7.64	**32.1**	19.7	*17.2*	31.0
s5	6.80	22.7	*18.8*	**34.7**	23.8
s6	4.34	**30.7**	24.6	*20.1*	24.7
s7	4.46	26.3	26.5	**28.7**	*18.5*
s8	7.32	*17.4*	20.5	28.9	**33.2**
avg	6.79				

s	std	players			
s1	9.14	*14.6*	21.4	28.0	**36.0**
s2	20.0	25.1	26.0	**48.9**	*0.00*
s3	20.7	16.3	**55.7**	*10.4*	17.6
s4	11.2	**37.3**	*14.0*	31.6	17.1
s5	17.5	33.5	17.3	**44.4**	*4.86*
s6	4.97	28.1	**29.4**	24.1	*18.4*
s7	16.9	**47.9**	*8.06*	25.9	18.1
s8	26.5	6.38	37.5	*0.00*	**56.2**
avg	15.9				

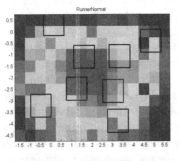
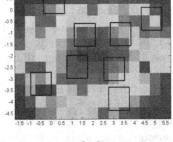
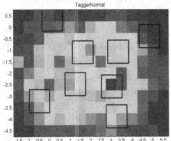
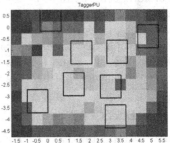

Fig. 3. Heatmaps of players' positions for the different versions, showing the locations of the power-ups with black rectangles. Runners' positions are shown in the top (T) images. In the left (L) images we show the positions in the baseline unmodified version of the game and in the right images the positions in the power-up version. TL: runners' in unmodified, TR: runners' with power-up, BL: taggers' in unmodified and BR: taggers' with power-ups.

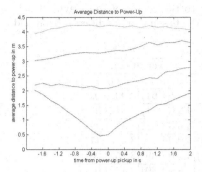

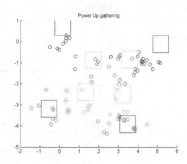

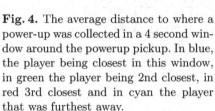

Fig. 4. The average distance to where a power-up was collected in a 4 second window around the powerup pickup. In blue, the player being closest in this window, in green the player being 2nd closest, in red 3rd closest and in cyan the player that was furthest away.

Fig. 5. The players position's when they gathered the different types of power-ups for tagger (black and red) and the runners(green and blue). The actual placement of the power-ups for the taggers (magenta) and for the runners (yellow) are shown with rectangles.

5.4 Power-Ups

We know that in tag, runners often move near the border of the playground and the taggers move near the center, see Figure 3. In this figure we can see that the distribution of location of players for the normal interactive tag version indeed follows this pattern. We have put power-ups in the ITP to see if we could change the location of players. We distributed the power-ups outside the 'standard' positions, power-ups for runners are in the center and power-ups for the taggers are at the edges of the playground.

We separately saved the positions of taggers and runners, as the power-ups were placed at different locations for these different roles. With this data we looked at Hypothesis 3. For every frame in the recordings of a session, we calculated the distance of runners and taggers to the center of the playground. Table 3 shows the average distance of runners and taggers to the center of the playground, and the standard deviation. A paired sample t-test does not show an effect on the average distance per group (N=8) between the baseline unmodified game and the power-up game for either runners or taggers.

Several reasons could help to explain the lack of effect. Only one player would gather the power-up and once gathered would directly leave that spot. In Figure 4 we plotted the average distance to the power-ups in the period surrounding a power-up being collected. We can see that players approach the power-up's position, and once its collected they move away again from this position. Furthermore, there were only a maximum of 12 power-ups to be collected each session and they appeared 10 seconds apart. Finally, the the size of the player's circle and of the power-up also diminishes the intended effect. The player's circle had to touch the power-up; the player himself did not need to be at the actual center

Table 3. Table showing the average distance to the center of the playing field, and standard deviation, for runners and taggers in the baseline unmodified version and the power-up game

s	baseline		power-up game	
	runner	tagger	runner	tagger
s1	3.82(1.71)	3.14(1.57)	4.62(1.61)	3.99(2.02)
s2	3.96(1.71)	3.81(1.84)	4.24(1.71)	3.81(2.06)
s3	3.84(2.04)	3.37(1.75)	4.62(1.87)	3.53(1.71)
s4	4.18(1.59)	4.15(1.63)	3.99(1.73)	3.47(2.11)
s5	4.54(1.78)	4.24(1.92)	4.04(1.69)	3.45(2.08)
s6	4.81(1.66)	3.73(1.49)	4.38(1.60)	4.12(2.01)
s7	4.27(1.79)	3.98(1.74)	4.30(1.55)	4.25(1.74)
s8	4.20(1.65)	3.92(1.67)	4.19(1.71)	3.48(1.94)
avg	4.20(1.74)	3.79(1.70)	4.30(1.68)	3.76(1.96)

position of the power-up but could remain a few steps away from it (see Figure 5).

We didn't find a significant effect in the locations visited by players. The players did however like the power-ups and over all sessions 85 from the 96 power-ups were gathered. Power-ups clearly are a useful mechanism to steer people, but not in the way we planned.

6   Conclusions and Future Work

We showed that it is possible to some extent to steer in various ways the behavior of participants during a game of interactive tag in the Interactive Tag Playground, although caution is needed in generalizing these results given the relatively low number of participants. The adaptive circles showed a clear balancing effect on the duration of each player being a tagger; the arrow pointing at someone showed an effect on whom would be tagged next. The power-ups did not lead to a visible effect on distribution of the locations of the players. Nonetheless, players did gather them and therefore went towards the chosen positions at least for a very short duration. Moreover, most players preferred the session with the power-ups. We believe this gives room for trying out other more long-lasting game mechanics to influence the position of players.

We believe the work we present shows an important aspect of successfully steering behaviors in playgrounds. In the future, this could be made adaptive, using the right timing and recognition of relevant player behavior to trigger such interventions, these behavior steering elements can help in attaining end goals such as promoting physical exercise and social interactions with a playful experience. We will use an improved playground implementation to explore these possibilities using measurements that indirectly indicate engagement, interactions and movement, e.g. person chased, distance walked or the average or top-speed of a player. As the power-ups did not show an effect yet, we will also look into other type of game mechanics to influence the locations of players. For instance, something similar to the shield power-up but making it affect a certain corner of the playing field.

The observation that people find ingenious strategies, such as hiding power-ups, and are able to incorporate shortcomings of a game as a feature, the lag, signifies the importance to look further into qualitative side-effects of introducing game elements as well. One aspect that has drawn our attention even more in our observations of childrens' non-instrumented play, is the 'break-down of play': play stopping, without the players agreeing to end the game, for several reasons including engagement drops, over-heated discussions or key-players leaving. In our research we will work towards a more thorough investigation on the break-down of play influenced by the interactive elements of the ITP and the endless possibilities of steering behavior to prevent this.

References

1. Björnsson, D., Fridriksson, R., Lund, H.: Adaptivity to age, gender, and gaming platform topology in physical multi-player games. In: Proceedings of ISAROB 2012 (2012)
2. Dalsgaard, P., Hansen, L.K.: Performing perception — staging aesthetics of interaction. ACM Trans. Comput.-Hum. Interact. 15(3), 13:1–13:33 (2008)
3. Derakhshan, A., Hammer, F., Lund, H.: Adapting playgrounds for children's play using ambient playware. In: IROS, Beijing, China, pp. 5625–5630 (2006)
4. Fogg, B.J., Hreha, J.: Behavior wizard: A method for matching target behaviors with solutions. In: Ploug, T., Hasle, P., Oinas-Kukkonen, H. (eds.) PERSUASIVE 2010. LNCS, vol. 6137, pp. 117–131. Springer, Heidelberg (2010)
5. Hamari, J., Koivisto, J., Pakkanen, T.: Do persuasive technologies persuade? - a review of empirical studies. In: Spagnolli, A., Chittaro, L., Gamberini, L. (eds.) PERSUASIVE 2014. LNCS, vol. 8462, pp. 118–136. Springer, Heidelberg (2014)
6. Her, J.J.: Playing interactivity in public space. In: Proceedings of MMEDIA 2010, Athens, Greece, pp. 22–28 (2010)
7. Hunicke, R.: The case for dynamic difficulty adjustment in games. In: Proceedings of ACE 2005, Valencia, Spain, pp. 429–433 (2005)
8. Landry, P., Pares, N.: Controlling and modulating physical activity through interaction tempo in exergames: A quantitative empirical analysis. J. Ambient Intell. Smart Environ. 6(3), 277–294 (2014)
9. Moreno, A., van Delden, R., Poppe, R., Reidsma, D.: Socially aware interactive playgrounds. Pervasive Computing 12(3), 40–47 (2013)
10. Mueller, F., Vetere, F., Gibbs, M., Edge, D., Agamanolis, S., Sheridan, J., Heer, J.: Balancing exertion experiences. In: CHI 2012, pp. 1853–1862 (2012)
11. Palmer, S., Popat, S.: Dancing in the streets. Interactions 15(3), 55–59 (2008)
12. Parés, N., Durany, J., Carreras, A.: Massive flux design for an interactive water installation: Water games. In: Proceedings of ACE 2005, Valencia, Spain, pp. 266–269 (2005)

Impact of Blinds Usage on Energy Consumption: Automatic Versus Manual Control

Bernt Meerbeek[1,2(✉)], Thijs van Druenen[2], Mariëlle Aarts[2],
Evert van Loenen[1,2], and Emile Aarts[2]

[1] Philips Research, High Tech Campus 34 1.064, 5656 AE Eindhoven, The Netherlands
{bernt.meerbeek,evert.van.loenen}@philips.com
[2] Intelligent Lighting Institute (ILI), Eindhoven University of Technology,
P.O. Box 513, 5600 MB Eindhoven, The Netherlands
{t.v.druenen,m.p.j.aarts,e.h.l.aarts}@tue.nl

Abstract. This paper reports a study on the impact of different usage patterns of an automated blinds system on the energy consumption for heating and cooling in a Dutch office building. A five-month observational field study in 40 offices resulted into a dataset on the blinds usage of four types of blind users. This data was used to simulate the effect of the blinds usage on the energy consumption for heating and cooling. The results of the field study show that a majority of the building occupants switched off the automatic mode of the blinds system permanently. The simulation results indicate that this significantly impacts the energy consumption in the building. The total daily average energy consumption for heating and cooling was significantly lower for occupants using the automatic mode than for the three groups of manual users (871W/day versus 2573W/day; T=-5.98, p=0.000).

Keywords: Blinds · Daylight · User control · Ambient intelligence · Energy

1 Introduction

1.1 Ambient Intelligence in the Office Environment

Technological advances in sensors, processing power, lighting, and networks in combination with an increasing attention for energy efficiency drive the development of so called 'Smart Buildings'. It is expected that office buildings will evolve into 'ambient intelligent' office environments [1]. Technology will be embedded into the office environment, aware of the context, personalized to individuals, and adaptive and anticipatory to their needs. This vision is starting to become a reality in today's office buildings. Simple forms of building automation such as occupancy sensing, daylight-based dimming, and automatically controlled blinds are already common practice. There are clear economical drivers for ambient intelligent office environments. For example, energy and cost savings can be realized by automatically switching off the electrical lighting when people are not in a room or by dimming the electric light if sufficient daylight is available. Such intelligent behavior should not only result in

© Springer International Publishing Switzerland 2014
E. Aarts et al. (Eds.): AmI 2014, LNCS 8850, pp. 158–173, 2014.
DOI: 10.1007/978-3-319-14112-1_14

energy and cost savings, but also make sure that occupants are satisfied with and feel in control of their working environment. A balance between energy efficiency and occupant comfort needs to be found. One particularly interesting topic in this respect is the control of daylight entrance in buildings, as this significantly impacts the energy usage in a building as well as occupants' feeling of comfort.

1.2 Daylight and Blinds

People generally have a clear preference for daylight over electric lighting as a source of illumination [2]. Studies have shown this preference for daylight in offices for reasons of enhanced psychological comfort, increased productivity, more pleasant office appearance, and assumed health benefits [3,4]. Christoffersen and Johnsen [5] found that employees prefer to sit near windows. The most positive aspects of a window according to this study in twenty Danish buildings are to have a view out, to be able to check the weather outside, and to have the ability to open the window. However, windows can also be a source of visual and thermal discomfort affecting the energy consumption in a building through heat gains and losses. Therefore, windows often come with blinds to regulate the daylight entrance.

Discomfort glare is known to be a primary factor driving blinds usage [6,7]. But the results of several studies indicate that people do not regularly change the blinds positions manually [e.g. 8,9]. People generally lower the blinds to block direct sunlight, but often forget to retract them. If people retract blinds, they mainly do this to increase daylight entrance, to save energy for electric lighting, or to create a view [10]. Interestingly however, Reinhart and Voss [11] – who studied the usage of automated exterior blinds with manual override options in German private and 2-person offices - found that in 88% of the cases when the blinds were lowered automatically, people manually raised them within 15 minutes, indicating poor acceptance of automatic blinds lowering. Based on a literature review, Galasiu and Veitch [10] concluded that photocontrolled lighting systems have best acceptance when there is individual override control. Integrated control for both lighting and shading can be acceptable, but have highest acceptance when a degree of manual control is provided.

Fig. 1. South facade of the office building (left) and a typical office room layout (right)

1.3   Research Questions

This study investigates the impact of the way building occupants use the automated exterior blinds system on the energy consumption for heating and cooling. More specifically, this first part of the study addresses the usage patterns of an existing automated exterior venetian blinds system. How do office workers use this system? How often are the blinds adjusted? What portion of the building occupants use the automatic mode? Can different type of blind users be distinguished? The second part of the study investigates the potential impact of blinds usage patterns on energy consumption for heating and cooling. What are the differences in energy consumption for heating and cooling for different blinds usage scenarios? Section 2 describes the earlier reported field study that investigated how office workers in 40 offices experience and use automatically controlled exterior venetian blinds - with manual override and option to switch off the automatic mode - in a real working environment over a period of five months, from July to December [12]. The blinds usage data that was collected during this field study was used as input to simulate the effect of the blinds usage on the energy consumption for heating and cooling. The simulation method and results are described in section 3. Discussion and conclusion are presented in section 4.

2   Field Study

2.1   Methodology

Setting

The field study was conducted in two- and three-person offices located at the south orientated façade of an office building on the High Tech Campus in Eindhoven, the Netherlands (see Fig. 1). Most employees in the building could be characterized as knowledge workers of a large multinational company with a high education level and from a variety of cultural backgrounds. The selected offices were located at the 3rd to 7th floor with an unobstructed view on natural scenery including a few buildings in the distance. The façade was equipped with automatic motorized exterior venetian blinds with manual override and option to switch off the automatic mode. These blinds were lowered automatically if the roof-top light sensors detected intensities exceeding a threshold value of 16kLux and were raised at fixed times (21:00) or with wind speeds exceeding 30 km/h (see Table 1). Furthermore, each room was equipped with three manually and individually operable indoor roller shades in the form of screens, and one controller for the exterior blinds. With this controller, occupants could choose to set the blinds in automatic or manual mode and use up and down keys to manually control the blinds height and slat angle. Each room was equipped with fluorescent lighting that was controlled automatically (on/off) based on occupant presence and daylight linked dimming only for the lights near the window. Occupants were not able to manually adjust the electric light. The daylight linked lighting was set up to provide a minimum of 500 lux on the desk. All the described blinds and lighting systems were unmodified commercially available products that were installed in the building a few years before this field study started.

Table 1. Explanation of blinds system

	Automatic mode 'on'	Automatic mode 'off'
Blinds go down	Manual adjustment possible between 6:00-21:00h If light intensity measured by roof top sensor exceeds 16 kLux (between 6:00-21:00h)	Manual adjustment possible between 6:00-21:00h
Blinds go up	Manual adjustment possible between 6:00-21:00h After 21:00h If wind speed exceeds 30km/h	Manual adjustment possible between 6:00-21:00h After 21:00h If wind speed exceeds 30km/h

Fig. 2. Schematic representation of the classified blinds positions with four different occlusion levels (from left to right 0%, 25%, 75%, 100% occlusion)

Data Collection and Analysis

All exterior blinds adjustments were monitored during a period of 21 weeks (July to December 2011). A webcam was installed facing the south façade of the building of interest. This camera captured an image of the façade every six minutes during the period of the field study. Only the images taken on working days (Monday to Friday) between 8:00 and 18:00 hours were selected for further processing. For privacy reasons, a low resolution camera was used such that participants could not be identified on the images. People were not informed that their blinds usage was monitored to avoid any deviation from their normal usage. The study was approved by the internal ethical commission for research with human subjects. A computer vision algorithm was developed to automatically process the images and classify the blinds position for a particular office at a particular time. In order to train the system to automatically classify the blinds position, a manual classification was done for a random set of images. Based on the training set, the software could automatically classify all remaining images with an accuracy of over 90%. Fig. 2 shows a schematic representation of the blinds position classification. Due to a temporary power cut of the monitoring system, the data of week 40 has been excluded from the analysis. Data of 100 working days remain for the analysis, resulting in a dataset of 400.000 images in total. A list of blinds adjustments was created by comparing the blinds position at time t with the blinds position at time t-1. Additionally, the type of adjustment was registered: 'system-triggered up' referring to a raise of the blinds initiated by the system, 'system-triggered down' referring to a lowering of the blinds initiated by the system, 'user-triggered up' referring to a raise of the blinds initiated by the user, or 'user-triggered down' referring to a lowering of the blinds initiated by the user. For a more detailed explanation of this classification method, as well as the data collection method and analysis, the reader is referred to [12].

2.2   Results

As shown in Table 2, 3433 blinds adjustments were registered of which 905 were system-triggered adjustments (26.4%) and 2528 user-triggered adjustments (73.6 %). Fig. 3 shows the total number of adjustments per week of the trial split per type of adjustment: user-triggered or system-triggered. Overall, there were more adjustments in the third trimester of the trial than in the first two trimesters. The number of system-triggered adjustments was relatively stable throughout the trial period, while the number of user-triggered adjustments varied largely. In particular in the last trimester of the trial the differences between the number of system-triggered and user-triggered adjustments are remarkable. When zooming in on the blinds adjustments per time of day, the results show that the largest number of adjustments was made between 8:00 and 9:00 (about 17% of all adjustments). The total number of adjustments gradually declined during the course of the day, with the lowest number of adjustments between 14:00-15:00 (about 5%), but slightly increases after 16:00 (to about 10%). System-triggered lowering of the blinds occurred most often in the early morning, while user-triggered lowering of the blinds mostly occurred in the late morning.

Table 2. Type and number of blinds adjustments (sum for all offices during trial)

	Number of adjustments	% of total
System-triggered up	130	3.8%
System-triggered down	775	22.6%
System-triggered adjustments (sum)	**905**	*26.4%*
User-triggered up	1173	34.2%
User-triggered down	1355	39.5%
User-triggered adjustments (sum)	**2528**	*73.6%*
Total up	1303	38.0%
Total down	2130	62.0%
Total adjustments (sum)	**3433**	*100.0%*

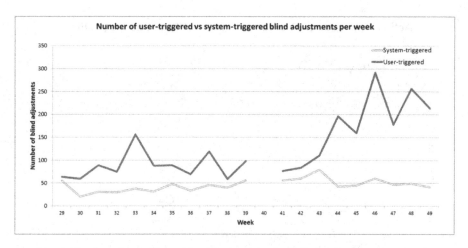

Fig. 3. Number of user-triggered and system-triggered blinds adjustments per week

The overall average of blinds adjustments per office during the trial period was 85.8, with a minimum of 0, a maximum of 198, and a standard deviation of 54.0. Hence, the average number of adjustments per working day was 0.86, but with a large spread across offices. Nine out of forty offices (22.5%) used the automatic mode of the blinds system throughout the trial period, while a large majority of offices (77.5%) never used the automatic mode or only during a small period of the trial. The first is referred to as the group 'auto mode' and the latter as the group 'manual mode'. The average number of adjustments for manual mode offices is much lower than for auto mode offices (73.6 respectively 127.9). Besides the large variation in the average total number of adjustments, there were also large differences in the type of adjustments (user-triggered versus system-triggered). In the auto mode group, on average, 39.6% of all adjustments were initiated by the user indicating a manual override of the automatic system. In the manual mode group, on average 92.4% of all adjustments in an office were initiated by the user. The remaining 7.6% of adjustments were triggered by the system and could be the result of manual mode users switching to automatic mode during a part of the trial, coincidentally adjusting the blinds at the same time and in an identical way as the automatic system, errors of the classification software, or special circumstances in which automatic adjustments are enforced upon the user (e.g. cleaning windows, high wind speed).

In Fig. 4, each office is indicated by a number and plotted in a two-dimensional space, in which the x-axis indicates the activity ratio and the y-axis the user control ratio. The activity ratio (A) and user control ratio (U) are calculated for each office (i) as described by the following equations where Bu refers to user-triggered blind adjustments and Bs to system-triggered blind adjustments:

$$A_i = \frac{Bu_i + Bs_i}{\overline{Bu_{i,n}} + \overline{Bs_{i,n}}} - 1 \tag{1}$$

$$U_i = \frac{Bu_i}{Bu_i + Bs_i} \tag{2}$$

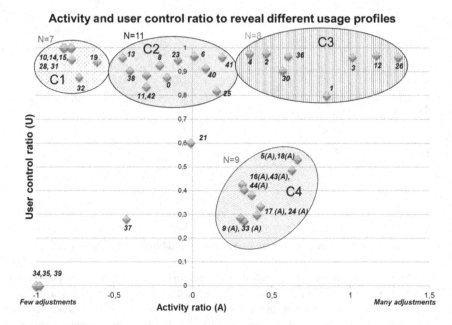

Fig. 4. Activity and user control ratio reveal different usage profiles

In the offices on the left side of the graph fewer adjustments of the blinds occurred than average, while in the offices on the right side more adjustments than average occurred. A higher user control ratio indicates relatively more user-triggered adjustments. Based on these two ratios, four clusters of offices with similar blinds usage are identified: C1 – few adjustments, mostly user-triggered (about 20% of offices); C2 – average adjustments, mostly user triggered (about 30% of offices); C3 – many adjustments, mostly user-triggered (about 20% of offices); C4 – system control with manual override (about 25% of users). Five offices could not be categorized into one of the four clusters and were left out of the energy simulation described in the next section.

3 Energy Simulation

3.1 Methodology

A simulation of heating and cooling loads was performed to gain insight in the difference in energy consumption that can be attributed to the ways the exterior venetian blinds are being controlled. The simulations were performed with IES Virtual Environment (IES VE). IES VE is a commercially available building performance analysis tool that is commonly used within the building services industry. The outcome of the simulations were matched with the dataset resulting from the field study reported in section 2 and were converted to hourly heating and cooling loads for all of the offices. Fig. 5 presents a schematic overview of the simulation method. Next, each step is explained in more detail.

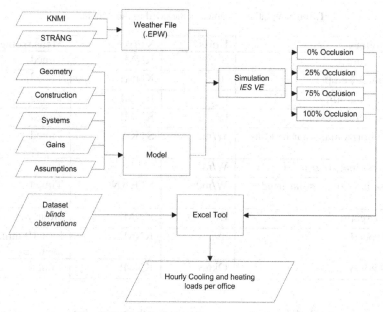

Fig. 5. Schematic overview of simulation method

Dataset Blinds Observations

A dataset was constructed from the blinds usage observations of the field study reported in the previous section. It consisted of a list of the blinds occlusion levels (0%, 25%, 75%, 100%) for each of the 35 offices for every 15 minutes on working days between 8:15 and 17:45.

Weather Data

Table 3 shows the weather parameters that were imported to the IES VE simulation software in an Energy Plus weather file. Most weather parameters were collected from a weather station of the KNMI (Royal Dutch Meteorological Institute) at the Eindhoven airport, 6.6km from the building of the field study: the outdoor temperature, dew point temperature, relative humidity, atmospheric pressure, wind direction and speed, and cloud cover. Solar irradiation values were collected from STRÅNG [13]. The STRÅNG model produces values of global radiation, direct normal radiation, and sunshine duration at a horizontal resolution of about 11 x 11 km and a temporal resolution of one hour. Global horizontal irradiance is the total amount of shortwave radiation received from above by a horizontal surface. Direct normal irradiance is the amount of solar radiation received per unit area by a surface that is always held perpendicular to the rays that come in a straight line from the direction of the sun at its current position in the sky. Diffuse horizontal irradiance is the amount of radiation received per unit area by a surface that does not arrive on a direct path from the sun, but has been scattered by molecules and particles in the atmosphere and comes equally from all directions.

Table 3. Weather parameters included in the simulation

Parameters	Units	Source	Measurement
Temperature	°C	KNMI	Timed
Dew point Temperature	°C	KNMI	Timed
Relative humidity	%	KNMI	Timed
Atmospheric pressure	hPa	KNMI	Timed
Global horizontal solar irradiation	W/m2	STRÅNG	Timed
Direct normal solar irradiation	W/m2	STRÅNG	Timed
Diffuse horizontal solar irradiation	W/m2	STRÅNG	Timed
Wind direction	Degrees	KNMI	Hourly average
Wind speed	m/s	KNMI	Last 10 min. average
Cloud cover	Oktas	KNMI	Timed

Table 4. Parameters and values used in the modelled office

	Parameter	Value
Office dimensions	Length x width x height	6.44 x 3.86 x 3.35 m³
Window dimensions	Base height	0.85 m
	Height	2.40 m
	Width	3.30 m
Thermal constructions	Internal walls (U-value)	2.878 W/m²·K
	External wall (U-value)	1.552 W/m²·K
	Glass (U-value)	1.185 W/m²·K
	Ceiling (U-value)	1.796 W/m²·K
	Floor (U-value)	1.796 W/m²·K
Thermal system	Heating set point	Following daily profile: 00:00h = 16°C 07:30h = 20°C 18:00h = 20°C 24:00h = 16°C
	Cooling set point (only if office is occupied)	Following daily profile: 00:00h = 28°C 07:30h = 23°C 18:00h = 23°C 24:00h = 28°C
Ventilation	Air exchange per hour	1.5

Building

The building consists of a concrete structure and the floors are created by concrete hollow-core slabs. The façade is formed by an uninsulated inner and outer leaf made of concrete. At the inside, the ceiling is constructed with a suspended ceiling and the inner walls are formed by metal studs and a gypsum layer. The floors are finished with carpet. The offices are designed to occupy two employees but the actual occupancy fluctuates between different offices and throughout the day. A model office room was constructed based on the information from the building specifications and building management system. An overview of the most important parameters of the model including room and window dimensions, U-values, and heating and cooling set points is shown in Table 4. The heating and cooling system used set points that varied over the day. For example, after 18:00 hour the heating is switched on when room temperature falls below 16°C, while between 07:30 and 18:00 it is switched on when room temperature drops below 20°C.

Another aspect that is included in the simulation model is the internal heat gain caused by sources inside the office. The following assumptions have been made to simulate the internal heat gains. First, when fully occupied an office contains 2 persons with a gain of 90 Watts per person. Furthermore, for electrical equipment (computers, mobile devices, etc.) an internal heat gain of 300 Watts was assumed with 2 persons in the office. Finally, internal gains for the lighting were estimated to be 120 Watts. Four lighting fixtures (TL5 54W fluorescent lights) in the ceiling were controlled by presence sensors (on/off) and two of those by daylight linked dimming. Because there is no occupancy data and dim levels available, the total heat gain from the four light sources was estimated to be 120 Watt. This estimation is based on a heat gain of 70% (30% visible radiation), which is considered normal for fluorescent lighting.

Assumptions

For the simulations, a number of assumptions had to be made in addition to the ones mentioned before. First, it was assumed that each office was occupied by two persons, while in reality some offices were occupied by three persons. Since the occupancy was not monitored, it was assumed that the offices were 100% occupied. Furthermore, it was assumed that the door was always closed and no additional ventilation or heat gain by opening of doors was modelled.

3.2   Results

Fig. 6 shows the average energy consumption for heating and cooling per working day over time per user group. It also shows the outside temperature during the trial. The average consumption for cooling for user group C4 (auto mode) is generally lower than for the user groups that switched off the automatic mode (C1-C3). However, in November and December with lower outside temperatures, the manual user groups (C1-C3) generally consume less energy for heating than the automatic mode group (C4).

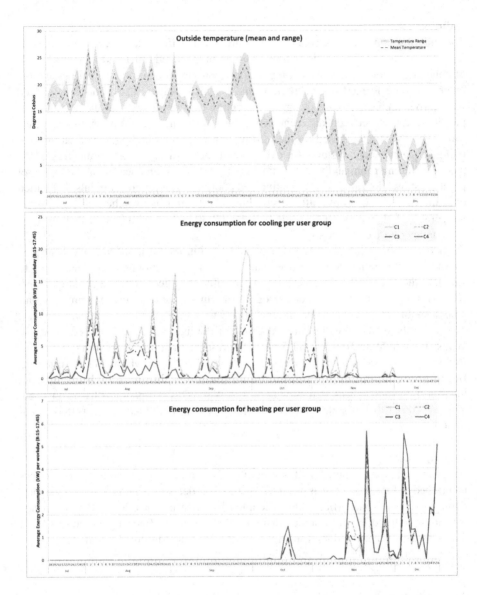

Fig. 6. Outside temperature (top), energy consumption for cooling (center), and energy consumption for heating (bottom) over time

Fig. 7 shows the average daily energy consumption (kW) in correlation with the daily average outside temperature for the four different user groups. The scatterplots indicate that in particular with higher outside temperatures, the energy consumption in the groups C1-C3 is higher than in group C4. For each group, a polynomial regression analysis was conducted to model the energy consumption (E) as a function of the outside temperature (t), resulting in the following equations:

$$E_{c1} = 10.7 - 1.872\, t + 0.08151\, t^2 \quad (S=2.95,\ R^2=54.9\%) \tag{3}$$

$$E_{c2} = 9.6 - 1.657\, t + 0.07002\, t^2 \quad (S=1.95,\ R^2=64.4\%) \tag{4}$$

$$E_{c3} = 8.029 - 1.365\, t + 0.05677\, t^2 \quad (S=1.37,\ R^2=69.3\%) \tag{5}$$

$$E_{c4} = 6.931 - 0.9890\, t + 0.03417\, t^2 \quad (S=0.82,\ R^2=62.7\%) \tag{6}$$

Occupants in the automatic mode on average used significantly ($T=3.50$, $p=0.001$) more energy for heating than the three groups of manual users (463W/day versus 330W/day), but significantly ($T=-6.63$, $p=0.000$) less energy for cooling (408W/day versus 2243W/day). The total daily average energy consumption for heating and cooling was significantly lower for occupants in automatic mode than for the three groups of manual users (871W/day versus 2573W/day; $T=-5.98$, $p=0.000$).

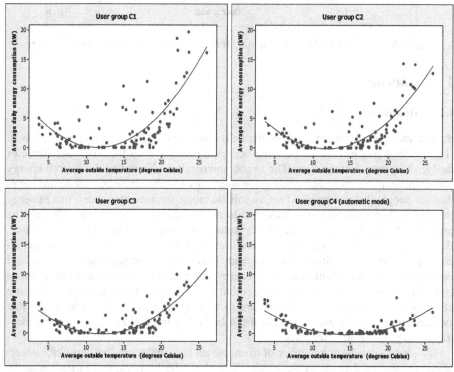

Fig. 7. Scatterplots of the average outside temperature (degrees Celsius) versus the average daily energy consumption (kW) for user group C1 – C4

Fig. 8 shows the boxplots of the average total energy consumption for heating and cooling during the trial per user group. The average consumption in user group C1 (few adjustments, mostly user-triggered) was 3.8 times higher than in the group C4 (system control with manual override). The most active user control group C3 used almost 40% less energy than the least active user control group C1, but still 2.3 times more than the automatic mode users C4.

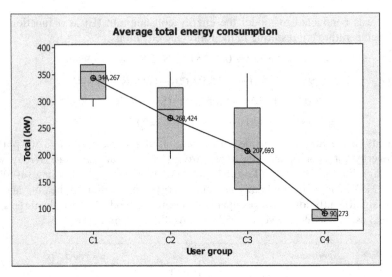

Fig. 8. Average total energy consumption for heating and cooling (kW) per user group

4   Conclusion

4.1   Discussion

An interesting and striking result of the field study reported in section 2, as well as in [11], is that a majority of the building occupants switched off the automatic mode of the blinds system permanently. The simulation results indicate that the overall energy consumption for heating and cooling for users that use the automatic mode are lower than for people that switched off the automatic mode. In particular, much more energy for cooling is needed in the offices that do not use the automatic mode. This can be explained by the fact that the blinds for automatic mode users are down more often. Especially, with higher outside temperature and solar heat gain, the difference increased. In November and December with lower outside temperatures, the manual user groups generally consume less energy for heating than the automatic mode group. This can be explained by the fact that the automatic mode users make less use of the solar heat gain, as their blinds are more frequently lowered, while people that switched off the automatic mode use the solar heat gain in winter and need less electrical energy for heating their room.

The simulations have a number of assumptions and limitations that introduce uncertainty and potential errors in the results. Therefore, the findings, and in particular the absolute numbers regarding the energy consumption, should be taken with care. Nevertheless, the relative differences in energy consumption for heating and cooling between different types of blinds users are interesting results and clearly indicate the negative consequences of switching of the automatic mode on energy consumption. Further studies are recommended to validate the results of this study. It is outside the scope of this work to specify the uncertainty levels introduced by the various parameters and indicate the error margins, but the main factors that might have impacted the generalizability and reliability of the simulation results will be described next

4.2   Limitations

With a large field study it is impossible to control for all variables and there are restrictions on the data that can be collected. Although the field study was one of the few large scale long-term studies on this topic, it still only involved one particular building at one particular location. Furthermore, one specific shading solution was used: automated exterior blinds (triggering at 16kLux at the rooftop sensor) with opt-out option and manual override in combination with manual interior roller shades. Due to technical and practical feasibility, only the exterior blinds usage was monitored with an accuracy of about 90%. The usage of interior shades might have been a confounding factor that was not measured throughout the field study. It is recommended to repeat this type of field studies in different settings with different blinds systems and algorithms. Moreover, no occupancy measures could be taken, as for privacy reasons this would require asking all building occupants for their consent to participate in the trial. However, the authors did not want to inform the occupants that they were part of the study, as this might have altered their blinds usage. Due to the absence of occupancy data, a 100% occupancy was assumed for the simulations which is not realistic.

Regarding the simulation results, it is important to mention that only the energy consumption for heating and cooling are included. Although this is a substantial part of the total energy consumption, other energy consumption aspects including energy for electric lighting and driving the motors of the exterior blinds are not included in the simulations. Moreover, assumptions had to be made that limit the generalizability of the results. The most important assumptions are related to the specific building construction (e.g. U-values), sources of internal heat gain, and thermostat control for heating. In reality, occupants could influence the room temperature with a thermostatic radiator valve by a rotating a dial between 0 (no flow of hot water) and 5 (max flow of hot water). Since the thermostatic radiator valve could not be monitored during the field trial, it was assumed for the simulations that it was in position 3. Also the assumption of 100% occupancy limits the generalizability and reliability of the results. From an online questionnaire among the building occupants (N=71) prior to the field study, 60% of the occupants indicate to spend between 50-75% of their working time behind their desk, while 32% of the occupants spend 75-100% of the time behind their desk. Assuming two occupants per office, this would mean that in approximately 10% of the time nobody is in the room. In this case, the cooling set point of 24 degrees Celsius would be deactivated, allowing room temperatures up to 28 degrees. Also, the internal heat gain from the human body would be absent. So in practice, the energy consumption levels for cooling would most likely be slightly lower with lower occupancy. Although the heating set point was not connected to the occupancy of the room, a lower occupancy level would most likely result in slightly higher energy consumption for heating as there is no internal heat gain from persons in the room. Although it would have been reasonable to assume an occupancy level of around 90%, it was decided to assume 100% occupancy for the simulation, because it was unknown which offices were unoccupied. This could further decrease the reliability of the simulations. Another factor that potentially reduces the reliability of the simulation results is the resolution of the measurements. The blinds occlusion levels were recorded every 6 minutes and grouped in four categories (0%, 25%, 75%, or 100% occlusion). In reality blinds could (although not very likely) move up and down within the 6 minutes time interval and the occlusion level could be any value between 0 and 100%. Furthermore, the weather data was collected at a weather station 6.6 km from the office building and the sunshine radiation data at a resolution of 11 x 11 km. This is an approximation of the real weather conditions at the exact location of the building.

4.3   Conclusions

To conclude, this paper reported a study on the impact of different usage patterns of an automated blinds system on the energy consumption for heating and cooling in a Dutch office building. A five-month observational field study in 40 offices resulted in a data-set on the blinds usage of four types of blinds users. This data was used to simulate the effect of the blinds usage on the energy consumption for heating and cooling. The field study results show that a majority of the building occupants (77.5%) switched off the automatic mode of the blinds system permanently. The effect of the blinds usage patterns for the four different user groups on energy consumption for heating and cooling were simulated. Although several assumptions were made that limit the reliability and generalizability of the results and possibly introduces errors, the simulations provide strong indications that the blinds usage pattern has a significant impact on the energy consumption in office buildings. The total daily average energy consumption for heating and cooling was significantly lower for occupants in automatic mode than for the three groups of manual users (871W/day versus 2573W/day; T=-5.98, p=0.000). Hence, it seems problematic from an energy saving perspective that a large majority of users switches of the automatic mode of an exterior blinds system. Further research is needed in other buildings, settings, and regions to increase the understanding and evidence about the impact of blinds usage on energy consumption. Furthermore, it seems worthwhile to investigate ways for improving the acceptance of automated blinds systems; not only for increased comfort of the building occupants, but also for a reduction of the energy consumption in buildings. One direction is the design of intelligent systems and improved algorithms that better match with personal comfort desires of building occupants, for example through self-learning systems. Another promising direction could be to make building occupants more aware of the way blinds systems work and their impact on the energy consumption in a building.

References

1. Aarts, E., Marzano, S.: The New Everyday: Views on Ambient Intelligence. 010 Publishers, Rotterdam (2003)
2. Boyce, P.R., Veitch, J.A., Newsham, G.R., Myer, M., Hunter, C., Heerwagen, J.H., Jones, C.C.: Lighting quality and office work: A field simulation study. LRC report, PNNL-14506 (2003)
3. Heerwagen, J.H., Heerwagen, D.R.: Lighting and psychological comfort. Lighting Design and Application 16(4), 47–51 (1986)
4. Veitch, J.A., Gifford, R.: Assessing beliefs about lighting effects on health, performance, mood and social behavior. Environ. Behav. 446–470 (1996)

5. Christoffersen, J., Johnsen, K.: Windows and daylight: a post-occupancy evaluation of Danish offices. In: Proc. Light 2000, CIBSE/ILE Joint Conference, pp. 112–120 (2000)
6. Van Den Wymelenberg, K.: Patterns of occupant interaction with window blinds: a literature review. Energy Build. **51**, 165–176 (2012)
7. O'Brien, W., Kapsis, K., Athienitis, A.K.: Manually-operated window shade patterns in office buildings: a critical review. Build. Environ. **60**, 319–338 (2013)
8. Inoue, T., Kawase, T., Ibamoto, T., Takakusa, S., Matsuo, Y.: The development of an optimal control system for window shading devices based on investigations in office buildings. ASHRAE Trans. **94**, 1049 (1988)
9. Rea, M.S.: Window blind occlusion: a pilot study. Build. Environ. **19**(2), 133–137 (1984)
10. Galasiu, A.D., Veitch, J.A.: Occupant preferences and satisfaction with the luminous environment and control systems in daylit offices: a literature review. Energy Build. **38**, 728–742 (2006)
11. Reinhart, C.F., Voss, K.: Monitoring manual control of electric lighting and blinds. Light Res Technol. **35**(3), 243–260 (2003)
12. Meerbeek, B.Te, Kulve, M., Gritti, T., Aarts, M., Van Loenen, E., Aarts, E.: Building automation and perceived control: A field study on motorized exterior blinds in Dutch offices. Building and Environment **79**, 66–77 (2014)
13. STRÅNG. http://strang.smhi.se/ (last visited August 07, 2014)

Discrete Control for Smart Environments Through a Generic Finite-State-Models-Based Infrastructure

Mengxuan Zhao[1(✉)], Gilles Privat[1], Eric Rutten[2], and Hassane Alla[3]

[1] Orange Labs, 28 Chemin du Vieux Chêne 38243 Meylan, France
{mengxuan.zhao,gilles.privat}@orange.com
[2] INRIA Grenoble, 655 av. de l'Europe, 38334 Montbonnot, St Ismier, France
eric.rutten@inria.fr
[3] GIPSA-Lab, 11 r. des Mathématiques, D.U., 38402 Saint Martin d'Hères Cedex, France
hassane.alla@gipsa-lab.fr

Abstract. Drawing requirements and models from reactive and real-time systems, we propose a self-configurable data mediation infrastructure for Smart Environments and the Internet of Things, showing how it can be used to effect discrete control in smart home environments by mediating and adapting generic rules through finite-state-machine models drawn from a domain ontology, representing observable & controllable "things" and space entities in this infrastructure.

Keywords: System architecture · Middleware · Domain ontologies · Discrete-event control · Finite-state automata · Reactive systems · Control theory

1 Introduction

Ambient Intelligence research [1] has tended to place a strong emphasis on the acquisition and processing of input data and its context, while often using basic solutions relying on unquestioned assumptions for the control part of AmI systems, when it exists at all. Sensing, extended to perceptual and contextual processing, has thus been addressed first as a broader and more interesting research challenge than mundane actuation. Yet the know-how of control theory and reactive systems should also be brought to bear to address both in tandem, even if most current AmI applications don't have the same kind of strict real-time and safety requirements as industrial control. The situation is somewhat similar in this regard for the Internet of Things domain, for which most present-day applications still boil down to straightforward remote monitoring and data acquisition from sensors, control being often left to a human operator, or considered unproblematic if it is automated at all. Evolving beyond these implicit assumptions requires questioning the functional engineering approach, inherited from mainstream ICT, whose data-processing-oriented models lack accurate temporal semantics. Most AmI context processing infrastructures are typical of this, being purely transformational data processing systems rather than reactive [2].

A shared AmI & IoT infrastructure should, in a given environment, support all AmI & IoT applications grounded in this environment. It should be more than a

© Springer International Publishing Switzerland 2014
E. Aarts et al. (Eds.): AmI 2014, LNCS 8850, pp. 174–190, 2014.
DOI: 10.1007/978-3-319-14112-1_15

regular AmI context middleware, more than a pure data processing or data brokerage platform. It should build upon a systemic, environment-specific yet environment-wide viewpoint, encompassing and capturing all temporal constraints and potential side effects that may result from physical sensing and actuation effects interwoven with network relationships. Such a shared infrastructure accounting for the bidirectional coupling between the IT and physical parts of AmI and IoT systems is what we rely on in this paper for the synthesis of discrete controllers, drawing for this on finite-state-machine models that have proved their relevance to capture the intrinsic and irreducible temporal properties of reactive systems [3].

We will borrow all of our examples from home environments, yet everything we present can be generalized to larger-scale similar environments such as smart buildings provided they are not one-of-a-kind (like e.g. factories or industrial facilities) and exhibit a measure of structural invariance from one instance to another, along the lines of what is explained for smart homes in the following.

2   Smart Homes Control Applications

Attempts towards the automation of so-called smart homes started long ago with fully custom-designed solutions, yet it is only in the last decade that generic ICT infrastructures and state of the art devices geared to these have become widely available, even if not yet widely used, to support their implementation. On this new basis of open and standards-based sensing and communication technologies [4], smart homes are a favorite application domain for ambient intelligence and smart environments research. In spite of this, most existing home control solutions still require a fully manual initial configuration and programming, and will not self-reconfigure if the environment changes. The most easy-to-use solutions are still those that rely on using exclusively hardware from the same manufacturer. A unified and widely used framework to seamlessly integrate all physical entities of the home, *including legacy appliances and non-network-connected entities,* is still missing. Moreover, few applications involve fully automatic control without any human in the control loop. All this imposes an undue cognitive overload on home users which is certainly the main reason for the lack of mass-market take-up of home automation.

2.1   Characteristics of Home Environments

Each instance of home environment may at first sight appear to be one-of-a-kind, stocked with widely heterogeneous networks and hardware, including mostly legacy equipment. Fully customized configuration of a home automation system for each instance of home environment would not adapt as the environment is evolving permanently with major or minor configuration changes, and its cost would be too high for most users.

The surface variability of home environments hides; however, a few key shared characteristics and a deeper structural invariance on which we may rely. Basic types and categories of physical entities are roughly similar from one instance of home environment to another: this includes common types of appliances that can be found in every home like lamps, radiators, washing machines, etc. as well as types of rooms like bedrooms, kitchens and bathrooms. The uniqueness of each home instance lies in the particular choice and configuration of these appliances and rooms, most of which belong to well-known categories.

Both the non-custom-design requirement and the property of structural invariance from one instance to another distinguish home control applications fundamentally from industrial control, where fully custom design is the norm. Our proposed models of physical entities rely on shared basic types and structural invariances of home environments to support generic design.

2.2   Examples of Smart Home Control Scenarios

The example below shows a few common legacy appliances, state-of-the-art devices and one room as one among thousands of possible configurations resulting from a composition of physical entities (appliances and rooms) belonging to generic well-known categories. We assume that these entities are observable and controllable, either through networked sensors (shown separately) and actuators for what concerns legacy appliances and rooms, or directly through a network API for state-of-the-art equipment [5].

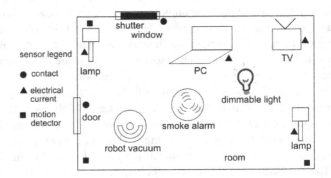

Fig. 1. Home instance example

Devices. A key distinction is made between the appliances that are the direct target of our proposed modeling and the most basic home devices, typically shared sensors and actuators connected to a home area network, which can play the role of network interfaces for legacy appliances and other non-networked entities such as rooms. These devices are considered to be stateless transducers and are not themselves the direct target of monitoring and control, they are used as intermediaries to monitor and control other entities. If we take the example of a passive infrared motion sensor, the infrared-radiating objects detected by the sensor, which may be all kinds of complex appliances as well as warm-blooded animals, are the "interesting" target of detection and monitoring whereas the sensor itself is but a dumb transducer. Other typical examples of such basic home sensor/actuator devices are water flow sensor, temperature sensor, electric switch, motorized water valve. They can be dedicated to one piece of equipment (e.g. a smart plug attached to the mains cord of an electrical appliance) but are most often shared to provide information about the behavior of several appliances (e.g. the home water meter providing clues about all appliances that use water in a home) or about the context (the ongoing activity in the room based on information of number of people, light intensity, noise, etc.). In the case of state-of-the-art appliances, they integrate the connectivity of devices together with a primary physical function that is the target of modeling proper.

Entities/subsystems. In this particular home instance, example relevant pieces of equipment considered as target-of-modeling subsystems are shown on Fig.1, together with a room that is itself also considered as a relevant subsystem in its own right, all called physical entities for short. PC, connected dimmable light-bulbs, robot vacuum cleaner, TV, smoke alarms are the entities with network connection which can update their functional states and receive commands directly through a network API ; others (lamp, motorized shutter and room) don't have a network connection of their own and can be monitored and controlled only through available networked sensors and actuators.

Control Objectives. We take as example a "home office" scenario where the following generic control objectives would apply:

- For safety, when there is someone in the room, there should be some light
- For energy efficiency, natural light is preferable to artificial light
- For productivity and comfort, when the person works
  - light should be bright
  - noise-making appliances (like robot vacuum, TV) should be deferred or delayed except for safety-related alarms
- For security and confidentiality, when the person begins a video conference, window blinds and doors to the home office should be closed to prevent interference from outside.

2.3   Corpus of Control Rules for Smart Home

We are interested in control applications whose control objectives expressed as rules similar to the ones above are specific to the home domain but are as much as possible generic to all home environment instances. We can see that the rules presented in this example are expressed in terms of generic categories or properties such as "light", "blind", "noise-making" that apply not only to particular instances of entities in this home environment instance, but also in most home instances which share the same generic entity categories. Using a shared infrastructure with self-configuration mechanisms that rely on these categories to identify entities [10], these rules should automatically apply in all instances of home environments without further customization. They make up a corpus of generic rules that constrain each other mutually. For example, one rule may require heating the room while another constrains the maximum instantaneous power. In the corpus, rules may be grouped into categories with different priorities, e.g. the category "safety" has higher priority than the category "energy efficiency" that has in turn higher priority than "comfort". These priorities are used to determine which rule overrides the other in a case where two rules imply contradictory actions on the same target. The contents of the corpus may be contributed by different home users in an incremental and participatory fashion, which implies that it should be open and accessible in a repository that can import and export rules in a standard format.

It should be noted that the type of discrete control we address here is fundamentally distinct from and complementary to both classical control and classical optimization based on multiple continuous variables. A comprehensive optimization application for home energy management such as proposed in [6], taking into account complex cost functions and multiple constraints on different time horizons would require a case-by-case design and manual parameter entry, by contrast to the minimal, lightweight, generic and self-configurable supervisory control we propose here.

2.4   Rule Execution Policy: Sequential vs. Parallel

The final results of the application of a set of rules depend on how they are executed within a concrete system implementation. In case of multiple rules triggered by a given transition, the execution policy may vary from parallel synchronous execution, which is widely applied in reactive systems [7], to sequential execution in some order (arbitrary from a declarative language or prescribed from an imperative language) which is commonly adopted in commercial business rule engines, such as open source Drools[1], and OpenRules[2].

More precisely, the "sequential execution of rules" we are speaking of here comprises two "sub-categories": implementations based on Rete algorithm and "sequential" ones. The main difference is that the former evaluates the rule conditions and selects the subset of rules which fulfill the conditions to execute (e.g. Drools), whereas the latter evaluates and executes rules one by one in a given order (e.g. OpenRules) so that the evaluation conditions of the next might no longer be satisfied because of the changes effected by the preceding rules. Each of these evaluation policies has its own advantages, so that efforts have been done in some implementations to bring features from their counterpart, like update() in Drools to make modification from a rule effective immediately after condition verification, or the "Rule Solver" component of OpenRules to better support declarative aspects in decision model.

Both policies still execute rules in a sequence and the resulting system behavior is not fully deterministic due to an arbitrary execution order chosen by the rules engine depending on system runtime context if all the rules are not placed in a total order of priority. Let's consider two rules appearing in the "home office" scenario:

---

[1] http://drools.jboss.org/
[2] http://www.openrules.com/

1. WHEN "videoconference[3]" THEN close window blinds and doors to keep privacy
2. WHEN "home office" THEN set bright light
3. WHEN bright light set THEN (open window blinds OR turn on lamp)

In the sequential condition evaluation policy, rules are executed from 1 to 3 with re-evaluation between each step. The consequence is obvious: deadlock between rule 1 and rule 3 as rule 3 doesn't take into account actions from rule 1 and prioritizes its first action "shutter opened". In the "evaluation once and fire all at the end" policy, a deadlock is also formed by 1 and 3 and the system reaches a different final state at the end of execution loop depending on the order in which the rules are executed as well as on the specific rule engine implementation whether an action should be completed before triggering the next.

In case of parallel synchronous execution, rules are examined together in a "compilation" step in order to obtain a deterministic behavior, corresponding to a stable state of the combined system *satisfying jointly all prescribed rules* inasmuch as they are compatible. If there is any conflict between rules, either a conflict resolution strategy is brought to bear, or the compilation phase will fail. If a "controller" is successfully compiled, it guarantees the examined rules to be executed and the system behavior is totally predictable with a final state that *provably* satisfies jointly the constraints dictated by all rules together. In the current example, the compiler will try out every possible state combination to find a stable system state where all the rules are respected, which is the state "shutter closed AND lamp on".

2.5   Discrete Control

In this paper, we show how discrete control can be used for Smart Environment applications through examples in the Smart Home domain. (Supervisory) discrete control consists of controlling automatically discrete event systems according to given control strategies, such as staying in a subset of states. The behaviors of entities are modeled by discrete-event finite-state machines (FSM) described with a synchronous programming language. Transitions from source state to target state are labeled with discrete-event firing condition c and an action a (c/a in following diagrams). Fig. 2a illustrates this with a reactive node for the control behavior of a delayable task. It can be idle, waiting or active. When it is in the initial idle state, the occurrence of the true value on input "r" requests the starting of the task. Another input "c" can either allow the activation, or temporarily block the request and make the automaton go to a waiting state. Input "e" notifies termination. The outputs represent, resp., "a": activity of the task, and "s": starting operation in the system's API. Such automata and data-flow reactive nodes can be reused by instantiation, and composed in parallel (noted in the concrete syntax ";") and in a hierarchical way, as illustrated in the body of the node in Fig. 2b, with two instances of the delayable node running in parallel.

---

[3] "videoconference" is a sub-state of "home office" , so that all rules that apply to the latter apply to the former.

A high level programming language [8] is available to describe the automata used by the Discrete Controller Synthesis (DCS), a formal operation on automata [3], within its compilation. The DCS method consists of partitioning variables into controllable and uncontrollable ones. For a given objective, DCS theory [9] automatically computes, by exploration of the state space, the constraint on controllable variables, so that the behavior satisfies the objective, whatever the values of the uncontrollable ones. The controller is maximally permissive, keeping all correct behaviors when more than one are possible, which gives the controlled system more flexibility. All example models in following sections use the notation described above with labeled (c/a) state transitions (a omitted if no action); even if all of them are not directly used for DCS.

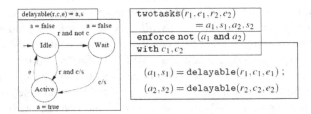

Fig. 2. (a) Delayable task ; (b) exclusion contract

3   Modeling Framework

We propose a modeling framework for smart environments, based on the example of smart homes, yet extensible to smart buildings, cities and other environments with similar characteristics. General models and their relationships are maintained in the framework, and are eventually enriched by drawing upon external ontologies and knowledge. System and subsystem models are designed with an orientation to control applications.

3.1   Generic Models for Home Entities

Discrete-event finite-state machines can be used as generic "modal" models for these, making it possible to identify them as an instance of parametric system identification problem through available sensors and actuators playing the role of network interface. Instead of attempting to provide an exact and comprehensive model for every existent entity (as would be done for state of the art devices in a Service Oriented Architecture such as UPnP, or for peripherals in a computer OS), only some of its most basic and essential properties are captured in a generic model. All equipment and space entities can thus be fully identified by the most approximate generic automata which may serve as their dynamic proxies for a large set of applications and services [10].

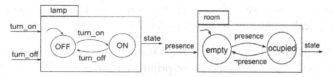

Fig. 3. Entity model of a) lamp; b) basic room

In the home instance example, (traditional) lamps are modeled by an automaton with 2 basic states "off"/"on" (Fig.3a). These states, also relevant for most electrical and ICT appliances, are observable and controllable through either a networked smart plug for mains-connected appliances, or a direct network interface if available. The room is also modeled through states corresponding to different activities, such as "empty"/"occupied" (Fig.3b). These states are non-controllable, yet observable through an aggregation and consolidation of data from multiple sensors, external data sources that can provide useful context information like weather, or eventually states of other entities/subsystems, e.g. the activation of VPN application on PC indicates that the room is in "home office" state (not shown in the basic model).

These generic models for home entities will be used as the "common denominator model" for the leaf categories in the structure described in the following sub section.

3.2   Generic Categories of Home Entities (Virtual Entities)

The most basic categories of entities are the "well-known" generic categories of appliances and rooms already mentioned, which are supposed to be drawn from a domain ontology. Another way to categorize these entities highly relevant to the purpose of their representation in a generic infrastructure is by properties that may cut across primary categories. Fig. 4 shows the ontology for the current home example environment, where the property "light emitting" category is linked not only the category "lamp" whose primary function is to emit light, but also, less obviously, to all categories of appliances which emit light by a side effect of their primary function, like TV and windows for natural light during daytime. Like taxonomic categories which have intermediate levels, properties also have intermediate levels representing finer categories to meet the demand of general control objectives, i.e. subdivision of "noise emitting" allow treating separately "alarm" and "non-crucial" for safety concern.

The categorization of entities according to such generic features is structured as a directed acyclic graph (DAG) which is a representation of a domain-specific ontology supposed to be known a priori. Virtual entities refer to the nodes in the DAG and each of them also has a common denominator finite-state model of its own which is meant to be as generic as possible for its characteristic features, so that it may be used both as intermediary abstraction of entities and provide a universal control interface similar to "interface" or parent class in object-oriented modeling, and as template to identify entities automatically through sensors and other entities that are in relationship with them. According to the received interpretation of a DAG, descendant d (closer to the leaf nodes) inherits properties from or "traits"/interfaces their ancestors a (closer to the root nodes) following an upward path of "d *Is_a* a" or "d *has property* a" /"d *has side effect* a" relationships. (Fig. 4, where "*has subclass*" is the inverse of "*Is_a*").

Advantages of such a way of structuring generic (concrete or abstract) characteristics of the physical world from an ontology are the following:

1. This DAG can easily be stored in a graph database to provide index-free adjacency and direct responses to all graph-based primitive queries.
2. It is possible to automatically attribute features to concretely existing object types by traversing the graph, compared to the more classical and commonly practiced methods which consist of tagging everything manually.
3. By contrast to the manual construction of functional groups by declaration in a static configuration file like in openHAB[4] which is a tedious procedure when the number of entities to be grouped increases, groups can be automatically created according to the nodes in the ontology. By doing so, a type of entity with multiple physical aspects may be included in different groups which are managed independently by different services. Dynamic changes of group members during runtime are also made possible by the dynamic nature of the group assignment procedure.

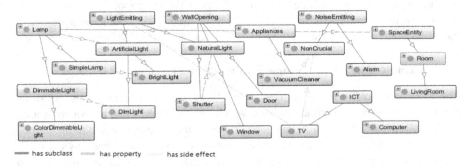

Fig. 4. Ontology/taxonomy graph for the home instance (graph made with protégé[5])

3.3   Establishing Hierarchical Relationship Between Virtual Entity Models

In order to always use the most generic relevant FSM model for monitoring and control of entity instances inheriting the states of such a model, the states should be carefully mapped between ancestor and descendant models in the DAG in order to keep every operation on one abstraction level valid on the other level as well. Hierarchical model pairs map their states according to the physical meaning presented by the state. For example, by common knowledge we know that a lamp emits light when it consumes electricity, thus a link is established to connect "lighting" in the model of "light-emitting" and "on" in "lamp" (Fig.5 on the right). The mapping is directly declared by the state in the descendant model, and is considered as one part of the following state machine ontology illustrated in Fig.5 on the left, based on the ontology proposed in [11], with the predicate *hasMappedState* declaring its corresponding state in one of its ancestors.

---

[4] http://www.openhab.org/, taking Drools as its rule engine.
[5] http://protege.stanford.edu/

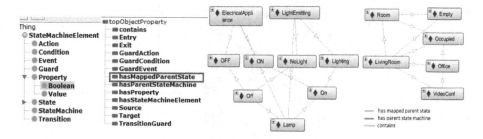

Fig. 5. FSM ontology and hierarchical state mapping

The states between the already known ancestor/descendant models should be mapped in such a way that state transition in the descendant model would never go out of the state space of the ancestor, and every state of the ancestor model can always find its corresponding state in any of its descendants. This assumption is made to keep our modeling framework generic and consistent instantaneously. A specific model lower down in the DAG should always be subsumable by one of its more generic ancestors for monitoring or control purposes. While it works as a specific modeled entity and goes to a state out of the state space of its ancestor model which is one of the subjects of a general control objective, the underlined control objective has no possibility to be accomplished as this entity is in an unknown state to it. To avoid such control failure due to inconsistency in state mapping, a strong hypothesis of descendant staying in ancestor's state space is necessary.

This mapping procedure is done manually for every parent/child pair and is just one method among the others which are valid as long as they satisfy the above assumption, without the need of knowledge of the method's details.

The principle of the proposed method is to consider ancestor/descendant models as hierarchical state machines where every state in a descendant model is a nested substate of a higher level state in its ancestor. The substate inherits the entire behavior (actions and property value) of its superstate as in the semantics of the synchronous language used for description [8]. If a state S_n of a hierarchical sub-automaton which is nested in the superstate S_s is active, both S_n and S_s are considered active, thus the result behavior of S_n to an outside observer is as if S_n has it specialized behavior plus all the behavior of its superstate S_s. This "behavioral inheritance" [12] in hierarchical state machines is very similar to the concept of "inheritance" in Object-Oriented programming (OOP). Taking again the example of "simple lamp" which is descendant of "bright light" and "electrical appliance". As declared explicitly in the model of "simple lamp", simpleLamp.on *hasMappedState* {brightLight.lighting, electrical-appliance.on} and simpleLamp.off *hasMappedState* {brightLight.no-light, electrical-appliance.off}, simpleLamp.on inherits automatically the value "lighing=true" from brightLight.lighting and "elec=true" from electrical-appliance.on, and simpleLamp.off inherits the value "lighing=false" from brightLight.no-light and "elec=false" from electrical-appliance.off. As result, simpleLamp.on has 2 inherited values from parent states as illustrated in Fig.6.

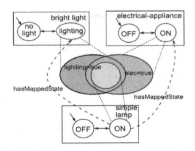

Fig. 6. Property inheritance from mapped parent state(s)

4   Smart Home System Representation

The representation of a particular home instance as a complete system captures and maintains direct, instantiated informational representations of entities from the physical environment based on data from the devices, drawing upon generic models from the modeling framework to provide a shared interface of the physical world to all smart home applications. The middle part of Fig. 7 details the system's architecture of 4 layers (remote applications excluded), always based on the example of the home instance.

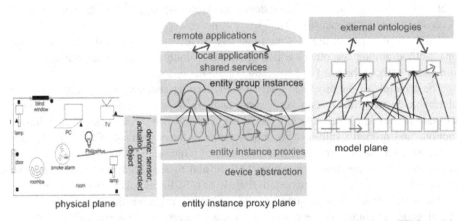

Fig. 7. Software representation of the smart home environment based on generic FSM models (model plane) instantiated in the instance proxy plane through different layers of abstraction

4.1   Device Abstraction Layer

The device abstraction layer is intended to hide different communication protocols and formats of data provided by various networked devices, in order to offer the upper level entity abstraction layer a unified data format. Several solutions are already available for this, such as openHAB[5], Prosyst HDM[6], which provide access to a range

---

[6] http://dz.prosyst.com/devzone/SmartHome

of devices. A common denominator REST interface is added on top of the above protocol adapters to provide a universal and uniform interface.

4.2   Entity Abstraction Layer

This layer provides a one to one mapping between physical entities and a set of proxies that maintain their states by instantiating corresponding models from the *model plane*. An entity proxy maps directly to a corresponding node in the model plane that provides a "modal" model/template, just as an object maps to a class in object-oriented software modeling. It provides an interface both to relevant devices to get actual sensor readings or forward control orders to actuators, and to higher layers of the infrastructures to provide information about current state and relevant variable values. Several instances of the same FSM can co-exist.

In this layer, entity instance proxies may have direct relationships other than hierarchical relationships mapped from their corresponding categories in the model plane. Examples are the relationship "located in" that links a lamp proxy and a room proxy if the lamp is in the room, or the relationship "owned by" that links several object proxies and a person if the objects belong to the person. These relationships are contingent on the configuration of the current environment instance and are distinguished as "instance relationships" from the generic environment-independent relationships mapped from the ontology DAG. Entity instance proxies together with the instance relationships connecting them make up a "graph of instances" that is maintained in the infrastructure and ready to be exposed to queries from applications and upper layers of the infrastructure.

4.3   Entity Group Layer

While virtual entities (described in section 3.2) are a categorization of identified physical entities by a specific type or by an intrinsic property and have a common denominator behavior model for each individual entity included in the category, entity group model represents the collective behavior of all the entities modeled by the identical common denominator model since the original purpose of the classification is to manage a set of entities together instead of the individuals. Thus they involve the composition of several identical individual entity models.

Entity group models are the ones provided to the upper level services as the system's behavior model, especially to the synthesized controller service. The advantages of managing entities by way of such groups are especially:

- Flexibility in configuration changes. The entity group hides completely the individual entities from upper level services or applications so that any change in the entity proxy layer, for example a new extra radiator added in the room during winter, is transparent for them. Only an update of mapping between present entity instances and their respective group is needed to get the correct input value for the entity group and transmit the output value to a valid entity instance instead of redesign or re-compilation of services.

- Reduction of state space for DCS to explore. Even the parallel composition of the most simple 2-state models would lead to a combinatorial explosion of the joint state space when the number of automata increases, a model representing the meaningful states after the parallel composition is one solution to reduce the state space that the DCS should deal with (e.g. with 3 2-state automata, $2^3 = 8$ states using classical DCS method vs. 3 states using the entity group model).

Examples will be given in the next section.

4.4   Services Layer

This layer hosts services and other applications that are tightly coupled to the infrastructure, need more knowledge of the semantics of entity models and may also mandate bounded latency constraints between system responses and actions. They can read all information from output of state model instances and perform actuation directly on the available inputs of the state models. Examples of services and applications in this layer are local light control (quick reaction to turn on light when presence is detected arrives), real-time electrical load shedding control from detection of overload.

This layer does also provide north bound interface to remote loosely-coupled applications which have less strict timing constraints and may be content with a "best-effort" REST interface through a wide-area network.

5   Discrete Control through the Proposed Infrastructure

5.1   Control-Oriented Entity Group Models

Entity group models can be dedicated to one purpose of use and one virtual entity (VE), and one VE could have more than one instantiated entity group with different models. For example, both on a group of radiators, an instance of entity group model containing a state *some radiator in frost protection mode* would be interesting for a safety control scenario (preventing frost danger in pipes), but totally insignificant for a comfort control scenario whose goal is to maintain the temperature at 24 degree. If in an environment instance, the above safety and comfort objectives coexist, each of them uses the entity group instance with its own corresponding model, thus 2 different entity group instances exist which are associated to the same VE. By contrast to the entity instance proxies which have a 1-to-1 mapping to physical entity, an entity group can be considered as an abstracted view of a set of entity instance proxies. Thus different "views" may be taken from different control objectives.

Group models are not provided directly by the model plane. Absent any more specific model, a very generic basic template is provided by the framework as a modeling tool, like representing groups of entities with 2 states (on/off) models through a 3-state (all off, all on, some on & some off) model.

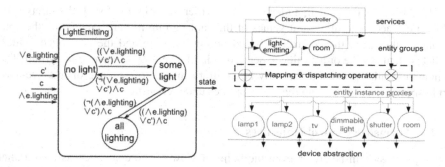

Fig. 8. a) Entity group model of "light-emitting" using template; b) Example of inter-layer data flow

An example is the group model of category "light-emitting", called in the first control objective, based on the 2-state VE model "no-light"/"lighting" which may model all present lamp entities, display entities (e.g. TV, screen) according to the ontology graph. The default group entity model is shown in Fig.8a, with 3 states "no light"/"some lighting"/"all lighting", taking as input the logic "OR" and "AND" operation of the states of all present "light-emitting" models and outputs the actual collective state that the entities are or should be in. The transitions are controllable which may be inhibited or enforced by 2 Boolean variables placed on transition labels (c and c').

Due to place limitation, other entity models involved in the scenario are presented in a simplified way. They are similar to the "lightEmitting" group by using the generic template.

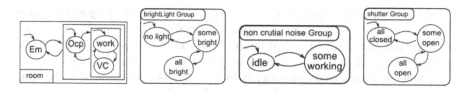

Fig. 9. Entity group models (simplified, only states are presented)

Data flow between entity groups and entity proxies is maintained by a mechanism we call "MDO" (Mapping & Dispatching Operator) to keep the input/output mapping of individual entity proxies and their corresponding group(s) updated. It does necessary operations on upwards data (e.g. logic "OR" or "AND" operation) specified by the entity group models and provide the final value to the controllers. The upwards information transmission is quite straight forward as long as the membership of a group and the operation to apply on input values are specified, whereas the downwards control order transmission is not always obvious and even complex.

Fig.8b shows the principle idea of control order transmission for r1, the safety rule. MDO has access to all output values of the entity group instance, including the controlled value from the controller. Based on current state and the controlled values, MDO calculates the order value to send to individual entity instance of the group. The choice of entity proxies to act may be arbitrary in case of absence of instance-and-rule-specific priority among the entity proxies under control.

5.2   Formalize Control Objectives

The global system behavior from the point of view of the controllers is the parallel composition of the relevant entity group models and necessary observer models. The control objectives invoked in the example home instance are formalized as Boolean expressions as follows:

- r1: ¬ (room.occupied ∧ lightEmitting.no_light) (safety)
- r2: ¬ (room.work ∧ brightLight.no_light) (productivity)
- r3: ¬ (room.work ∧ nonCrucial.working) (productivity)
- r4: ¬ (room.videoConf ∧ shutter.open) (security)

In which the control target objects are nodes presented in Fig.4 with models in Fig 9.

To be as modular as possible, one controller corresponds to one scenario in order to give user the possibility to combine scenarios they need. DCS generates the controller guarantees that the system will remain invariantly inside the subset of its global states according to the 4 rules at the entity group level.

6   Simulation

A first validation of the functional architecture together with the proposed modeling framework has been performed on the basis of a simulation environment: entity proxies are created manually and context information or events are sent to them either by reading a configuration file or manually via the system's web interface. The Java code of the controllers generated automatically by the DCS tool is associated to the upper interface of the entity group layer. The observation of the system is made on the current state of each FSM entity proxy as well as its other possible output values.

We have developed MiLeSEnS (**M**ulti **L**evel **S**mart **En**vironment **S**imulator) as a testing ground based on Siafu, an open-source context simulator written in Java [13], which provides a GUI and basic and simple physical models such as moving people and physical areas (Fig.10). These are toy models with no pretense of physical plausibility, yet they may provide enough environmental elements and interactions between actuators and sensors to validate key properties of the models and controllers. The implemented infrastructure runs on top of the simulator which provides simulated sensor readings and takes actuator signals on the runtime. Adaptation to configuration changes during runtime can also be validated by the simulator: a newly identified vacuum cleaner at its very first usage is taken into consideration by the controller which stays unchanged; one lighting appliance (TV screen included) is lit up by the system if there is no light in the occupied room, for which the choice of appliance is either arbitrary or prescribed by the newly modified configuration. Unlike the environment without control where undesired behaviors of simulated entities are observed, the controlled one respect all the rules even when the configuration changes.

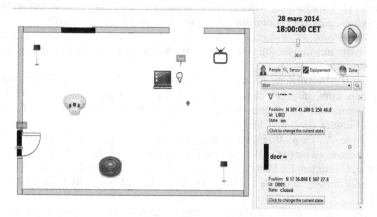

Fig. 10. Initial configuration of the simulation in MiLeSEnS

7   Conclusion and Perspectives

We have introduced a smart environment/IoT mediation infrastructure based on a discrete-event control-oriented modeling framework, in which physical entities are modeled by generic FSM models, to be regrouped by similar properties that are significant for either monitoring, context-awareness or control objectives. DCS is performed on the basis of these groupings to derive controllers corresponding to rules drawn from a generic corpus.

Validation in a mixed environment (combining simulation with pieces of real hardware equipment) is now under development. Further work includes the automatic management of potential conflicts between rules applying to the same entities and the application in an actual Smart Home environment including both legacy equipment and state-of-the-art ICT devices together with the new breed of non-ICT connected devices. Generalization and validation of these ideas in other smart environments and IoT application domains will be studied first in smart cities with a sharing of a similar infrastructure between applications that have remained so far completely isolated and did not share any piece of their respective infrastructures. Real-time requirements are more critical that in the home domain and justify further the adoption and extension to non-custom designed and platform-based systems of approaches inherited from the design of reactive systems such as have always been used for the (fully custom) design of e.g. transportation safety systems.

References

1. Streitz, N., Privat, G.: Ambient Intelligence. In: Stephanidis, C. (ed.) The Universal Access Handbook, pp. 60.1–60.17. CRC Press, Taylor & Francis Group (2009)
2. Halbwachs, N.: Synchronous Programming of Reactive Systems, vol. 215. Springer (1992)
3. Cassandras, C.G., Lafortune, S.: Introduction to Discrete Event Systems. Springer (2008)
4. Gomez, C., Paradells, J.: Wireless home automation networks: A survey of architectures and technologies. IEEE Communications Magazine 48(6), 92–101 (2010)
5. Zhao, M., Privat, G., Rutten, E., Alla, H.: Discrete control for the internet of things and smart environments. In: 8th International Workshop on Feedback Computing. USENIX, Berkeley, CA (2013)
6. Joumaa, H., De-Oliviera, G., Ploix, S., Jacomino, M.: Energy management problem in dwellings: combining centralized and distributed solving approaches. In: 2012 3rd IEEE PES International Conference and Exhibition on Innovative Smart Grid Technologies (ISGT Europe), pp. 1–8. IEEE (2012)
7. Benveniste, A., Caspi, P., Edwards, S.A., Halbwachs, N., Le Guernic, P., De Simone, R.: The synchronous languages 12 years later. Proceedings of the IEEE 91(1), 64–83 (2003)
8. Delaval, G., Rutten, E., Marchand, H.: Integrating discrete controller synthesis into a reactive programming language compiler. Discrete Event Dynamic Systems 23(4), 385–418 (2013)
9. Ramadge, P.J., Wonham, W.M.: The control of discrete event systems. Proceedings of the IEEE 77(1), 81–98 (1989)
10. Hu, Z., Privat, G., Frenot, S., Tourancheau, B.: Self-configuration of home abstraction layer via sensor-actuator network. In: Keyson, D.V., Maher, M.L., Streitz, N., Cheok, A., Augusto, J.C., Wichert, R., Englebienne, G., Aghajan, H., Kröse, B.J. (eds.) AmI 2011. LNCS, vol. 7040, pp. 146–150. Springer, Heidelberg (2011)
11. Dolog, P.: Model-driven navigation design for semantic web applications with the uml-guide. In: ICWE Workshops, pp. 75–86 (2004)
12. Samek, M., Montgomery, P.Y.: State oriented programming. Embedded Systems Programming 13(8), 22–43 (2000)
13. Martin, M., Nurmi, P.: A generic large scale simulator for ubiquitous computing. In: MobiQuitous 2006. IEEE Computer Society, San Jose, California, USA (July 2006)

Learning and Recognizing Routines and Activities in SOFiA

Berardina De Carolis, Stefano Ferilli, and Giulio Mallardi

Dipartimento di Informatica, Università di Bari, Bari, Italy
{berardinadecarolis,stefanoferilli}@uniba.it,
giuliomallardi@gmail.com

Abstract. In order to promote an effective and personalized interaction, smart environments should be endowed with the capability of understanding what the user is doing. To this aim we developed a system called WoMan that, using a process mining approach, is able to incrementally learn user's activities and daily routines as workflow models. In order to test its efficacy in a real-world setting, we set up a smart office environment, SOFiA, equipped with a sensor network based on Arduino. Then we collected an annotated dataset of 45 days and from this dataset we learned the workflow models of the user daily routines and of the activities performed in the office. Then we performed some experiments that show how our approach perform in learning and recognizing activities and routines. In particular, we achieve in average the accuracy of 82% for tasks and the accuracy of 98% for the transitions among tasks. Moreover we test the real-time performance of the approach with sensor data coming from the SOFiA sensors and the system started to make a correct prediction since the fourth execution in 82% of the cases.

1   Introduction

As other types of smart environments, smart offices aim at supporting workers during their daily activities so as to support the automatization of their tasks in a non intrusive way. According to [1], compared to a generic smart environment, a smart office is characterized by several factors that may simplify this task. For instance, office work is often highly automatizable and strictly connected to the use of devices and specific tools, offices may be used for several purposes (i.e. meeting, discussion with colleagues, etc.) and therefore adapting the kind of support to the recognized activity is important. Moreover during work the use of sensing technology is considered less intrusive and undermines less the users' privacy since, very often, these environments are already video controlled or accessible to the pubic. These considerations lead us to think that applying ambient intelligence solutions in a office is more acceptable by users than in other environments such as smart homes, etc..

In order to provide adaptive support to office work, successful recognition of human activities in the office is crucial for a number of applications such as, surveillance, context-aware reminder, service recommendations, etc. Enabling the environment to learn the user's most common behaviors becomes an important step towards

© Springer International Publishing Switzerland 2014
E. Aarts et al. (Eds.): AmI 2014, LNCS 8850, pp. 191–204, 2014.
DOI: 10.1007/978-3-319-14112-1_16

this objective. In particular, modeling the user's daily routines can be used not only for predicting his/her needs but also for comparing the actual situation with the expected one in order to detect anomalies in his/her behavior. While manually setting up process models in business and factory environments may be cost-effective, building models of the user processes is infeasible. Hence the interest in automatically learning them from examples of actual behavior is fully justified.

Research in automatic recognition of human activities in smart environments has explored two main approaches that can be also combined. The first approach is based on the monitoring and analyzing visual information, such as images and surveillance videos, as means to recognize activities. Recent research has moved towards the use of multiple sensors embedded in the environment. These sensors are used to acquire the data required for the process of activity recognition.

Following the latter approach we developed the SOFiA (Smart OFfice with Arduino) project that aims at supporting office workers in their daily activities through the user of a network of Arduino [2] sensors and actuators. Starting from sensors data we learn two-level models of the user behavior in the office. At the higher level we learn the model of daily routines of the user and at the lower level we learn the model to recognize single activities (i.e. reading, sitting, looking for books, …). In doing so, we exploits the WoMan (acronym for 'Workflow Management') system to incrementally learn and refine users routines represented in First-Order Logic (FOL) and the WoGue ("Workflow Guesser") system to recognized the current routine or activity for the learned models [3].

In this paper, after providing a brief overview on the related work in Section 2, a brief description of the representation formalism on which our proposal is based and of the WoMan algorithm are described in Section 3. Then, in Section 4, we show how the approach has been exploited in the context of SOFiA, and, to this aim, we presents some evaluation experiments that show the effectiveness of the proposed approach. Lastly, Section 6 concludes the paper and outlines future work directions.

2   Related Work

Several examples of application of Ambient Intelligence to Smart Offices can be found in the literature [1]. In [4] smart offices are defined as environments that are able to adapt to the user needs, release the users from routine tasks they should perform, to change the environment to suit to their preferences and to access services available at each moment by customized interfaces. To this aim reasoning on the user's behavior is a crucial task in order to support the user effectively in her work [20].

Understanding what the user is doing in a smart environment can be performed at two different levels of abstraction. At the lower level it is important to understand what the user is doing, which specific activity is doing in the environment, then, at a higher level what is the workflow of these activities during the day, the user routine.

As far as activity recognition is concerned, there are two main approaches: vision-based and sensor-based activity recognition. Vision-based approaches monitor the user's behavior in the environment analyzing and extracting knowledge by camera-based facilities present in the environment (i.e. surveillance systems) (for instance [5]). Besides the complexity of detecting and recognizing activities from video in real world settings, since this approach uses camera to record what people does in the environment, it is perceived invasive and as violating the user's privacy. These reasons moved research efforts towards the use of multiple miniature dense sensors embedded within environments. Sensor data are collected and are usually analyzed using data mining and machine learning techniques to build activity models and perform further the recognition of the activity correctly performed in the environment. In this approach, sensors can be attached to either an actor under observation or objects that constitute the environment. Sensors attached to humans, i.e., wearable sensors often use inertial measurement units (e.g. accelerometers, gyroscopes, magnetometers), vital sign processing devices (heart rate, temperature) and RFID tags to gather an actor's behavioral information [6,7].

As far as learning and using models of daily routines and activities there are different approaches that can be followed. These are mainly based on Data Mining and Machine Learning techniques. Since an analogy can be drawn between tasks/activities and patterns (intended as relevant configurations of sensor-based events) [8], pattern mining methods can be used to identify the configurations of sensor events that are typically associated to the occurrence of an activity. Among the Machine Learning techniques, HMM [9], CRF [10] and SCCRF [11] are the most widely used. HMM-based approaches are more suitable for representing sequential activities from a stream of sensor events. Since HMMs and CRF cannot model concurrency, some variants, such as Coupled HMMs, SCCRFs, have been proposed to handle parallel activities. However these approaches are computationally expensive and require a large amount of training data. Another shortcoming of these approaches is that they cannot integrate common-sense background knowledge, that is important in any activity recognition system, nor can they provide human-readable models. This can be overcome by approaches that use logical formalisms for representing activity recognition models [12]. For instance, Riboni and Bettini [13] adopted a knowledge-based perspective, using ontological reasoning. In particular, they use the enhanced expressiveness of OWL-2 to model and reason about complex human activities. Recently, Helaoui et al. [14] combined the data-driven and knowledge-based approaches, using probabilistic ontological reasoning to deal with the variability of complex activities. Aztiria et al. [15] proposed a layered approach in order to first identify frequent sequences of actions using the Apriori algorithm and then, using a process mining approach based on the work in [16], learn the topology of frequent actions as workflow.

In our approach we exploits process mining in order to start from the activities performed by some agent to carry out a given process and to identify the valid patterns of activities that support that process [21]. Using more technical terminology, process mining aims at inferring workflow models from examples of cases. Workflows are established formalisms that have been used in AmI contexts for modeling the user's daily routines in order to endow the environment with the capability of recognizing users' needs and responding with situation-aware services [17].

According to these considerations, the WoMan system was proposed, that was shown to be able to learn efficiently complex workflow models that are able to deal with concurrent activities and with noise [18,19]. Moreover, the learned model are complete, irredundancy and minimality (it is as simple and compact as possible). For these reasons, we adopted it in this work.

3   A Brief Overview on the WoMan System

At a higher level of abstraction learning the habits of the user by building models of his daily routines in order to both make prevision of the next possible user's actions and detect the conformity of the user behavior is important especially in the assisted living, lifelogging and smart diaries application contexts. At a lower level of abstraction, it is important as well to learn frequent pattern sensor data configuration that denote a particular activity. In order to perform these two tasks we employ the WoMan system and therefore we learn models represented as workflows [18,19].

In our approach, a process is a sequence of events associated to actions performed by agents [6]. A workflow is a (formal) specification of how a set of tasks can be composed to result in valid processes, including sequential, parallel, conditional, or iterative execution [20]. Each task may have preconditions (that should hold before it is executed) and postconditions (that should hold after execution of the task). An activity is the actual execution of a task. A case is a particular execution of actions in a specific order compliant to a given workow, along an ordered set of steps (time points) [14]. WoMan can be considered as a Declarative Process Mining system, since it adopts FOL representations. FOL provides great expressiveness, useful to handle complex domains in which variable numbers of objects are involved, and several interplays among them can take place. It also provides a single unifying framework in which case descriptions, process models, and conditions on activities may be expressed and brought to cooperation both for learning and for enactment purposes.

In order to understand the examples in this paper, we provide here a short description of the employed formalism.

In WoMan, a trace element is represented as a 6-tuple **(T,E,W,P,A,O)** where **T** is the time/date the event occurred, **E** is the type of the event (begin of process, end of process, begin of activity, end of activity), **W** is the name of the workflow the process refers to, **P** is a unique identifier for each process execution, **A** is the name of the activity, and **O** is the progressive number of occurrence of A in P. This is a standard formalism that allows describing explicitly the flow of activities (both sequential and parallel). An example is provided in the following:

```
entry(20121001073047,begin_of_process, monday,rl1,none,none).
entry(20121001073049,begin_of_activity,monday,rl1,act_ComputerWork,1).
entry(20121001073523,end_of_activity,monday,rl1,act_ComputerWork,1).
entry(20121001080940,begin_of_activity,monday,rl1,act_Coffe,1).
entry(20121001083002,end_of_activity,monday,rl1,act_Coffe,1).
entry(20121001093028,begin_of_activity,monday,rl1,act_Students,1).
entry(20121001093028,begin_of_activity,monday,rl1,act_Telephone,1).
entry(20121001150033,end_of_activity,monday,rl1,act_Telephone,1).
entry(20121001150033,end_of_activity,monday,rl1,act_Students,1).
entry(20121001150036,begin_of_activity,monday,rl1,act_Lecture,1).
entry(20121001153007,end_of_activity,monday,rl1,act_Lecture,1).
...
entry(20121002073524,end_of_process,monday,rl1,none,none).
```

As context and activities are detected or entered by the user, the corresponding entries are provided to the WoMan system that, applying the algorithm described in [18], learns activities and relations among them. The task flow of a case is internally expressed in WoMan as a conjunction of ground atoms built on the following predicates:

- **activity(S,T)** : at step S task T is executed
- **next(S',S'')** : step S'' follows step S'

Argument T of the *activity/2* predicate is taken from a (fixed and context-dependent) set of constants representing the allowed tasks. Steps are denoted by unique identifiers, they are associated to events and can be implemented as timestamps denoting the associated events. The *next/2* predicate allows to explicit represent parallel executions in the task flow. This avoids the need to infer/guess the parallelism by means of statistical considerations, which may of course be wrong and thus mislead the workflow learning process. Any trace represented in the 6-tuple format previously introduced can be automatically translated into this internal format. For instance, the previous sample trace for the 'monday' would be expressed as:

For instance, the previous sample trace for the 'monday' workflow/routine would be expressed as:

activity(s0,act_ComputerWork),   next(s0,s1),   activity(s1,act_Coffee), next(s0,s2) activity(s2, Lecture), next(s1,s3), activity(s3, act_Students), next(s3,s4), activity(s4,act_Telephone), ...

The first activity ('ComputerWork') is associated to step s0. Activity 'Coffee' is associated to step s1, and has a 'next' relationship to 'ComputerWork' as the (only) most recently closed activity and so on.

Workflow structure is described as a conjunction of atoms built on the following predicates:

- **task(t,C)** : task t occurs in cases C;
- **transition(I,O,p,C)** : transition p, that occurs in cases C, consists in ending all tasks in I (that must be running), and starting the execution of new instances of all tasks in O.

Argument C represents a history of those tasks/transitions, and thus can be exploited for computing statistics on their use.

WoMan may run in 3 modes. The *learning* mode allows learning a process model from logs of activities. The *supervision* mode allows applying a learned model to new cases of the process in order to check that they are compliant with the model. The *prediction* mode allows applying a learned model to new cases of the process in order to foresee the most likely subsequent activities that the user will perform at a given moment of the execution.

Models are built by the WoMan system according to the procedure reported in Algorithm 1.

The described approach is fully incremental: it can start with an empty model and learn from one case (while others need a large set of cases to draw significant statistics), and can refine an existing model according to new cases whenever they become available (introducing alternative routes, even adding new tasks if they were never seen in previous cases, and updating the statistics). This peculiarity is an advance to the state-of-the-art, because continuous adaptation of the learned model to the actual practice can be carried out efficiently, effectively and transparently to the users.

Algorithm 1 Refinement of a workflow model according to a new case

---

Require: $\mathcal{W}$: workflow model
Require: c: case having FOL description D
  for all activity$(s,t) \in c$ **do**
    if $\exists$ task$(t,C) \in \mathcal{W}$ **then**
      $\mathcal{W} \leftarrow (\mathcal{W} \setminus$ task$(t,C)) \cup \{$ task$(t,C \cup \{c\})$ $\}$ /* update statistics on task t */
    else
      $\mathcal{W} \leftarrow \mathcal{W} \cup \{$ task$(t,\{c\})) \}$ /* insert new task and initialize statistics */
    end if
    refine_precondition$(\mathcal{W}, t(s)$:- $D|_s)$
    refine_postcondition$(\mathcal{W}, t(s)$:- $D)$
  end for
  for all next$(s',s'') \in c$ **do**
    $I \leftarrow \{t'|$ activity$(s',t') \in c\}$
    $O \leftarrow \{t''|$ activity$(s',t'') \in c\}$
    if $\exists$ transition$(I,O,p,C) \in \mathcal{W}$ **then**
      $\mathcal{W} \leftarrow (\mathcal{W} \setminus$ transition$(I,O,t,C)) \cup \{$ transition$(I,O,t,C \cup \{c\})$ $\}$
      /* update statistics on transition p */
    else
      $p \leftarrow$ generate_fresh_transition_identifier()
      $\mathcal{W} \leftarrow \mathcal{W} \cup \{$ transition$(I,O,p,\{c\})) \}$
      /* insert new transition and initialize statistics */
    end if
  end for

A graphical representation of a portion of the learned model for the Monday workflow is shown in Figure 1.

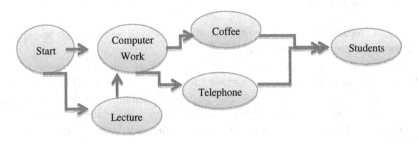

Fig. 1. An example of the graphical representation of learned workflow

In order to endow the smart office with the capability to recognize at runtime activities and daily routine patterns, we developed a simple algorithm in Prolog called WoGue (Workflow GUEsser) that uses the WoMan system in a supervision mode and assess how much the current user's behavior is compliant with a model learned previously.

For each data coming from sensors WoGue will return the names of the workflow models that are compliant with the pattern of activated sensors, then each workflow in the list will be dynamically ranked on the basis of the WoMan answer (OK/Error). At each step the active workflows will be reordered on the basis of their compliance ranking returning a confidence level that will be used to determine the most probable activity. The same approach is applied for determining the compliance of the current routine to the learned models.

4   Evaluation of the Approach in SOFiA

We evaluated the described approach in the context of SOFiA.

SOFiA (Smart OFfice with Arduino) is the name of the project and of the smart office. It uses a network of sensors and actuators with the aim of gathering a annotated dataset of routines and activities in a smart office, learning models starting from the collected dataset and evaluate the performance of the approach described previously in recognizing the routines and activities that happen in the office. The hardware used to set up the sensor network of SOFiA is based Arduino since it offers a wide variety of cheap sensors, it is easy to program and it is well supported by an active community of developers.

An outline of the sensor and actuator network developed in the context of the SOFiA project is shown in Figure 2.

In particular, in the office that was employed for the experiment we used motion, brightness, light and temperature sensors in the room and pressure sensors on the chairs. Moreover the main chair in the office, the one usually used by the user, has got two sensors: one on the sitting and one on the seatback in order to get also information about the back position (i.e. relax vs. attentive).

There are other touch sensors on the desks in order to get information about activities, such as writing on paper that usually happens on the desk. The other desk, the one aside on which the user usually put the computer in order to work, has been endowed with a wrist-resting pillow containing two touch sensors. These sensors give information about the use of computer during the office work (at present we are not interesting at monitoring which application the user is using on the computer). There are also sensors on the closet containing books and teaching material. In order to get information about the status of the door (open, partially open or closed) we used a magnetic sensor. In addition to these sensors, we put a NFC tag on the main desk in order to activate an android-based smartphone application that allows to the user to annotate the start and the end of an activity in the office. These annotations have been combined with the videos recorded in office in order to have a very accurate annotation.

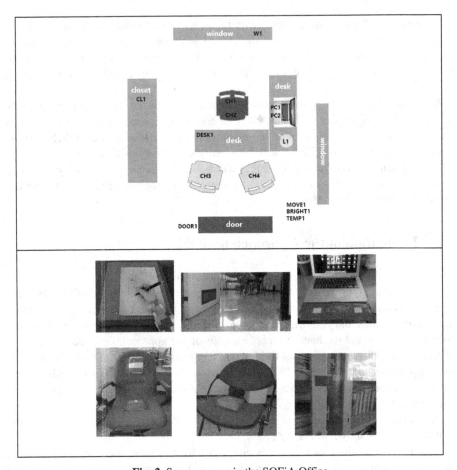

Fig. 2. Some sensors in the SOFiA Office

4.1   Dataset Collection

The testbed that we are using to validate our algorithms is an office located at the Computer Science Department at University of Bari in Italy. As shown in Figure 2, the smart office testbed includes several sensors.

Sensor data is captured using a sensor network that was designed and controlled with the Arduino Mega board and stored in a database. For our experiments, we collected sensor data and annotated these data with activities labels in order to have also the structure of the routines.

Data were collected for one subject (woman, 49 y.o, assistant professor) for a period of 45 working days (from Monday to Friday) since we could equipped only one office with the necessary sensors. In total we collected, at the lower level, about 90.000 sensor events and, at the highest level 450 instances of execution of activities.

Each sensor event was identified by the sensor ID and was stored together with the timestamp of the event and the sensor value.

In order to annotate the activities and routines we used a combination of a self-reported annotation using a smartphone application allowing to the user to annotate the start and the end of an activity in the office. These annotations have been combined with the videos recorded in office in order to have a very accurate annotation.

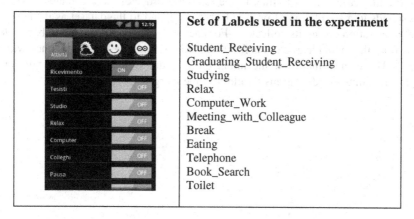

	Set of Labels used in the experiment
	Student_Receiving
	Graduating_Student_Receiving
	Studying
	Relax
	Computer_Work
	Meeting_with_Colleague
	Break
	Eating
	Telephone
	Book_Search
	Toilet

Fig. 3. A screenshot of the mobile application for annotating activities and the set of labels used in the experiment

Figure 3 shows the screenshot of the main activity of the mobile application with the list of labels available for annotating the activity by switching on and off the appropriate button. The user could also add a label that was not in the initial list.

In terms of privacy video recording was allowed since, besides the permission of the subject that accepted to participate to the experiment, in the Department there are advertisements informing people that the spaces are monitored by video cameras. These collected data were then transformed automatically in the WoMan format (see Section 3). Here we report an example of entries that we provide to WoMan in order to learn models of an activity (working at the computer in this case) from raw sensor data:

```
entry(20130416105518,begin_of_process,computer,computer2538,none,none).
entry(20130416105518,begin_of_activity,computer,computer2538,ch2,1).
entry(20130416105520,begin_of_activity,computer,computer2538,pc2,1).
entry(20130416105846,end_of_activity,computer,computer2538,pc1,1).
entry(20130416105902,begin_of_activity,computer,computer2538,pc2,0).
entry(20130416105939,begin_of_activity,computer,computer2538,pc2,1).
...
entry(20130416110119,begin_of_activity,computer,computer2538,ch1,1).
...
```

4.2   Incremental Learning of Activities and Routines

From the collected annotated dataset the model for each weekday has been learned and each model has been validated in terms of correctness and accuracy.

As far as learning is concerned we performed first a test in order to determine the effectiveness of WoMan in learning the activity model. We leveraged the incremental behavior of the system by considering the whole dataset and fed the system with the daily training cases one at a time, in the temporal order of the associated days. This corresponds to a simulation of on-line learning applied to the dataset as if the system were in operation during its collection. For each case, we counted the number of deviations from the model learned thus far (0 deviations meaning full compliance with the model). The idea is that after the initial days, if the system has caught the correct model, the number of deviations should become marginal.

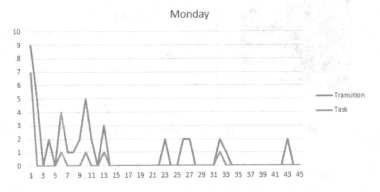

Fig. 4. Learning behavior of the "Monday" routine

For instance the graphic in Figure 4 shows the learning behavior along the 45 days reporting for each day the numbers of deviations from the learned model.

As far as tasks are concerned, of the 11 activities (see Figure 3) that are present in the dataset for the Monday routine, 7 were learned immediately from the first day. Concerning transitions, every peak denotes a failure of the current model, and at the same time causes a refinement thereof, so that the next applications will benefit from an improved model. The shape of the graphic, showing smaller and sparser peaks as long as the days go by, confirms both that the behavior of the tracked persons has a significant routinary component, and that WoMan is able to capture such a component.

In order to have a more thorough insight both as regards the system and as regards the dataset. The dataset was split into 10 folds in order to run a cross-validation. The experimental results are summarized in Table 1. It is vertically organized into sections, reporting some statistics expressed both in number of occurrences and in associated percentages (columns denoted by %).

The 'Learning %' columns report about the training phase, specifying the percentage of tasks and transitions that were learned (considering as ground truth the model learned in the previous experiment from the full set of cases). The 'Learning' columns report the same statistics in absolute number of tasks and transitions. The values are reported for each day separately and on average. They show that, using only 1/10 of the dataset for training, 82% of the tasks and 98% of the transitions are learned on average, yielding a recognition error on the test set of just 1% for tasks and 28% for transitions.

Table 1. 10-fold cross validation of the SOFiA dataset

	Learning		Learning %	
	Nr.Task	Nr.Transition	%Task	%Transition
Monday	8,9000	43,8000	81	97,33
Tuesday	10,0000	65,6000	83	97,91
Wednesday	9,0000	52,8000	82	97,78
Thursday	8,0000	51,3000	80	98,65
Friday	9,8000	55,1000	81	96,67
AVG	***9,1400***	***53,7200***	***81,55***	***97,67***
VAR	0,6380	62,0370	0,0002	0,0001
DEV	0,7987	7,8764	0,0123	0,0073

4.3   Recognition of Activities and Routines

Besides validating the learning performance of the system, we conducted an experiment aiming at evaluating at runtime how much the recognition task was accurate using our approach. In particular we focused on activity recognition, but the same procedure could be applied to daily routines.

First of all we learned the model of the following activities that were the most frequent in the dataset: *studying, student_receiving, graduating_students_receiving, relax*. Then for one week during the working hours we sent sensor data to the WoGue algorithm as explained previously.

On average we found out that the workflow correspondent to the correct activity has been identified after the fourth execution corresponding to a change in the sensor data. For instance, the following Figure 5 shows how the initially there are two possible workflow models corresponding to what is happening in the office, student_receiving and graduating_student_receiving that are similar in their nature. However after the fourth execution of the WoGue ranking the workflow corresponding to the activity student_receiving received, correctly, a higher ranking becoming a candidate for the model that is more compliant to what the user is currently doing.

In order to test the accuracy of the prediction, for each activity that has been learned in this second experiment we compared the WoGue response with the real activity that the user was actually performing by looking at the video of each day and the workflow corresponding to the current activity was correctly ranked as the most compliant in 82% of the cases.

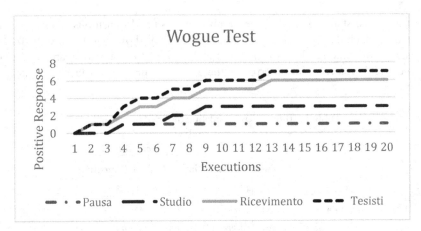

Fig. 5. An example of ranking for the recognition of the activity student_receiving on four possible activities
(pausa=relax, studio=studiyng, ricevimento=student_receiving,
tesisti=graduating_student_receiving)

5   Conclusions and Future Work

Learning and using a model of the routines of people and of the activities they execute in the environment allow to trace their behavior, understand their goals and determining problematic situations as deviations from the routine. We proposed an approach based on WoMan for learning these models in a smart office. WoMan adopts a Process Mining perspective to learn models of daily routines and activities from examples of the actual user behavior. Differently from the past proposals in the literature, it is fully incremental, has a powerful representation model that can handle routines of any complexity.

In order to confirm its efficiency and effectiveness, we experimented the approach on a real smart environment. To this aim we set up a smart office environment, SOFiA, equipped with Arduino sensors and effectors and we developed an algorithm WoGue that, using the WoMan functionalities, is able to recognize which is, among the learned workflows, the most compliant to what the user is doing in the environment.

In order to do so, we first collected a dataset of real-world data, then we annotated the dataset using a combination of self-reported annotation using a smartphone application and analysis of video that we recorded during the 45 working days of the experiment and then from the dataset we learned the workflow models of the user daily routines and of the activities performed in the environment. In order to test the accuracy of the learning task we run a 10-fold cross-validation. The experimental results shows that in average 82% of the tasks and 98% of the transitions are learned correctly.

In order to test the real-time performance of the approach we performed another experiment with sensor data coming from the SOFiA sensors and, as far as activity recognition is concerned, the WoGue algorithm started to make a correct prediction since the fourth execution in 82% of the cases.

These results encourage us to go on with our research in several directions.

First of all, while in the reported experiment we used the raw sensor data as they were provided in the dataset, we are currently working on processing them to obtain a higher-level description of the contextual situation. This would make easier to use our approach also for learning contextual user preferences depending on possibly complex interactions of environmental factors.

Finally, we aim at collecting a new dataset in a work environment that takes into account also data concerning affective (emotion and mood) aspects. We believe that this is important to improve the modeling of the user's situation by taking into account extra-rational factors and consequently to provide a more "empathic" adaptation of the environment to the user's situation.

Acknowledgments. This work is partially funded by the projects: "PUGLIA@SERVICE - Internet-based Service Engineering enabling Smart Territory structural development" (PON02_00563_3489339) and "VINCENTE – A Virtual collective INtelligenCe ENvironment to develop sustainable Technology Entrepreneurship ecosystems" (PON 02_00563_3470993) both funded by the Italian Ministry of University and Research (MIUR).

References

1. Ramos, C., Marreiros, G., Santos, R., Freitas, F.C.: Smart Offices and Intelligent Decision Rooms. In: Handbook Ambient Intelligence Smart Environ VII, pp. 851–880. Springer (2010)
2. http://www.arduino.cc/ (last consulted on the August 19, 2014)
3. Anonymized
4. Marsa-Maestre, I., de la Hoz, E., Alarcos, B., Velasco, J.R.: A hierarchical, agent-based approach to security in smart offices. In: Proceedings of the First International Conference on Ubiquitous Computing (ICUC-2006) (2006)
5. Fiore, L., Fehr, D., Bodor, R., Drenner, A., Somasundaram, G., Papanikolopoulos, N.: Multi-Camera Human Activity Monitoring. Journal of Intelligent and Robotic Systems **52**(1), 5–43 (2008)
6. Parkka, J., Ermes, M., Korpipaa, P., Mantyjarvi, J., Peltola, J., Korhonen, I.: Activity classification using realistic data from wearable sensors. IEEE Transactions on Information Technology in Biomedicine **10**(1), 119–128 (2006)
7. Patterson, D.J., Fox, D., Kautz, H., Philipose, M.: Fine-grained activity recognition by aggregating abstract object usage. In: Proc. of IEEE International Symposium on Wearable Computers, pp. 44–51 (2005)
8. Gu, T., Wang, L., Wu, Z., Tao, X., Lu, J.: A Pattern Mining Approach to Sensor-Based Human Activity Recognition. IEEE Transactions on Knowledge and Data Engineering **23**(9), 1359–1372 (2011)
9. van Kasteren, T.L.M., Englebienne, G., Kröse, B.: Human Activity Recognition from Wireless Sensor Network Data: Benchmark and Software. In: Activity Recognition in Pervasive Intelligent Environments, Atlantis Ambient and Pervasive Intelligence series. Atlantis Press (2010)
10. Kim, E., Helal, S., Cook, D.: Human activity recognition and pattern discovery. IEEE Pervasive Computing **9**, 48–53 (2010)

11. Hu, D.H., Yang, Q.: Cigar: Concurrent and interleaving goal and activity recognition. In: 23rd AAAI Conference on Artificial Intelligence (AAAI'08), pp. 1363–1368 (2008)

12. Chen, L., Nugent, C., Mulvenna, M., Finlay, D., Hong, X.: A Logical Framework for Behaviour Reasoning and Assistance in a Smart Home. Int'l J. Assistive Robotics and Mechatronics 9(4), 20–34 (2008)

13. Riboni, D., Bettini, C.: OWL 2 modeling and reasoning with complex human activities. Pervasive and Mobile Computing 7(3), 379–395 (2011)

14. Helaoui, R., Riboni, D., Stuckenschmidt, H.: A probabilistic ontological framework for the recognition of multilevel human activities. In: International Conference on Ubiquitous Computing (UbiComp2013), pp. 345–354 (2013)

15. Aztiria, A., Augusto, J.C., Basagoiti, R., Izaguirre, A., Cook, D.J.: Learning Frequent Behaviors of the Users in Intelligent Environments. IEEE T. Systems, Man, and Cybernetics: Systems 43(6), 1265–1278 (2013)

16. Weijters, A.J.M.M., van der Aalst, W.M.P.: Rediscovering workflow models from event-based data using little thumb. Integr. Comput.-Aided Eng. 10(2), 151–162 (2003)

17. Serral, E., Valderas, P., Pelechano, V.: Supporting runtime system evolution to adapt to user behaviour. In: Pernici, B. (ed.) CAiSE 2010. LNCS, vol. 6051, pp. 378–392. Springer, Heidelberg (2010)

18. Anonymized

19. Anonymized

20. Cook, D.J., Das, S.K.: How smart are our environments? an updated look at the state of the art. Pervasive Mobile Computing 3(2), 53–73 (2007)

21. van der Aalst, W., Weijters, T., Maruster, L.: Workflow Mining: Discovering Process Models from Event Logs. IEEE Trans. on Knowl. and Data Eng. 16(9), 1128–1142 (2004)

On-line Context Aware Physical Activity Recognition from the Accelerometer and Audio Sensors of Smartphones

David Blachon[1,2,3,4]([✉]), Doruk Coşkun[1,2,3], and François Portet[1,2,3]

[1] Laboratoire d'Informatique de Grenoble, 41 rue Mathématiques,
BP 53, 38041 Grenoble Cedex 9, France
{david.blachon,doruk.coskun,francois.portet}@imag.fr,
david.blachon@st.com
[2] Univ. Grenoble Alpes, LIG, 38000 Grenoble, France
[3] CNRS, LIG, 38000 Grenoble, France
[4] STMicroelectronics, 12 rue Jules Horowitz, BP 217,
38019 Grenoble Cedex, France

Abstract. Activity Recognition (AR) from smartphone sensors has become a hot topic in the mobile computing domain since it can provide services directly to the user (health monitoring, fitness, context-awareness) as well as for third party applications and social network (performance sharing, profiling). Most of the research effort has been focused on direct recognition from accelerometer sensors and few studies have integrated the audio channel in their model despite the fact that it is a sensor that is always available on all kinds of smartphones. In this study, we show that audio features bring an important performance improvement over an accelerometer based approach. Moreover, the study demonstrates the interest of considering the smartphone location for on-line context-aware AR and the prediction power of audio features for this task. Finally, another contribution of the study is the collected corpus that is made available to the community for AR recognition from audio and accelerometer sensors.

Keywords: Data Science · Sensing and Reasoning Technology

1 Introduction

Automatic human Activity Recognition (AR) is recognised as an important process for human behaviour monitoring (health, well-being, sport) [8] but it is also extensively studied for the provision of context-aware services for smart objects (smartphones, robots...) and smart spaces (smart homes, smart rooms, public spaces...) [7]. Though AR is a hot topic in the community, according to the application, the activities under study can be very different (e.g., walking, getting money at an ATM, screw driving, etc.) and there is still not a clear definition of the different levels of activities that can be modelled and processed. In this article, we aim at detecting basic physical activities from smartphone

© Springer International Publishing Switzerland 2014
E. Aarts et al. (Eds.): AmI 2014, LNCS 8850, pp. 205–220, 2014.
DOI: 10.1007/978-3-319-14112-1_17

i.e., activities involving basic movements with low level of semantics such as walking, standing still or sitting. These are a subset of the Compendium of Physical Activities [1] that are classified according to the semantics they share and effort magnitude. For instance, the group *Bicycling* lists different activities of bicycling in several environments (e.g., mountain) and at different speeds. Basic physical activities have the advantages of being well defined, can be captured by means of sensors and can be used to reconstruct higher-level activities. They are also directly related to the health and sporting activities of the user and can greatly inform the context of smartphones.

The emergence of smartphones introduced new ways to perform human activity recognition. Indeed, they embed accelerometers for sensing, and resources for storage and data transmission. Hence, data collection is comparable to previous studies such as the one of Bao et al. [3]. Beyond the availability of accelerometer, smartphones usually embed many different sensors. For instance, it is common to find other inertial sensors (e.g., gyroscope), ambient sensors (e.g., microphone, barometer, magnetometer) which can be used for human activity recognition. Also, thanks to their design, smartphones are easy to carry so they might be used to collect new kinds of activities in realistic conditions. Studies report their use for tasks about locomotion activities [12,17] or daily activities [10].

Smartphones also embed large resources in terms of computation, storage, battery, which could allow to perform online embedded activity recognition. However, according to a survey from Incel et al [11], online activity recognition is an under explored area. They report that most studies deal with offline classification and that classifiers still require much resource for embedding them on smartphones. Yet, some recent work have started studying online AR classification, using Decision Tree and K-Nearest Neighbors (KNN) [12,17].

Beyond those temporary limitations of resources, other issues need to be tackled with. First, the large variability of sensors does not seem to be standardized yet, which means that one should not make a system depend on the availability of such a sensor on every smartphone. For instance, accelerometer is quite common but proximity sensor or barometer are far less common. Hence, a system of human activity recognition should deal with this variable sensor availability. Also, unlike the previously mentioned study of Bao et al [3], sensor location and orientation may change in time. Indeed, smartphone users can carry them in different locations. A survey [6] performed among 55 volunteers reported the preferred locations for users to carry their smartphones. The 4 most frequent answers were hand, pants pocket, bag and jacket pocket. The change of location may make it more difficult for a system to infer user activity, yet it needs to be taken into account.

In this paper, we present an approach for online basic physical AR from microphone and accelerometer data streams collected on smartphones. Indeed, these two kinds of sensors are found on most smartphones (if not all). If accelerometers are very popular, microphones are far less used in the domain despite their strong informative potential. Another contribution of the study is the explicit modelling of the smartphone location context and its use as input information for AR. This AR framework is described in detail in Section 3 after a short description of the state of the art in Section 2. Since no dataset composed of microphone and accelerometer data is available, we collected our own dataset on different smartphone brands to evaluate the method. This data collection, that we made publicly available, is described in Section 4. Three different state of the art classification models were learned from this dataset in different conditions to assess the impact of the audio channel and the smartphone context on classification performance. These results are detailed in Section 5 and discussed in Section 6. The paper finishes with a short conclusion and an outlook on further works in Section 7.

2   Related Work

A first study dealing with basic physical activities is the one of Kose et al [12]. Authors report a high F-Measure value of 92% for a clustered KNN classifier on a set of basic physical activities (running, walking, standing, sitting). Another study is from Yang et al [21] focusing on a similar set of basic physical activites and using different classifiers such as Decision Tree, Naive Bayes, KNN and Support Vector Machine (SVM). This study reports 90% of accuracy using the Decision Tree. Moreover, the survey of Incel et al [11] shows that most reported studies rely on the use of accelerometer. GPS and radio communications such as WiFi are sometimes used while audio is hardly present in studies. Also, the survey shows that for most studies reported, the number of subjects was less or equal than 20.

Accelerometer appears to be the most popular sensor for the domain. However, we previously noticed in the introduction that smartphone location and orientation might change due to the habits of users that can carry it in different locations. This can have an impact on accelerometer readings as Alanezi et al [2] report. They collected accelerometer data from two different positions: hand holding and pants pocket. Magnitudes of acceleration hardly reached the value of 15 m/s^2 when in hand while they often exceeded 15 m/s^2 and even reached 20 m/s^2 in pants pocket. The difference was also noticeable on standard deviations of readings. Hence, as the authors concluded, accelerometer data are affected by smartphone position. However, studies reported different solutions to address this issue. First one is to train classifiers for each different location considered. Reddy et al [17] trained Decision Tree cascaded with Hidden Markov Models (HMM) for each different location and compared results to the same type of classifier trained with data from all concerned locations. They report similar performances for transportation mode recognition. Another reported technique includes a gravity-based feature for estimating orientation. Park et al [15] used this technique for recognizing different smartphone locations. Using a SVM classifier, they reported accuracy values of 99.6% when including the gravity-based feature and only 82% when excluding it. Despite those solutions, Incel et al consider in their review [11] that smartphone location and orientation still remain open points.

Leveraging the many sensors of smartphone can also help for activity recognition. Among them, one rarely used is the microphone that could be a source of information very relevant regarding such conditions. Indeed, a microphone can be found on every smarptthone. Although audio readings might suffer from frictions between microphone and direct context (e.g., fabric of pants) as reported Alanezi et al [2], some studies have promising results with microphone. For instance, Miluzzo et al [14] proposed a system to distinguish various smartphone locations thanks to environment sounds but it was successfully tested only on two locations: inside a pocket and outside a pocket. Diaconita et al [9] presented a technique to recognize smartphone position and user's environment based on the emission of a sound pulse and then the classification of the reverberation (classifiers were trained on such reverberations in order to recognize user's environment and smartphone position). They report 97% of accuracy using Mel Frequency Cepstral Coefficients (MFCC) as features classified with KNN. However, to the best of our knowledge, the use of audio for smartphone location recognition and human activity recognition is not optimal and can still be improved.

3 Method

This section describes the method designed for online activity recognition. The activities of interest as well as the smartphone context are first defined, then the global architecture, the extracted features and the different classification schemes are introduced.

3.1 Activities and Smartphone Context

In this article we focus on basic physical activities such as walking, running, etc. leaving apart high level activities (e.g., making coffee, cleaning the house) and fine grained gestures (e.g., screw driving, raising the phone over the head).

The activity set is presented Table 1. It is composed of i) 8 frequent daily activities which are a subset of the Compendium of Physical Activities [1] and ii) an Unstable activity which groups every data not belonging to any of the 8 previously defined activities (e.g., making coffee, cleaning). In any of these daily activities, the user is likely to wear his/her smartphone. This cannot be assumed in some other activities of the compendium (e.g., snorkeling).

Table 1. The 8 activities considered in the study and the UNSTABLE class

Stationary	Sitting	Standing Still
Lying	Running	Walking
Jumping	Stairs	UNSTABLE

Though the above activities are well defined, the observations recorded by a smartphone can be highly dependent on the location of this device with respect to the user. For instance, as exemplified by Figure 1(a), if someone is running, the observations collected will be very different if the smartphone is in the hand (in that case most of the dynamic will be those of the arm), in the bag (in that case the smartphone captures the bag jerks) or in the pocket (in that case most of the dynamic will be those of the legs). To take the different interaction dimensions between the user and the smartphone into account, we defined the smartphone context space represented Figure 1(b).

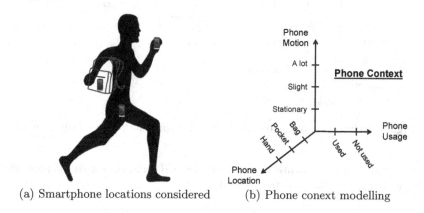

(a) Smartphone locations considered   (b) Phone conext modelling

Fig. 1. Smartphone locations considered and smartphone context modelling

The first axis concerns phone motion. It is indeed very informative to assess which amount of movement the smartphone is subject to. This can help infer activity as well as whether the smartphone is with the user or not (e.g., put on a table far away from the user). The second axis, phone usage, has two values respectively used and not used. By phone usage we focus on the interaction with the phone. For example, typing an SMS is a direct interaction and listening to music is an indirect one, but both are considered as 'used' in our definition. On the opposite, carrying the phone in a bag without interacting with it is considered as not used. This information is a useful context component to build applications that can prompt user when she/he is paying attention to her/his smartphone. The third axis, smartphone location, represents the different locations in which a smartphone can be with respect to the user's body. For the kind of activities addressed in the study this is the most important information, therefore throughout the rest of the paper we will concentrate on the dependence between AR and smartphone location.

3.2 Architecture

The AR system architecture is depicted Figure 2. Data streams are continuously acquired. Every w windows, a buffer is sent for feature extraction. Features are computed over a 2-second long buffer with 50 % overlapping. From the feature vector obtained, the most likely location of the smartphone is extracted. Then,

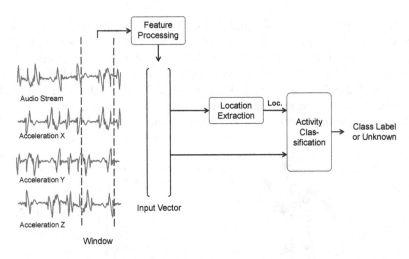

Fig. 2. Architecture of the online activity recognition system on smartphone

the location and the feature vector feed the AR module which decides which activity (if any) is observed from the data.

3.3 Features

Our set includes features from acceleration and audio data. They are listed below:

- Average of accelerometer magnitude
- Variance of accelerometer magnitude
- Energy of accelerometer magnitude
- Variance of acceleration along each axis (x, y, z)
- Subband energy at 3 Hz and 4 Hz

Average, variance and energy are very popular features for activity recognition task [11]. Since acceleration is directly related to motion, they estimate quantity and variability of motion within the window. Also, frequency parameters can help focus on human motion and avoid some noise added by data collection.

Regarding audio features, we used frequency based one but no temporal-based ones. Indeed, microphone is an ambient sensor that records data coming from different sources, including many external ones (e.g. radio, speech). Separating information due to motion from the one due to external source is a challenging task, if not impossible, using temporal domain features. However, frequency domain features can leverage energy distribution along frequencies allowing then to isolate spectrum subbands more sensitive to motion variation. For instance, as we reported in Section 2, a smartphone located in a pocket may involve frictions on the microphone which can in turn generate sounds. Finding subbands of spectrum of these frictions could be very helpful. Our set of audio features contains spectrum power estimation of 40 subbands spread along the Mel scale frequencies. Mel-scales are inspired from human ability of hearing and they are basically perceptual scales of pitches judged by listeners to be equal in distance from one another. In theory, the computation of Mel filter banks is implemented in 3 steps 1) the signal is windowed (e.g., with a hamming window), 2) Fast Fourier transform is applied, 3) spectrum power estimation obtained is mapped onto the mel scale. For the experiments presented in this paper, spectrum power estimation is performed on 200 ms long frames and only spectrum magnitude coefficients are saved (phase is removed). From this audio feature set, speech content cannot be retrieved with today techniques.

3.4 Classification Models

Three different models were implemented to perform AR. Decision trees are the standard method used in the literature and was used as baseline system. Random Forest is the scheme that has gained interest recently since it showed the most promising performance in AR from smartphone and worn sensors [8]. The third model is Conditional Random Field (CRF) which is a sequence model which has demonstrated impressive performance in related field of AR [20]. These three models and their learning strategy are briefly introduced below.

Decision Trees. The induction of a decision tree is based on the "divide and conquer" principle to partition a training set TS, composed of individuals described by several attributes, into homogeneous subgroups. Let the classes of the individuals be $\{C_1, C_2, \ldots, C_k\}$, there are four possibilities:

1. TS contains individuals belonging to only one class C_j. In this case, this is a leaf named C_j.
2. TS is empty. In this case this is a leaf for which the class is defined by information other than TS (e.g. the most frequent class of the parent).
3. TS contains individuals belonging to several classes. Thus, a test T is chosen, based on a single attribute that has the exclusive outcomes $\{O_1, O_2, \ldots, O_n\}$ which are used to partition TS into the subsets $\{TS_1, TS_2, \ldots, TS_n\}$ where TS_i contains all the individuals in TS that have outcomes O_i. The decision tree for TS consists of one branch for each outcome. This mechanism is then reapplied recursively on each subset TS_i.
4. TS contains individuals belonging to several classes but for which no test can be found. In this case this is a leaf for which the class is defined by information from TS (e.g. the most frequent class in TS) or other than TS.

In this paper, we use the well known C4.5 method [16] which uses the gain ratio to choose the test T. The gain ratio can be described as the gain of information (based on the entropy) for T normalized by the potential information of dividing TS into n outcomes. Therefore, the decision tree chooses the most discriminant tests (best separation of the information).

Random Forest. Random forests is an ensemble classifier composed of several 'weak' decision trees whose each individual output are combined (by voting strategy) to generate the final decision. The method to induce Random Forest models [5] combines bagging and random attribute selection. Briefly, if the dataset contains N individuals described by M attributes, the learning consists in drawing a subset of individuals randomly with replacement to constitute a training set (keeping the rest as test set) which is used to induce a decision tree with m attributes ($m << M$) randomly selected. Each tree is grown to the largest possible extent without pruning. The most important parameters for the learning are the maximum number of trees and m the number of attributes. Random forest is very efficient on large datasets and has a very good accuracy on many datasets without over-fitting (even if some study downplayed this advantages with some noisy datasets [18]). In fact, RF has shown impressive performances for AR on worn sensors [8].

Conditional Random Fields. Conditional random fields (CRF) are graph based models to perform discriminative probabilistic inference over a set of variables in classification tasks [13]. Similarly to HMM, CRF can classify a label y for a given sample x taking into account its relations with neighbour samples when they are organized in a sequence $X = x_1, \ldots, x_T$. CRF model the conditional distribution $p(Y|X)$, but without requiring to model the distribution of the variable X. In the case of activity recognition, we can consider the X a set of temporal windows, and Y as the activity to infer.

Formally, a CRF model is a undirected graph $G = (V, E)$ such that $Y = (Y_v)_{v \in V}$, so that Y is indexed by the vertices of G. Then (X, Y) is a conditional random field if the following Markov property with respect to the graph is respected $p(Y_v|X, Y_w, w \neq v) = p(Y_v|X, Y_w, w \sim v)$, where $w \sim v$ means that w and v are neighbours in G. The simplest of the CRF model is a simple chain. This is the model that we adopt in this paper. In that case, X represents a sequence of observations and Y represents a hidden state variable (activity) that must be inferred given X.

CRF are generally implemented as log linear models by means of feature functions f_k, in the case of chain-like conditional random fields $p(Y|X)$ is estimated by equation 1.

$$p(y|x) = \frac{1}{Z(x)} exp \left\{ \sum_{k=1}^{K} \lambda_k f_k(y_t, y_{t-1}, x_t) \right\} \qquad (1)$$

where the features functions f_k impose a bias in the model, they take the value of 1 if its variables take a certain configuration and 0 otherwise, y_t is the class (activity) to be estimated at current time, x_t is the observation sequence at current time, y_{t-1} is the (previous) neighbour, Z is a normalization factor, λ_k is a parameter to assign a weight to the feature function f_k. These weights are estimated during the learning phase using an iterative gradient method. Finally, for chain-like model, inference is performed through an adapted version of the Viterbi algorithm [19].

4   Experiment

To validate the approach, datasets containing audio and accelerometer data labelled with physical activities were required. However, although a fair number of datasets with accelerometer data are available, we did not find a dataset including audio data. Therefore we ran our own experiment to collect data from 19 people by using 4 smartphones which were located in 3 different locations. This section describes the method employed to collect this dataset, the specific scenarios that were designed and finishes with a summary of the collected data.

4.1   Protocol

Each recording involved one experimenter and one participant as well as five smartphones. At the beginning of the experiment, the participant was fit with 2 smartphones in a bag, 1 in the pocket and 1 in the hand. Each participant performed the 9 activities introduced in Table 1 (walking, running, jumping, stairs, lying, standing still, stationary, sitting and the remaining one we call unstable) and 5 different secondary activities (calling, listening to music, sending sms, using an application on the phone, none) with predefined order which was determined by a data collection scenario. During that time, the experimenter was always with the participant to trigger changes of activities with his own smartphone. The own smartphone of the participant was never used. All smartphones were equipped with the RecordMe application[1] that acquires all sensors and smartphone activity data on the fly. Accelerometer data were sampled at a rate of 50 Hz and audio sampled at a rate of 44.1 kHz. More details of the RecordMe application can be found [4].

If the participant did not have a bag (e.g., own handbag) a backpack already filled with some stuff was used (e.g., pens, thermos bottle, sheets of paper). All the experiments happened within the lab in different places (office, corridors, stairs, close outside, cafeteria) at calm and rush hours. Before experiment, the participant was explained the aim of the study, the risk of undertaking this experiment so that she/he could give a signed informed consent to undertake the experiment and to let the data be used for research purpose. It was also explained that the raw audio data were not kept but only coefficients from which raw signal cannot be reconstructed.

4.2   Scenarios

To make sure all activities and smartphones will be uniformly mixed, our data collection consisted of 3 main scenarios. The organisation of each scenario was implemented by using the modelling of the smartphone context and human activities. All possible smartphone contexts and human activities that can be performed within relevant protocol were indicated. Table 2 summarises these 3 scenarios.

---

[1] http://lig-membres.imag.fr/blachon/download/recordme.apk

Table 2. Abstracted view of the scenarios used for data collection

scenario ID	Phone Usage	Phone Motion	Smartphone Location				Activities
			SP1	SP2	SP3	SP4	
1	Yes/No	Yes/No	bag	hand	pocket	bag	All activities + secondary act.
2	No	No	pocket	bag	hand	bag	Stationary
3	No	Yes/No	hand	pocket	bag	bag	All activities

In scenario 1, the participant is interacting with the phone (also carrying it). She/he has a phone in the hand (another one in the pocket and two in the bag) and performs all activities one after the other. To add naturalness to the collected data, the scenario included 'secondary activities'. These are performed with the smartphone in hand and contain activities such as calling or sending a SMS. These were added for representing the changeable hand movement of the participants. In daily life, people can carry their phones in their hand with different gestures. These gestures were modelled by the secondary activities. Then, in scenario 2 the participant is not carrying the phone in the hand. Instead, s/he puts it on a table and stays around quietly. While in scenario 3 the participant is carrying the phone (but not interacting with it) and perform again physical activities, most of them outdoors.

These 3 scenarios were performed sequentially without any interruption. Unlike many data collections in which activities are collected separately from each other, we wanted to reproduce the real life in which activities are part of a whole day. Indeed, systems to be deployed in the wild must deal with transitions between activities and not predefined activities.

A 'phone switch' sequence was inserted between the execution of each scenario so that smartphones were not always at the same place. Initial position of smartphone was uniformly distributed over the participants to secure the same amount of data per location × activity. That is to say, smartphones SP1-3 were not recording an activity always in the same location.

4.3   Acquired Data

At the end of the experiment, 20 hours of data were collected from 19 participants (14 males, 5 females) between 19-29 years old. Four smartphones were used: Motorola Defy Mini, MTT, Samsung Galaxy S2 and Nexus 4. Each experiment took 15 to 20 minutes to be performed. Figure 3 displays time distribution over the activities. Repartition of recorded time per smartphone is of 50 % for bag location, and 25 % for pocket and hand locations. All the data were annotated according to two dimesnions: Phone Location, and physical Human Activity. This dataset is available at http://getalp.imag.fr/xwiki/bin/view/Projects/SmartPhoneHumanActivityData

After data collection, the annotation performed during the experiment was manually checked in the time and label domains. Some data are still not cleaned and checked.

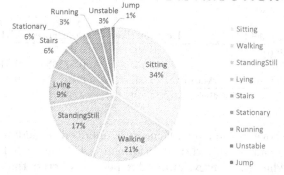

Fig. 3. Activity duration distribution over all 9 activities

5 Results

Model training and tests were performed offline. However, the classification task simulated online conditions since only the present data vector was known by the classifier. The tasks of activity recognition and smartphone location recognition were run on 3 different feature sets: 1) Accelerometer features; 2) Audio features; and 3) Accelerometer plus audio features. We used 50 trees for Random Forest. All models were acquired and tested using a 10 times x 10 fold cross validation and precision, recall and F-Measure were computed for each run. For each result, statistical significance test were computed against either the Decision tree (reference model) or accelerometer results (reference feature set).

5.1 Basic Human Activity Recognition

The first experiment was to test how well the models perform on the three different feature sets without using smartphone location information. Table 3 summarises the F-measure obtained for each combination. It turned out that Random Forest performed better than the two other algorithms in every feature sets. This increase of performance was for each set significantly better than Decision Tree. On the contrary, CRF performed worse than Decision Tree. Also, one can notice that Random Forest performed better with audio feature set than with accelerometer set. A significance test was performed to test whether audio features play a role in the performance increase. Each Model performance for the Accel+Audio feature set was compared to the Accel feature set. Apart for CRF model, improvements were significant ($p < 0.01$). Thus, it seems that audio features may play an important role for physical activity classification from smartphone.

5.2 Context-Aware Human Activity Recognition

To assess the impact of smartphone location on activity classification, the learning has been run again but adding the ground truth location in the feature

Table 3. Overall F-measure of activity classification for each Model and feature set without smartphone location

Feature set	Decision Tree	Random Forest	CRF
Accelerometer	0.59	0.65***	0.37
Audio	0.55	0.67***	0.31
Accelerometer + Audio	0.64	0.73***	0.42

*** means statistically significant difference at $p < 0.01$

vector. Table 4 provides the global F-measure obtained by adding the location. Apart for CRF, it can be noticed that performances have increased for all feature configurations. Thus the context-aware AR performs better than classical AR without location information. Statistical test between these two experiments for the Accel+Audio feature set revealed a significant difference ($p < 0.01$). Once again, Random Forest has the highest score and it is significantly better than Decision Tree in all conditions while CRF is worse than decision tree. Statistical tests still show a significant impact of audio features on the classification and once again, Random Forest performs better with audio feature set than with accelerometer one.

Table 4. Overall F-measure of activity classification for each Model and feature set with ground truth smartphone location

Feature Set	Decision Tree	Random Forest	CRF
Accelerometer + location	0.64	0.69***	0.38
Audio + location	0.60	0.71***	0.31
Accelerometer +Audio+ location	0.68	0.76***	0.42

*** means statistically significant difference at $p < 0.01$.

5.3 Inferring Smart-Phone Context

Since the smartphone location has a positive impact on AR, it was tested whether smartphone location can be inferred from the data. In this experiment, smartphone location was used as class to assess the feasibility of building a location predictor. Results are presented Table 5. Once again, Random Forest performed significantly better than Decision Tree. Unlike previously reported experiments, CRF performance is very close to these of the two other classifiers. It can be seen that very good performance can be reached with Accel+Audio data (F-measure of 91% for Random Forest). Similarly to previous experiments, performances with audio feature set exceed these with accelerometer feature set, for Decision Tree and Random Forest. Moreover, apart for CRF, all classification results for Accel+Audio feature set were significantly superior to results with Accel feature set only. This means that audio features might have a high predictive power for smartphone location.

Table 5. Overall F-measure of smartphone location classification for Decision Tree, Random Forest and CRF Models and feature set

Feature Set	Decision Tree	Random Forest	CRF
Accelerometer	0.79	0.84***	0.83
Audio	0.80	0.89***	0.69
Accel+Audio	0.86	0.93***	0.86

*** means statistically significant difference at $p < 0.01$.

5.4 Inferred Context-Aware Human Activity Recognition

We complete our experiments by launching again the human activity recognition task with feature sets including smartphone location inferred from a first classifier. Here, we cascaded a smartphone location classifier with a human activity classifier. In order to avoid over-fitting, a portion of the dataset (20 %) was used for training the smartphone location classifier which was then used to predict location on the remaining dataset. The resulting dataset (enhanced with inferred location) was then used for activity recognition classifier in a 10-fold cross-validation way. Table 6 summarizes results (because CRF performed worse than DT for this AR task, it was not used for this experiment). Results are inferior to those in Table 4 (which is not surprising since here location is inferred while it was groud truth on previous experiment) and slightly improved when compared to Table 3. Results should be analysed with caution since both classifiers were trained on reduced datasets for reasons explained before.

Table 6. Overall F-measure of activity classification for Decision Tree and Random Forest and feature set with inferred smartphone location

Feature Set	Decision Tree	Random Forest
Accelerometer + inferred location	0.60	0.65***
Audio + inferred location	0.56	0.67***
Accel+Audio + inferred location	0.65	0.74***

*** means statistically significant difference at $p < 0.01$.

6 Discussion

One of the main findings of the study is the interest of audio features both for AR and smartphone location recognition. Regarding smartphone location, audio features alone make it possible to overcome the model with accelerometer features alone (F-measures of 89% for audio vs 84% for accelerometer). But, as shown in Table 5, the most interesting outcome is that audio and accelerometer features are very complementary. Indeed, the dataset with full features shows an increase of Recall for 'hand' (93%) and 'pocket' (91%) well above the one obtained in audio alone (hand: 89%, pocket: 84%) and accelerometer alone (hand: 86%, pocket: 83%). For activity classification, audio features are competitive since results are very similar to the ones with accelerometer feature

sets, and even exceed them with Random Forest. However, it must be emphasized that accelerometer features bring far better results with the running and
jumping activities than audio features do, which is not surprising. Despite this
advantage, the fusion of both feature sets shows again the complementariness
of the audio and accelerometer features since performances always significantly
increase in that case for AR. However, some subsequent analyses are needed to
understand which exact part of the location and activity acoustic signal captures. In particular, a finer feature selection might optimize the current feature
set.

Another important finding of the study is the role of the context for improved
AR. In this work, the location was simply used as an input feature. If this has
brought improvement in all cases, further research must be investigated to know
whether location information can be used later in the process. For instance, it
might be interesting to train classifiers for every considered location and to use a
voting strategy to improve the classification accuracy [17]. In any case, location
inference is an important element of the context that can be useful in many
applications others than activity recognition.

Three models were tested for AR including a sequence model. Overall, the
best model was by far the Random Forest which always showed significant best
performance for AR and location classification. RF has showed superiority over
decision tree in numerous tasks and is known to handle particularly well imbalanced data sets. Therefore, these results confirms recent studies of the community in similar tasks [8]. The less performing model was Conditional Random
Fields that exhibited poor performance for the AR task. It was however competitive for the SP location task. CRF is known to require a high amount of
data for training and in the location task only 3 classes with balanced number of
instances are provided (about 8400 instances per classes) while in the AR task
9 classes with unbalanced number of instances are provided (from 8400 to 300
instances per class). This suggests that with an increased number of data, CRF
could exhibit much better performances.

The data collection also revealed some limits of the smartphone sensor data
acquisition. Indeed, we noticed that some smartphones block the acquisition
when screen is off. For the data collection, we had to use a screen locker to keep
it on and to allow the recording to continue. Thus, real on-line AR system must
find solution to react to this unexpected behaviour if they plan to be largely
deployed.

The study reported good performance using accelerometer and audio data.
These two channels were selected because they are always present on modern
smartphones. However, there are opportunities to improve the classification accuracies even more. For instance, it would be interesting to investigate the data
that come from other sensors or phone logs when available. Although data from
every possible sensor and phone logs were collected, only accelerometer and
microphone were used. For instance, hand location could be inferred from a combination of different clues: a phone call event, no headset or bluetooth device
is plugged and motion detected through accelerometer data. Using this kind of

information could increase activity recognition accuracy and also diminish the battery usage.

7 Conclusion

The first contribution of this paper is the corpus that was used for the task of activity recognition. Collected from 4 smartphones worn by 19 participants, the data contains both accelerometer and audio samples labeled with 8 different basic physical activities and 3 smartphone locations on volunteers. Moreover, the data was acquired in a sequential way scheduled by scenarios. To the best of our knowledge, this is the first dataset made available with such features.

Beyond the corpus, the main contribution is the importance of audio features for the AR task. The audio feature set proved to be competitive with the accelerometer feature set for the AR task and even outperformed it with some of the 3 state of the art classifiers used. Moreover, the best performance was achieved when combining both feature sets together.

Finally, our study highlights the importance of smartphone location. Our approach includes it as an attribute of the feature set. This resulted in an increase of AR performances which confirmed our assumption. Yet, smartphone location information can be integrated in other ways in such a system of recognition (e.g., classifiers are trained for different locations and a voting strategy selects one).

These results will be useful for the ambient intelligence community by shedding light on the role of audio features for AR as well as on the importance of modelling the smartphone context for the applications. Nevertheless, we plan to undertake more studies to assess the interest of sequence models and to collect data "in the wild" to validate the approach in real ecological situations.

References

1. Ainsworth, B.E., Haskell, W.L., Herrmann, S.D., Meckes, N., Bassett, D.R., Tudor-Locke, C., Greer, J.L., Vezina, J., Whitt-Glover, M.C., Leon, A.S.: 2011 compendium of physical activities: a second update of codes and met values. Medicine and Science in Sports and Exercise 43(8), 1575–1581 (2011)
2. Alanezi, K., Mishra, S.: Impact of smartphone position on sensor values and context discovery. http://digitool.library.colostate.edu/exlibris/dtl/d3_1/apache_media/L2V4bGlicmlzL2R0bC9kM18xL2FwYWNoZV9tZWRpYS8yMTIyNjM=.pdf
3. Bao, L., Intille, S.S.: Activity recognition from user-annotated acceleration data. In: Ferscha, A., Mattern, F. (eds.) PERVASIVE 2004. LNCS, vol. 3001, pp. 1–17. Springer, Heidelberg (2004)
4. Blachon, D., Portet, F., Besacier, L., Tassart, S.: RECORDME: A Smartphone Application for Experimental Collections of Large Amount of Data Respecting Volunteer's Privacy. In: Hervás, R., Lee, S., Nugent, C., Bravo, J. (eds.) UCAmI 2014. LNCS, vol. 8867, pp. 345–348. Springer, Heidelberg (2014)
5. Breiman, L.: Random forests. Machine Learning 45(1), 5–32 (2001)

6. Chon, Y., Talipov, E., Cha, H.: Autonomous management of everyday places for a personalized location provider. IEEE Transactions on Systems, Man, and Cybernetics, Part C: Applications and Reviews **42**(4), 518–531 (2012)

7. Coutaz, J., Crowley, J.L., Dobson, S., Garlan, D.: Context is key. Communications of the ACM **48**(3), 49–53 (2005)

8. Cvetković, B., Kaluža, B., Milić, R., Luštrek, M.: Towards human energy expenditure estimation using smart phone inertial sensors. In: Augusto, J.C., Wichert, R., Collier, R., Keyson, D., Salah, A.A., Tan, A.-H. (eds.) AmI 2013. LNCS, vol. 8309, pp. 94–108. Springer, Heidelberg (2013)

9. Diaconita, I., Reinhardt, A., Englert, F., Christin, D., Steinmetz, R.: Do you hear what i hear? using acoustic probing to detect smartphone locations. In: 2014 IEEE International Conference on Pervasive Computing and Communications Workshops (PERCOM Workshops), pp. 1–9. IEEE (2014)

10. Eagle, N., Pentland, A.: Reality mining: sensing complex social systems. Personal and Ubiquitous Computing **10**(4), 255–268 (2006)

11. Incel, O.D., Kose, M., Ersoy, C.: A review and taxonomy of activity recognition on mobile phones. BioNanoScience **3**(2), 145–171 (2013)

12. Kose, M., Incel, O.D., Ersoy, C.: Online human activity recognition on smart phones. In: Workshop on Mobile Sensing: From Smartphones and Wearables to Big Data, pp. 11–15 (2012)

13. Lafferty, J.D., McCallum, A., Pereira, F.C.N.: Conditional random fields: Probabilistic models for segmenting and labeling sequence data. In: Proceedings of the Eighteenth International Conference on Machine Learning, ICML 2001, pp. 282–289 (2001)

14. Miluzzo, E., Papandrea, M., Lane, N.D., Lu, H., Campbell, A.T.: Pocket, bag, hand, etc.-automatically detecting phone context through discovery. In: Proc. PhoneSense 2010, pp. 21–25 (2010)

15. Park, J.-G., Patel, A., Curtis, D., Teller, S., Ledlie, J.: Online pose classification and walking speed estimation using handheld devices. In: Proceedings of the 2012 ACM Conference on Ubiquitous Computing, pp. 113–122. ACM (2012)

16. Ross Quinlan, J.: C4.5: Programs for Machine Learning. Morgan Kaufmann Publishers Inc., San Francisco (1993)

17. Reddy, S., Mun, M., Burke, J., Estrin, D., Hansen, M., Srivastava, M.: Using mobile phones to determine transportation modes. ACM Transactions on Sensor Networks (TOSN) **6**(2), 13 (2010)

18. Segal, M.R.: Machine learning benchmarks and random forest regression. Technical report, University of California (2004)

19. Sutton, C., Mccallum, A.: Introduction to Conditional Random Fields for Relational Learning. MIT Press (2006)

20. van Kasteren, T.L.M., Englebienne, G., Kröse, B.J.A.: An activity monitoring system for elderly care using generative and discriminative models. Personal and Ubiquitous Computing **14**(6), 489–498 (2010)

21. Yang, J.: Toward physical activity diary: motion recognition using simple acceleration features with mobile phones. In: Proceedings of the 1st International Workshop on Interactive Multimedia for Consumer Electronics, pp. 1–10. ACM (2009)

Real-Time Event Detection
for Energy Data Streams

Aqeel H. Kazmi$^{(\boxtimes)}$, Michael J. O'Grady, and Gregory M.P. O'Hare

School of Computer Science and Informatics,
University College Dublin, Dublin 4, Ireland
Aqeel.Kazmi@ucdconnect.ie,
{Michael.J.OGrady,Gregory.OHare}@ucd.ie

Abstract. Appliance specific energy monitoring is perceived as a prerequisite for reducing energy usage in households. A number of approaches exist, however, Non-Intrusive appliance Load Monitoring is considered to be the most promising and scalable method. This method can also facilitate Ambient Intelligent applications with the hope activity recognition of the resident is of paramount importance. In this paper, we propose an event detection algorithm to support non-intrusive energy monitoring. A performance evaluation of this algorithm has been carried out on a reference dataset.

Keywords: Non-Intrusive Appliance Load Monitoring · Event Detection

1 Introduction

Reducing energy consumption is an imperative, nationally, commercially, and individually. However, energy conservation is challenging, one of the major reasons being consumers' lack of awareness about energy usage patterns [5]. As a first step towards energy conservation, greater transparency over the traditional invisibility of energy usage must be engendered. AUTHENTIC [10] is one example of an Ambient Intelligence (AmI) solution that seeks to make energy consumption visible to occupants within their homes. Recent research activity in the area of energy monitoring resulted in a number of solutions that range from low-cost to high-cost methodologies [8]. Non-Intrusive appliance Load Monitoring (NILM) is considered as the most promising and scalable solution to acquire appliance-specific energy information [3]. The two major approaches of NILM are often referred to as event-based, and non event-based methods [2].

Event-based load disaggregation approach uses an event detection mechanism to detect events in an energy signal. These events occur whenever appliances are turned on and off. To disaggregate appliance-specific energy usage the power signal is analyzed to identify these events. Detected events are then classified into appliance types by making a reference to an appliance training dataset. Due to the dynamic nature of appliances, existing event detectors face a key challenge of

© Springer International Publishing Switzerland 2014
E. Aarts et al. (Eds.): AmI 2014, LNCS 8850, pp. 221–225, 2014.
DOI: 10.1007/978-3-319-14112-1_18

keeping a low false alarm rate. We propose Real-time Energy Activity Classification Technique (REACT) a simple real-time event detection method for NILM and present a performance evaluation on a publicly available dataset [9].

2   Related Work

Generally, an event detector algorithm looks for a change (i.e. between two steady states) in an aggregated power signal. If the change exceeds a specified value of threshold, an alarm event is flagged. A number of statistical-based methods have been presented to identify these events. Of those, Generalised Likelihood Ratio Test (GLR) and mean-difference based methods are frequently used. These methods are mostly applied in an offline based manner, i.e. passing the whole data stream to the algorithm. However, this differs from real-time event detection (online based) techniques where the energy measurements are passed to the algorithm one by one. Moreover, existing approaches often require periodic training to adjust the required parameters in order to keep a low false alarm rate. The authors in [2] discuss a number of event detection algorithms proposed for NILM.

Authors in [4], present a modified version of the generalized likelihood ratio (GLR) test. The algorithm works well to detect sudden changes in the stream but fails to detect slower ones. Moreover, if events occur close to each other, the stronger event dominates the smaller ones. The work in [7] discusses a near real-time event detection method using Chi-square test for Goodness of Fit (GOF) to detect events in a power signal. However, this algorithm requires a training process. In [1], the author presents a real-time version of an event detector presented in [6]. An event is recorded if a power change (in the sample being observed) differs from the baseline beyond a fixed threshold. Reported accuracy was 96%, however, the experiment was carried out on only four test appliances.

3   Event Dectection

The event detection algorithm is presented in Algorithm 1. The algorithm requires the setting of two parameters: sliding window size, and a power threshold. In a sequential change detection scenario, a test statistic is usually computed on a data stream using a window technique. We choose sliding window technique that supports incremental queries on the data stream. The size of the window is chosen based on the event types (in terms of duration) to be detected. For example, if a smart meter reports data at a frequency of 3 seconds, a window size of 10 (observations) will only detect events that last 15 seconds or more in duration. The power threshold is the minimum power change value used to detect events. The algorithm works as follows. Sliding window of size N is loaded with data points of the energy signal being received over time, and then divided into two samples of size N/2. Data points in both samples are then subtracted from each other (one by one) and compared against the threshold. This returns a vector of decisions containing TRUE and/or FALSE values (TRUE if the difference exceeds the given threshold or FALSE otherwise). An event is detected if the product of the decision vector values is TRUE. This event is then classified as an ON or OFF event by calculating the mean difference of both samples. The location of the event is the first data point of second sample. Information about event location and the mean difference is stored in an event queue.

Algorithm 1. REACT: a real-time event detection algorithm for NILM.

Require: $window.size \geq 4$, $threshold \geq 1$
  while receiving observations **do**
    $window \leftarrow data[next.observation]$
    if $window[window.size] = loaded$ **then**
      $sample1 \leftarrow window[1 : window.size/2]$
      $sample2 \leftarrow window[window.size/2 + 1 : window.size]$
      if $prod(abs(sample1 - sample2) \geq threshold)$ **then**
        if $(mean(sample2) - mean(sample1)) > 0$ **then**
          $event.queue \leftarrow event.start(index + window.size/2, mean1)$
        else
          $event.queue \leftarrow event.end(index + window.size/2, mean1)$
        end if
        $window[1 : window/2] \leftarrow sample2$
        $window[window.size/2 + 1 : window.size] \leftarrow empty$
      end if
    else
      $window \leftarrow data[next.observation]$
    end if
    $index \leftarrow index + 1$
  end while

---

4   Experimental Results

To evaluate the performance of REACT, we conducted an experiment on a publicly available dataset called Reference Energy Disaggregation Dataset (REDD) [9]. The dataset consists of whole-house and appliance specific energy measurements obtained in 6 home in the U.S. over a period of several months. The dataset contains both high frequency and low frequency data. The low frequency data is chosen in which the mains are measured at a rate of 1 second and the appliances are measured every 3 seconds. This is because sampling frequency of the available smart meters fall into this category. We use appliance/circuit specific data as ground truth to evaluate the performance of event detector. Figure 1 provides a comparison of detection accuracy (for house 2 data containing 8 test appliances) between REACT and two popular GLR and mean-difference based event detectors.

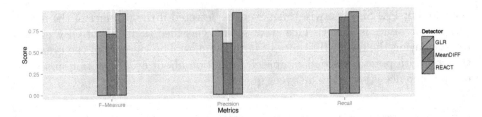

Fig. 1. Analysis of REACT using the dimensions of Precision, Recall and F-measure. The power threshold and the window size are set to 20 and 10 respectively.

5   Conclusion

In this paper, we proposed a simple yet powerful event detection algorithm named REACT for detecting events in energy data streams. Performance of the algorithm was then evaluated on the REDD dataset. REACT achieves the event detection accuracy of 95%. This shows a superior performance when compared with two other common approaches; GLR and mean-difference based event detection techniques.

Acknowledgments. This work is part funded by IRCSET Embark Postgraduate Research Scholarship in conjunction with Intel. In addition this work is supported by Science Foundation Ireland under grant 07/CE/I1147. The support of Enterprise Ireland under grant TC20121002A is also acknowledged.

References

1. Alasalmi, T., Suutala, J., Rning, J.: Real-time non-intrusive appliance load monitor - feedback system for single-point per appliance electricity usage. In: SmartGreens, pp. 203–208. SciTePress (2012)
2. Anderson, K., Berges, M., Ocneanu, A., Benitez, D., Moura, J.: Event detection for non intrusive load monitoring. In: IECON 2012 – 38th Annual Conference on IEEE Industrial Electronics Society, pp. 3312–3317 (October 2012)
3. Armel, C.K., Gupta, A., Shrimali, G., Albert, A.: Is disaggregation the holy grail of energy efficiency? the case of electricity. Energy Policy 52(C), 213–234 (2013)
4. Berges, M., Goldman, E., Matthews, H., Soibelman, L., Anderson, K.: User-centered nonintrusive electricity load monitoring for residential buildings. Journal of Computing in Civil Engineering 25(6), 471–480 (2011)
5. Fischer, C.: Feedback on household electricity consumption: A tool for saving energy? Energy Efficiency 1, 79–104 (2008)
6. Hart, G.W.: Nonintrusive appliance load monitoring. Proceedings of the IEEE 80(12) (1992)
7. Jin, Y., Tebekaemi, E., Berges, M., Soibelman, L.: Robust adaptive event detection in non-intrusive load monitoring for energy aware smart facilities. In: 2011 IEEE International Conference on Acoustics, Speech and Signal Processing (ICASSP), pp. 4340–4343 (May 2011)

8. Kazmi, A.H., O'Grady, M.J., Delaney, D.T., Ruzzelli, A.G., O'Hare, G.M.P.: A review of wireless-sensor-network-enabled building energy management systems. ACM Trans. Sen. Netw. 10(4), 66:1–66:43 (2014)

9. Kolter, J.Z., Johnson, M.J.: REDD: A Public Data Set for Energy Disaggregation Research. In: SustKDD Workshop on Data Mining Applications in Sustainability (2011)

10. Lillis, D., O'Sullivan, T., Holz, T., Muldoon, C., O'Grady, M., O'Hare, G.: Smart home energy management. Recent advances in ambient intelligence and context-aware computing. IGI Global (in press)

Developing a Face Monitoring Robot
for a Desk Worker

Ryosuke Kondo, Yutaka Deguchi, and Einoshin Suzuki[✉]

Department of Informatics, ISEE, Kyushu University,
744 Motooka, Nishi, Fukuoka 819-0395, Japan
2ie13013g@s.kyushu-u.ac.jp, yutaka.kyushu@gmail.com,
suzuki@inf.kyushu-u.ac.jp
http://www.i.kyushu-u.ac.jp/~suzuki/slabhomee.html

Abstract. We have developed an autonomous mobile robot which monitors the face of a desk worker. The robot uses three kinds of information observed with its Kinect to search for the desk worker and adjusts its position for monitoring. The monitoring is based on incremental clustering of the faces. Our experiments revealed that not only Animation Units (AUs) features, which represent deviations from the neutral face, but also the pitch angle of the face normalized in a new way are necessary for a valid clustering under specific conditions. Our robot lost sight of a desk worker only once in experiments for 8 persons for about 50 minutes. The resulting clusters correspond to "yawning", "smiling", and "reading" for a half of the desk workers with high NMI (normalized mutual information), which is an evaluation measure often used in clustering.

Keywords: Human monitoring robot · Clustering · Face tracking

1 Introduction

One of the important ways humans display emotions is through facial expressions [7,15]. With the proliferation of human-computer intelligent interaction systems including those in the ambient intelligence domain [1], the problem of automatically recognizing human emotions through his/her facial expressions has been attracting much attention of the research community [10,12,15,19–21]. From the ambient intelligence perspective, such a technique should be deployed in a real situation, enabling in the long run a truly "intelligent" system which "understands" the target person by his/her look. This requirement necessitates an adequate design of the whole system as well as coping with various challenges met in the deployment.

Having seen the recent rapid advancement of consumer mobile robots, e.g., Eddie[1], TurtleBot 2[2], as well as successful applications [4–6,8,18], we believe that a system which includes an autonomous mobile robot is a promising solution.

---

[1] http://www.parallax.com/product/28992
[2] http://www.turtlebot.com/

© Springer International Publishing Switzerland 2014
E. Aarts et al. (Eds.): AmI 2014, LNCS 8850, pp. 226–241, 2014.
DOI: 10.1007/978-3-319-14112-1_19

Compared to the prevailing monitoring systems based on fixed cameras, such a monitoring system is less invasive to privacy, more flexible to changes, and more focused in its observation due to its ability to move to the right position when necessary [18].

Our previous work [18] identified three major obstacles in developing such a system: (1) diverse targets, (2) massive data, and (3) huge management cost. The targets of the monitoring vary significantly, e.g., each aged person has his/her own behaviors, habits, preferences, requirements, and prohibitions. The observed data by the robots are massive, e.g., under a typical setting, a Kinect device[3] [17] outputs an image file of about 4.5MB in size every 1/30 seconds, which results in about 4.0PB in 1 year. Management of multiple robots is still in its infancy, e.g., even preparing a demonstration of such a system in an exhibition requires considerable skill and labor. With these obstacles we tackled the problem of discovering fall risks[4] successfully [5,6,18] with an incremental clustering BIRCH [22][5] and sometimes a data stream management system (SoCQ) [9]. In these systems, one or two autonomous mobile robots would continuously observe a person walking in a room and at the same time cluster his/her skeletons observed with Kinect. These papers showed promising results in terms of the discovered clusters and the robot control [5,6].

Our initial trials for imitating their systems for our face-monitoring problem of a desk worker failed due to the following difficulties. The face tracking application of Kinect is less accurate than its skeleton tracking application due to the much smaller size of a face than the whole body[6]. Our initial robot easily lost sight of the human due to the frequent, abrupt changes of the face orientations. Even after resolving this difficulty, the clusters learnt by the robot were mostly counter-intuitive. In this paper, we propose our solution that has almost overcome the first difficulty and gives promising results for the second difficulty.

2   Autonomous Mobile Robot

We followed [5,6,18] and used a consumer mobile robot TurtleBot 2 as the platform. A Kinect device and a notebook PC are mounted on the platform as in [5,6,18]. Figure 1 left shows our autonomous mobile robot. The notebook PC is Panasonic's Let's Note CF-SX2DETBR with 4GB memory and Corei7 Processor. The OS is Windows 8.1 to easily use Kinect for Windows and TurtleBot 2. Using the face tracking application, the robot can observe and store a color

---

[3] http://research.microsoft.com/en-us/projects/vrkinect/

[4] Among the various problems the elderly face in their daily lives, accidental falls are critical, e.g., in the U.S., falls occur 30–60% of older adults each year, and 10–20% of these falls result in injury, hospitalization, and/or death [13].

[5] Compared to its successors [2,11,16], BIRCH is fast, simple, and adequate for onboard clustering.

[6] We used the first generation of Kinect for Windows. The newer generation of Kinect would possibly give superior result, though we have to adapt our method to the new set of features provided by its face tracking application.

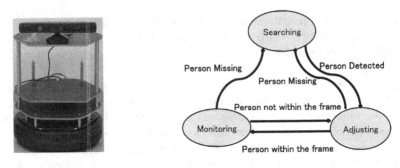

Fig. 1. (Left) Our autonomous mobile robot. (Right) Behavior of the robot as a 3-state finite automaton.

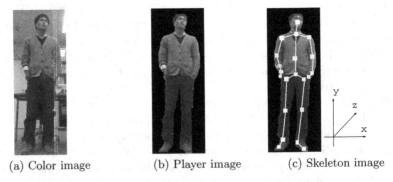

(a) Color image   (b) Player image   (c) Skeleton image

Fig. 2. Examples of data observed with Kinect

image, facial features, and the orientation of a face at about 6.25fps. Details will be given in Section 3.1. Note that Kinect also provides the player region, which allows us to estimate the regions of the person in the color and depth images. A skeleton consists of the 3D coordinates of the 20 joints inferred by Kinect. Figure 2 shows (a) the color image, (b) the player image in the player region in (a), and (c) the skeleton overlaid on (b).

We followed a conventional approach also adapted by [6] and modeled the behavior of the robot as a 3-state finite automaton, which we show in Figure 1 right. The three states are searching, monitoring, and adjusting. Since the face of a desk worker moves less distance than the skeleton of a walking person, our implementations of the three states are different from those of [6]. Note also that Kinect was initially developed as an input device for a video game console. It is less effective to a desk worker, who is sitting on a chair, than to a walker. A Kinect-equipped robot with a straightforward control program can easily lose sight of the person. To circumvent this problem, we devised a controlling algorithm which utilizes the color image, the depth image, the skeleton, and the face tracking information simultaneously. We implemented searching as a rotation of the robot, adjusting as a forward/backward move and a rotation of the robot.

Execution of monitoring is decided by a relatively complex procedure which relies not only faces but also skeletons and color images for coping with noise.

The pseudo code of the behavior control of our robot is shown in Algorithm 1, where player means the target person. With the algorithm, the robot can keep its distance to the person appropriately and take an appropriate action according to the actions of the person. In the pseudo code, function Update($colorMat$, $depthMat$, $playerMat$) updates the color, depth, and player matrices $colorMat$, $depthMat$, and $playerMat$, respectively. Function $GetPlayer()$ returns the number of the persons (players) in sight. Function moveRobot(v_x, v_a) moves the robot with the velocity v_x of the forward move and the velocity v_a of the anticlockwise yaw. x_{ORG} represents the x coordinate of the origin of the image region, which corresponds to the horizontal direction of the sight of the robot.

We assumed that the appropriate distance between the robot and the face of the person is 1.5 [m]. The person is hidden behind the desk with a shorter distance and the accuracy of Kinect deteriorates with a longer distance. The condition in line 17 was determined by the plausible distance between the robot and the face of a standing person at around 1.5 [m]. It is because the robot has detected the person, who is assumed to be standing or moving, and has to find his/her face. The next action in line 18 represents that the robot moves at its safe, fastest speed (0.3 [m/s]) until its distance to the face becomes less than 2.2 [m]. On the other hand, the condition in line 32 was determined by assuming that the person is sitting still, coping with the noise in the depth image. The next action in line 33 represents that the robot moves at a slower speed (0.2 [m/s]) to the appropriate distance. Other parameters were also determined empirically. The condition in line 11 is relatively strict (width 1 [m]) to keep on spotting the person at the center of the sight. The turning action in the next line was devised to slow down when the person is located near the center. On the other hand, the turning action in lines 25 - 28 is for a person under observation. We adopted very loose conditions (below 280 [pixel] or above 360 [pixel]) to continue the observation as long as possible. Loosening these conditions further would increase the risk of missing the person considerably. Finally, the turning speed in line 7 was found empirically. A faster speed prevents the robot from detecting the person.

3   Clustering Faces

3.1   Face Tracking Application

Microsoft provides face tracking application for Kinect[7]. It can measure 17 facial features, the orientation of the face, and 87 tracking points. The 17 facial features consist of 6 Animation Units (AUs), which represent the deviations from the neutral face, and 11 Shape Units (SUs), which represent particular shapes and positions of the facial parts such as mouth, brows, and eyes. We explain these

---

[7] Microsoft, Microsoft Developer Network, "http://msdn.microsoft.com/en-us/library/jj130970.aspx" (2014/7/14).

Algorithm 1. Behavior control of our robot

```
 1: v_x ← 0
 2: v_a ← 0
 3: while true do
 4:     Update(colorMat, depthMat, playerMat)
 5:     num_player ← GetPlayer()
 6:     if Face is not found OR num_player = 0 then
 7:         (v_x, v_a) ← (0, 0.6) [m/s, rad/s] // Search state (rotate anticlockwise)
 8:     else if num_player > 0 then
 9:         (v_x, v_a) ← (0, 0) [m/s, rad/s] // Stop
10:         x_0 ← (the x-coordinate of the hip center joint)
11:         if x_0 − x_ORG > 0.5 [m] OR x_0 − x_ORG < −0.5 [m] then
12:             v_a ← min(0.3(x_0 − x_ORG), 0.3) [rad/s] // Adjusting state
13:         else
14:             v_a ← 0 [rad/s]
15:         end if
16:         head_z ← (distance to the head joint)
17:         if z_3 < 1.9 [m] OR z_3 > 2.2 [m] then
18:             v_x ← min(0.3(z_3 − 2.2), 0.3) [m/s] // Adjusting state
19:         else
20:             v_x ← 0 [m/s]
21:         end if
22:     else if Face is found then
23:         (v_x, v_a) ← (0, 0) [m/s, rad/s] // Monitoring state (Stop)
24:         centerFacePoint ← (center of gravity of the face)
25:         if centerFacePoint_x < 280 [pixel] then
26:             v_a ← 0.1 [rad/s] // Adjusting state
27:         else if centerFacePoint_x > 360 [pixel] then
28:             v_a ← −0.1 [rad/s] // Adjusting state
29:         else
30:             v_a ← 0 [rad/s]
31:             face_z ← (distance to the center of gravity of the face)
32:             if face_z > 1.55 [m] OR face_z > 1.3 [m] then
33:                 v_x ← min(0.2(face_z − 1.5), 0.3) [m/s] // Adjusting state
34:             else
35:                 v_x ← 0 [m/s] // Monitoring state (Stop)
36:             end if
37:         end if
38:     end if
39:     moveRobot(v_x, v_a)
40: end while
```

features in the Appendix. The orientation of the face is represented by 3 angles: pitch, yaw, and roll as shown in Figure 3. Each angle takes a value between -90 [degree] and 90 [degree].

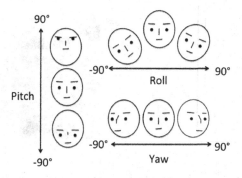

Fig. 3. 3 angles for representing the face orientation

3.2 BIRCH

We followed [5,6,18] and adopted BIRCH (Balanced Iterative Reducing and Clustering using Hierarchies) [22] as the clustering method. BIRCH first transforms a set $X = \{x_1, x_2, \ldots, x_n\}$ of instances each x_i of which is described with numerical features into a set $V = \{v_1, v_2, \ldots, v_m\}$ of CFs (clustering features), clusters the CFs, and if required translates the clusters of the CFs into the corresponding clusters of instances. Here n and m represents the numbers of instances and CFs, respectively. Each CF v_j corresponds to an abstract representation of a neighboring instances and is represented as follows when the corresponding instances are $x'_1, x'_2, \ldots, x'_p$.

$$v = \left(p, \sum_{i=1}^{p} x'_i, \sum_{i=1}^{p} \| x'_i \|^2 \right) \tag{1}$$

One of the two virtues of the CF is that various kinds of inter-cluster distances can be calculated from the corresponding CFs of the clusters only, i.e., the original instances are not necessary in the calculation. For instance, the average inter-cluster distance $D_2(E_1, E_2)$ can be calculated from the corresponding CFs as follows, where $E_1 = \{x_1, x_2, \ldots, x_{n_1}\}$ and $E_2 = \{x_{n_1+1}, x_{n_1+1}, \ldots, x_{n_1+n_2}\}$.

$$D_2(E_1, E_2) \equiv \sqrt{\frac{\sum_{i=1}^{n_1} \sum_{j=n_1+1}^{n_1+n_2} \| x_i - x_j \|^2}{n_1 n_2}} \tag{2}$$

$$= \sqrt{\frac{n_2 \sum_{i=1}^{n_1} \| x'_i \|^2 + n_1 \sum_{j=n_1+1}^{n_1+n_2} \| x'_j \|^2 - 2 \sum_{i=1}^{n_1} x'_i \cdot \sum_{j=n_1+1}^{n_1+n_2} x'_j}{n_1 n_2}} \tag{3}$$

The other virtue is that a CF can be updated without the original instances when a new instance is added. This characteristic holds due to the definition of

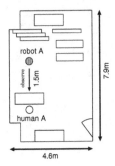

Fig. 4. (Left) Map of the environment of the experiments. (Right) Snapshot of the experiments

the CF. Note that instances can be safely forgotten and BIRCH needs to store CFs only. CFs are stored in a height-balanced tree similar to the B+ tree. An added new instance follows the path from the root node to a leaf, updating the CFs of the nodes on the path. It is absorbed into an existing leaf if the average inter-cluster distance between the CF of the leaf and the CF that consists of the instance only is below an absorption threshold θ.

3.3   NMI

When a ground-truth, i.e., the correct cluster label for each instance, is available, NMI (normalized mutual information) is often used to evaluate the goodness of a clustering result.

$$NMI = \frac{-2\sum_{i=1}^{|C_A|}\sum_{j=1}^{|C_B|} N_{ij} \log \frac{N_{ij}N}{N_i N_j}}{\sum_{i=1}^{|C_A|} N_i \log \frac{N_i}{N} + \sum_{j=1}^{|C_B|} N_j \log \frac{N_j}{N}} \tag{4}$$

where C_A and C_B represent the true and the actual sets of clusters, respectively. N_i, N_j respectively represent the numbers of instances contained in C_A and C_B. N_{ij} and N represent the number of instances contained in both C_A and C_B, and the total number of instances, respectively. NMI takes a value between 0 and 1, which respectively correspond to the worst and the best results.

4   Experiments

4.1   Conditions of the Experiments

We conducted experiments in an office, where the subject is mostly sitting on a chair and the robot is located at 1.5 [m] distant from him/her. Figure 4 shows the map of the office and a snapshot of the experiments. All experiments were conducted with the window shade down to avoid direct sunlight[8].

---

[8] We admit that this is an artificial condition.

Table 1. Statistics of the experiments for each subject

Subject ID	Gender	Date	Time	# of frames	# of lost sight
1	male	14/06/07 16:20	6m23s	2408	0
2	male	14/07/16 20:23	6m34s	1816	0
3	female	14/07/16 20:13	6m54s	1251	1
4	male	14/07/16 20:32	6m45s	2249	0
5	female	14/07/25 16:30	6m01s	1617	0
6	male	14/07/25 16:09	7m14s	1862	0
7	male	14/09/26 14:37	6m14s	1374	0
8	male	14/09/26 20:50	7m26s	2048	0

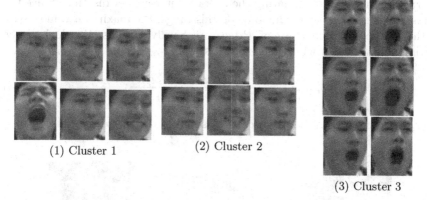

(1) Cluster 1   (2) Cluster 2

(3) Cluster 3

Fig. 5. Examples of clusters with their representative instances with AUs only as features

We employed eight subjects in Table 1, each of whom was first standing up behind the table. The robot found the subject, adjusted its position, and began monitoring him/her. The subject confirmed that the robot was monitoring him/her and then sat down on a chair to read a book for about 6 minutes. The monitoring lasted during this period, which resulted in about 1600–2400 frames. Table 1 also shows that the robot almost never lost sight of the subjects. The single exception is due to a rapid seating of Subject 3.

4.2   Results with AUs only

Initial experiments revealed that SUs have a negative effect on clustering probably due to its slower changing rate than that of the facial expressions. Thus we first used AUs only as features. Contrary to the abundance of supervised facial expression recognition, unsupervised methods are rare. In this paper, we compare several methods in our approach.

Figure 5 shows examples of clusters with their representative instances. The Figure shows that the clusters are not so homogeneous. For instance, expressions such as "yawning", "smiling", and "reading" are mixed in these three clusters.

4.3   Incorporation of the Pitch Angle

After analyzing the results of the experiments, we found that some of the values of the AUs are not reliable, probably due to the small size of the observed color image (50 × 50 pixels). We also noticed that the pitch angle $Pitch_t$ of the face orientation at time t, which is shown in Figure 3, is often related with the expressions of the subjects. For instance, 4 out of 8 subjects, before laughing, typically raised his/her face up because a colleague had talked to him/her. These subjects, before yawning, often moved his/her face up and down. In addition, $Pitch_t$ is relatively accurate compared with AUs. Thus we decided to reflect $Pitch_t$ in our clustering by adding a new feature to represent an instance[9].

Since $Pitch_t$ takes a value between -90 [degree] and 90 [degree], it must be normalized to avoid dominating the average inter-cluster distance. Since the pitch angle does not take a value outside this range, the maximum value P_{MAX} and the minimum value P_{MIN} of $Pitch_t$ are hardly outliers. We devised the following normalization which relies on these values.

$$p'_t = \frac{Pitch_t - 0.5(P_{MAX} + P_{MIN})}{0.5(P_{MAX} - P_{MIN})} \tag{5}$$

In this series of experiments, we used 6 AUs and p'_t to represent an instance.

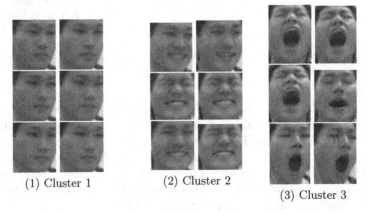

(1) Cluster 1   (2) Cluster 2

(3) Cluster 3

Fig. 6. Examples of clusters with their representative instances with AUs and our pitch feature

Figure 6 shows examples of clusters with their representative examples. Note that this time the three classes "yawning", "smiling", and "reading" are clearly separated in these three clusters. We show the results of NMI with AUs and our pitch feature in Figures 7(a)–(h).

---

[9] We also tried to reflect roll and yaw angles in various ways without greater success, which explains our confinement to the pitch angle.

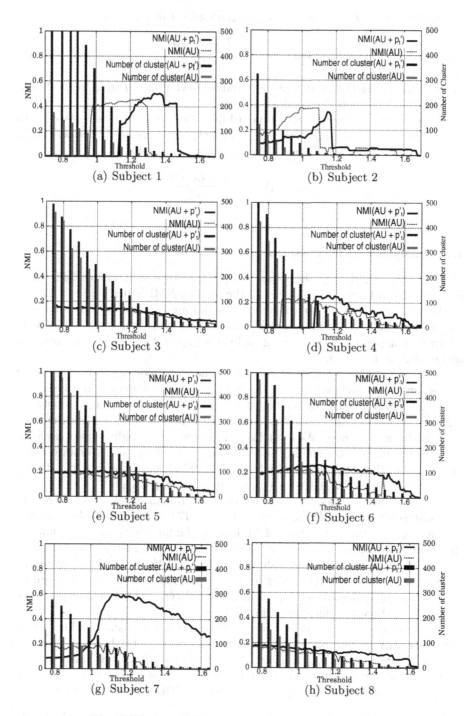

Fig. 7. Results of NMI with AUs and our pitch feature

We also tested Z-score $p_{t,\text{z-scoreStd}}$ to normalize $Pitch_t$.

$$p_{t,\text{z-scoreStd}} = \frac{Pitch_t - \bar{p}}{\sigma_p} \tag{6}$$

where $\bar{p}$ and σ_p are the mean and the standard deviation of $Pitch_t$, respectively. Figures 8 (a)–(h) show the results.

In z-score normalization, the standard deviation is sometimes replaced with the absolute deviation $MAD_p = \frac{1}{T}\sum_{t=0}^{t=T}(Pitch_t - \bar{p})$ because the former can be dominated by an outlier. Figures 9 (a)–(h) show the results.

$$p_{t,\text{z-scoreMad}} = \frac{Pitch_t - \bar{p}}{MAD_p} \tag{7}$$

4.4   Analysis and Discussions

Figure 7 (a), (d), (f), (g) show that our pitch feature p'_t leverages NMI while Figure 7 (b), (c), (e), (h) not. In (g), the highest NMI is 0.599 ($\theta = 1.12$ and 46 clusters), which shows the effectiveness of our approach under this condition. The latter 4 subjects often yawned while reading and their pitch angles were relatively not related with yawning and smiling. The two kinds of z-scores are also ineffective for them.

We found that the degree of relatedness between looking up and changing expressions is a good indicator of the improved NMI. A person in our experiments is usually reading by looking down (the average pitch angle is between -12 [degree] and -11 [degree]). We defined that a face is upward when the pitch angle is above -8 [degree]. We formalized the degree of relatedness as α, which is given by the ratio of the smiling and yawning expressions among upward faces. In the figure, the values of α are 0.588, 0.379, 0.535, 0.897 for (a), (d), (f), (g) and 0.304, 0.360, 0.392, 0.370 for (b), (c), (e), (h), respectively[10].

Kinect often returns a wrong pitch angle when it mistracks the face region. The mistrack rates were highest with 0.450%, 0.174%, and 0.120% for Subjects 5 (e: a scarf of a muslim female), 4 (d: hair on the forefront), and 3 (c: low-cut shirt with chest open), respectively. We are further investigating this issue.

In Figure 7, our pitch feature shifts the plots of NMI to the right because its addition increases the inter-cluster distance. Note also that the range of values of the AUs, $p_{t,\text{z-scoreStd}}$, and $p_{t,\text{z-scoreMad}}$ are different. These facts explain the difference of the values for θ for high NMI.

NMI are relatively higher in Figure 7 than in Figures 8 and 9, which shows the superiority of our pitch feature to the z-scores. Note that the values of $p_{t,\text{z-scoreStd}}$ and $p_{t,\text{z-scoreMad}}$ can be greater than 1 while an AU takes a value between -1 and 1. For instance, the numbers of images in which $p_{t,\text{z-scoreStd}}$ or $p_{t,\text{z-scoreMad}}$ exceeds 1 for Subject 1 are 285 and 356, respectively. Out of the

---

[10] The sole exception is between (d) and (e). The former shows lower α despite an increase in NMI.

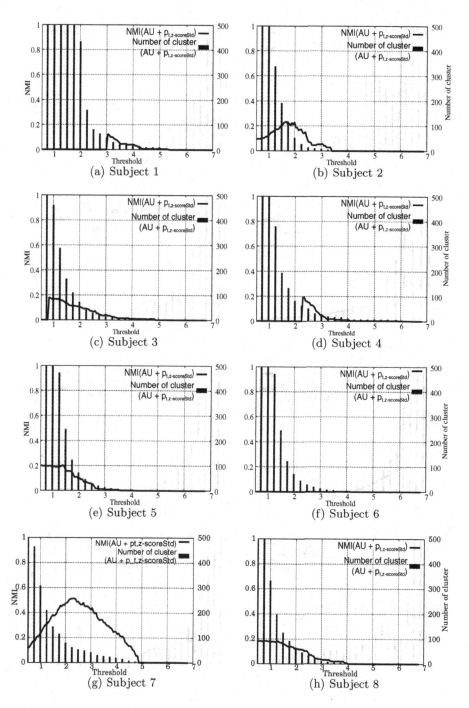

Fig. 8. Results of NMI with AUs and the pitch feature obtained by the z-score with the standard deviation

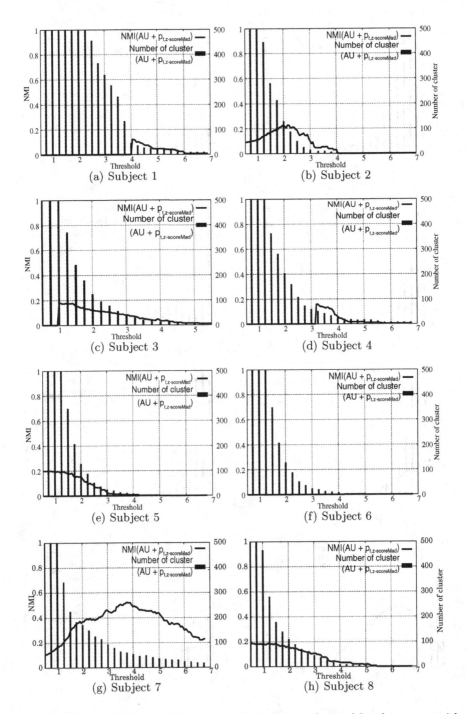

Fig. 9. Results of NMI with AUs and the pitch feature obtained by the z-score with the absolute deviation

285 and 356 images, 282 and 303 images correspond to either "yawning" or "smiling", respectively. These images are often scattered to small clusters due to the wide variety of values for $p_{t,\text{z-scoreStd}}$ and $p_{t,\text{z-scoreMad}}$. For example, even at the highest NMI 3.2 in Figure 8 (a), 128 out of the 285 images belong to clusters each of which consists of less than 4 images.

Though the absolute deviation MAD_p is robust against noise, even $p_{t,\text{z-scoreMad}}$ has a deficiency. The face can move abruptly, resulting in a very large value (around 3 to 5) of $p_{t,\text{z-scoreMad}}$. In such a case, the inter-cluster distance between two CFs is dominated by $p_{t,\text{z-scoreMad}}$, which deteriorates NMI. A typical example of this phenomenon is found in Figure 9 (f).

We see from these experiments that not only deviations (AUs) from the neutral face but also the pitch angle of the face normalized in our own way are necessary for a valid clustering under specific conditions. Our robot recovered "yawning", "smiling", and "reading" of the desk worker with high NMI for half of the subjects by clustering, which is an important step toward personalized monitoring based on discovery by an autonomous mobile robot.

5 Conclusions

We have developed a face monitoring robot. The robot observes the face of the desk worker and clusters them. Our experiments revealed that incorporation of the pitch angle is necessary for avoiding counter-intuitive clusters. We assume that the clusters should be inspected by a human analyzer. One natural extension is to automate this inspection procedure so that the robot conducts the task and decides the next action. Realizing such a loop is trivial if we resort to an ad-hoc procedure. Our ambitious goal is to realize the loop in a systematic way so that the robot is capable of adapting to various people with little man labor. We believe lifelong learning [14] gives a promising direction.

A Animation Units and Shape Units

AUs and SUs were defined based on the Candide 3 Model [3]. The AUs are deviations from the neutral face: all AUs are 0 for the neutral face. Each AU is expressed as a numeric weight varying between -1 and +1 [11]. A SU defines a deformation of a standard face towards a specific face. It is an estimate of a particular shape of the user's head, e.g., the neutral position of their mouth, brows, eyes. The shape parameters should be invariant over time but specific to each individual[12]. Animation parameters naturally vary over time.

Tables 2 and 3 show definitions of the AUs and the SUs in the face tracking SDK application, respectively. Note that they are slightly different from those in the Candide 3 Model.

---

[11] Microsoft,   Microsoft   Developer   Network,   "http://msdn.microsoft.com/en-us/library/jj130970.aspx" (2014/7/14).

[12] We observed that SUs do change over time but more slowly than the AUs.

Table 2. Definition of AUs (See http://msdn.microsoft.com/en-us/library/jj130970. aspx for images)

AU	AU value and its interpretation
AU0 - Upper Lip Raiser (AU10 of Candide 3)	0=neutral, covering teeth; 1=showing teeth fully; -1=maximal possible pushed down lip.
AU1 - Jaw Lowerer (AU26/27 of Candide 3)	0=closed; 1=fully open; -1= closed, like 0.
AU2 - Lip Stretcher (AU20 of Candide 3)	0=neutral; 1=fully stretched (joker's smile); -0.5=rounded (pout); -1=fully rounded (kissing mouth).
AU3 - Brow Lowerer (AU4 of Candide 3)	0=neutral; -1=raised almost all the way; +1=fully lowered (to the limit of the eyes)
AU4 - Lip Corner Depressor (AU13/15 of Candide 3)	0=neutral; -1=very happy smile; +1=very sad frown
AU5 - Outer Brow Raiser (AU2 of Candide 3)	0=neutral; -1=fully lowered as a very sad face; +1=raised as in an expression of a deep surprise

Table 3. Definition of SUs

SU name	SU ID in Candide 3
Head height	0
Eyebrows vertical position	1
Eyes vertical position	2
Eyes, width	3
Eyes, height	4
Eye separation distance	5
Nose vertical position	8
Mouth vertical position	10
Mouth width	11
Eyes vertical difference	n/a
Chin width	n/a

Acknowledgments. This work was partially supported by the grants-in-aid for scientific research (24650070, 25280085) from the Japanese Ministry of Education, Culture, Sports, Science and Technology. We appreciate Rachel Pang for her technical assistance.

References

1. Aarts, E., Encarnacao, J.: Into Ambient Intelligence. In: True Vision - The Emergence of Ambient Intelligence, pp. 1–16. Springer-Verlag (2006)
2. Aggarwal, C.C., Han, J., Wang, J., Yu, P.S.: A Framework for Clustering Evolving Data Streams. In: Proc. VLDB 2003, pp. 81–92 (2003)
3. Ahlberg, J.: Candide-3 An Updated Parameterised Face. Technical Report LiTH-ISY-R-2326, Dept. Elec. Eng., Linköping University Sweden (2001)
4. Coradeschi, S., et al.: GiraffPlus: Combining Social Interaction and Long Term Monitoring for Promoting Independent Living. In: Proc. HSI, pp. 6–15 (2013)

5. Deguchi, Y., Suzuki, E.: Skeleton Clustering by Autonomous Mobile Robots for Subtle Fall Risk Discovery. In: Andreasen, T., Christiansen, H., Cubero, J.-C., Raś, Z.W. (eds.) ISMIS 2014. LNCS, vol. 8502, pp. 500–505. Springer, Heidelberg (2014)
6. Deguchi, Y., Takayama, D., Takano, S., Scuturici, V.-M., Petit, J.-M., Suzuki, E.: Multiple-Robot Monitoring System Based on a Service-Oriented DBMS. In: Proc. Seventh ACM International Conference on Pervasive Technologies Related to Assistive Environments (PETRA 2014) (2014)
7. Erna, A., Yu, L., Zhao, K., Chen, W., Suzuki, E.: Facial Expression Data Constructed with Kinect and Their Clustering Stability. In: Ślęzak, D., Schaefer, G., Vuong, S.T., Kim, Y.-S. (eds.) AMT 2014. LNCS, vol. 8610, pp. 421–431. Springer, Heidelberg (2014)
8. Fischinger, D., et al.: HOBBIT - The Mutual Care Robot. In: Proc. ASROB (2013)
9. Gripay, Y., Laforest, F., Petit, J.-M.: A Simple (yet Powerful) Algebra for Pervasive Environments. In: Proc. EDBT, pp. 359–370 (2010)
10. Hossny, M., et al.: Low Cost Multimodal Facial Recognition via Kinect Sensors. CISR, Deakin University, Australia, Technical report (2013)
11. Kranen, P., Assent, I., Baldauf, C., Seidl, T.: The ClusTree: Indexing Micro-Clusters for Anytime Stream Mining. Knowledge and Information Systems 29(2), 249–272 (2011)
12. Lyons, M.J., Akamatsu, S., Kamachi, M., Gyoba, J.: Coding Facial Expressions with Gabor Wavelets. In: Proc. Third International Conference on Face and Gesture Recognition (FG), pp. 200–205 (1998)
13. Rubenstein, L.Z.: Falls in Older People: Epidemiology, Risk Factors and Strategies for Prevention. Age and Ageing, ii37–ii41 (2006)
14. Ruvolo, P., Eaton, E.: ELLA: An Efficient Lifelong Learning Algorithm. In: Proc. ICML 2013, vol. 1, pp. 507–515 (2013)
15. Sebe, N., Lew, M., Sun, Y., Cohen, I., Geners, T., Huang, T.: Authentic Facial Expression Analysis. Image and Vision Computing 25, 1856–1863 (2007)
16. Seidl, T., Assent, I., Kranen, P., Krieger, R., Herrmann, J.: Indexing Density Models for Incremental Learning and Anytime Classification on Data Streams. In: Proc. EDBT 2009, pp. 311–322 (2009)
17. Shotton, J., Fitzgibbon, A., Cook, M., Sharp, T., Finocchio, M., Moore, R., Kipman, A., Blake, A.: Real-Time Human Pose Recognition in Parts from Single Depth Images. In: Proc. CVPR 2011, pp. 1297–1304 (2011)
18. Suzuki, E., Deguchi, Y., Takayama, D., Takano, S., Scuturici, V.-M., Petit, J.-M.: Towards Facilitating the Development of Monitoring Systems with Low-Cost Autonomous Mobile Robots. In: Kawtrakul, A., Laurent, D., Spyratos, N., Tanaka, Y. (eds.) ISIP 2013. CCIS, vol. 421, pp. 57–70. Springer, Heidelberg (2014)
19. Valstar, M.F., Jiang, B., Mehu, M., Pantic, M., Schrer, K.: The First Facial Expression Recognition and Analysis Challenge. In: Proc. International Conference on Face and Gesture Recognition (FG), pp. 921–926 (2011)
20. Verma, A., Sharma, L.K.: A Comprehensive Survey on Human Facial Expression Detection. Int'l J. Image Processing 7(2), 171–182 (2013)
21. Yong, C., Sudirman, R., Chew, K.: Facial Expression Monitoring System Using PCA-Bayes Classifier. In: Future Computer Sciences and Application (ICFCSA), pp. 187–191 (2011)
22. Zhang, T., Ramakrishnan, R., Livny, M.: BIRCH: A New Data Clustering Algorithm and its Applications. Data Mining and Knowledge Discovery 1(2), 141–182 (1997)

A Benchmarking Model for Sensors in Smart Environments

Andreas Braun[1(✉)], Reiner Wichert[1], Arjan Kuijper[1,2], and Dieter W. Fellner[1,2]

[1] Fraunhofer Institute for Computer Graphics Research IGD, Darmstadt, Germany
{andreas.braun,reiner.wichert,arjan.kuijper,
dieter.fellner}@igd.fraunhofer.de
[2] TU Darmstadt, Darmstadt, Germany

Abstract. In smart environments, developers can choose from a large variety of sensors supporting their use case that have specific advantages or disadvantages. In this work we present a benchmarking model that allows estimating the utility of a sensor technology for a use case by calculating a single score, based on a weighting factor for applications and a set of sensor features. This set takes into account the complexity of smart environment systems that are comprised of multiple subsystems and applied in non-static environments. We show how the model can be used to find a suitable sensor for a use case and the inverse option to find suitable use cases for a given set of sensors. Additionally, extensions are presented that normalize differently rated systems and compensate for central tendency bias. The model is verified by estimating technology popularity using a frequency analysis of associated search terms in two scientific databases.

Keywords: Benchmark · Smart environments · Modeling · Sensor technology

1 Introduction

When designing a new application or system for a specific purpose, the parties involved have to make a number of decisions regarding the different components, processes and methods that are to be used. Benchmarking is a method mostly used in business practice to compare the performance of processes, products and market entities against one another. A single or a set of different indicators are used to act as metric or calculate an overarching metric of performance that can be compared to other entities [1]. This tool is widely used for supporting decisions in different domains. Looking at smart environments, a common challenge is to select a specific sensor technology for any given application. While the majority of systems are following a structured approach in the design process, e.g. by ranking available systems or performing an iterative trial & error routine, so far there has been no generic model that would allow to evaluate the expected performance of a system based on a specific sensor technology. This is particular in complex domains, such as Ambient Assisted Living (AAL) that involve constant interaction of actors within the environment, third parties that exchange information with the smart environment, and a variety of

© Springer International Publishing Switzerland 2014
E. Aarts et al. (Eds.): AmI 2014, LNCS 8850, pp. 242–257, 2014.
DOI: 10.1007/978-3-319-14112-1_20

different sensor systems measuring certain aspects of the environment. In this work we introduce a formal benchmarking model that allows estimating the performance of applications in smart environments based on a specific sensor technology. Using a set of common features and an adaptive weighting model we are able to cover a high number of different applications in a specific domain and thus support the decision process at an early stage of the application design. We are presenting related works ranging from technology benchmarking to selection of specific metrics before discussing features that are relevant for smart environments. After introducing the model formalism we evaluate the method by performing a popularity analysis within scientific works. For this we use a set of search terms on two scientific databases. Furthermore, we discuss several normalization and compensation techniques that cope with specific effects we observed in the benchmarking process.

2   Related Works

Benchmarking is a tool that is widely used in computing technology [2]. Hardware benchmarks compare the performance of different single systems, often seen for GPUs or CPUs to evaluate both theoretical and real-life performance. Some metrics that are used for theoretical comparison in CPUs are FLOPS (floating point operations per second), e.g. measured by Linpack [3], or MIPS (million instructions per second), e.g. measured by Dhrystone [4]. Regarding GPUs the benchmarks include Texel rate (how many triangles can be processed per second) and Pixel rate (how many pixels are processed per second. Real-life benchmarks for CPUs typically included timing specific tasks on applications that are demanding for certain aspects of the CPU, such as video processing, image processing or audio encoding. For GPUs many PC games provide benchmarking tools that allow evaluating the real-life performance of different graphics cards at different settings, e.g. resolution or detail level. The typical metric here are FPS (frames per second) that denote how often the screen content can be rendered in a second.

System benchmarks are a step up from single component benchmarks and combine the performance measurements of various components in different scenarios to evaluate the estimated behavior in numerous real-life situations. There are several standardized test suites that provide this functionality, such as SPEC [5]. A common single index that is available for all newer Windows machines (Vista and beyond) is the Windows System Assessment tool that calculates the WEI (Windows Experience Index), a combined score of CPU performance, 2D and 3D graphics performance, memory performance and disk performance. For determining the lowest score of all single metrics is chosen to determine a lower bound for expected real-life performance.

If different systems of the same category are compared, technology reviewers often use a single index that is calculated based on various aspects of the system. Smith introduced different potential combined metrics that can be used for this purpose [6]. Three different approaches are mentioned, geometric mean, arithmetic mean and harmonic mean. Additionally varieties with a specific weighting are mentioned.

There has been considerable work in the domain of identifying suitable metrics for a given benchmark. Crolotte argued that the only valid benchmark for decision support systems is the arithmetic mean of different single benchmark streams, as it is valid for normalized and time-relevant benchmarks [7]. Jain and Raj dedicate several chapters of their book to introduce methods and considerations for metric selection in benchmarking computer systems [8].

In smart environments a number of different benchmarks have been proposed that cover aspects similar to our approach. Ranganathan et al. introduced benchmarking methods and a set for pervasive computing systems [9]. They distinguish system metrics, configurability and programmability metrics and human usability metrics. Another example for benchmarking whole systems is the EvAAL competition that aims at evaluating different technologies that are applicable in Ambient Assisted Living [10]. There are various tracks, including indoor localization and activity recognition. Apart from technical metrics, such as precision, a focus of this competition is on a more holistic approach and thus includes metrics like installation time, user acceptance and interoperability of the solution. Santos et al. presented a model to evaluate human-computer interaction in ubiquitous computing applications, based on trustability, resource-limitedness, usability and ubiquity [11]. In order to assess how well ubiquitous computing applications cover privacy aspects, Jafari et al. propose a set of five abstracted metrics that are applied to whole systems [12]. While these are all benchmarking models within smart environments, they are either aiming at evaluating whole systems or singular aspects not directly related towards sensor technology.

3   Sensor Features

One of the most challenging aspects of benchmarking is selecting the appropriate metrics to be included. In order to identify relevant sensor features for technologies to be applied in smart environments we take inspiration from sensor technology overviews [13] and the pervasive model presented by Ranganathan et al. [9]. Accordingly, we can identify three different groups of sensor features: sensor performance characteristics, pervasive metrics and environmental characteristics. These different groups are detailed in the following sections. We are giving an overview of different potential members of the groups, discuss their relevancy for the benchmarking model and create a feature matrix, as a basis for the feature scoring model.

3.1   Sensor Performance Characteristics

This group of sensor features is related to specific technical properties of the given sensing device, as they would be typically put into the datasheet. A first important characteristic is the sensitivity or resolution of a sensor, which is the smallest change of a measured quantity that is still detectable. For example an accelerometer might be able to only detect changes that are above 0.1g. Another important characteristic is the update rate of a sensor. This denotes the number of samples the sensor is able to measure in a certain timeframe. Typically, the number of samples in a second is noted as frequency, thus a sensor may have an update rate of 20 Hz, generating 20 samples in a second. Another factor that is particularly important for embedded systems or wearables is the power consumption of the sensor that may limit the time it can operate on battery, independent of a power source. A last example is the detection range, denoting the maximum distance between the measured object and the sensing device. This can be a significant distance for cameras (e.g. satellite images), whereas we are primarily looking at smaller smart environments, where it is rare that distances of 20 meters are exceed. Other technologies such as capacitive proximity sensors may not work at this distance [14].

3.2 Pervasive Metrics

Pervasive metrics can be identified as features that specify how well a given sensor system will perform in collaboration with smart environments, when networked with other devices and when placed into existing surroundings. An example for the latter is the obtrusiveness of a sensor device. If it is clearly visible when applied, if there are disturbing signals generated, or if certain privacy concerns are associated to the sensor device, the acceptance by the user and thus the applicability is reduced. If the sensor is operating in a larger network of other devices, the bandwidth required to submit signal to an analyzing node should be kept low. Equally, if the processing capabilities are limited, less complex data processing is preferable. The overall system cost is increasing if single sensors are particularly expensive, thus limiting the potential applications. The system and attached sensors should be robust, both in terms of physical design and quality of service. Finally, the sensors are more readily applicable if the systems are interoperable to each other.

3.3 Environmental Characteristics

The third group is the environmental characteristics of a sensor system. Any sensor is affected by a certain disturbance caused by factors in the environment that are similar to the measured quantity, also called noise. For example an optical sensor is influenced by ambient light sources. In this context it is relevant how frequent those influences are in a certain environment and how robust the sensor is against noise. In many cases the presence of noise can be detected and counteracted with a calibration towards the changed environmental factors. The complexity of this calibration is another interesting factor in this regard. Finally, all sensors have some unique limitations, e.g. specific materials that absorb certain wavelengths of the electromagnetic field are difficult to detect for sensors that work in this specific frequency range.

3.4 Discussion of Feature Selection

We want to select the three most relevant features of each category. This allows a more manageable overall model, however, requires a selection of the presented features. In this work the selection is based on the authors' analysis of the related works. In future it is advisable to use more sophisticated methods, such as surveying AmI experts and calculating inter-rater reliability [15]. Of the sensor performance characteristics group we will select resolution, update rate and detection range. Resolution is a critical feature in any application, determining precise any detection is and if particular objects may be detected at all. Update rate is equally important if fast objects are to be detected and if we want to have reactive systems that respond in real-time. The importance of detection range correlates with the size of the environment and may lead to a reduction of required sensors. Of the mentioned features we omit power consumption. The actual power consumption of a whole system is a more interesting metric but very difficult to predict from the energy usage of a single sensor [16]. Of the pervasive metrics group we select unobtrusiveness, processing complexity and robustness. Unobtrusiveness of the sensor device is a desired feature in many different scenarios, where it should not impede the environment.

Table 1. Feature matrix denoting capabilities required for a certain rating

Feature	--	-	o	+	++
Resolution (res)	very coarse	coarse	normal	fine	very fine
Update Rate (upd)	< once per second	slower real-time	real-time	faster real-time	> 100 times per second
Detection Range (det)	touch	less than one meter	less than 5 meters	less than 20 meters	more than 20 meters
Unobtrusiveness (unob)	open large system	open small system	hidden, large exposure	hidden, noticeable exposure	invisible
Processing Complexity (proc)	single sensor CPU	10+ sensors CPU	single sensor embedded chip	10+ sensors by single chip	no further processing
Robustness (robu)	single point of failure	error detection	quality of service	self-recovery	fully redundant
Disturbance Frequency (disfr)	very frequent	frequent	average	unlikely	highly unlikely
Calibration Complexity (calco)	very hard	hard	normal	easy	very easy
Unique Limitations (uniql)	very critical	critical	average	not critical	none

While microprocessors are becoming ever faster processing complexity is still crucial if the number of sensors is increasing. A dedicated chip will require a more complex architecture and lead to more cost, higher energy usage and more potential points of failure, leading to the final chosen feature of robustness, both against physical abuse, but also in terms of system design, where it should be resilient towards failure of single components. We omitted the required bandwidth, as this metric is not important for many sensors, as they have low bandwidth requirements in general, but also the available bandwidth in wired and wireless systems is increasing continuously. In the last group of environmental characteristics we choose frequency of the disturbing factor, calibration complexity and unique limitations. If the disturbing factor occurs only rarely it is not critical and therefore should be part of the benchmark. Calibration complexity combines both the processing complexity and time that is required to recalibrate the system. This is highly important in real-time systems that have to monitor the environment continuously. Finally, unique limitations are a rather broad metric that is difficult to quantify. However, in many scenarios it is obvious that a specific limitation might arise, e.g. if the smart environment is in an area with a lot of human noise, microphones could be regularly disturbed. Including this metric allows modeling those applications into the benchmark with a strong weight penalizing unsuited sensors.

3.5   Feature Matrix

From the selected metrics we want to create a feature matrix that allows us to associate specific capabilities to a specific rating that is used later in the scoring process of the benchmark model. Each feature is mapped to five different ratings on an ordinal rating scale comprised of the items "least favorable" (--), "not favorable" (-), "average" (o), "favorable" (+) and "very favorable" (++). This leads to the feature matrix shown in Table 1, which will be discussed briefly.

- *Resolution* is ranging from "very coarse" to "very fine". We are using this unspecific rating, as the range may vary strongly between different sensor types. A mapping to actual should depend on the application and object that has to be detected. If the object is large a sensor that would be ranked "coarse" for smaller objects can be ranked as "fine".
- *Update Rate* is rated around real-time performance that is often rated at around 20 samples per second. Slower sensors might miss various events, while faster sensors allow detecting highly dynamic events. It should be noted that for certain sensor categories that measure fast events can require considerably faster update rates.
- *Detection Range* is rated around the 5m distance mark, that is typically enough to cover the entirety of a single apartment room. For larger rooms sensors with a higher detection distance are favorable, many sensors only react to touch.
- *Unobtrusiveness* is ranging from exposed systems placed in the environment (one example would be the Microsoft Kinect) to invisible systems that integrate seamlessly into the environment.

- **Processing Complexity** has a range from dedicated CPUs that are required to process the data of a single sensor to smart sensors that require no further processing, which allows to apply numerous sensors without adding additional processing capabilities to the environment.
- **Robustness** is following criteria for quality of service. The least favorable system fails, if only a single node is present and failing. The preferred system is fully redundant.
- **Disturbance Frequency** is ranging from frequently occurring disturbing signals, to highly unlikely disturbing signals, resulting in a better rating.
- **Calibration Complexity** is a combined metric including the calibration time, the required processing capabilities and if external aid is required in the calibration process, leading to a rating from "very hard" to "very easy".
- **Unique Limitations** should be ranked according to their criticality, as previously explained they may be suitable to penalize certain sensors or emphasize the prevalence of a disturbing factor in a noisy environment.

Now that the feature matrix is complete, the next step is presenting the formalized benchmarking model and how we can use the presented features and their rating to calculate a benchmark score that allows us to compare different sensor categories with regard to different applications.

4   Benchmarking Model

In this section we will describe a formal model that will allow us to determine a benchmark score for a given application and a given sensor technology. As previously explained the different applications are distinguished by applying a different set of weights to the known features. We will begin by discussing the process of this feature weighting and giving some examples about proper application. Afterwards, we will introduce a formal model that deduces a single score benchmark for any sensor technology and any application. The overall process is shown in Figure 1 and will be detailed in the following sections, including an example.

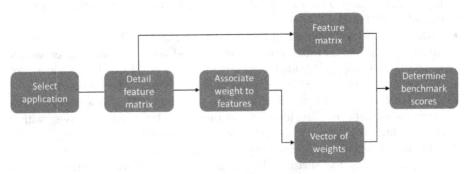

Fig. 1. Benchmarking process

4.1 Feature Score and Weighting

The presented feature matrix has some ratings that need detailing in order to be quantifiable in the specific application. The ordinal measurements of the feature matrix should be assigned a quantifiable measure. Taking "Unobtrusiveness" the open system can be detailed as "visible by users" and "large system" as size larger than 100 x 100 x 100 mm. Similar levels of detail can be applied to the other features, leading to the application-specific detailed feature matrix that is used in the scoring process. The different ratings are assigned different numeric values, namely 0.00 (--), 0.25 (-), 0.5 (o), 0.75 (+) and 1.00 (++). The weight of the features for the specific application is also rated on a 5-point ordinal scale, denoted as "not important" (numeric value 0.0), "less important" (0.25), "moderately important" (0.5), "important" (0.75) and "very important" (1.00). Thus for each application we have a distinct detailed feature matrix and a vector of associated weights that can be applied to a set of sensor technologies in order to calculate the benchmark score. We will now introduce the formal modeling that allows us to determine the calculation for this scoring process.

4.2 Modeling

The model is supposed to formalize a benchmark for any application and any sensor technology in any domain. We will start with the following definitions:

- Set of n domains $D = \{d_1, \dots, d_i, \dots d_n\}$
- Set of m applications $A = \{a_1, \dots, a_j, \dots a_m\}$
- Set of o features $F = \{f_1, \dots, f_k, \dots f_o\}$
- Set of p sensor technologies $S = \{s_1, \dots, s_l, \dots s_p\}$

In any domain d_i we have a set of potential applications $A_{d_i} \subseteq A$ and a set of relevant features $F_{d_i} \subseteq F$. For each feature f_{k,d_i} there is the associated feature score $r_{F_{d_i}}$ as explained in the previous section. Each sensor technology s_l has a specific feature score $r_{s_l,F_{d_i}} \in [0,1]$. The combined feature scores result in the following vector.

$$\overrightarrow{r_{s_l,F_{d_i}}} = \begin{pmatrix} r_{s_l,f_{1,d_i}} \\ \vdots \\ r_{s_l,f_{o,d_i}} \end{pmatrix} \tag{1}$$

The weights $w_{f_o} \in [0,1]$ associated to a specific application a_j in a domain d_i have the same cardinality $|w|$ as the vector of feature scores $\left|\overrightarrow{r_{s_l,F_{d_i}}}\right|$.

$$\overrightarrow{w_{a_j}} = \begin{pmatrix} w_{f_1,a_j} \\ \vdots \\ w_{f_o,a_j} \end{pmatrix} \tag{2}$$

The feature scores and associated weights allow us to determine a benchmark score b_{s_l} for a specific sensor technology s_l for any application a_j by using the scalar product of feature score and respective weight and apply normalization with regard to the weight.

$$b_{s_l} = \frac{\overrightarrow{r_{s_l,F_{d_i}}} \cdot \overrightarrow{w_{a_j}}}{\sum_{k=1}^{o} w_{f_k,a_j}} \tag{3}$$

We can now compare different sensor technologies by calculating and comparing the different benchmark scores for a given set of sensor technologies $S_p \subseteq S$ and receive a set B_{S_p} with $t = |S_p|$.

$$B_{S_p} = \{b_{s_l,1}, \ldots, b_{s_l,t}\} \tag{4}$$

Thus in order to determine the optimal (chosen) sensor technology b_c for an application a_j and given the prerequisites regarding non-negativity of weights and feature scores, we can evaluate the set for the maximum element.

$$b_c = \max(B_{S_p}) \tag{5}$$

4.3   Feature Score Normalization

With regards to actual benchmarking the problem of bias towards a specific technology may occur. If the average features ratings are different between two technologies the calculated benchmark score will increase. In many instances this might be beneficial, yet if comparing numerous technologies to a set of different applications a trend might be more important than absolute scores. Thus, we provide an optional step of calculating the normalized feature vector $\overrightarrow{r_{s_l,F_{d_i},norm}}$ with regard to the average associated value of 0.5, using the following equation.

$$\overrightarrow{r_{s_l,F_{d_i},norm}} = \begin{pmatrix} r_{s_l,f_{1,d_i}} \\ \vdots \\ r_{s_l,f_{o,d_i}} \end{pmatrix} \cdot \frac{o \cdot 0.5}{\sum_{p=1}^{o} r_{s_l,f_{p,d_i}}} \tag{6}$$

The feature-normalized benchmark score is accordingly determined with the following equation.

$$b_{s_l,norm} = \frac{\overrightarrow{r_{s_l,F_{d_i},norm}} \cdot \overrightarrow{w_{a_j}}}{\sum_{k=1}^{o} w_{f_k,a_j}} \tag{7}$$

4.4   Benchmark Scoring

Now with the formal model and the available set of feature matrix and weights we are able to calculate the benchmarking score for a set of sensor technologies. As an example we are choosing the application indoor localization in a public shopping area to monitor customer behavior. As a first step the feature matrix has to be detailed according to the specific requirements of the application. These include a tracking accuracy of 50 cm, with a large area to cover and potentially fast moving persons. Thus the importance ratings for performance characteristics are moderately important for resolution, important for update rate and very important for detection range. The system can also be used for security purposes, thus unobtrusiveness is less important. There can be dedicated servers, so processing complexity is not important, but the system should be difficult to disturb, thus robustness is important. Disturbance frequency is moderately important, as a large number of persons is monitored, leading to statistically significant results, even if single measurements are disturbed. The environment is fairly static, thus calibration complexity is less important. It is possible that a crowded shop produces a lot of acoustic noise, therefore no unique limitations towards acoustic disturbances should be present and this is moderately important. The resulting vector of weights is:

$$\vec{w_a} = (0.50\ 0.75\ 1.00\ 0.25\ 0.00\ 0.75\ 0.50\ 0.25\ 0.50)^{\mathrm{T}} \tag{8}$$

This vector of weights is static for the benchmarking of this specific application. As a next step it is necessary to determine the feature scores for a sensor technology. In this case, we assume a selection based on previous experiences and best practice for this application and choose a system based on numerous stationary cameras. The system has high resolution cameras, with an update rate of 30 samples per second and a high detection range of more than 20 meters. The cameras are external, not hidden from view but attached on the ceiling. The processing complexity is very high, requiring a dedicated CPU per camera. Since they are out of reach they are robust towards human intervention and independent from each other. In the given setting visual disturbance is unlikely, calibration is difficult but not required regularly and the system is not disturbed by acoustic noise. This results in the following rating vector:

$$\vec{r_{s,f}} = (1.00\ 0.75\ 1.00\ 0.25\ 0.00\ 0.50\ 0.75\ 0.25\ 1.00)^{\mathrm{T}} \tag{9}$$

Using those two vectors we can calculate the final scoring for this sensor system using the equations of the previous section, leading to $b_s \approx 0.76$ and a feature-normalized score of $b_{s,norm} \approx 0.63$. Determining the feature rating vector for other technologies is possible in a similar fashion, whereas the optimal technology has the highest score b_s or $b_{s,norm}$.

5   Evaluation

In order to evaluate the method we propose a discussion based on previous successful works in the domain of smart environments. We will select three different application areas and for each benchmark three different sensor technologies. In order to estimate how popular a certain technology is for a given application we will be using the ACM Digital Library[1] (from now on referred to as ACM DL) to query scientific publications with respective author keywords. This method is limited, as the chosen keywords may not catch all relevant publications. Therefor we will slightly increase the

---

[1] http://dl.acm.org

focus by using multiple associated search terms for each application and technology. Additionally we will also perform respective searches using the Google Scholar[2] (referred to as GS) database that has a much broader scope-The advantages of the latter are the huge collection of scientific resources and no strong selection bias. However, there are various associated issues that may affect the method. The search results vary on the search term, additionally there will be results that mention the search term but do not necessarily rely on the technology for their respective system. Therefore, the results should be considered as an indicator for popularity in the research community. Similar to the ACM DL search we are also looking for synonyms and calculate an average between the search results.

As applications we choose hand gesture interaction, a marker-based identification system and obstacle avoidance for an autonomous system. The technologies are camera systems, radio-based systems, depth or stereo cameras and ultrasound devices.

5.1   Scoring

At first we determine the weights of the different applications with regards to the features. The results are shown in Table 2. For the tables in this section we are using short notation of the features in order of appearance in Section 3.4.

Table 2. The importance weighting of different applications, based on the features

	res	upd	det	unob	proc	robu	disfr	calco	uniql
Hand Gesture	++	++	-	+	o	o	+	+	-
Identification	--	-	++	++	o	++	+	-	+
Obstacle Avoidance	-	+	-	o	+	+	++	++	+

Table 3. Feature rating of the different sensor technologies

	res	upd	det	unob	proc	robu	disfr	calco	uniql
Camera	++	o	+	-	o	o	o	-	o
Radio	-	+	++	+	o	o	o	o	-
Depth camera	+	o	o	-	-	o	-	o	o
Ultrasound	-	+	o	o	+	o	+	o	o

The rating of the different technologies and the resulting score is shown in Table 3. Here it is possible to follow different strategies regarding the rating. In terms of unbiased comparison looking at the equations it would be necessary that all technologies have the same average feature rating. The second strategy is to apply an absolute ranking to all technologies, independent of the given application. This might lead to certain technologies being unsuited for a given task, or technologies that have the best benchmark score regardless of application. In this specific case the average rating according to equation (iii) is 0.53 for cameras, 0.58 for radio, 0.44 for depth cameras

---

[2] http://scholar.google.com

and 0.56 for ultrasound devices. The importance weights and feature ratings are translated to numerical values, as shown in equations (ix) and (x). Table 4 displays the different calculated benchmark scores for the combinations between applications and technologies. As we are comparing numerous technologies and applications the feature-normalized benchmark score (equation (viii)) is also included.

Table 4. Regular and normalized benchmark score matrix of different applications and technologies

		Camera	Radio	Depth Camera	Ultrasound
Hand Gesture	b_{s_l}	0.53	0.57	0.46	0.55
	$b_{s_l,norm}$	0.50	0.48	0.51	0.50
Identification	b_{s_l}	0.49	0.64	0.40	0.57
	$b_{s_l,norm}$	0.46	0.55	0.45	0.51
Obstacle Avoidance	b_{s_l}	0.47	0.56	0.42	0.59
	$b_{s_l,norm}$	0.44	0.48	0.47	0.53

The effect of the normalization is easily visible. Particularly radio has a high feature rating and is negatively affected by the normalization. The only example with a negative average feature rating is the depth camera. After applying the normalization it becomes competitive in some applications.

Finally, Table 5 shows the search results regarding the different technologies and applications. Particularly the ACM DL keyword search can generate empty results if the search terms are too specific. Thus, the search terms we were using are "gesture", "identification and "obstacle" in this regard and add synonyms for the different technologies. For each sensor category we allowed the following synonyms. "Camera" and "video" for the first technology, "radio", "rf" and "wifi" for the second, "depth camera", "stereo camera" and "Kinect" for the third and "ultrasound" as well as "ultrasonic" for the last one. All search results were averaged according to the number of synonyms used For the Google Scholar search we used more specific terms, "hand gesture", "user identification" and "obstacle avoidance" with the same synonyms to prevent an excessive number of search results and prevented inclusion of patents and citations. All searches were performed on January 30th, 2014.

Table 5. Search result frequency given specific applications, sensor technologies and synonyms for ACM Digital Library (DL) and Google Scholar (GS)

	Camera		Radio		Depth Camera		Ultrasound	
	DL	GS	DL	GS	DL	GS	DL	GS
Hand Gesture	66	14100	27	7350	32	6850	3	1660
Identification	81	5590	162	4920	10	3957	5	599
Obstacle Avoidance	8	24000	1	13017	17	12278	8	14500

5.2   Discussion of Benchmarking Strategy

In this evaluation we included both benchmark score types to outline their differences. "Camera", "radio" and "ultrasound" have a feature rating above average, whereas "depth cameras" had a lower than average rating. The feature-normalized benchmark score is thus adapted accordingly. Regarding the application of "hand-gesture recognition" this leads to "depth cameras" being considered the optimal technology as opposed to "cameras" that had a higher score before normalization. For the other applications there is no change in optimal technology. The preferred strategy for applying feature-normalized or non-feature-normalized benchmark scoring should depend on the specific benchmarking. If we are comparing numerous technologies and applications at once, the feature-normalization might be helpful to get a tendency regarding the optimal system. However, if the application is very specific it might be preferred to get a clear ranking and penalize unsuited technologies, regardless of their average feature weight. Accordingly, it is possible to refrain from normalization.

5.3   Discussion of Search Results

Looking at the search results we can draw several conclusions. The prevalence is unequally distributed between the different technologies. Both in keywords and general occurrence cameras are the most commonly occurring sensor device, with radio and depth camera ranked behind. Ultrasound on the other hand is less frequently occurring. This may be explained by the higher versatility of the other options. Regarding the "hand gesture" application, cameras have both the highest benchmark scores and most results in the database searches. The benchmark score for "user identification" and "radio" are matched for the ACM DL. However, there are more GS results for "camera". As already mentioned cameras are more commonly used, yet, the difference in keyword search results is significant. "Obstacle avoidance" is least common in the ACM DL, however quite popular in GS. Accordingly, "ultrasound" sensors are significantly more common in both searches, as opposed to the previous applications. Nonetheless, "stereo cameras" are the most common sensor device for this application. They are commonly used in automotive scenarios, where the detection range of ultrasound is insufficient, as the objects are moving fast [17]. Therefore, the application scenario might have to be redefined for fast-moving object detection in open areas as opposed to obstacle avoidance for robots in home scenarios.

5.4   Querying Scientific Databases

We additionally have to discuss the method of using database searches for verifying the benchmarking method, as opposed to expert opinion. Surveys of a specific application or certain technologies are common in scientific literature. However, while they might be comprehensive and cite several hundred different applications, the ACM DL database covers more than 2.2 million entries and GS searches can lead to more than 9.7 million results. Therefore, the index searches are preferable in terms of broadness. The search for keywords in ACM DL results in few hits compared to the database size. As they are chosen by the authors there is a large variety in word choice, spelling or number of keywords. While extending the number of different searches might lead to more results overall, it may also lead to additional overshoot, including work that does not cover the desired topics. The GS searches are very prone to overshooting, and should be preferably used to discover trends in data, as opposed to narrowly clustered results. The presented approach is just a first attempt on using these databases to evaluate the popularity of different research topics. Potential extensions to the presented approach could use automated querying of similar search terms, a specific weighting of keyword or creating yearly queries to discover more recent trends. Additionally, one could consider preferring frequently cited articles, thus including the scientific impact of certain works into the results. While the ACM DL is more focused on computer science and has a well-defined database, GS provides an open and fast search that can be more easily fed using scripts. Therefore, it is suited for more complex searches.

5.5   Central Tendency Bias

We want to briefly discuss the tendency of the benchmark scores to crowd around 0.5. While the benchmark score has a range between 0 and 1 the two normalization processes the average is close to 0.5. Thus, even smaller differences close to this average may have a higher significance. This effect is called central tendency bias and is a common occurrence on Likert-scale questionnaires and rating systems [19]. Experts scoring technologies, just like survey respondents have a tendency to avoid extreme responses to a question. While experience of the person executing the benchmarking process might avoid this problem, it is also possible to use a corrective term in the calculation of the final benchmarking score. The primary purpose of this corrective term is to make the comparison between different scores easier to the reader. The following equations can be used to fix either regular or normalized benchmarking scores, resulting in the modified benchmarking score m_b, respectively $m_{b,norm}$:

$$m_b = (b_{s_l} + 0.5)^a \qquad m_{b,norm} = (b_{s_l,norm} + 0.5)^a \qquad (10)$$

The exponent a should be a value higher 1 and chosen according to the level of adjustment that is desired. As an example, Table 6 shows adaptations of b_{s_l} and $b_{s_l,norm}$ for cameras and ultrasound from Table 4. The different values for a are 1, 5 and 10.

Table 6. Central tendency bias correction for different exponents a

		Camera			Ultrasound		
		a=1	a=5	a=10	a=1	a=5	a=10
Hand Gesture	m_b	1.03	1.16	1.34	1.05	1.28	1.63
	$m_{b,norm}$	1.00	1.00	1.00	1.00	1.00	1.00
Identification	m_b	0.99	0.95	0.90	1.07	1.40	1.97
	$m_{b,norm}$	0.96	0.82	0.66	1.01	1.05	1.10
Obstacle Avoidance	m_b	0.97	0.86	0.74	1.09	1.54	2.37
	$m_{b,norm}$	0.94	0.73	0.54	1.03	1.16	1.34

6   Conclusion and Future Work

On the previous pages we have introduced the benchmarking model that calculates a benchmark score as an indicator for the suitability of a sensor technology for a certain application. Additionally, it is possible to use the inverse option and benchmark a single sensor technology for a number of applications. The model was derived based on a set of common features for sensor technologies and a weighting factor determining their importance for smart environment systems. It was tested using a frequency analysis of related search terms in the ACM DL and GS scientific databases. Furthermore, we have discussed the effects of different normalization and bias compensation techniques on the benchmarking score.

As future work we want to improve our verification by using survey data to determine a more definite set of sensor features. We are planning to use the benchmarking model for actual validation of different sensor technologies within smart environments. Using this on a large set of potential application domains lets us verify existing applications or identify novel use cases, if a good score is calculated for a domain where the sensor technology has not been used yet. A good candidate is capacitive proximity sensing that our group worked with extensively in the past.

References

1. Camp, R.C.: Benchmarking: the search for industry best practices that lead to superior performance. Quality Press, Milwaukee (1989)
2. Lewis, B.C., Crews, A.E.: The evolution of benchmarking as a computer performance evaluation technique. MIS Q, 7–16 (1985)
3. Dongarra, J.J., Luszczek, P., Petitet, A.: The LINPACK benchmark: past, present and future. Concurr. Comput. Pract. Exp. **15**, 803–820 (2003)
4. Weicker, R.P.: Dhrystone: A synthetic systems programming benchmark. Commun. ACM **27**, 1013–1030 (1984)
5. Henning, J.L.: SPEC CPU2000: Measuring CPU performance in the new millennium. Computer (Long. Beach. Calif.) 33, 28–35 (2000)
6. Smith, J.E.: Characterizing computer performance with a single number. Commun. ACM **31**, 1202–1206 (1988)
7. Crolotte, A.: Issues in Benchmark Metric Selection. In: Nambiar, R., Poess, M. (eds.) TPCTC 2009. LNCS, vol. 5895, pp. 146–152. Springer, Heidelberg (2009)
8. Jain, R.: The art of computer systems performance analysis. John Wiley & Sons, Chichester (1991)
9. Ranganathan, A., Al-Muhtadi, J., Biehl, J., Ziebart, B., Campbell, R.H., Bailey, B.: Towards a pervasive computing benchmark. In: Proceedings PerCom, pp. 194–198 (2005)
10. Barsocchi, P., Chessa, S., Furfari, F., Potorti, F.: Evaluating Ambient Assisted Living Solutions: The Localization Competition. IEEE Pervasive Comput. **12**, 72–79 (2013)
11. Santos, R.M., de Oliveira, K.M., Andrade, R.M.C., Santos, I.S., Lima, E.R.: A Quality Model for Human-Computer Interaction Evaluation in Ubiquitous Systems. In: Collazos, C., Liborio, A., Rusu, C. (eds.) CLIHC 2013. LNCS, vol. 8278, pp. 63–70. Springer, Heidelberg (2013)

12. Jafari, S., Mtenzi, F., O'Driscoll, C., Fitzpatrick, R., O'Shea, B.: Measuring Privacy in Ubiquitous Computing Applications. Int. J. Digit. Soc. **2**, 547–550 (2011)
13. Wilson, J.S.: Sensor technology handbook. Elsevier (2004)
14. Braun, A., Wichert, R., Kuijper, A., Fellner, D.W.: Capacitive proximity sensing in smart environments. J. Ambient Intell. Smart Environ. (in press)
15. Fleiss, J.L.: Measuring nominal scale agreement among many raters. Psychol. Bull. **76**, 378 (1971)
16. Landsiedel, O., Wehrle, K., Götz, S.: Accurate prediction of power consumption in sensor networks. In: Proceedings Workshop on Embedded Networked Sensors (2005)
17. Bertozzi, M., Broggi, A.: GOLD: A parallel real-time stereo vision system for generic obstacle and lane detection. IEEE Trans. Image Process. **7**, 62–81 (1998)
18. Crawford, L.E., Huttenlocher, J., Engebretson, P.H.: Category effects on estimates of stimuli: Perception or reconstruction? Psychol. Sci. **11**, 280–284 (2000)

Multi-view Onboard Clustering of Skeleton Data for Fall Risk Discovery

Daisuke Takayama[1], Yutaka Deguchi[1], Shigeru Takano[1],
Vasile-Marian Scuturici[2], Jean-Marc Petit[2], and Einoshin Suzuki[1(✉)]

[1] Dept. Informatics, ISEE, Kyushu University, Fukuoka 819-0395, Japan
{takayamad,yutaka.kyushu}@gmail.com, {takano,suzuki}@inf.kyushu-u.ac.jp
http://www.i.kyushu-u.ac.jp/~suzuki/slabhomee.html
[2] LIRIS, Université de Lyon, CNRS, INSA, Lyon, France
{marian.scuturici,jean-marc.petit}@insa-lyon.fr
http://liris.cnrs.fr/membres

Abstract. We propose a multi-view onboard clustering of skeleton data for fall risk discovery. Clustering by an autonomous mobile robot opens the possibility for monitoring older adults from the most appropriate positions, respecting their privacies[1], and adapting to various changes. Since the data that the robot observes is a data stream and communication network can be unreliable, the clustering method in this case should be onboard. Motivated by the rapid increase of older adults in number and the severe outcomes of their falls, we adopt Kinect equipped robots and focus on gait skeleton analysis for fall risk discovery. Our key contributions are new between-skeleton distance measures for risk discovery and two series of experiments with our onboard clustering. The experiments revealed several key findings for the method and the application as well as interesting outcomes such as clusters which consist of unexpected risky postures.

Keywords: Skeleton Clustering · Service-oriented DBMS · Human Monitoring · Mobile Robots

1 Introduction

Ambient intelligence, which refers to the electronic environments that is sensitive and responsive to the presence of people, has mainly employed fixed cameras and sensors for monitoring people, e.g., [2,3,11,13,20,24]. Mobile robots have significant advantages over fixed sensors because the former can observe from the most appropriate positions, move away when necessary to protect the privacies of the persons, and are highly adaptive to various changes of the environment [8,9,16,25]. Falls of older adults are considered as significant events which should be handled by such robots due to their rapid increase in number [19], the severe

---

[1] The robot can move away when instructed by the monitored person.

© Springer International Publishing Switzerland 2014
E. Aarts et al. (Eds.): AmI 2014, LNCS 8850, pp. 258–273, 2014.
DOI: 10.1007/978-3-319-14112-1_21

effects of falls among the older adults [21], and the importance of its early prediction from relevant, common activity [21]. Detection of their falls by mobile robots has been successfully achieved in large-scale EU projects such as GiraffPlus and Hobbit [7,12].

By exploiting consumer device Kinects, commercial robots TurtleBot 2 with Kobuki, and hand-crafted robots of which prices are less than one-tenth of the above robots, we have been working on fall risk discovery by analyzing skeletons of gaits, i.e., ways of walking [8,9,26]. Gaits deserve special attention as they are ranked as the second cause (17%) of older adults' falls right after unexpected accidents due to the environment (31%) [24]. Our challenge here lies not only in the use of far less expensive robots but in the realization of discovery from sensing by autonomous robots. We have realized such discovery [8,9,26] based on a clustering method BIRCH [28], which is appropriate for data stream [14]. In the realization, similar risky postures are discovered in a few clusters.

The onboard clustering by a single robot [26], although yielding promising results, has a space for improvement in terms of the NMI (normalized mutual information)[2] of the obtained clusters: safe postures and risky postures were not separated so clearly. We believe that our imbalanced features extracted from skeletons are incomplete and subject to improvement. Inventing new imbalanced features is in some sense an endless endeavor and increases the number of factors counted in the distance function on which BIRCH depends. The latter fact can worsen clustering quality by making the distance function counter-intuitive, which is related to the curse of high dimensionality. This paper proposes a completely different approach which uses the original imbalanced features and the skeletons simultaneously. It corresponds to adopting multiple views in the onboard clustering of skeleton data for fall risk discovery.

2 Target Problem

Our problem is defined as onboard clustering of skeletons S of a human $\mathbf{H}$ by an autonomous mobile robot $\mathbf{R}$ operating in a room. We assume that $\mathbf{H}$ is standing or walking because we focus on the gait. $\mathbf{R}$ uses a Kinect[3], which is a calibration-free, consumer device embedding several sensors including an RGB camera, an infrared (IR) emitter, and an IR depth sensor[4] [23]. We consider the case where Kinect observes one skeleton at a time.

At time t, $\mathbf{R}$ either observes a single skeleton $s_t \in S$ or fails to observe one, which situations we denote with $\tau_t =$ TRUE and $\tau_t =$ FALSE, respectively. We call τ_t the observation state of a skeleton at time t. Hence, $S = \{s_{t_1}, s_{t_2}, \ldots, s_{t_T}\}$ ($t_1 < t_2 < \cdots < t_T$), where t_i and T represent the time tick with $\tau_{t_i} =$ TRUE and the total number of the observed skeletons, respectively.

---

[2] NMI is often used as an evaluation measure for clustering methods. Intuitively it measures how close the clusters are to the instances' class labels, which are used for evaluation purpose only. Its definition is given in Section 4.3.

[3] http://research.microsoft.com/en-us/projects/vrkinect/

[4] http://www.microsoft.com/en-us/kinectforwindows/

Table 1. Identifiers and names of the joints

ID Name	ID Name
1 Hip Center	11 Wrist Right
2 Spine	12 Hand Right
3 Shoulder Center	13 Hip Left
4 Head	14 Knee Left
5 Shoulder Left	15 Ankle Left
6 Elbow Left	16 Foot Left
7 Wrist Left	17 Hip Right
8 Hand Left	18 Knee Right
9 Shoulder Right	19 Ankle Right
10 Elbow Right	20 Foot Right

We use Kinect for Windows, which returns a skeleton of 20 joints with their tracking states (either tracked or inferred) when $\tau_t = \text{TRUE}$. We include both tracking states as they are unreliable, i.e., many tracked joints are incorrect and several inferred joints are correct, and thus $s_t = \{p_{t,1}, p_{t,2}, \ldots, p_{t,20}\}$, where $p_{t,j}$ represents the 3D coordinate of the jth joint observed at time t. Hence $p_{t,j} = (p_{t,j}.x, p_{t,j}.y, p_{t,j}.z)$, where $p_{t,j}.x, p_{t,j}.y, p_{t,j}.z$ represent the x, y, and z coordinates of $p_{t,j}$, respectively. Here the x, y, and z axes correspond to the horizontal, vertical, and depth directions, respectively, as shown in Figure 1.

The 20 joints are shown in black circles in Figure 1 and as IDs[5] in Table 1. Note that the skeleton observed with a Kinect is a mirror image and the left and right joints in the Table refer to those of the image. For instance, ID 6 (elbow left) in an image of the front body corresponds to the left elbow of a human body.

S is converted to a set E of examples by transforming each s_t to example e_t at time t. The transformation may be achieved by simply retaining the 60 coordinates for the 20 joints in the original space. As we will explain in the next section, it can also be achieved by using the two numerical features which can be extracted from s_t and storing their values as e_t.

Our robot applies its incremental clustering algorithm A to E and discovers a set $\{C_1, C_2, \ldots, C_{n(E,A)}\}$ of clusters, where $n(E, A)$ represents the number of clusters discovered with A from E. By incremental clustering, we mean that the robot updates its clusters each time it observes s_t. The updates, which we call onboard clustering, are executed in its computing device without any help from an external computing device. In the ideal case several clusters contain only safe skeletons while other clusters contain only risky skeletons, and the risky clusters vary in terms of their constituting skeletons.

---

[5] Note that Kinect for XBOX has different joint IDs.

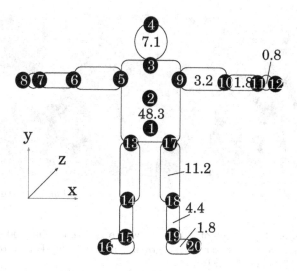

Fig. 1. Joint IDs tracked by Kinect (black circles) and mass ratios of body parts

3   Proposed Method

3.1   Clustering Method

BIRCH [28] is a distance-based clustering algorithm which builds an index structure CF (clustering feature) tree and then clusters its leaves each of which contains a micro cluster as a compressed set of similar examples. It is recognized
as one of the first algorithms of data squashing [10], which is an approach to
compress huge input data so that a conventional machine learning algorithm
can be used instead of developing a novel algorithm. Compared to its successors
[1,14,15,17,18,22], BIRCH is fast, simple and adequate for onboard clustering.
We employ BIRCH as our onboard clustering algorithm which builds a CF tree
and then agglomerates the leaves as output clusters. We neglect other post-
processing such as its refinement of the CF tree with another data scan, which
can interrupt the observation in an incremental setting.

A CF corresponds to the pseudo data that accurately reproduce the moments.
Clustering CFs is done highly efficiently as the number of CFs is drastically
smaller than the number of examples in the data set. For a set U which consists of
examples $x_1, x_2, \ldots, x_N$, the CF $\gamma(U)$ is a triplet $\gamma(U) = \left(N, \sum_{i=1}^{N} x_i, \sum_{i=1}^{N} \|x_i\|^2\right)$.
It is straightforward to show that, for two sets U_1, U_2 of examples, various
extended distance measures between U_1 and U_2 can be calculated with $\gamma(U_1)$
and $\gamma(U_2)$ only [28]. Such extended distance measures include the average inter-
cluster distance $\left(\frac{\sum_{i \in U_1} \sum_{j \in U_2} d(x_i, x_j)^2}{|U_1||U_2|}\right)^{\frac{1}{2}}$ and the average intra-cluster distance
$\left(\frac{\sum_{i \in U_1 \cup U_2} \sum_{j \in U_1 \cup U_2} d(x_i, x_j)^2}{(|U_1|+|U_2|)(|U_1|+|U_2|-1)}\right)^{\frac{1}{2}}$, where $d(x_i, x_j)$ represents the Euclidean

Stable posture   Imbalanced posture

Fig. 2. Two kinds of postures of a person, where a green point and the red point represent a joint and the center of the gravity, respectively. The second posture is exaggerated for the sake of clarity.

distance between x_i and x_j. Note that the CF satisfies additivity, i.e., for two sets U_1, U_2 of examples, $\gamma(U_1 + U_2) = \gamma(U_1) + \gamma(U_2)$. This fact guarantees that when new examples are added to a CF, the CF can be updated with the new examples only, which enables us to safely forget the original examples.

A CF tree is a height-balanced tree with three parameters: branching factor β_{internal} for an internal node, branching factor β_{leaf} for a leaf, and an absorption threshold θ of the CF in a leaf. When the average inter-cluster distance between the CF which consists of the input example and the CF of a leaf is no greater than θ, the example is absorbed to the leaf. Let m be the number of nodes in the tree. When θ is small and the number of entries in a leaf can be regarded as a constant, CF tree allows an efficient execution of membership and insert operations in $O(\log m)$, which is same with the B+ tree [6]. Moreover, as the membership operation of an example to a leaf may be judged with the example and the CF with threshold θ, an approximate membership operation is executed in $O(\log m)$ if the number of leaves involved is constant.

Entries in leaves form a bidirectional linked list as each of them has pointers to its predecessor and successor, enabling the operation of listing the entries of the leaves is executed in $O(m)$. We simplified the bidirectional linked list to a unidirectional linked list, which is sufficient for agglomerating a pair of leaves of which inter-cluster distance are less than θ. Note that this operation does not interrupt the observation because it is executed only when the clusters are requested and the number of leaves is drastically smaller than the number of examples in the data set.

3.2   Multi-view Distance Measure

As explained in the previous section, BIRCH relies on a distance measure between a pair of examples to build the CF tree. For fall risk discovery from gait skeletons, we wish to distinguish the two kinds of postures shown in Figure 2, the left being stable and the right imbalanced. In a series of initial experiments, we found that the sum of the Euclidean distances between the same joints [23], which we call the first distance measure, turned out to be inappropriate for this purpose.

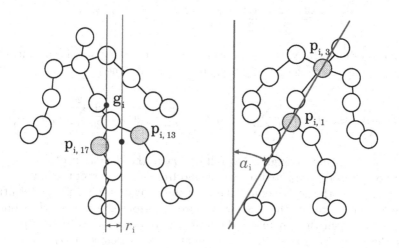

Fig. 3. Initial two kinds of imbalanced features

This finding is apparent in hindsight since the problem is Kinematic and requires considering imbalance of the body, which is different from clustering for gait verification [4]. The most standard approach in pattern recognition to the consideration is to extract imbalanced features in data preprocessing. Among such features, for a skeleton s_i, we have first chosen the deviation r_i of the center of the gravity of the body from the center of the hip left $p_{i,13}$ and hip right $p_{i,17}$ both projected on the ground, and the angle a_i of the upper body, i.e., the line segment between $p_{i,1}$ and $p_{i,3}$, and the y axis. We show these features in Figure 3.

Our second distance measure between a pair of skeletons s_i and s_j was defined as the Euclidean distance between two normalized 2D points of (r_i, a_i) and (r_j, a_j). Note that the dimensions of r_i and a_i are different so we use the z-score normalization $z = \frac{v-\mu}{\sigma}$, where v, μ, and σ represent the measured value, the average of the measured values, and the standard deviation of the measured values, respectively. Note that the standard deviation σ is often dominated by outliers so we also use the z-score normalization with the absolute deviation for comparison.

As a preliminary to introducing these features, let us consider the weights of the parts each segmented by the joints. Figure 1 shows also the mass ratios of body parts investigated experimentally [5]. We assume that the mass of a part can be regarded as concentrated at the center of the part and the joints of the part are distributed so that each of their centers coincides with the center of the part[6]. These assumptions allow us to consider that each joint i owns the evenly distributed sum of the masses of the body parts as its concentrated mass w_i.

$$(w_1, \ldots, w_{20}) = \left(\frac{48.3}{7}, \frac{48.3}{7}, \frac{7.1}{2} + \frac{48.3}{7}, \frac{7.1}{2}, \frac{3.2}{2} \right.$$
$$+ \frac{48.3}{7}, \frac{3.2}{2} + \frac{1.8}{2}, \frac{1.8}{2} + \frac{0.8}{2}, \frac{0.8}{2}, \cdots, \left. \frac{1.8}{2} \right)$$

The 3D coordinate $(g_t.\mathrm{x}, g_t.\mathrm{y}, g_t.\mathrm{z})$ of the center of gravity of s_t is the linear sum of the coordinates of the joints j weighted by w_j at time t.

$$(g_t.\mathrm{x}, g_t.\mathrm{y}, g_t.\mathrm{z}) = \left(\frac{1}{20} \sum_{j=1}^{20} w_j \mathrm{p}_{t,j}.\mathrm{x}, \frac{1}{20} \sum_{j=1}^{20} w_j \mathrm{p}_{t,j}.\mathrm{y}, \frac{1}{20} \sum_{j=1}^{20} w_j \mathrm{p}_{t,j}.\mathrm{z} \right)$$

The first feature r_t is given as follows. r_t is the deviation of the center of gravity of the body projected to the ground from the center of the left and right hips and reflects the degree of imbalance of the body on the x-z plane. Intuitively the more the center of the gravity deviates horizontally and deeply from the midpoint between the left and right hips, the more imbalanced the posture of the skeleton is. Note that the y coordinates are neglected as r_t captures the horizontal and depth imbalance.

$$r_t = f \left(\frac{\mathrm{p}_{t,13} + \mathrm{p}_{t,17}}{2}, g_t \right) \tag{1}$$

$$f(\mathrm{q}_i, \mathrm{q}_j) \equiv \sqrt{(q_i.x - q_j.x)^2 + (q_i.z - q_j.z)^2} \tag{2}$$

where q_i and q_j represent two 3D coordinates while $q_k.x$ and $q_k.z$ are the x and z coordinates of point q_k, respectively.

The angle a_t of the upper body intuitively represents the degree of imbalance of the upper body. We employ the hip center joint $\mathrm{p}_{t,1}$ and the shoulder center joint $\mathrm{p}_{t,3}$.

$$a_t = \arctan \left[\frac{f(\mathrm{p}_{t,3}, \mathrm{p}_{t,1})}{\mathrm{p}_{t,3}.\mathrm{y} - \mathrm{p}_{t,1}.\mathrm{y}} \right] \tag{3}$$

Figure 4 shows two examples of postures to insist the importance of the two features. From left to right, each posture has a high value of r_t and a_t. Their corresponding values of the two statistics of the z-score normalization are $(r_t, a_t) = (1.8, 0.21)$ and $(-0.96, 2.57)$, respectively.

As we explained previously, our second distance measure achieved a limited success, which led us to adopt multiple views. We thus employed the first and second distance measures simultaneously, which has been achieved by extending CF to a quadruplet $\left(N, \sum_{i=1}^{N} \mathrm{x}_i, \sum_{i=1}^{N} \|\mathrm{x}_{\mathrm{pos},i}\|^2, \sum_{i=1}^{N} \|\mathrm{x}_{\mathrm{uf},i}\|^2 \right)$, where $\mathrm{x}_{\mathrm{pos},i}$ and $\mathrm{x}_{\mathrm{uf},i}$ represent the coordinate value vector (60 dimensions) and the

---

[6] We admit that this assumption is strong.

Large r Large a

Fig. 4. Two kinds of postures to show the necessities of the two imbalanced features

---

Algorithm 1. Moving robot state transitions

Require: $\eta_x^{\min}$, $\eta_x^{\max}$, $\eta_z^{\min}$, and $\eta_z^{\max}$: thresholds specified by the user; $p_{t,1}.x$, $p_{t,1}.z$:
    hip center coordinates;
Ensure: $rstate$: moving robot state.
1: **if** $(\tau_t = \text{TRUE}) \wedge (\eta_x^{\min} < p_{t,1}.x < \eta_x^{\max}) \wedge (\eta_z^{\min} < p_{t,1}.z < \eta_z^{\max})$ **then**
2:     $rstate \leftarrow monitoring$
3: **else if** $(\tau_t = \text{TRUE})$ **then**
4:     $rstate \leftarrow adjusting$
5: **else**
6:     $rstate \leftarrow searching$
7: **end if**
8: **return** $rstate$

---

normalized imbalanced feature value vector (2 dimension) of x_i, respectively. It is straightforward to show that both distance measures can be computed from a pair of the quadruplet. As the absorption threshold, we use θ and ϕ for the first and second distance measure, respectively.

3.3 Positioning Strategy

As the positioning strategy of the robot $\mathbf{R}$, we adopted a finite state automaton with three states: monitoring, adjusting, and searching, which we show in Figure 5 and Algorithm 1. The state is monitoring if the skeleton is tracked and the hip center, i.e., the joint 1, is in an appropriate position in terms of x and z axes (along the horizontal and depth directions). The state is adjusting if and only if the skeleton is tracked but the hip center is located inappropriately along at least one of the two axes. Otherwise, the state is searching. The state recognition can be represented as a decision list as follows, where $\eta_x^{\min}$, $\eta_x^{\max}$, $\eta_z^{\min}$, and $\eta_z^{\max}$ are thresholds of which values are specified by the user.

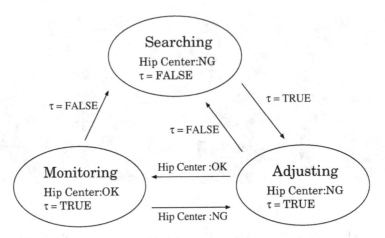

Fig. 5. Positioning strategy. Each oval contains a state with its definitions and an arrow from a state to another one represents the transition with its condition.

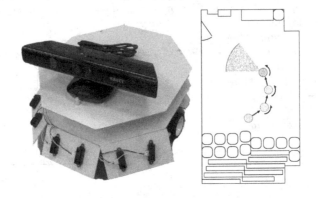

Fig. 6. Autonomous mobile robot with a Kinect and a map of the environment

In this strategy, when the state is monitoring, the robot stops its motors, observes the person, and clusters the skeletons. In the adjusting state, the robot rotates left or right and/or moves forward or backward depending on the values of $p_{t,1}.x$ and $p_{t,1}.z$ and their thresholds, respectively. The rotation and the move are for a transition to the monitoring state. In the searching state, the robot iterates approximately a 20 degree left rotation and a 10cm forward move until it makes a transition to another state.

4   Experimental Evaluation

4.1   Autonomous Mobile Robots

Figure 6 left shows our hand-crafted autonomous mobile robot. Its size is approximately of length 30cm × width 30cm × height 20cm. It weighs about 4.0kg and

Fig. 7. Snapshot of the experiments with elderly experience equipment

its maximum velocity is at most 42cm/s. It is equipped with a notebook PC of CPU 2.30GHz with RAM 4GB, a MPU board Arduino 16MHz for motor control, and a Kinect for Windows, which allows it to observe at most 30 frames per second. Preliminary experiments revealed that our incremental onboard clustering with other actions works with approximately at most 20 skeletons per second, which corresponds to 20fps (frames per second).

4.2   Experiments and their Results

As a first step toward fall prevention of older adults, a young student acted as the person to avoid accidents. Sanwa's Elderly experience equipment kit[7] enables us to experience the daily life of an elderly and has been widely used in Japan mainly for educational purpose. Note that this kit enables us to conduct experiments much more safely than monitoring elderlies with difficulties in their gaits. The student walked without any restriction in the environment. The initial position of the robot was approximately the center of the room.

We conducted two series of experiments: 1) the person occasionally took imbalanced postures without elderly experience equipment (F1 - F5). 2) the person occasionally took imbalanced postures and did hobbling behavior with elderly experience equipment (T1 - T6). Fig. 7 shows a snapshot of the experiments and Fig. 6 right shows a map of the environments.

In the experiments, the frame rate was 5fps for the searching mode and 15fps for the remaining modes. The reduction of the frame rate in the searching mode is due to blurs during large moves. For the other modes, we allowed a safe margin and adopted a smaller value than 20fps.

Table 2 shows the statistics of the eleven runs of the experiments, including those of the skeletons s_i and states. The number T of total skeletons vary from

---

[7] http://www.sanwa303.co.jp/products/medicare/teaching-material/104-994?
gclid=CM-B67Tj374CFY9vvAodcRIAUw

Table 2. Parameters and statistics

	F1	F2	F3	F4	F5	T1	T2	T3	T4	T5	T6
T	336	238	198	139	230	187	121	198	198	209	290
Stable s_i	289	209	186	117	207	176	107	179	189	189	261
Risky s_i	47	29	12	22	23	11	14	19	9	20	29
Time(sec)	60	198	223	186	243	426	89	214	345	162	178
Searching time	43.6%	60.8%	55.3%	58.3%	58.9%	70.5%	30.4%	65.7%	75.9%	74.0%	49.8%
Adjusting time	22.6%	27.2%	35.8%	34.2%	31.7%	25.1%	56.0%	25.0%	18.3%	13.1%	33.9%
Monitoring time	33.8%	12.0%	8.9%	7.5%	9.5%	4.4%	13.6%	9.3%	5.7%	12.9%	16.3%
Searching images	20.5%	30.2%	27.6%	26.6%	30.2%	48.4%	53.2%	36.6%	56.2%	45.9%	9.3%
Adjusting images	31.9%	42.0%	52.8%	55.3%	48.2%	41.0%	34.3%	40.8%	29.8%	21.9%	52.7%
Monitoring images	47.6%	27.8%	19.6%	18.1%	21.6%	10.7%	12.5%	22.6%	14.0%	32.2%	38.0%

121 to 336 and the ratios of stable skeletons to risky skeletons are diverse. The time length of each run is not proportional to T because it depends on the searching, adjusting, monitoring time lengths. Note also that these time lengths do not necessarily determine the numbers of the images taken in these states.

For the parameters, $\eta_x^{max}, \eta_x^{min}, \eta_y^{max}, \eta_y^{min}$ were set to 0.4, -0.4, 3.2, 2.4, respectively, and we adopted $\beta_{internal} = \beta_{leaf} = 5$. We compared our method against a simplified version with the Euclidean distance.

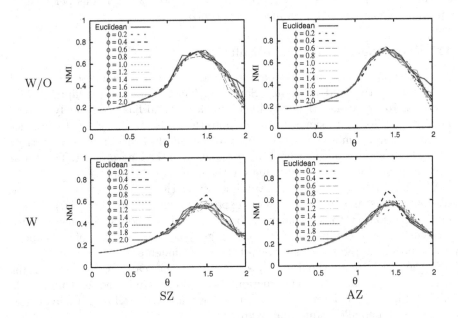

Fig. 8. NMI of the two series of experiments, where W/O and W represent without and with the elderly equipment, respectively. SZ and AZ represent the z-score normalization with the standard and the absolute deviations, respectively.

cluster 1

cluster 2

cluster 3

cluster 4

cluster 5

cluster 6

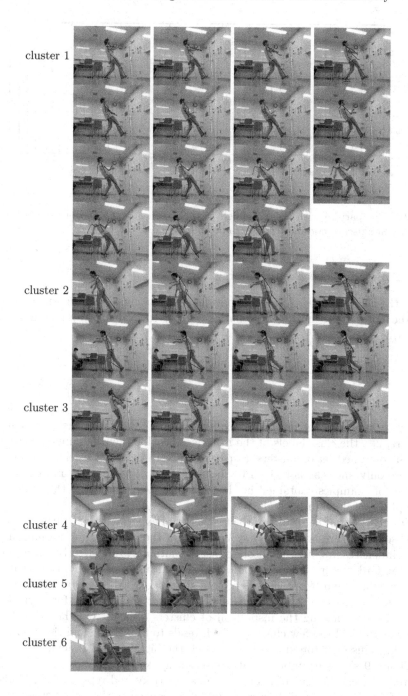

Fig. 9. Examples of the all constituting skeletons of six out of ten clusters obtained by our method with the absolute z-score normalization in the first series of the experiments with $\theta = 1.4, \phi = 0.4$.

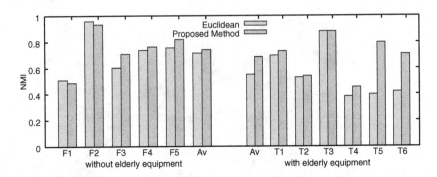

Fig. 10. Comparison with the simplified method with $\theta = 1.4$ and our method with the absolute z-score normalization with $\theta = 1.4, \phi = 0.4$.

4.3 Analyzing the Experiments

Since the number $n(E, A)$ of clusters depends on clustering algorithm A, we use the normalized mutual information (NMI) to evaluate the goodness of a clustering result.

$$NMI(C, D) = \frac{-2 \sum_{i}^{|C|} \sum_{j}^{|D|} N_{ij} \log \left(\frac{N_{ij} N}{N_i N_j} \right)}{\sum_{i}^{|C|} N_i \log \left(\frac{N_i}{N} \right) + \sum_{j}^{|D|} N_j \log \left(\frac{N_j}{N} \right)}$$

where N represents the number of examples and C and D are the correct set of clusters, i.e., the class labels of the instances provided by the human evaluator, and the obtained set of clusters, respectively. Note that C is used for evaluation purpose only and was not given to the clustering algorithm. N_i represents the number of examples contained in cluster i while N_{ij} represents the number of examples contained in both clusters i and j.

Figure 8 shows the results of the two series of experiments in which we varied the absorption thresholds θ and ϕ. We see that the two kinds of normalizations yield similar results but the absolute z-score normalization slightly outperforms the standard z-score normalization, which confirms our expectation that the latter is weak against outliers. The plots show that NMI usually peaks around $\theta = 1.4$, which yields 2 to 15 clusters. Note that small values for θ yield too many clusters, making the inspection of clusters difficult. On the other hand, large values yield too few clusters, which tends to mix stable and risky postures in a same cluster. Around $\theta = 1.4$, $\phi = 0.4$, the highest NMI is achieved.

Figure 9 shows examples of all constituting skeletons of six out of ten discovered clusters. We see that all skeletons are risky and represent six kinds of risks of falls, some of which were actually overlooked in the initial stage of our research. These results give an evidence that our motivation for discovering risky postures has been satisfied.

Figure 10 shows the results of the simplified method that uses the Euclidean distance of each joint with $\theta = 1.4$ and proposed method with the absolute z-score normalization with $\theta = 1.4, \phi = 0.4$ for the 11 runs. The null hypothesis that the difference between our method and the compared method is insignificant was rejected with paired t-test with the significance level of 5%.

5 Conclusions

We aimed at discovering clusters that consist of risky skeletons with our onboard clustering. We believe supervised learning is inappropriate for this purpose because specifying risky gaits in advance would cause serious overlookings due to the large diversity of the older adults. On the other hand, unsupervised learning may be better able to accommodate variations in individual behavior.

As far as we know, research employing a cutting-edge data mining algorithm on a physical system is scarce. One of the few examples of onboard incremental clustering on an autonomous robot is [27], which clusters color bags[8] for outlier detection. Though fundamental, color processing is known to have various flaws. It should be noted that our method is interesting from the viewpoint of fall risk discovery, which unlike color bag clustering has obvious direct merits.

As the directions for our future works, selecting data to observe next opens the possibility for extending this work to active online clustering, in which the robot decides its observation according to the patterns it discovers online and onboard. It can be recognized as the first step toward building a discovery robot, that strategically balances its observation, discovery, and action.

Acknowledgments. A part of this research was supported by a Bilateral Joint Research Project between Japan and France funded by JSPS and CNRS (CNRS/JSPS PRC 0672), and JSPS KAKENHI 24650070 and 25280085.

References

1. Aggarwal, C.C., Han, J., Wang, J., Yu, P.S.: A Framework for Clustering Evolving Data Streams. In: Proc. VLDB 2003, pp. 81–92 (2003)
2. Aghajan, H., Augusto, J.C., Wu, C., McCullagh, P., Walkden, J.-A.: Distributed Vision-Based Accident Management for Assisted Living. In: Proc. Int. Conf. Smart Homes Health Telemat, pp. 196–205 (2007)
3. Ayers, D., Shah, M.: Monitoring Human Behavior from Video Taken in an Office Environment. Image and Vision Computing 19(12), 833–846 (2001)
4. Ball, A., Rye, D., Ramos, F., Velonaki, M.: Unsupervised Clustering of People from 'Skeleton' Data. In: Proc. HRI, pp. 225–226 (2012)
5. Clauser, C.E., McConville, J.T., Young, J.W.: Weight, Volume, and Center of Mass of Segments of the Human Body. Technical Report AMRL-TR-69-70, Wright Patterson Air Force Base, Ohio, USA (1969)
6. Comer, D.: The Ubiquitous B-Tree. ACM Computing Surveys 11(2), 121–137 (1979)

---

[8] A bag, which is a generalization of a set, consists of possibly duplicating members.

7. Coradeschi, S., et al.: GiraffPlus: Combining Social Interaction and Long Term Monitoring for Promoting Independent Living. In: Proc. HSI 2013, pp. 6–15 (2013)

8. Deguchi, Y., Suzuki, E.: Skeleton Clustering by Autonomous Mobile Robots for Subtle Fall Risk Discovery. In: Andreasen, T., Christiansen, H., Cubero, J.-C., Raś, Z.W. (eds.) ISMIS 2014. LNCS, vol. 8502, pp. 500–505. Springer, Heidelberg (2014)

9. Deguchi, Y., Takayama, D., Takano, S., Scuturici, V.-M., Petit, J.-M., Suzuki, E.: Multiple-Robot Monitoring System Based on a Service-Oriented DBMS. In: Proc. Seventh ACM International Conference on Pervasive Technologies Related to Assistive Environments (PETRA 2014) (2014)

10. DuMouchel, W., Volinsky, C., Johnson, T., Cortes, C., Pregibon, D.: Squashing Flat Files Flatter. In: Proc. KDD 1999, pp. 6–15 (1999)

11. Fiore, L., Fehr, D., Bodor, R., Drenner, A., Somasundaram, G., Papanikolopoulos, N.: Multi-camera Human Activity Monitoring. J. Intelligent & Robotic Systems 52(1), 5–43 (2008)

12. Fischinger, D., et al.: HOBBIT - The Mutual Care Robot. In: Proc. ASROB (2013)

13. Gjoreski, H., Lustrek, M., Gams, M.: Context-Based Fall Detection Using Inertial and Location Sensors. In: Proc. AmI 2012, pp. 1–16 (2012)

14. Guha, S., Meyerson, A., Mishra, N., Motwani, R., O'Callaghan, L.: Clustering Data Streams: Theory and Practice. IEEE Trans. Knowl. Data Eng. 15(3), 515–528 (2003)

15. Jain, A., Zhang, Z., Chang, E.Y.: Adaptive Non-Linear Clustering in Data Streams. In: Proc. CIKM 2006, pp. 122–131 (2006)

16. Kouno, A., Takayama, D., Suzuki, E.: Predicting the State of a Person by an Office-Use Autonomous Mobile Robot. In: Proc. 2012 IEEE/WIC/ACM International Conference on Intelligent Agent Technology (IAT 2012), pp. 80–84 (2012)

17. Kranen, P., Assent, I., Baldauf, C., Seidl, T.: The ClusTree: Indexing Micro-Clusters for Anytime Stream Mining. Knowledge and Information Systems 29(2), 249–272 (2011)

18. Lühr, S., Lazarescu, M.: Incremental Clustering of Dynamic Data Streams using Connectivity Based Representative Points. Data Knowl. Eng. 68(1), 1–27 (2009)

19. Lutz, W., Sanderson, W., Scherbov, S.: The Coming Acceleration of Global Population Ageing. Nature 451(7179), 716–719 (2008)

20. Rashidi, P., Mihailidis, A.: A Survey on Ambient Assisted Living Tools for Older Adults. IEEE J. Biomedical and Health Informatics 17(3), 579–590 (2013)

21. Rubenstein, L.Z.: Falls in Older People: Epidemiology, Risk Factors and Strategies for Prevention. Age and Ageing 35(suppl. 2), ii37–ii41 (2006)

22. Seidl, T., Assent, I., Kranen, P., Krieger, R., Herrmann, J.: Indexing Density Models for Incremental Learning and Anytime Classification on Data Streams. In: Proc. EDBT 2009, pp. 311–322 (2009)

23. Shotton, J., Fitzgibbon, A., Cook, M., Sharp, T., Finocchio, M., Moore, R., Kipman, A., Blake, A.: Real-Time Human Pose Recognition in Parts from Single Depth Images. In: Proc. CVPR 2011, pp. 1297–1304 (2011)

24. Stone, E.E., Skubic, M.: Evaluation of an Inexpensive Depth Camera for In-Home Gait Assessment. Journal of Ambient Intelligence and Smart Environments 3(4), 349–361 (2011)

25. Sugaya, S., Takayama, D., Kouno, A., Suzuki, E.: Intelligent Data Analysis by a Home-Use Human Monitoring Robot. In: Hollmén, J., Klawonn, F., Tucker, A. (eds.) IDA 2012. LNCS, vol. 7619, pp. 381–391. Springer, Heidelberg (2012)

26. Suzuki, E., Deguchi, Y., Takayama, D., Takano, S., Scuturici, V.-M., Petit, J.-M.: Towards Facilitating the Development of Monitoring Systems with Low-Cost Autonomous Mobile Robots. In: Kawtrakul, A., Laurent, D., Spyratos, N., Tanaka, Y. (eds.) ISIP 2013. CCIS, vol. 421, pp. 57–70. Springer, Heidelberg (2014)
27. Suzuki, E., Matsumoto, E., Kouno, A.: Data Squashing for HSV Subimages by an Autonomous Mobile Robot. In: Ganascia, J.-G., Lenca, P., Petit, J.-M. (eds.) DS 2012. LNCS, vol. 7569, pp. 95–109. Springer, Heidelberg (2012)
28. Zhang, T., Ramakrishnan, R., Livny, M.: BIRCH: A New Data Clustering Algorithm and its Applications. Data Mining and Knowledge Discovery 1(2), 141–182 (1997)

WATCHiT: A Modular and Wearable Tool for Data Collection in Crisis Management and Training

Simone Mora[(✉)] and Monica Divitini

Department of Information and Computer Science, NTNU, Trondheim, Norway
{simone.mora,monica.divitini}@idi.ntnu.no

Abstract. We present WATCHiT, a prototype of sensor-augmented wristband computer for data collection during crisis response work. During crises, information about the environment (e.g. to map the territory) and the rescuers (e.g. for assessment of workers' condition) offers help to support coordination of work, post-emergency debriefing and to build realistic training scenarios. Being each crisis nearly unique it is important to collect data from every single occurrence, yet it is difficult to foresee the type of data and context information that is relevant to capture. WATCHiT features: (1) wearable sensors, (2) easy customization of the type of information sensed, including both quantitative and qualitative data; (3) an intuitive, distraction-free user interface for controlling the data capturing procedure. Our design process has been driven by user studies during training events characterized by a high degree of realism; our prototype has been successfully evaluated with experts against technology acceptance.

Keywords: Wearable computers · Crisis response · Crisis training · Sensor data · Tangible interface

1   Introduction

Capturing information about the condition of the environment and of workers is critical in crisis response, e.g. in case of earthquakes, overcrowding, and flooding. This information might include, e.g. location of rescuers, number of injureds and environmental data (air and soil contamination, temperature).

Information captured from a disaster scene is useful (i) to provide support for decision-making processes along the command chain [1], (ii) to support cooperation among different agents and roles in the field [2, 3], (iii) to inform post-crisis debriefings to understand what happened and learn from mistakes [4, 5]; and (iv) to recreate crisis scenarios in training exercises [6].

User studies [7, 8] report that rescue workers, in particular first responders, currently play a central role in capturing data on action and throughout the duration of a crisis. Agents broadcast over vocal radio communications sensor readings taken by multiple handheld devices (e.g. GPS, Geiger counter); often contextualizing raw data with comments and qualitative observations. In general this practice is prone to error and demanding for workers [7], whose primary focus has to remain on giving

© Springer International Publishing Switzerland 2014
E. Aarts et al. (Eds.): AmI 2014, LNCS 8850, pp. 274–289, 2014.
DOI: 10.1007/978-3-319-14112-1_22

assistance to the persons in need. With that, information captured might get biased by factors like attention distribution and impediments in operating tools for data collection while activating rescue protocols (e.g. carrying someone on a stretcher). Those errors affect both the ability to react timely to events and the completeness and correctness of logs to be used in debriefings.

Mobile and wearable sensors could improve information collection on a crisis scene. They have recently moved from being expensive tools to be used under the supervision of professionals in controlled environments; for example for logging human's vital signs in sports or safety-critical jobs, to commercial products for everyone.

Our research started as an investigation on the use of consumer sensors and applications to collect data during crisis exercises, yet our user studies soon revealed that user interfaces in many wearable sensors-based apps featured touch-screens or voice interaction and cannot be used on a crisis scene. Workers wear heavy gloves that make interaction with touchscreen almost impossible, voice-based command might get distorted by noise on the field (e.g. explosions, alarms). Furthermore workers' hands are most of the time busy using tools (e.g. stretchers, cutters or hammers) and concerns were shared about any computer interface that distract from rescue operations.

In this paper we report the design, implementation and evaluation of WATCHiT, a prototype of wearable computer for supporting modular data collection during crisis response work. WATCHiT addresses three requirements gathered during our user studies: (1) it is wearable, (2) it provides easy customization of the type of information sensed, including both quantitative and qualitative data; (3) it provides an intuitive, hands-free user interface for controlling the data capturing process.

Our focus is on data collection, how the data is used goes beyond the scope of this paper. Being data captured with WATCHiT broadcasted using standard protocols it is possible to complement existing systems for decision support (DSS) and tools for supporting debriefing, like [9].

In the following sections, after related works, we present the research methodology that lead to the current prototype of WATCHiT. We then describe design challenges we identified, followed by the final prototype implementation and evaluation. We conclude the paper tracing out future works.

2   Related Works

Research in hardware development in the field of pervasive computing, has brought to a degree of miniaturization that allow for embedding sensors in garments like wristbands, shirts and socks. While usually a sensor module is designed to work out-of-the-box for a specific application domain just a few works have focused on modularization and customization of data collection tools.

In [10] Zehe et al. created a toolkit for rapid prototyping of wearable sensing applications using sensors embedded in LEGO bricks that can be stacked on top of a base module and communicate information wirelessly to a server. Their focus is in automatic sensing and logging of information like body movements and environmental data. Aiming at simplifying the design process of sketching sensor-based modular applications, DUL radio modules [11] are small hybrid modules able to capture and broadcast data from sensors connected to them; while [12] presents a software and hardware toolkit that allow non-experts to experiment with building different sensors applications.

Due to the reduced size and limited capability of information display, wearable computers require novel interaction techniques. Several works investigated the use of "Body-centric interactions" [13] in order to exploit body movements for interaction. In [14] Pasquero et al. investigate exploiting eyes-free active tactile interactions on a wristband prototype for acquiring information from a companion mobile device. The wrist is used as an anchor point over to perform hand gestures like cover-and-hold, shake and swipe. Similar to this work, the "Gesture watch" [15] investigates contact-free hand gestures over a watch-like device to control media players. Getting more physical, the Stane project [16] investigates scratch, rub and tap gestures over a textured surface, to control another device like a mobile phone or a music player. While the above-mentioned projects use the wrist or a surface as anchor points for gestures recognition, [17] exploits free-form forearm gestures in the air captured by a accelerometer embedded in a armband. They experimented with 12 different specific gestures commands achieving a relatively high recognition rate, considering the use of a single 3-axis accelerometer sensor. Yet none of those related works directly address data collection during crisis nor the need of distraction-free user interfaces.

3   Research Approach

WATCHiT has gone through three user-centered design iterations. User studies and tool evaluations were conducted during simulated crisis events organized for training purposes. Although traditional field studies claim that a work practice is best understood observing the real environment [18], there are issues associated with doing ethnography and testing technology in settings characterized by traumas and emergencies [19], such as hospitals and crisis scenes. Moreover real crisis poses researchers' safety at risks and are largely unforeseeable in time and space. The simulations we base our field study on are organized to provide a high degree of realism, involving dozens of agents; and to recreate working conditions that are as close as possible to real crises.

Data collected during the studies included video recording of parts of the events, notes from one observer, and interviews.

The two first versions of WATCHiT we developed acted as technology probes [20]. Despite their usability issues, they were essential for us and for users to create new scenarios and identify technological challenges.

3.1   User Studies

During the first design iteration we performed observation and shadowing of emergency workers during a three-days simulation emergency response work held in Italy, in October 2011 (Figure 1-a). Different crisis scenarios were simulated both at day-time and nighttime, including flooding, earthquake and a massive car crash. The simulation involved different units (ER units, civil protection, police, dog units, …), and people with different roles (disaster managers, team coordinators, volunteers, injured figurants, …). The simulation was conducted in a physical environment that resembled as much as possible a real emergency (e.g. broken trees, debris, broken cars). Rescue exercises involved in sequence: police forces to handle traffic and fence the operation area; firefighters to explore and secure undisclosed areas; dog units to search for survivors; and paramedics to activate triage and medical assistance. ICT support for sharing information such as check-in locations, activities or sensor data readings was limited to vocal audio transceivers (also known as walkie-talkies). Some agents were furnished with handheld sensors for hazardous gas and for acquiring GPS traces. Those devices did not share a common user interface nor communicate data automatically. Call dispatchers in a coordination room were in charge of logging radio communications and of updating a digital map with the location of team of workers.

Fig. 1. Design iterations

Likewise what reported in the study by Kyng et al. [7], we observed that the system in place presents several pitfalls that makes difficult to maintain an overview of the incident site and to log operations. Information is distributed across people along the command chain and the coordination team easily fails in keeping track of information such as number of the rescued and injureds, or location of available resources; often requiring field agents to transmit twice the same information. This is worsened by the use of different radio systems among heterogeneous workgroups that cannot communicate with each other, requiring workers to use personal cellphones or have to find each other physically to coordinate [7].

This study allowed us to get familiar with the work setting and to identify main design challenges for devices suitable to be used during crises.

Building on our analysis and exploiting the Arduino[1] rapid prototyping platform, we developed our first prototype of wearable sensor for data capturing (Figure 1-b) [21] and we tested technology acceptance with experts. Results were encouraging and pushed us towards improving wearability and deepening our understanding of which types of information are relevant to be captured.

Based on the results, we created a second version of the prototype adopting a watch-like form factor (Figure 1-c). Furthermore in April 2012 we ran a second focus group with 10 emergency workers to evaluate the prototype, to investigate new interaction techniques and to refine scenarios of use. Workshop participants had different roles and different levels of experience.

Addressing the requirements for wearability, modularity and user control gathered over the first two iterations, we eventually designed the third and current version of WATCHiT (Figure 1-d). Our prototype, described in detail in section 5, is wearable and can be worn under the work uniform. It empowers emergency workers to capture information while being on a crisis scene and without interrupting the rescue work. Data captured by sensor modules might include both information from the individual (for example stress level, mood and personal notes) and information sensed from the environment (like temperature, gas or radioactive exhalations). Data captured, including an identifier of the transmitter, is wirelessly broadcasted to ZigBee-compatible[2] receivers, enabling data logging and integration with existing information systems.

In the rest of the paper, we build upon the three iterations to draft design challenges as suggestions for driving the development of wearable computers for supporting data capture in crisis management. Later on we describe how we implemented the challenges, formalized in system requirements, in our current prototype (Figure 1-d).

4   Design Challenges and Requirement Analysis

Analyzing the data gathered during three user studies we were able to define the following challenges to drive the design of data capturing tools for crisis work.

DC1. Mobility of work and sensing – Due to the nature of crises, sensing information with static sensors embedded in the environment is not always a viable solution. While urban environments, especially big cities, are getting populated by many sensors, there are large areas of the world that are not instrumented, or not instrumented with the right type of sensors. It is therefore important to complement data from static sensors with mobile ones. The degree of mobility is also important. While rescue vehicles can be equipped with sensors, the highest degree of mobility is

---

[1] Arduino – http://arduino.cc
[2] ZigBee protocol - http://www.zigbee.org/

achieved with sensors worn by the workers. Indeed, rescue protocols require vehicles to be operated in areas that are already secured, while walking units are first to explore undisclosed environments.

DC2. Different crises, different relevant data – Experts stressed that being each crisis almost unique, it is difficult to define which data might be relevant based on generic typologies of crises. One kind of information acquired on the field that might be relevant for a crisis could be useless for another kind of emergency. For example a Geiger counter sensor provide relevant information during a nuclear plan accident, but it is nearly useless information during other type of accidents. Moreover data is also depending on the role of the worker.

DC3. Different types of data – Three classes of information have emerged from our studies:

a) Information for assessment of the worker's safety and wellbeing (e.g. stress level)
b) Information for mapping the territory and the work (location, temperature, humidity, etc..)
c) Information related to the rescued people (e.g. pathology, protocols actuated, medical supplies used).

In the current practice, some information is collected in writing using coded language; some is not collected at all.

DC4. Sensor data and user-submitted data – Some data (e.g. quality of air) is quantitative in nature and can be collected with dedicated sensors, possibly through highly standardized protocols. Workers might however provide critical qualitative data that cannot be measured with sensors, for example the perceived level of panic in an area. Data from different sources, sensors and humans, might help in building a more complete perspective.

DC5. Different use, different sharing – Some types of information can be very useful for real-time coordination of different forces. For example it is important that the first responders map the territory including safe and dangerous zones for the next rescue units to come, experts say. Therefore those data should be shared among co-workers in real time. Instead, information relevant for self-assessment of the worker conditions (e.g. stress-levels, engagement, ..) are core information for personal reflection that often can't or don't want to be transmitted real time during the emergency, or to be reported in formal documentation. Those are sensible data that the owner could choose or not choose to share with colleagues and supervisors. If shared those data could also help to activate an after-work psychological support for the worker.

DC6. Intuitive, hands-free interaction – Experts drew attention on the need for simple and intuitive user interaction approaches that leaves hands free for the work. The focus of the workers must be as much as possible on the rescue operation and not on data capturing and logging, they say. Most of the tasks a field worker is engaged in require both hands to be free; for example to carry someone on a stretcher, to break into a building or to set up a field hospital as quick as possible. (*"Forearms and* *hands are needed to be free for movements and to raise weights"* experts say). It is also considered unfeasible to use consumer technology like smartphones because it's nearly impossible to use touchscreens with gloves and the use of a smartphones at work could be misinterpreted in some cultural settings. Because of the harsh working environment audio and visual feedbacks could be problematic but also haptic feedbacks could not be a proper choice because the thick jacket worn by the workers would soften the vibration feedback; unless the device is worn underneath the uniform.

DC7. Automate and discrete capturing – There are two different approaches to data capturing: automatic capturing and discrete capturing. During automatic capturing sensors systems continuously monitor and capture information. Examples of these sensors can be a GPS that track the path of the worker and a chest band that sense heart pulse. That information must be analyzed either by human or computers to extract peaks and connect the raw data to context information needed to link to work episodes. During discrete capturing the system doesn't automatically capture information and it's up to the user to trigger the capture of precise information at a precise time/location, via a user interface. In this case the information captured is highly contextualized. On the other side field rescue work needs a user interface suitable to be used on the field and compatibly with rescue protocols.

The identified challenges have been formalized in three core requirements to the supporting technology:

Wearability, to address Design Challenges 1,3

Wearability impacts on form-factors and raw material for building the device. The design space of wearables for emergency workers is very narrow. For example working uniforms are highly standardized in protocols that strictly limit the areas of the body a device can be worn on. Pockets are assigned to specific tools or part of the body must be left free for operating tools. The technology might also limit the wearability; for example an hear-pulse sensor device must be worn on-skin and underneath clothes, while environmental sensors have to be worn on top of clothes in direct contact to the harsh environment typical of crisis (high temperature or humidity, for example). Wearables for crisis must be small and light enough to not hamper or distract from work duties but at the same time resilient to endure simulated rescue operations. In fact, although prototypes are not meant to be used during real-life operations, simulated exercises are set up to resemble real emergency; including the continue exposure of workers to fire, water and extreme temperatures.

Modularity, to address Design Challenges 2,3,7

Modularity deeply impacts on hardware and software architecture design. Modularity in system architecture is required to make wearables that are customizable to specific contexts of use and user groups. Crises present very varying peculiarity. Although classifications of crises both for severity and typology are available each crisis is nearly unique and it is likely to not be replicated in the future. Capturing the relevant information is critical, yet it is difficult to foresee the type of data and context information that is relevant to be captured. Building a wearable device that embed every sensor for the data relevant for any crisis would make the device too big and power-consuming to be wearable. Modularity can address the need for capturing the relevant data by allowing a generic wearable device to be customized with sensor modules relevant before a specific crisis.

Distraction-free User Interaction, to address Design Challenges 4,5,6

Distraction-free interaction impacts on hardware, software and wearability. Once more, the specific domain narrows down the design space of wearables, this time in terms of user interface. For example the use of touch-screen interfaces is not doable to workers wearing heavy gloves. The user interface paradigm for WATCHiT need to disrupt as little as possible the user's concentration and hands, to not interfere with rescue protocols and the current use of existing tools.

5   WATCHiT Design

Leveraging rapid prototyping techniques we designed a WATCHiT prototype which addresses the identified requirements. The prototype is fully functional and it has been evaluated during training events.

WATCHiT is a wearable computer sewn in a wristband to be worn under the work uniform (Figure 2). It allows emergency workers to capture information while being on a crisis scene and without interrupting the rescue work. Data captured might include both information from the individual, for example stress level, mood and personal notes; and information sensed from the environment like temperature, gas or radioactive exhalations.

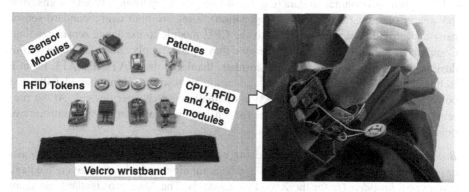

Fig. 2. WATCHiT parts

WATCHiT doesn't constitute an application itself, like any input devices it has to be considered as a user interface to specific application logics, simple template code for system integration and APIs are available at [22].

WATCHiT makes use of physical *sensor modules* for transient customization of the device functionalities, and RFID tokens to implement a *distraction-free* user interface for tagging data captured with useful context information. A Velcro wristband is used as mounting platform for the modules (Figure 2) and 3D-printable hard shells protect the device when in use.

5.1   Modularity

We designed a completely modular device. Our architecture allows experts to customize the device to address the need for capturing data in specific emergencies and for different user groups. It also introduces opportunities for designers to build applications that are not limited by a pre-defined hardware: each application can be designed to work with a specific set of modules or to provide extended functionalities when additional modules are available. On top of that a modular design allows new functionalities and sensors to be introduced into the system in the future.

WATCHiT modules fall in three categories:

Core – are mandatory modules for the device to work. They provide CPU, battery and RFID capabilities. A CPU module includes a microprocessor, memory, I/O connectors, status LEDs and a tiny vibration motor to provide haptic feedbacks. The battery module powers up all modules daisy chained with 3-wires patches and include a rechargeable battery and mini-USB connector for charging. The RFID module allows the wristband to read textual labels encoded in passive tokens when the wristband is hovered onto them (at a distance of 0-3cm). The RFID is needed to implement the body shortcut interaction technique described in the next sub-section.

Sensor – are modules that embed sensors for specific data types. These modules can either capture environmental data (e.g. hazardous gas, temperature) or vital signs from the wearer (e.g. heart-rate, blood oxygenation). They are built using standard sensor parts and provide a 1-wire interface to the CPU module to exchange sensor reading. Compared to traditional handled sensors they hinder application developers from dealing with multiple data-exchange formats, thanks to the WATCHiT API. From a technical point of view, sensor modules optimize resources (one shared CPU and power source), allowing the construction of smaller and cheaper devices. At the present time we have prototyped modules for sensing time, location (GPS), temperature, noise and heart rate.

Broadcaster – enable sharing of data using wireless protocols. At least one broadcaster is required to connect WATCHiT to a device running an application layer. We have prototype a *broadcaster* for the Xbee Pro standards. The Xbee pro standard can share data with receivers in a range of 2Km, allowing multiple WATCHiTs to interact with a centralized system, e.g. for logging data.

While modules are daisy-chained to share the power source, each module requires an additional 1-wire connection to the CPU for data exchange, limiting the number of module simultaneously connected to 7. This is a limitation of the current prototype that will be addressed in future design iterations.

5.2   Distraction-Free User Interaction via RFID Tokens

WATCHiT's RFID tokens empower users to (i) activate specific sensors, (ii) tag the collected information with user-generated information.

Tagging sensor raw data with human-readable information has multiple benefits: (i) can describe a context for a data-point helping making sense processes, especially when a piece of information is reviewed later in time (ii) can classify data captured discerning between relevant data and noise, (iii) can be used to set a level of privacy for the information captured.

In our prototype we experimented tagging sensor data with text messages reporting on workers' stress levels and activities on the field; this information can be useful to support debriefings and reflection. For example a worker can tag location data captured with the GPS sensor module with text messages about her actions and behavious like "Here I rescued a person" or "Here I don't feel confortable with this situation". With tags we also address the need for capturing both quantitative and qualitative data.

Introducing tags required to design a user interface for tagging, in real time and without interrupting the work, the information acquired by sensors. Designing a user interface to interact with WATCHiT we built on prior works on mnemonical body shortcuts [23, 24], and body-centric interaction [13].

In [24] Guerreiro et al. propose the use of body locations as a placeholders to trigger pre-defined, programmable digital operations to be a more intuitive alternative to voice or key shortcuts in mobile contexts. Such digital operations are triggered by temporary holding a smartphone on pre-defined body areas. For example, holding the phone on the wrist can set an alarm on your Google calendar; while holding the device on the mouth could initiate a phone call. Chen et al. [13] further included body shortcuts techniques in the broader class of *Body-Centric Interaction with Mobile Devices*, highlighting that people can apply their associative experience to semantically relate their body parts to certain digital actions. Furthermore the kinesthetic sense [25] would allow a person to reach the body parts with reduced visual attention.

WATCHiT leverages mnemonic body shortcuts for tagging raw sensor data with a set of pre-defined textual labels encoded in RFID tokens; and we extend the use of body shortcuts to also include interactions with objects. Yet, instead of holding a phone on body locations, the user holds the wrist wearing WATCHiT on areas marked by RFID tokens. The WATCHiT wristband embeds an RFID reader (as *core* module) to read the textual labels and append them to the raw data samples that are being sensed. Raw data and textual labels are eventually broadcasted. In this way we aim at providing an interface that is less disruptive for the work compared to handheld devices currently in use, voice or touch-based interaction.

The semantic of textual data written onto RFID tokens can be set to address the need of tracking a specific work practice or the role, or even to control or pause data acquisition. Developers can therefore easily create new tokens driven by a specific application logic or visualization. A typical customization procedure for WATCHiT is the following.

Tokens are configured by adding textual contents using RFID transceivers ot enabled smartphones, and get visually labeled with mnemonic aid (Figure 3-a). Then tokens are appended on parts of working uniform or tools used on action (Figure 3-b), leveraging associative users' experience to create mappings that are easy to execute, understand and remember [13]. For example by sticking an RFID token encoding the label "Injured rescued" on a stretcher a worker could easily tag locations of rescue operations with a quick interactions that might become part of her work routine. Eventually, once a token is read by hovering WATCHiT (Figure 3-c) raw data being captured gets tagged with the textual label encoded in the token (Figure 3-d). The richer information is finally send (thru *broadcaster* modules) to receivers the users is acknowledged by haptic feedbacks on the wrist. Receivers use the data to trigger digital operations or change in visualization according to specific application logics.

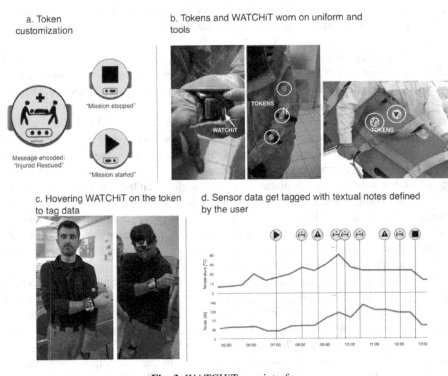

Fig. 3. WATCHiT user interface

5.3   Scenario of Use

In the following we describe a possible scenario of use for WATCHiT from the point of view of a fictional character named Giacomo.

Background. Giacomo is a firefighter. One day, Giacomo's team is alerted for a wildfire in a nearby chemical plant, several people are reported to be missing.

Scene 1. While getting ready for the rescue mission Giacomo receives a WATCHiT configured with modules for sensing location, noise, temperature and a module for Xbee broadcasting to the control room the data he acquires.

Scene 2. Furthermore Giacomo receives from his team manager RFID tokens for tagging the location where a missing person is found and for tagging sensor data with a self-assessment of his stress level via three emoticons.

Scene 3. Giacomo wears WATCHiT on his right wrist and ties the tokens on his left arm using Velcro laces (Figure 3-b). He is now ready.

Scene 4. Giacomo breaks into a building on fire and rescue an injured person, he broadcasts the location and air quality measurement where he found a person by hovering WATCHiT on the relative token (Figure 3-c).

Scene 5. When a token is read, a sensor reading is acquired, tagged with the information embedded in the token, eventually broadcasted or stored in the device according with privacy setting.

Scene 6. After a token is read, and the data broadcasted to the coordination room, Giacomo is acknowledged by a haptic feedback on the wrist.

Scene 7. Thanks to the information collected and sent in by Giacomo through WATCHiT, the coordinator knows that it is safe to send in more units.

Scene 8. Later on Giacomo feels he cannot hold up anymore to his task. He tags data captured when he's checking out from duty with a "high stress-level" tag. He will later analyze data captured during the mission to reflect on his experience.

6   Implementation

The final prototype of WATCHiT has been developed around a core module which hosts Arduino Pro Mini board [26]. The core module also embeds a backup memory for the information captured. Default modules includes:

- Power module which includes a 800mAh battery to guarantee a 4-hours autonomy during normal operations
- Broadcaster module based on a Xbee S1 PRO chipset, which guarantees communication within a 1.5Km range in open air.
- RFID tags can be read thanks to a module which embeds an ID Innovations ID-12 chipset for scanning of 125KhZ RFID tags within a 10cm range.

The set of sensor modules prototyped so far include a location module built with a Fastrax UP501 GPS chipset and a hearth-pulse sensor built with the pulsesensor.com finger worn sensor. WATCHiT runs a firmware developed with the Arduino IDE. The code is available under an open source license at [22]. WATCHiT broadcasts data in a simple JSON format and it can be programmed leveraging the Arduino IDE to address specific application needs. Template code is provided at [22].

Shells to protect modules during user evaluation have been designed 3D printed. The total cost for the components is about 250 USD.

7   Evaluation

The evaluation of our final prototype took place during a two days training event for field rescue operations. Classroom teaching of rescue practices was complemented by simulated rescue missions in a city park setting where inexperienced rescue workers were shadowed by disaster managers. Each mission consisted in finding a dummy hidden in the grass, simulating a BLS (Basic Life Support) practice directly on place (Figure 4), under the supervision of experts, and finally carrying the dummy to an ambulance using a stretcher.

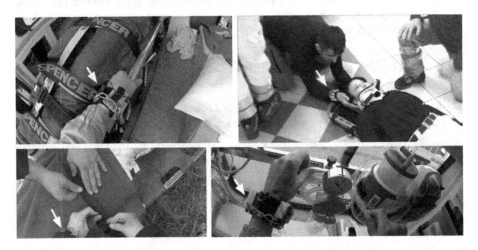

Fig. 4. Emergency workers during training

Two rescue workers took part to the evaluation of WATCHiT: a young inexperienced field rescuer and an experienced team coordinator. One of the two participants also took part in a previous evaluation of the system. Two WATCHiT were set up with a module for location sensing and four tokens for the sensor were customized with the tag-messages "Found a person", and the description of moods: "Happy", "So and so", "Sad". The two agents were asked to wear WATCHiT and append the tokens on the uniform where they find less intrusive. They were asked to use the system to report the location where they find the dummy to be rescued and use the moods tokens to give an assessment of their performances at each step of the BLS procedure; which is activated after the discovery of a injured. The simulation was recorded using a head-mounted camera and the video footage was later analyzed. The goal was to understand whether the WATCHiT prototype and the token-driven interaction it features can be successfully used during a rescue operation (although simulated) and find suggestion for improvement of the system.

Results from the video analysis and a post-simulation meeting with the users show that the interaction technique based on mnemonic body shortcuts was well accepted. The workers could easily fit WATCHiT underneath the heavy work uniform and they appreciated the distraction-free interaction and the freedom of movement.

We validated that body gestures (e.g. shaking or crossing arms), which leave hands free as much as possible, are a suitable approach for the interaction with the device, to trigger the capture of a particular data without interrupting the work. Tokens can be worn on the work uniform using bands and Velcro (work uniforms observed in action already used Velcro bands for attaching labels like the name and field role).

Participants also reported to have clearly perceived all the tactile feedback patterns on the wrist.

On the other side WATCHiT and its modules are too fragile to be used during a simulation and consequently during a real emergency. The perceived fragility of the devices made them keep focus on protecting the device from shocks and contributed to distract the workers from the action. Indeed one of the two WATCHiT got partially damaged during the experiment.

An interesting behavior was observed, the experienced worker used the mood-tokens to evaluate and rate the work of the young worker rather than to give an assessment of his own stress level. Although it is complicated to understand whether that behavior was due to the training purpose of the simulation and would not be observed during a real crisis, this can be seen as a tentative to hack the system being WATCHiT used to collect information about another individual rather than oneself or the environment.

Since the first design iteration, experts said that WATCHiT could play an important role especially in the early stages of an emergency where the first responders need to map the territory for the other units to come and coordinate the rescue operations. In this agitated phase there's often a lack of coordination among the different forces in stake and WATCHiT could fill the gap by facilitating sharing of data intra and inter different teams. Moreover information collected could help in the debriefing phase of the emergency and the information could be used in case studies during training of new personnel, experts say. Currently, data sharing with colleagues is handled by vocal communication over analog radio devices. Experts believe that while radio communication should still be used as the main cooperation tool towards implementing rescue protocols, some information could be collected and shared by WATCHiT, to avoid overloading radio operators.

8   Conclusion and Future Works

Through an iterative design process that has involved target users from the very beginning, we created a modular wearable tool for situated data capturing of quantitative and qualitative data on a crisis scene. We designed for our tool a hands-free user interface which exploits tokens attached to the worker's body and tools. We validated that our interaction technique is compatible with emergency work and the captured information can assist the phases of coordination and debriefing in crisis response.

Future work is planned in four main directions. First, we plan to generalize the interaction model to support more complex interactions, e.g. controlling the degree of sharing. This will include a study to clarify sustainable complexity. Second, we want to investigate different forms of wearability, for example integrating the modules into rescuers' jackets, in line with initial work presented in [21]. Third, we plan to develop a tool to support users in the definition of their own tokens, supporting better the "hacking" processes that we observed in the field. Finally, we plan to make WATCHiT available for long-term use to investigate how it integrates into rescue practices.

Acknowledgments. This work is co-funded by EU-ICT 7FP MIRROR (http://www.mirror-project.eu). We thank Mr. Gianni della Valle for his insight into crisis work and helping with the organization of the evaluation, the students who helped with the development, and the workers who joined the user studies.

References

1. Keramitsoglou, I., Kiranoudis, C.T., Sarimvels, H., Sifakis, N.: A Multidisciplinary Decision Support System for Forest Fire Crisis Management. Environmental Management **33**, 212–225 (2004)
2. Vivacqua, A.S., Borges, M.R.S.: Taking advantage of collective knowledge in emergency response systems. Journal of Network and Computer Applications **35**, 189–198 (2012)
3. Frassl, M., Lichtenstern, M., Khider, M., Angermann, M.: Developing a system for information management in disaster relief-methodology and requirements. In: Proc. of the 7th International ISCRAM Conference (2010)
4. Turoff, M., Chumer, M., Van de Walle, B., Yao, X.: The design of a dynamic emergency response management information system (DERMIS). Journal of Information Technology Theory and Application (2004)
5. Mora, S., Boron, A., Divitini, M.: CroMAR: Mobile Augmented Reality for Supporting Reflection on Crowd Management. International Journal of Mobile Human Computer Interaction (IJMHCI), 88–101 (2012)
6. Boin, A., Hart, P.T.: The crisis approach. Handbook of disaster research, 42–54 (2007)
7. Kyng, M., Nielsen, E.T., Kristensen, M.: Challenges in designing interactive systems for emergency response. In: Proc. of the 2006 Design Interactive Systems Conference (DIS). New York, USA (2006)
8. Mora, S., Divitini, M.: WATCHiT: Towards wearable data collection in crisis management. Work-in-progress at the Eight International Conference on Tangible, Embedded and Embodied Interaction, TEI. Munich, Germany, 1–6 (2014)
9. Mora, S., Divitini, M.: Supporting debriefing with sensor data: A reflective approach to crisis training. In: Proc. of ISCRAM-MED. Toulouse, France, 71–84 (2014)
10. Sebastian Zehe, T.G.T.H.: BRIX - An Easy-to-Use Modular Sensor and Actuator Prototyping Toolkit. In: Proc of the 4th International Workshop on Sensor Networks and Ambient Intelligence, 1–6 (2012)
11. Brynskov, M., Lunding, R., Vestergaard, L.S.: The design of tools for sketching sensor-based interaction. In: Proc. of the Sixth International Conference on Tangible, Embedded and Embodied Interaction (TEI), 213–216 (2012)
12. Spelmezan, D., Schanowski, A., Borchers, J.: Rapid prototyping for wearable computing. In: Proc. of the 12th IEEE International Symposium on Wearable Computers, 109–110 (2008)

13. Chen, X., Marquardt, N., Tang, A., Boring, S., Greenberg, S.: Extending a mobile device's interaction space through body-centric interaction. In: Proc. of MobileHCI 2012, 151–160 (2012)

14. Pasquero, J., Stobbe, S.J., Stonehouse, N.: A haptic wristwatch for eyes-free interactions. In: Proc. of CHI 2011 (2011)

15. Kim, J., He, J., Lyons, K., Starner, T.: The Gesture Watch: A Wireless Contact-free Gesture based Wrist Interface. In: Proc. of the 2007 IEEE International Symposium on Wearable Computers ISWC 15–22 (2007)

16. Murray-Smith, R., Williamson, J., Hughes, S., Quaade, T.: Stane: synthesized surfaces for tactile input. In: Proc. of the 2008 IEEE International Symposium on Wearable Computers ISWC (2008)

17. Cho, Il-Yeon, Sunwoo, J., Son, Y.-K., Oh, M.-H., Lee, C.-H.: Development of a Single 3-Axis Accelerometer Sensor Based Wearable Gesture Recognition Band. In: Indulska, J., Ma, J., Yang, L.T., Ungerer, T., Cao, J. (eds.) UIC 2007. LNCS, vol. 4611, pp. 43–52. Springer, Heidelberg (2007)

18. Beyer, H.R., Holtzblatt, K.: Apprenticing with the Customer. Commun. of ACM 38, 45–52 (1995)

19. Brown, D.S., Motte, S.: Device Design Methodology for Trauma Applications. In: Proc. of CHI 2008. New York, USA (1998)

20. Hutchinson, H., Mackay, W., Westerlund, B., Bederson, B.B., Druin, A., Plaisant, C., Beaudouin-Lafon, M., Conversy, S., Evans, H., Hansen, H., Roussel, N., Eiderbäck, B.: Technology probes: inspiring design for and with families. In Proc. of CHI 2003 (2003)

21. Cernea, D., Mora, S., Perez, A., Ebert, A., Kerren, A., Divitini, M., Gil de La Iglesia, D., Otero, N.: Tangible and Wearable User Interfaces for Supporting Collaboration among Emergency Workers. In: Herskovic, V., Hoppe, H., Jansen, M., Ziegler, J. (eds.) CRIWG 2012. LNCS, vol. 7493, pp. 192–199. Springer, Heidelberg (2012)

22. WATCHiT Github repository. https://github.com/simonem/WATCHiT

23. Guerreiro, T., Gamboa, R., Jorge, J.: Mnemonical body shortcuts: improving mobile interaction. In: Proc. of ECCE 2008 (2008)

24. Guerreiro, T., Gamboa, R., Jorge, J.: Mnemonical Body Shortcuts for Interacting with Mobile Devices. Gesture-Based Human-Computer Interaction and Simulation 5085, 261–271 (2009)

25. Tan, D.S., Pausch, R., Stefanucci, J.K., Proffitt, D.R.: Kinesthetic Cues Aid Spatial Memory. In: Proc. of CHI Extended Abstracts 2002. New York, USA (2002)

26. Arduino pro mini. http://arduino.cc/en/Main/ArduinoBoardProMini

Truck Drivers as Stakeholders in Cooperative Driving

Freek de Bruijn[✉] and Jacques Terken

Departement of Industrial Design, Technische Universiteit Eindhoven,
P.O. Box 513, 5600 MB Eindhoven, The Netherlands
freek@fdebruijn.com, j.m.b.terken@tue.nl

Abstract. Cooperative driving for trucks has been claimed to bring substantial benefits for society and fleet owners because of better throughput and reduced fuel consumption, but benefits for truck drivers are questionable. While most work on cooperative driving focuses on the technology, the current paper focuses on the consequences for drivers and how to deal with those. Two concepts are proposed and evaluated. One concept supports drivers in coordinating cooperative driving with other truck drivers to locate, join, and quit platoons. The other concept provides drivers of following trucks with situation awareness by means of a "see through" system displaying camera images from the lead vehicle. A user evaluation in a driving simulator confirms that cooperative driving may have largely negative benefits for truck drivers, and that concepts such as the ones described in this paper may help to improve the cooperative driving situation for truck drivers.

Keywords: Cooperative driving · Platooning · Human Factors · User Experience

1   Introduction

Cooperative driving has been identified as one of the applications of Ambient Intelligence 6. With cooperative driving, vehicles drive in platoons (or road trains, see Fig. 1) at short distance (0.2 or 0.3 s). The short distance is possible because the acceleration and braking behavior are communicated from the lead vehicle of a road train to the following vehicles in the train, reducing the latency in braking or acceleration/deceleration that occurs with manually driven vehicles or radar/lidar controlled ACC to virtually 0s. In this paper, we focus on cooperative driving for trucks.

Cooperative driving is claimed to offer substantial benefits, both with respect to road capacity 1 and fuel consumption: since the following vehicles drive in the slipstream of the preceding vehicles, estimates for reduction in fuel consumption amount to as high as 20% for trucks 2.

While benefits for society and for fleet owners may be clear, the advantages of cooperative driving for individual drivers may be more ambivalent. On the one hand, driving at ultra-short distance is safer when longitudinal control is taken away from the individual drivers. Furthermore, forms of cooperative driving that combine longitudinal and lateral control resemble high or full automation, and thus reduce the risks

© Springer International Publishing Switzerland 2014
E. Aarts et al. (Eds.): AmI 2014, LNCS 8850, pp. 290–298, 2014.
DOI: 10.1007/978-3-319-14112-1_23

Fig. 1. A road train of cooperatively driving trucks (http://newsroom.scania.com/en-group/2012/04/04/scania-lines-up-for-platooning-trials/)

Fig. 2. Rear of truck in front driving at close distance

associated with multitasking that exist now. On the other hand, driving at ultra-short distance minimizes the view of the driver on the road ahead (see Fig. 2), therewith seriously impeding the situation awareness 310 of the driver. In addition, looking at the rear of the truck in front from a close distance for an extended period is likely not to be experienced as very exciting. (Obviously, drivers will deal with this situation by engaging in other activities, as high or full automation will make multitasking less risky, but we assume that drivers will still desire to maintain a satisfactory level of situation awareness.)

Given the expected benefits of cooperative driving for society and fleet owners, it is likely that individual drivers will have little choice to engage in cooperative driving. Therefore, the best we can do is to supplement the research efforts on the technological innovation with research on the human perspective, and to propose ways to alleviate the above-mentioned disadvantages for drivers. So far, most work in the area of cooperative driving has focused on the technology, and relatively little work has focused on the human perspective (for some exceptions see 29). In the current paper, we present the results of a project that aimed to explore cooperative driving from a driver's perspective, to propose applications improving the driving experience and to elicit the drivers' opinions about how such applications might treat the expected disadvantages of cooperative driving for individual drivers.

1.1   Approach

After an initial orientation through conceptual analysis and user research employing different methods including contextual inquiry, ideas for applications were generated and implemented as experiential prototypes. The experiential prototypes were evaluated in a driving simulator with a mixed group of participants including professional truck drivers. The driving simulator was chosen as a testing platform since developing fully working prototypes and evaluating them in a field study with trucks driving cooperatively was beyond the scope of the current research.

In the following sections we present the initial user research, the application concepts and the evaluation. We end with some conclusions and directions for further study.

2   User Requirements for Cooperative Driving

User requirements for cooperative driving were collected employing two different methods. In a first study, the CoConstructing Stories (CCS) method was applied to obtain feedback on initial concepts 8. In the CCS method, depth interviews are conducted consisting of two phases. In the first phase, the interviewee is sensitized to the topic under discussion by inviting him to describe his current experiences in the relevant context. In the second phase, one or more concepts are presented and the interviewee is asked to comment on them by imagining how they would affect the experiences described in the first phase and to provide feedback about their positive and negative aspects. In the current study, five participants were interviewed including one truck driver. In the second phase, the topic under discussion was automated driving. The opinions were mixed. Participants saw clear advantages, e.g. for visually impaired people or when being tired and on long distances with traffic jams, but also disadvantages and issues such as trust and the lack of engagement.

In a second study, a contextual inquiry 5 was conducted with one truck driver, RV, who was accompanied during a regular working day of eleven hours where deliveries had to be made at 29 locations in central Netherlands. During the trip, the driver was observed, and questions were asked about how he experienced his work, about his use of driver assistance systems and information appliances, and about his opinion about cooperative driving. RV was mostly positive about cooperative driving, as the external control of the speed would make driving more relaxed. He was aware of the negative aspects of platoon driving such as looking at the rear of the truck in front, but did not have many issues with that as he mentioned the opportunity of doing other things such as playing videogames.

Finally, project directions and preliminary concepts were discussed with the same truck driver RV as before and with experts from a truck manufacturer. In this round, two preliminary concepts were discussed: one concept aimed at supporting the communication between drivers in a platoon; and one concept would allow drivers to transfer control of the platoon between the trucks in the platoon (based on transmitting camera images from the lead vehicle to the following vehicles). While the first idea was well received, the "transfer control" idea was considered unrealistic. On the other hand, the element of transmitting camera images from the lead vehicle to the following vehicles was received well as a means for improving situation awareness.

3   Concept Development

3.1   Supporting Communication Between Truck Drivers

In the context of cooperative driving, we expect that communication between truck drivers is needed in three different phases. In the first phase, drivers need to form a new or locate and join an existing platoon. Although part of this activity may be strategic and therefore considered to be the responsibility of the fleet manager (e.g. when working out a trip schedule), we expect that also at the tactical level the individual truck driver may need support to form a platoon with other trucks or locate a suitable platoon. Once a group of trucks has been identified that might merge into a platoon, or a platoon has been located, the drivers need to coordinate forming the platoon or joining the platoon with their fellow truck drivers. Therefore, the concept should include functionality enabling communication between truck drivers.

For the second phase, when driving in a platoon, we assume that drivers will like to have updates of various types of information concerning the platoon and again will like to stay in touch with the other platoon members. Concerning the updates, we assume that truck drivers may need different types of information about the platoon and the platoon members (see Fig. 3). The display shows the following pieces of information: The order of the trucks in the platoon together with the associated load for each truck (lower half), the nicknames of the truck drivers, the amount of time each truck drove as the leading truck and the time left until the next break (top half), since the driving time is legally bound. The question whether the time spent driving in a following truck should be considered as driving time is the subject of discussion, but is beyond the scope of the current discussion. It was also discussed with drivers whether the nicknames should be combined with portrait photo's, but this was rejected by drivers. Instead, they preferred to be able to choose an avatar from a collection of cartoon figures. For staying in touch with the other platoon members, the application allows drivers to communicate to each other by texting or talking.

For the third phase, quitting from a platoon or dissolving a platoon, again we assume that drivers will need facilities to communicate with the other platoon members, if only to say goodbye. The functionality for messaging or oral communication from the second phase can be used for this. Also, for quitting the platoon, the interface should provide functionality for transferring control to the driver again.

The interface providing access to the different functions is shown in Fig. 4. The interface can be shown on a head-down display or a head-up display projected onto the windshield. In the latter case, the driver may access the different functions through gestures registered for instance through a Leap motion controller.

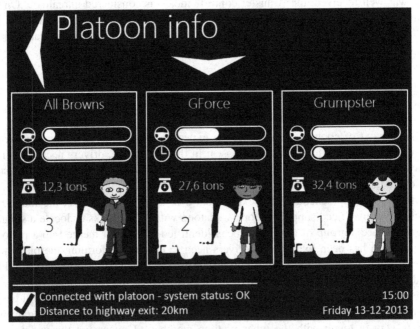

Fig. 3. Display for platoon driving showing different types of information. Bars after the steering wheel icon denote time spent as lead vehicle, bars after the clock symbol denote the time left until the next break according to legal regulations. Bottom half: order of vehicles in platoon and load.

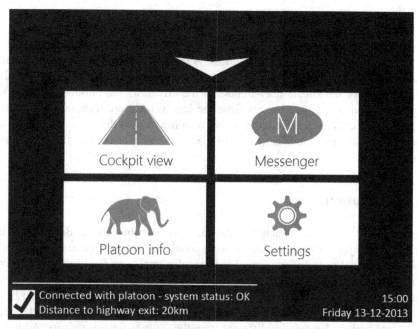

Fig. 4. Driver interface for platoon driving

Fig. 5. Impression of "see through" functionality providing drivers of following vehicles a view of the road ahead. The arrows are navigation widgets for the UI.

3.2   Supporting Situation Awareness

As mentioned in the introduction, one of the problems with cooperative driving for trucks, in particular at ultra-short distances, is that the driver is looking at the rear of the truck in front and has little to no information about what is happening ahead. In order to improve the situation awareness of the driver, a "see through" concept was proposed, by which camera images from the lead vehicle are transmitted to the following vehicles, where they may be shown on a head-down display or a head-up display projected on the windshield (see Fig. 5). A similar "see through" concept has been presented in 9.

4   Evaluation

A user test was set up to evaluate the two concepts described above. Because no fully working prototypes of the concepts were available yet and because cooperative driving functionality is not yet available in regular trucks, no field test could be conducted. Instead, a setup was created with a driving simulator. Although the driving simulator is tuned towards experiments with private cars, a truck setting can be selected as well. In this case, the driver is in an elevated seating position and the acceleration and braking behavior is different from the settings for private cars. Additional changes were made, so that the truck could drive to the rear of a platoon and join the platoon. Once the truck was within close reach of the truck at the rear of the platoon, the system switched to automated mode.

Two runs of test sessions were conducted. One run involved a convenience sample of ten students and staff member from the Dept. for Industrial Design of TU Eindhoven. The other run involved three professional truck drivers. During the test, participants drove in a highway scenario for several kilometers after which they encountered a platoon. They were asked to join this platoon and stay with it until the first exit (after about 10 minutes). The total test time was fifteen minutes. After the ride, interviews were conducted to hear participants' opinions about platoon driving and the proposed concepts. Since the tests were done individually, the communication functionality was not included in the test. The "see through" functionality was emulated. Rather than showing actual simulator images as the leading truck would see them, video footage recorded from a truck driving on the highway was projected on the screen of the simulator with a projector, as shown in Fig. 5.

The interview data clearly indicated that cooperative driving is boring. Although participants understood the benefits of platoon driving as stated in the Introduction, they were not pleased with the associated experience. The platoon statistics as shown in Fig. 3 were considered useful. The participants saw the relevance of the messaging functionality for platoon driving but did not find messaging (sending text messages) interesting for themselves and suggested that other ways of communication might be more suitable. Suggestions were made for improving the functionality to support platoon joining and quitting. The "see through" concept was overall very well received.

5   Conclusion and Discussion

While cooperative driving with trucks has clear benefits for society and fleet owners, the benefits for truck drivers may be questionable: their boredom and disengagement may increase, and their situation awareness may decrease. Therefore, we need to think about ways to alleviate the negative consequences and about design opportunities to make cooperative driving more pleasant. In a user-centered design process two concepts were developed to support cooperative driving. One concept aims to support drivers in locating, joining and quitting platoons and coordinating these activities with fellow truck drivers. The other concept offers "see through" functionality providing truck drivers with a view of what is happening before the platoon, improving the situation awareness of drivers in following trucks. The concepts were evaluated with two groups of participants, one a convenience sample and the other a smaller group of professional truck drivers. Participants confirmed the need to coordinate with other truck drivers and saw the value of functionality supporting the activities of locating, joining and quitting platoons. Also, they provided suggestions for further elaboration and modification of the concept. All participants understood the added value of the "see through" concept.

Obviously, the current study is limited in important aspects. In the first place, the concepts were evaluated in a driving simulator, and the fidelity of the simulations was low (but considered sufficient for the current purpose). Also, not all the functionality was implemented or simulated. Finally, the duration of the test was short, while the adoption and appropriation of such services usually takes time. Therefore, there is a need for further work in this area to study how truck drivers might employ such functionality in real driving situations.

References

1. van Arem, B., van Driel, C.J.G., Visser, R.: The Impact of Cooperative Adaptive Cruise Control on Traffic-Flow Characteristics. IEEE Transactions on Intelligent Transportation Systems 7(4), 429–436 (2006)
2. Damböck, D., Kienle, M., Bengler, K., Bubb, H.: The H-metaphor as an example for cooperative vehicle driving. In: Jacko, J.A. (ed.) Human-Computer Interaction, Part III, HCII 2011. LNCS, vol. 6763, pp. 376–385. Springer, Heidelberg (2011)
3. Endsley, M.R.: Toward a theory of situation awareness in dynamic systems. Hum Factors 37(1), 32–64 (1995)
4. Gomes, P., Olaverri Monreal, C., Ferreira, M.: Making Vehicles Transparent through V2V Video Streaming. IEEE Transactions on Intelligent Transportation Systems 13(2), 930–938 (2012)
5. Holtzblatt, K., Jones, S.: Contextual Inquiry: A Participatory Technique for System Design. In: Namioka, A., Schuler, D. (eds.) Participatory Design: Principles and Practice. Erlbaum, Hillsdale (1993)
6. ITEA. ITEA technology roadmap for software-intensive systems, second ed. Information Technology for European Advancement (ITEA). Office Association. (May 2004). https://itea3.org/article/itea-technology-roadmap-for-software-intensive-systems-edition-2.html

7. Matsumoto, S., Kawashima, H.: Fundamental study on effect of preceding vehicle information on fuel consumption reduction of a vehicle group. Journal of Communications and Networks **15**, 173–178 (2013)
8. Ozcelik Buskermolen, D., Terken, J.: Co-constructing stories: a participatory design technique to elicit in-depth user feedback and suggestions about design concepts. In Proceedings of the 12th Participatory Design Conference: Exploratory Papers, Workshop Descriptions, Industry Cases (PDC 2012), vol. 2, pp. 33–36. ACM, New York (2012)
9. Rakotonirainy, A., Demmel, S., Gruyer, D.: Articulating cooperatives systems and driver behaviour theories. In: 16th ITS World Congress, September 21-25, Stockholm, pp. 3849–3854 (2009)
10. de Winter J.C.F., Happee R., Martens M.H., Stanton N.A.: Effects of adaptive cruise control and highly automated driving on workload and situation awareness. A review of the empirical evidence. Transportation Research Part F: Traffic Psychology and Behaviour (in press, 2014)

Hands-on-the-Wheel: Exploring the Design Space on the Back Side of a Steering Wheel

Alexander Meschtscherjakov[✉], David Wilfinger, Martin Murer,
Sebastian Osswald, and Manfred Tscheligi

Christian Doppler Laboratory for "Contextual Interfaces", HCI and Usability Unit,
ICT & S Center, University of Salzburg, Salzburg, Austria
`alexander.meschtscherjakov@sbg.ac.at`

Abstract. The phrase "eyes on the road and hands on the wheel" has
gained acceptance as a maxim for safe driving. Many driver interfaces do
not adhere to this simple rule. We explore interaction possibilities which
follow this principle by introducing the Back-of-the-Steering-Wheel
(BotSW) as an automotive input design space. Since the steering wheel
is in the peripheral vision of the driver when looking ahead this space
can be seen as an ambient interaction space for the driver. In order to
explore this design space, we follow a research through design approach.
We present the development of three "explorations" which we consider
as evolutionary prototypes built to investigate the BotSW design space:
two-sliders, *six-buttons*, and *braille-keyer*. Based on our experiences, we
discuss the BotSW design space systematically by identifying its interaction design related properties: *ring shape*, *rotating*, *not visible*, *supporting bimanual and multi fingers interaction*. The intention of our work
is to show possibilities of interaction at the back of the steering wheel
and inspire designers to envision novel solutions to interact with the car
while leaving the hands on the wheel.

Keywords: Automotive user interfaces · Back-of-device interaction ·
Design space · Exploration · Steering wheel

1 Introduction

Everyday people die every day, often because the driver is distracted[1]. What
makes driver-computer interaction in the car dangerous is the fact that a driver
always has a primary task: to drive safely. Secondary tasks, such as controlling
the air conditioner or switching the radio station, compete with the driving task.
The primary task is usually not interruptible unless the driver pulls over. Most
often, distraction becomes apparent when driver's eyes stray from the road and
his/her hands leave the steering wheel (e.g. when entering a new destination
into the navigation system). Thus, automotive user interfaces should follow the
simple maxim "eyes on the road and hands on the wheel" [9], however many
driver interfaces do not.

---

[1] see e.g., http://www.distraction.gov for actual numbers in the U.S.

© Springer International Publishing Switzerland 2014
E. Aarts et al. (Eds.): AmI 2014, LNCS 8850, pp. 299–314, 2014.
DOI: 10.1007/978-3-319-14112-1_24

To enable interaction in cars, drivers have been offered different input and output devices with regards to modality and placement [11]. One major drawback of most of these systems is that they require the user to take at least one hand off the steering wheel during driving. In order to allow for leaving hands on the wheel, many modern cars are equipped with input devices on the steering wheel. So far, most of them have been placed on the front side and the rim of the steering wheel. We claim that the back of the steering wheel offers potential to enable interaction with in-car systems leaving both hands on the wheel providing an ambient way to interact with the vehicle. Up to today, the possibilities of this space have not been sufficiently exploited.

1.1 Objectives

In this paper, we present a systematic effort which introduces the Back-of-the-Steering-Wheel (BotSW) as a *design space* for driver input. The objectives are to explore the back of the steering wheel and to inspire interaction designers. The central contribution of the paper is a structured description of this design space, including ergonomic properties grounded in an analysis of solutions of existing cars. This design space is intended to provide a basis for analyzing and discussing different user interface modalities on the back of a steering wheel and to identify new opportunities for ambient interaction.

In line with Westerlund [25], we conceive a design space as a representation of all possible solutions which cannot be fully described because of its complexity and size. We see it as a conceptual tool during the entire design process which helps us to understand its properties and guide us in our design. In order to grasp the design space in a holistic way, there is a need to build, feel, and experience possible solutions within this design space [7]. We argue to see the exploration of the design space as an evolutionary process. Therefore, we have built three prototypes, henceforth referred to as *explorations*, that show our efforts in exploring BotSW interaction. In line with Gaver and Martin [8], these explorations can be seen as placeholders which cover parts of the design space without necessarily being the best possible solutions but providing valuable insights.

For that purpose, we analyze related work on automotive user interfaces in HCI in both academia and industry. We investigate steering wheel interaction in order to identify potentials of this area and to help define the BotSW design space. Thereafter, we provide background on back-of-device interaction. Then, we present three BotSW interaction explorations we have been researching in order to explore the BotSW design space. Finally, properties of this design space are described in detail and implications for interaction designers are presented.

2 Related Work

Automotive user interfaces have been investigated within the HCI community over the last years in various ways [22]. Kern et al. [11] provided a first design space for driver-based automotive user interfaces that allows a comprehensive description of input and output devices in a car with regards to placement and modality. Driver interaction areas can be divided into the windshield (e.g., for head-up displays), the dashboard (often visualizing information behind steering wheel), the center console (often used as the main input area with buttons, touch screens or multifunctional knobs), the steering wheel (divided into front and back side of the steering wheel), the floor (for pedals), and the periphery (e.g., side - and rear-view mirrors) [11].

2.1   Steering Wheel Interaction

In the context of our research, we are focussing on the steering wheel as a location input modalities. In modern cars, steering wheels are often cluttered with buttons, switches and thumbwheels. These controls are not configurable and only very limited predefined tasks can be accomplished, applying the metaphor of remote controlling the more powerful system in the central console. They are clustered in different areas. Conceptually, we divide steering wheel interaction areas into four parts: the front of the steering wheel, the steering wheel rim, the back of the steering wheel, and behind the steering wheel.

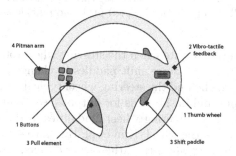

Fig. 1. Interaction elements are located (1) at the front of the steering wheel e.g., buttons, thumb wheels; (2) at the steering wheel rim e.g., vibro-tactile feedback; (3) mounted on the back of the steering wheel e.g., shift paddles; (4) located behind the steering wheel e.g., pitman arms.

Figure 1 shows different interaction areas on and near the steering wheel. At the front of the steering wheel many modern cars offer buttons and wheels. Academia has located this area as a playground for different kinds of interaction modalities, such as touch screens (e.g., [17], [15], [4]). The rim of the steering wheel (i.e. the area of the steering wheel which is grabbed with the hands when being turned) has been suggested as place for touch pads [9] (see Figure 2c) and buttons [21] (see Figure 2d). Others used the whole rim for vibro-tactile feedback [24], [6] (see Figure 3a and d).

With the "back of the steering wheel" we mean approaches which have input or output elements *mounted* on the back side of the wheel. These elements need to be connected to the steering wheel in a way that they follow the movement

Fig. 2. From left to right: (a) multi-touch steering wheel [17]; (b) touch screen on steering wheel [15]; (c) touch pad for thumb interaction mounted on steering wheel rim [9]; (d) buttons for chording with three fingers mounted on the inside of the rim [21].

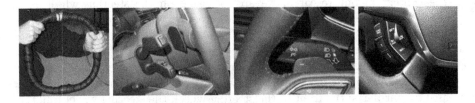

Fig. 3. From left to right: (a) pneumatic steering wheel [6]; (b) two pitman arms and a shift paddle in an Audi from a side view; (c) the upper pitman arm and the visible part of the shift paddle from a front view; (d) push and pull elements in a Ford Focus.

of the steering wheel (i.e., rotate when the steering wheel rotates). Examples for an input modality in this area are shift paddles to change gears (see Figure 3b and c). Finally, the area behind the steering wheel typically has elements such as pitman arms for input and dashboards for output (see Figure 3b and c). These differ from the back of the steering wheel modalities in the sense that they do not follow the rotation of the wheel. Kun et al. [13] have explored tap sequences on the back of the steering wheel to authenticate drivers. Our work is based on previous approaches by Murer et al. [14] and Osswald et al. [16].

2.2   Back-of-Device Interaction

Our efforts in addressing the back of the steering wheel as design space, go along with a movement in the HCI community that identified the back of devices as promising spaces for user input. Baudisch et al. [2] found that using the devices' back sides allows for the creation of smaller devices. With their RearType system, Scot et al. [23] found text input with a keyboard on the back of a device to be comparable with touchscreen text input in terms of speed. Text input via a keyboard is, especially by more experienced users, often conducted eyes free which is why typing on the back of the device can result in comparable speeds. In that case, tactile feedback is crucial for blind interaction. Robinson et al. [18] have presented TapBack, a system that uses audio gestures (i.e. taps on the back side of mobile devices) to control telephone services. Touch screens have also shown their potential to be implemented at the back of the device improving the interaction with it. Wigdor et al. [26] used a "see through approach" in their

LucidTouch concept. It creates the illusion of a semi-transparent screen, allowing users to acquire targets on the back of a device without obstructing them with their own hand.

3   Back-of-the-Steering-Wheel Explorations

Now that we have identified the steering wheel as a common place for interactive elements, we want to draw our attention to the back of the steering wheel design space. We have built a prototyping environment containing a set of tools that make different interaction designs possible to be explored in. The prototypes are seen as evolutionary prototypes [19] making the exploration of the design space an evolutionary process. We aimed for low-fidelity, flexibility, and reusability. Thus, we decided to reduce interface designs to a minimum and focused an the exploration of different interaction scenarios. Within this prototyping environment, we have built a set of prototypical interaction implementations (as we call them: *explorations*). These explorations are placeholders within the BotSW design space not mentioned to be the perfect solution [8] but the materialization of different ideas which are crucial to feel the design space [7].

3.1   Prototyping Environment

For the prototyping environment, we set up a laboratory driving simulation setting. It included a driver's seat, foot pedals for acceleration and breaking, and a Fanatec Porsche GT3 steering wheel[2] mounted on a rod system. The steering wheel was connected to a Simulator PC running different driving simulators (e.g., Lane Change Test (LCT) as specified in ISO 26022). Two loudspeakers were used for sound output. The driving simulation was projected with a video projector to a white wall in front of the mock-up.

In order to implement our explorations, we used the back of the Fanatec steering wheel. It is equipped with two shift paddles (one on each side of the steering wheel). We detached these paddles and used the mounting points for attaching input elements to the wheel. These input elements were connected to an Arduino sensor board and to a Prototyping PC, allowing for implementing various input scenarios. For output, we decided to implement a simulated Head-Up-Display (HUD). We projected the HUD with a black background on top of the driving simulator software using a second video projector which was mounted in front of the car mockup. A self-made JAVA tool enabled us to quickly change settings of the HUD, such as position and font size.

With this prototyping environment as a base, we implemented three BotSW explorations. The first exploration uses two touch sensors mounted on the left and right side of the steering wheel (see Figure 4a). The second uses three buttons on both sides of the steering wheel (see Figure 4b). For the third prototype, we implemented Braille input using the six-buttons hardware.

---

[2] http://www.fanatec.com/

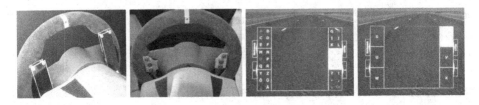

Fig. 4. From left to right: (a) two slider elements on both sides of the steering wheel; (b) six buttons placed on the back of the steering wheel; (c) letters S-X are selected in the simulated HUD; (d) within the subset S-X the letter T is selected.

3.2   Two-Sliders

The two-sliders exploration consisted of two touch sensitive sensors mounted on each side of the back of the steering wheel in the position of the shifting pedals [14] (see Figure 4a). Both sensors were covered with acrylic glass allowing for a smooth movement of the fingers over the surface. With these elements we could achieve sliding gestures (up and down) as well as pressing (i.e. pulling the slider element strong enough to trigger a click event from the shift paddle of the steering wheel). In order to increase the number of possible press events, we divided the active area of the slider into three zones: top, middle and bottom. A press event was then achieved by reading the zone of the sensor (top, middle or bottom) and the shift paddle click event. This setup enabled us to have three different input areas on each side of the steering wheel. Additionally, we could use up and down slider gestures.

As an application scenario for the two-sliders exploration, we chose text input while driving since it is increasingly important for automotive infotainment systems [12]. Additionally, text entry is challenging with a limited amount of input controls. For typing text with the two-sliders exploration, we applied a keyboard using the six available areas described beforehand. For the input of a letter, we used the Tiki'Notes[3] concept. This concept devides the input of a single character in two steps; first, a subset of letters is chosen and then the desired letter of this subset is selected to complete the second step.

Since we had six available areas, we divided the alphabet into six groups consisting of six letters each as well as punctuation characters (A-F, G-L, etc.). These groups of six letters or symbols were arranged in a 2x3 rectangular cell and visualized in the HUD. Each group corresponded with one of the six slider zones. For example, if the driver wants to enter the letter T, pulling the top of the left slider resulted in the selection of the group S-X in the top left off the HUD (see Figure 4c). Now that the subset of letters S-X was selected the HUD visualized this selection: 'S' in the top left cell, 'U' in the middle left cell, 'W' in the bottom left cell, 'T' in the top right cell, etc. Pulling the matching slider zone (top right cell) resulted in entering of the wanted character 'T' (see Figure 4d).

---

[3] http://tikilabs.com/app/tikinotes/

After this step input is completed, the letter is visualized in the center of the HUD, the character group is left, and a new letter can be typed in.

In addition to text input by pulling the slider, sliding gestures were used for various purposes including backspace and the quick switching of keyboard sets, e.g., from letters to numbers by sliding up and down. As feedback, the area on the slider which was currently touched by the fingers of the driver was highlighted on the HUD.

We explored the two-sliders approach in various informal sessions. To run an informative evaluation, we asked researchers of our group to type words in driving and non-driving conditions. The general feedback was positive, yet the exploration of the system revealed some drawbacks; specifically, we missed haptic feedback for the different zones of the slider elements. Another finding was, that it is important to be able to allow fingers to be rested on the elements without making an input. Finally, sliding gestures were difficult to perform while simultaneously turning the steering wheel. These flaws motivated us to use the very same text input scenario with different input elements: six-buttons.

3.3   Six-Buttons

For the second exploration, we aimed for having physical feedback on the touched areas and discarded the sliding gestures. This exploration was inspired by Scot et al. [23] and their RearType system. We replaced the two touch elements with three hardware buttons on each side of the steering wheel (see Figure 4c). Buttons were aligned in an ergonomic way which allowed users to leave their fingers (fore, middle, and ring finger) on the buttons while steering, and also while pressing one button. The haptic feedback made it easier to target single buttons. For text input, we again used the Tiki'Notes concept described above. Instead of slider gestures for deleting or moving back and forth in the text, we used a combination of more than one button. For example, backspace was done by pressing the top left and and middle left buttons.

To evaluate the six-buttons approach, we conducted a user study. The study was part of a publicity event of our university and visitors were asked to freely explore the system. Participants were asked to provide demographic data, fill in a System Usability Scale (SUS) questionnaire and rate two additional items. Overall, 17 people (13m, 4f) with an average age of 34 years (SD=12.7 years) participated in our study. On the SUS, a score of 69.4 was reached which can be considered as good [1]. Participants answers on the two additional items which had to be rated on a 5-point Likert-scale (1=not, 5=very), revealed a very high confirmation about leaving the hands on the steering wheel (M= 4.3, SD=1.02), as well as an average agreement to the statement about the system allowing the eyes to stay on the road (M= 3.1, SD=1.21).

The study results show potentials of the six-buttons approach in terms of hands on the wheel. But they reveal also that information visualization in a HUD does not necessarily raise the feeling of keeping the eyes on the road. Since the input of a letter required two steps (first subset selection, then letter selection) there was a need for displaying the letters in the HUD. If we could find a way to enter text without the need for displaying which characters match which keys, we could even get rid of the HUD visualization. We needed a way to interact blindly with the input elements. This was when we decided to explore how blind people are writing.

3.4 Braille-Keyer

For the third exploration we used two concepts already applied in HCI research: keyer concepts and braille codes. A chorded key set is an input device that allows to enter commands by simultaneously pressing a set of keys as already introduced by Douglas Engelbart in the 1960s [5]. By using a chorded key set with the six-buttons input approach, we could achieve $2^6=64$ different combinations—enough for each letter in an alphabet. But how to assign chords to letters in a prudent way? Fortunately, we found in the braille language exactly what we were looking for. It was developed by Louis Braille [3] to allow blind people to read through haptic sensation. This is achieved by means of physically raised dots in a 3x2 binary matrix which is called a braille cell. Characters are identified within this cell through the tactile perception of different dot combinations. Braille can be used for reading but also for writing. For example, Romero et al. [20] developed the BrailleTouch concept for eyeless text input on mobile devices. With their prototype braille writing is possible on a tablet or a smartphone.

To implement braille in our system, we reused the six-buttons approach [16]. These six buttons exactly match a braille cell as can be found in the braille language. The advantage of the braille-keyer approach is that a character or command can be entered with only a single input combination without the need to look at the buttons for input. For example, the 'A' is entered by pressing the top left button. Additionally, we added commands for moving the cursor and character manipulation (e.g., backspace). Feedback after entering a letter could be visualized in the HUD. We also implemented auditive feedback by playing the corresponding character sound file from a database of MP3 files. To be able to measure performed action (e.g. errors, timestamps), we implemented a logging tool. Finally, we connected the braille-keyer to a twitter account.

Again, we evaluated and iterated the system with twelve participants. After freely exploring the braille-keyer, participants had to learn seven characters (A, B, E, L, M, R, and T) of the braille alphabet using a learning tool we have developed. Thereafter, participants were asked to enter five predefined words consisting of four letters each, built from the learned characters (e.g., LAMA, MAMA, etc.) and send them via the Twitter application. Writing was done while driving. Errors could be fixed with a delete combination of buttons. The message was sent by pressing all six buttons. After the tasks, participants had to complete the SUS questionnaire and answer predefined questions.

In total, 12 people (7m, 5f) participated in the study with an average age of 27.7 years (SD=2.89). Six participants praised the immediate system reaction and two users stated that their hands were able to "memorize" the movements after a short time which made it easier to remember letters. Seven participants mentioned that the interaction requires a lot of learning and is not intuitive.

Nine participants remarked that it was fun that the input system differs so much from common devices and that they would like to see a score on how well they performed. The SUS scored a value of 73.75 which can be considered as good [1]. The error rate during the tasks was rather low. Participants made in total 21 errors when entering overall 240 characters.

Summarizing, it can be concluded that the three explorations allowed us to investigate different interaction approaches. Our hands-on experiences enabled us to improve our understanding of the BotSW design space. Based on the explorations we were able to identify various properties. These properties characterize the design space by providing different perspectives on it. This structured view on the BotSW design space enabled us to discuss implications relevant for interaction designers.

4   Back-of-the-Steering-Wheel Design Space

Based on the previously described related work and the three explorations, we now can draw some conclusions about the properties of the back of the steering wheel design space. We will provide a structured analysis of ergonomic characteristics, as well as interaction implications for the BotSW design space. Figure 5 is visualizing the BotSW design space. It is nested in a three dimensional Cartesian coordinate system with its origin in the center of the steering wheel rotating around y-axis. Based on our experiences we identified the following properties:

– It is shaped like a ring.
– It is rotating.
– The area of interaction is not visible.
– It supports bimanual and multi fingers interaction.

We do not claim that this list is complete. It covers aspects which we consider as being highly relevant for understanding the BotSW design space. These properties can be seen as a boundary box for interaction designers. In the following section, we will discuss each of these properties and discuss what implications these they have for the design space.

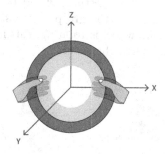

Fig. 5. BotSW design space nested in a three dimensional Cartesian coordinate system with its origin in the center of the steering wheel. The green area visualizes the shape of the design space.

4.1 Ring Shape

The area where we can put interactive elements on the back of the steering wheel is shaped like a ring. This is true if we make two assumptions. First, the steering wheel is circular (as most traditional steering wheels are). Second, the driver's hands embrace the steering wheel in a way that thumbs are resting on the front side of the steering wheel and fingers are positioned on its back side. The width of the ring is determined by two factors. The outer circle of the ring is dependent on the radius of the steering wheel itself. It has to be smaller than the steering wheel, otherwise it could not be easily operated with the fingers. The inner circle of the design space is limited by the length of the driver's fingers.

Implications. In order to reach input elements when grasping the steering wheel in a comfortable way, the potential interaction area is rather narrow. This implies that interaction within the xz-plane from the origin towards the outer circle or from the outer circle towards the origin (i.e. radial movements) needs to be little (see Figure 6). This kind of interaction is only possible if the hand stays on one position of the steering wheel. Fingers have to flex and stretch out.

Fig. 6. Radial gestures within the xz-plane needs to be little

Interaction within the xz-plane along the ring (e.g., up and down) have the same orientation as the turning steering wheel (see Figure 7). In this case, we could use the wrist to support the movements of the fingers. If we allow the hand moving along the steering wheel with the thumb on the front side and the fingers on the back side, other gestures would be possible. The drawback here is that the hand has to leave the grasp of the steering wheel. Combined with the fact that the steering wheel is rotating, this might lead to positioning problems and unintended input might occur.

Fig. 7. Gestures within the xz-plane along the ring (e.g., up and down) have the same orientation as the turning steering wheel

When we combine these two modes (radial movements and interactions along the ring), more advanced gesture inputs would be possible. This could include writing numbers or letters on touch surfaces mounted on the back of the steering wheel (see Figure 8). In this case, it has to be considered that writing on the back of a device is mirror-inverted—either for the fingers or for the brain. Nevertheless, Baudisch et al. [2] have shown that the key to touch-enabling very small devices is to use touch on the device back side. This makes us confident that micro gestures on the back of the steering wheel are a promising approach.

Fig. 8. Writing letters on touch surfaces mounted on the back of the steering wheel

Interactions along the y-axis (e.g., press a button or push a unit away with the back of the fingers) have the advantage of not lying in the rotation plane of the steering wheel (see Figure 9). This reduces unintended input. Rotating the wheel for steering (a movement within the xz-plane) and using it as an input modality (interactions along the y-axis) are orthogonal to each other. This kind of interaction was used in the six-buttons exploration. Another, approach could be to use tap gestures for interaction, as in [18]).

Fig. 9. Interaction along the y-axis (e.g., press a button) has the advantage of not lying in the rotation plane of the steering wheel

4.2 Rotating

What makes the back of the steering wheel design space especially challenging is the fact that it is rotating around the y-axis. It rotates in both directions (clockwise and anti-clockwise) sometimes more than 180 degrees. Since the design space has the shape of a ring this might be no problem for interaction—but it is.

Implications. Rotation makes interaction within the xz-plane complicated. As experienced with the two-sliders prototype, interacting with a rotating slider element is problematic. Gestures within the xz-plane along the ring (see Figure 7) are difficult when the wheel is rotating. How can the system know if the driver is steering or performing a sliding gesture? Interactions along the y-axis (see Figure 9) are more accurate as we could experience with the six-buttons exploration.

It is recommended that hands should grasp the steering wheel in a 10 and 2 o'clock position [9]. Due to the risk of injuries caused by air bags in this position some argue that drivers should place hands at 9 and 3 o'clock or slightly lower at 8 and 4 o'clock[4]. Since we want the driver to keep his/her hand on the steering wheel, the area between 8 and 10 o'clock for the left hand and between 2 and 4 o'clock for the right hand is preferable to position input devices. When the steering wheel is rotating, these areas are rotating as well.

For example, in our explorations, input elements were positioned at 9 (left input element) and 3 o'clock (right input element). When the steering wheel is turned 90 degrees clockwise the left input element is at 12 and the right input element is at 6 o'clock. With the two-sliders prototype this implicates that an up gesture with the left element is now a slide from left to the right. If we turn around the steering wheel for another 90 degrees (overall 180 degrees) things get even more complicated. The left slider element is now on the right side and the right slider element is on the left side and gestures are upside down. This problem also occurred with the six-buttons and braille-keyer prototypes. Text input was nearly impossible when the steering wheel was turned around 180 degrees.

A possible solution could be to use the dialing technique (i.e. circular movements on a touchscreen) as in Gonzalez and colleagues' approach [9]. Dialing allows for one-dimensional movement by either clockwise or counter clockwise motion and orientation remains the same when rotated. Another approach could be to use rotating input elements (see e.g., [10]). These elements could orientate dependent on the steering wheel angle.

4.3   Invisibility

Interaction on the back side of the steering wheel is invisible for the driver. To be more concrete, the position on which the fingers may interact with the input element is invisible. This makes blind interaction necessary.

Implications. Drivers need to be able to feel a haptic input device. Different input elements need to be distinguishable in order to provide orientation for fingers. Exploring input elements by touching them without making input should be facilitated. In this sense, the six-buttons prototype outperformed the two-sliders approach. With the buttons, orientation was easy and fingers could rest

[4] California Driver Handbook: www.dmv.ca.gov/pubs/hdbk/signaling.htm

on the buttons during entering a character. With the slider elements, we needed a visualization of the fingers position in the HUD and unused fingers had to be lifted when entering a character. In comparison to traditional touch elements, the occlusion problems (i.e. fingers obscure input elements) did not arise.

Blind interaction needs feedback aside the place where input was made. With our prototypes, we explored visualizations in the HUD, as well as audible feedback. With the HUD drivers could keep their eyes on the road, even though information shown in the HUD increases mental workload. Additionally, blind input is more error-prone. Thus, designing for the back of the steering wheel should focus on preventing errors and allow for recovery from errors. Another challenge is how to teach drivers that there are input elements on the back of the steering wheel in the first place. For example, Ford labeled these elements on the front side (see Figure 3b-d). Another idea could be to implement a "see through approach" as Wigdor et al. [26] showed with mobile devices. But then again, drivers eyes would have to leave the street and look at the steering wheel.

Blind interaction in the car is challenging, but also holds some potentials. Since many automotive user interfaces attract the driver's visual attention the BotSW design space offers potentials to educate drivers to not look at these visual attractions, but keep their eyes on the road.

4.4 Bimanual and Multi Fingers Interaction

Assuming that both hands are resting on the steering wheel in a 9 and 3 o'clock position, the two thumbs are on the front side and four fingers of each hand are on the back side of the steering wheel. These eight fingers might be used for interaction. This setup makes bimanual and multi fingers interaction possible.

Implications. First, input can be achieved by using one hand or both hands. Here, it has to be mentioned that there are dedicated input elements for the right hand and for the left hand. These elements cannot be exchanged (unless the steering wheel is turned 180 degrees). It is also not desirable to have both hands on one side of the steering wheel.

Since eight fingers are available for input, multitouch gestures such as pinch and zoom are possible. For our two-sliders approach, we did not use multitouch. However, more sophisticated interaction approaches can be envisioned. For the braille-keyer exploration, we utilized the possibility of entering chorded keys. This was beneficial for the implementation of the braille alphabet. Due to ergonomic reasons we placed only three buttons on each side of the steering wheel (instead of four). This limited the amount of possible chorded keys, but made finding the right button easier.

In summary, the discussed properties are essential characteristics of the BotSW design space. The ring shaped form and its rotating nature fosters interaction along the y-axis in comparison to gestures within the xz-plane. When designing for the back of the steering wheel the movement of hands while steering and the rotation of the steering wheel have to be considered. Blind interaction should be fostered through haptic input elements and fingers need to be able to rest on these elements. Bimanual and multi fingers approaches hold the potential to explore new interaction modalities.

5   Conclusion

"Eyes on the road and hands on the wheel!" is one of the most common rules for safe driving. Unfortunately, many automotive interfaces do not support this simple rule and cockpits are often cluttered with buttons, knobs, and screens. So far, both research and industry have been focusing mainly on the front side of the steering wheel as interaction space. Our approach expands the possibilities of traditional interaction beyond the front side of the steering wheel to the back side providing an ambient way to interact with the car. This approach allows for interaction and simultaneously leaving both hands on the steering wheel while driving.

In order to explore the BotSW design space, we have set up a prototyping environment. We presented three explorations to grasp the design space of BotSW interaction. The first used two sliding sensors placed on the left and right of the back of the steering wheel. The second had six tactile buttons (two times three) and the third exploration used the Braille alphabet for entering text. These explorations enabled us to experience the BotSW design space, to try things out, and to explore unconventional ideas such as using the Braille language for text input while driving. Although, all our explorations take text input as an example driver task the interaction design is adaptable to other types of applications, such as volume chaining or selection tasks.

Equipped with this knowledge, we discussed the BotSW design space systematically by identifying its interaction design related properties. We discussed the ring shape of the design space and its rotating nature. We explained why blind interaction is needed and explored the potentials and drawbacks of bimanual and multi fingers interaction. We do not claim that these properties are exhaustive, but we want to inspire interaction designers to think of the BotSW design space in a different way. Further research should focus on output modalities such as tactile actuators or thermo elements integrated into the steering wheel.

Of course, one could argue that all distractive activities have to be banned from cars while driving. This has been tried in many countries by prohibiting to use mobile phones in cars, let alone texting. Reality shows that people ignore such laws. The US government report that a large number of drivers in the US state that they text on their phones while steering a vehicle[5]. Thus, we see the need to explore ways to make interaction in the car safe for the driver. Designing for the back of the steering wheel could help to solve these problems. Our intention is to show new interaction possibilities in the BotSW design space and inspire designers to think of novel solutions to interact with the car while leaving the hands on the wheel for safer driving.

---

[5] http://www.distraction.gov/ - last accessed 1.10.2014

Acknowledgments. The financial support by the Austrian Federal Ministry of Science, Research and Economy and the National Foundation for Research, Technology and Development and AUDIO MOBIL Elektronik GmbH is gratefully acknowledged (Christian Doppler Laboratory for "Contextual Interfaces").

References

1. Bangor, A., Kortum, P., Miller, J.: Determining what individual sus scores mean: Adding an adjective rating scale. Journal of Usability Studies 4(3), 114–123 (2009)
2. Baudisch, P., Chu, G.: Back-of-device interaction allows creating very small touch devices. In: Proceedings of the 27th International Conference on Human Factors in Computing Systems, CHI 2009, pp. 1923–1932. ACM, New York, NY, USA (2009)
3. Braille, L.: Procedure for Writing Words, Music and Plain Song Using Dots for the Use of the Blind and Made Available to Them. Royal Institution of Blind Youth, Paris (1829)
4. Döring, T., Kern, D., Marshall, P., Pfeiffer, M., Schöning, J., Gruhn, V., Schmidt, A.: Gestural interaction on the steering wheel: reducing the visual demand. In: Proceedings of the 2011 Annual Conference on Human Factors in Computing Systems, CHI 2011, pp. 483–492. ACM, New York, NY, USA (2011)
5. Engelbart, D., English, B.: A research center for augmenting human intellect. In: Proceedings of the 1968 Fall Joint Computer Conference, San Francisco, CA, vol. 33, pp. 395–410, (December 1968)
6. Enriquez, M., Afonin, O., Yager, B., Maclean, K.: A pneumatic tactile alerting system for the driving environment. In: PUI 2001: Proceedings of the 2001 Workshop on Perceptive User Interfaces. pp. 1–7. ACM Press, New York, NY, USA (2001)
7. Fernaeus, Y., Sundström, P.: The material move how materials matter in interaction design research. In: Proceedings of the Designing Interactive Systems Conference. DIS 2012, pp. 486–495. ACM, New York, NY, USA (2012)
8. Gaver, B., Martin, H.: Alternatives: exploring information appliances through conceptual design proposals. In: Proceedings of the SIGCHI Conference on Human Factors in Computing Systems, CHI 2000, pp. 209–216. ACM, New York, NY, USA (2000)
9. González, I.E., Wobbrock, J.O., Chau, D.H., Faulring, A., Myers, B.A.: Eyes on the road, hands on the wheel: thumb-based interaction techniques for input on steering wheels. In: GI 2007: Proceedings of Graphics Interface 2007, pp. 95–102. ACM, New York, NY, USA (2007)
10. Hinckley, K., Pierce, J., Sinclair, M., Horvitz, E.: Sensing techniques for mobile interaction. In: Proceedings of the 13th Annual ACM Symposium on User Interface Software and Technology, pp. 91–100. ACM (2000)
11. Kern, D., Schmidt, A.: Design space for driver-based automotive user interfaces. In: Proceedings of the 1st International Conference on Automotive User Interfaces and Interactive Vehicular Applications, pp. 3–10. ACM, New York, NY, USA (2009)
12. Kern, D., Schmidt, A., Arnsmann, J., Appelmann, T., Pararasasegaran, N., Piepiera, B.: Writing to your car: handwritten text input while driving. In: CHI EA 2009: Proceedings of the 27th International Conference Extended Abstracts on Human Factors in Computing Systems, pp. 4705–4710. ACM, New York, NY, USA (2009)
13. Kun, A.L., Royer, T., Leone, A.: Using tap sequences to authenticate drivers. In: Proceedings of the 5th International Conference on Automotive User Interfaces

and Interactive Vehicular Applications, AutomotiveUI 2013, pp. 228–231. ACM, New York, NY, USA (2013). http://doi.acm.org/10.1145/2516540.2516567

14. Murer, M., Wilfinger, D. Meschtscherjakov, A., Osswald, S., Tscheligi, M.: Exploring the back of the steering wheel: Text input with hands on the wheel and eyes on the road. In: Proceedings of the 4th International Conference on Automotive User Interfaces and Interactive Vehicular Applications, AutomotiveUI 2012, pp. 117–120. ACM, New York (2012)

15. Osswald, S., Meschtscherjakov, A., Wilfinger, D., Tscheligi, M.: Steering wheel-based interaction: Potential reductions in driver distraction. In: International Joint Conference on Ambient Intelligence, AmI 2011 (2011)

16. Osswald, S., Meschtscherjakov, A., Mirnig, N., Kraessig, K.-A., Wilfinger, D., Murer, M., Tscheligi, M.: Back of the steering wheel interaction: The car braille keyer. In: Paternò, F., de Ruyter, B., Markopoulos, P., Santoro, C., van Loenen, E., Luyten, K. (eds.) AmI 2012. LNCS, vol. 7683, pp. 49–64. Springer, Heidelberg (2012)

17. Pfeiffer, M., Kern, D., Schöning, J., Döring, T., Krüger, A., Schmidt, A.: A multitouch enabled steering wheel: exploring the design space. In: CHI EA 2010: Proceedings of the 28th of the International Conference Extended Abstracts on Human Factors in Computing Systems, pp. 3355–3360. ACM, New York, NY, USA (2010)

18. Robinson, S., Rajput, N., Jones, M., Jain, A., Sahay, S., Nanavati, A.: Tapback: towards richer mobile interfaces in impoverished contexts. In: Proceedings of the 2011 Annual Conference on Human Factors in Computing Systems, CHI 2011, pp. 2733–2736. ACM, New York, NY, USA (2011)

19. Rogers, Y., Sharp, H., Preece, J.: Interaction design: Beyond human computer interaction (2002)

20. Romero, M., Frey, B., Southern, C., Abowd, G.D.: Brailletouch: designing a mobile eyes-free soft keyboard. In: MobileHCI 2011, pp. 707–709. ACM, New York, NY, USA (2011)

21. Sandnes, F.E., Huang, Y.P., Huang, Y.M.: An eyes-free in-car user interface interaction style based on visual and textual mnemonics, chording and speech. In: Proceedings of the 2008 International Conference on Multimedia and Ubiquitous Engineering, pp. 342–347. IEEE Computer Society, Washington, DC, USA (2008)

22. Schmidt, A., Dey, A.K., Kun, A.L., Spiessl, W.: Automotive user interfaces: human computer interaction in the car. In: Proceedings of the 28th of the International Conference Extended Abstracts on Human Factors in Computing Systems, CHI EA 2010, pp. 3177–3180. ACM, New York, NY, USA (2010)

23. Scott, J., Izadi, S., Rezai, L.S., Ruszkowski, D., Bi, X., Balakrishnan, R.: Reartype: text entry using keys on the back of a device. In: Proceedings of the 12th International Conference on Human Computer Interaction with Mobile Devices and Services, MobileHCI 2010, pp. 171–180. ACM, New York, NY, USA (2010)

24. Van Erp, J., Van Veen, H.: Vibro-tactile information presentation in automobiles. In: Proceedings of Eurohaptics, vol. 2001, pp. 99–104. DTIC Document (2001)

25. Westerlund, B.: Design space conceptual tool-grasping the design process. In: Proceedings of the Nordic Design Research Conference, pp. 29–31 (2005)

26. Wigdor, D., Forlines, C., Baudisch, P., Barnwell, J., Shen, C.: Lucid touch: a seethrough mobile device. In: Proceedings of the 20th annual ACM Symposium on User Interface Software and Technology, UIST 2007, pp. 269–278. ACM, New York, NY, USA (2007)

Driver-to-Driver Communication on the Highway: What Drivers Want

Chao Wang, Jing Gu, Jacques Terken$^{(\boxtimes)}$, and Jun Hu

Departement of Industrial Design, Technische Universiteit Eindhoven,
P.O. Box 513, 5600 MB Eindhoven, The Netherlands
{ch.wang,j.m.b.terken,j.hu}@tue.nl, j.gu@student.tue.nl

Abstract. Drivers need to coordinate with each other to share the road infrastructure. The social relationship between drivers also influences the driving behavior. With everywhere available connectivity and the broad penetration of social network services, the relationship between drivers on the road may gain more transparency, enabling social information to pass through the steel shell of the cars and giving opportunities to reduce anonymity and strengthen empathy. In this paper, we investigate what sort of social communication drivers consider useful for a highway scenario and which factors influence their willingness to receive or send the information concerned. We utilized the "CoConstructing Stories" method to investigate 30 novel scenarios with 22 participants. We find that driver-to-driver communication relating to Safety and Efficiency is well accepted. In order to account for the acceptance of driver-to-driver communication concerning the Social relation between drivers and their Identity, additional information is required. Some relevant factors are considered in the discussion, and steps for future research are suggested.

Keywords: Social car · Connected car · Automotive User Interfaces · Interactive Vehicular Applications · Social Computing

1 Introduction

Usually, driving occurs in a situation where there are other road users. Accordingly, drivers need to coordinate with each other to share the infrastructure. Besides, the social relationship between drivers also influences the driving behavior [1]. But when we sit in "iron cages", there are only a few channels to exchange information between drivers. Lights, horn and speed information are the most frequently used tools to exchange information, limiting both the range and the bandwidth of the connectivity. This awkward situation leaves drivers with few ways of understanding the intentions of co-located drivers, and makes them struggle to figure out why other people do what they do [2]. Cars appear as machines, lacking any anthropomorphic (human-like) features [3]. With everywhere available connectivity and the broad penetration of social network services, the relationship between drivers on the road may gain more transparency, enabling social information to pass through the steel shell of the cars and giving opportunities to reduce anonymity and strengthen empathy as well as

© Springer International Publishing Switzerland 2014
E. Aarts et al. (Eds.): AmI 2014, LNCS 8850, pp. 315–327, 2014.
DOI: 10.1007/978-3-319-14112-1_25

eliminate boredom, loneliness and stress. This connectivity will lead to a boom of social applications on the road, which is gradually drawing attention both from the industry and academia. But this phenomenon has not been interpreted from a social computing perspective, and the acceptance of this trend by drivers is not clear.

Schroeter et al [4] discussed the social and geo-car concept, which enables the exchange of urban information and social expression, offering new opportunities for in-vehicle applications in the future. After an ideation workshop with urban informatics research experts, a rich list of concepts emerged. The authors established a model that combined the geo dimension and people dimension to illustrate the design space of the people layer of social information on the road. But they did not investigate the acceptance of these ideas and the factors that may influence the acceptance. Riener et al. [5] compared the state of drivers' current in-vehicle technology use and investigated their needs and wants for plausible new vehicle area network (VAN) services. But being based on an online survey, it was difficult to extrapolate to the future situation.

In this paper, we conduct s more in-depth investigation of what kind of social information drivers find useful and which factors influence the drivers' judgments.

1.1   Social Graph of the Future Road

The relationship on the road can be represented by a traditional social graph, such as Multigraph [6], which depicts multiple channels of social connection between actors. There are two levels of relationship in the driving situation: The Event layer, which represents the activities based on locations, and the community layer, which represents the social connection between drivers.

Figure 1 shows the current driving situation. From the perspective of location based events: sharing the road infrastructure is the only event that connects drivers on the road today. From the perspective of the community between drivers: when they sit in cars, the drivers see others as machines rather than social actors, lacking any anthropomorphic features. This lack has also been shown to contribute towards aggressive, selfish and anti-social driving behavior [3].

Recently, this situation has been changed by the everywhere available connectivity of the internet and the broad penetration of social network services [4]. Figure 2 shows the possible picture of the future driving activities.

For the event layer, connectivity allows drivers not to be restricted by physical time and space, which means drivers are able to participate in activities on other places and asynchronously. For example, driver A (Figure 2) who is currently involved in driving event 1, encountered ice on the road in driving event 2. The drivers C in event 2 are able to interact with the "shadow" of A (A1 in Figure 2) to receive a warning about the icy road. Furthermore, other kinds of information based on location may be generated, such as information about landscape, fuel discount and weather. These events provide opportunities for cooperation rather than competition on the road. For the community layer, a series of communities will be established to bring more transparency to the relationship between drivers. Different levels of relatedness humanize the car, evoking social awareness and preventing anti-social driving behavior. In addition, the communities allow personal expression, which is another way of identity besides the styling of the car.

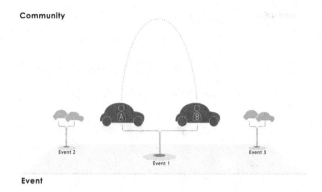

Fig. 1. Social graph of current driving activity

According to this social graph, if the connection between cars is established, plenty of information and social activities will emerge, which results in a boom of applications on the road.

1.2   Existing Initiatives Toward the Social Car

Nowadays, millions of social status updates and photos with location information are uploaded through Twitter, Facebook and Flicker etcetera every day. As a part of mobile Internet/Web, this wave is also emerging in the automotive domain. During the CES 2012 in Las Vegas, Mercedes Benz with its 2013 SL-Class model, showed an in-car platform able to connect and interact with Facebook. Drivers were able to insert messages by selecting pre-set messages with touch screen interfaces. In 2013, Volkswagen and Google launched an Android app called SmileDrive (smiledrive.vw.com), which enabled drivers to share their travelogue, filled with the captured photos, maps of the trip, status updates, as well as other memories that are collected on a single URL. Waze (www.waze.com), which has been acquired by Google at 1.1 billion dollars [7], is a highly engaged community of users willing to provide real-time traffic information. Beside apps based on the smart phone, automotive companies, IT companies and web companies have the ambition to establish platforms that provide an SDK for third party developers to create applications for the road. Although the understanding of connected cars in the future may be different, GM AppShop, Ford SYNC and the latest Apple's CarPlay allow third party apps running on their system, which may tremendously enrich in-vehicle applications.

The amount of applications will boom with the enhancement of the connectivity between drivers. But different organizations have distinct understanding of the future services based on the connected car. Because of the lacking of general rules underlying the structure of the social graph on the road and the difficulty in investigation of future concepts, it's hard to make predictions which direction will offer more opportunities among users.

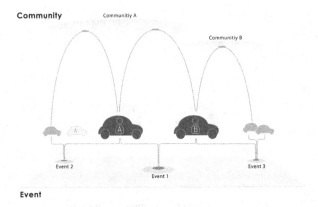

Fig. 2. Social graph of future driving activity

In this study, we applied the "CoConstructing Stories" Method [8] and integrated a group brainstorming method to generate initial concepts for social activities on the road, aiming to identify factors that influence people's acceptance as a reference for innovative design of social applications on the highway.

As the diversity of driving scenarios makes the research more complex, this research only focuses on highway driving, which requires less mental effort of drivers and concerns fewer elements (no pedestrians, traffic lights etc) than urban scenarios.

2   Methodology and Approach

The research involved two steps. In the first step, a brainstorm was conducted to obtain a set of ideas to discuss with potential users. In the second step, interviews were conducted with potential users using the "CoConstructing Stories" method. The CoConstructing Stories method is a participatory design technique for early, formative concept evaluation to elicit in-depth user feedback and suggestions. The development of the technique was motivated by the link between experiences, memories and dreams [8], and was based on the assumption that users are better prepared to judge whether novel design concepts will enable valuable experiences in the future if they revive their past experiences first. The social communication on the highway which is made possible by the development of ITS (Intelligent Transport Systems) technology, auto- pilot technology and novel HMI (Human-Machine Interface) technology, does not exist in current driving. As a result, we consider the CoConstructing stories method as an appropriate method by which researchers may create and evaluate fictional scenarios with participants.

2.1   Approach

Group Brainstorming and Categorization
The purpose of group brainstorming was to generate sufficient ideas for extensive analysis in the phase of CoConstructing stories. Three rounds of group brainstorming

sessions were run with 16 researchers and students of different disciplinary backgrounds (including bckgrounds such as industrial design, and computer science).

First, a warming-up session was conducted, in which participants were asked to write down 10 things they like/dislike about driving. Then they were asked 2 questions that guided the ideation: What kind of ideas you would like to exchange with other people on the highway? What kinds of information and data could you imagine to be conveyed to drivers in the future? The participants were required to write down these ideas on paper cards and pass on the cards to the person sitting next to them every 2 minutes for three times. They were encouraged to freely think of any ideas inspired by their own past experience.

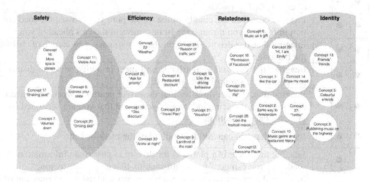

Fig. 3. The classification of concepts

After data clustering through all three brainstorming sessions, 30 ideas were generated in total. Initially, the ideas were categorized into briefly 8 themes: safety, comfort, efficiency, lifestyle, skill rating, sharing trips, free offers and communication. Later, the 8 categories were combined into 4 according to different levels of need [9] (see Figure 3). The hierarchy of categories from basic needs to higher needs is: Safety, Efficiency, Relatedness and Identity. The bordered categories are overlapping, because some of the concepts belong to both of them. Table 1 shows the description of all the concepts and the categories they belong to.

Table 1. Description of all the concepts. S, E, R, I indicate the category each concept belongs to. S: Safety; E: Efficiency; R: Relatedness; I: Identity. Some concepts belong to more than one category

S	E	R	I	Concepts
●				Imagine that you can remind the car behind you to keep distance..
●				Imagine that your seat vibrates from left to right to indicate that a car is going to overtake you from your rear of your left.
●				Imagine that your music volume goes down once the car in front of you suddenly breaks.
●	●			Imagine that you can discover a car running near yours cruises its way through automatic cruise control, self-driving etc.

Table 1. (*continued*)

●	●			Imagine your car can express your state: "I'm really in hurry!"
●	●			Imagine that you can check the driving skill of the driver whose car is in front of yours.
	●			Imagine that you are driving on the highway at night and can discover the nearest cars in front of you.
	●			Imagine that a driver whose child is seized with a serious sickness asks for priority on the emergency lane.
	●			When you are nearing your destination, you can get weather information there from other drivers in real time.
	●			Imagine that you can get fuel discount information if your fuel is low.
	●	●		Imagine that a driver on the road invites you to group with him for "group discount" in a restaurant.
	●	●		Imagine once you are caught in the traffic jam, you can see the road condition in front of you through the front camera of the cars ahead of you.
	●	●		Imagine that if a driver gives you the way to pass, you can "like" his driving behavior.
	●	●		Imagine that you and your friends will meet in a city; you can discuss the travel plan with your friends while driving.
	●	●		Imagine that you can discover that the driver nearby is working in a similar position or in the same industry as yours and that you are separated by two professional connections.
	●	●		Imagine that you can ask the landlord of the road for help
		●		Imagine that there is a platform for drivers to post some information on the road, and you can get filtered information that is relevant to you.
		●		Imagine that when you see a trendy car, you can ask for permission of his Facebook.
		●		Imagine that you can discover places that are recommended by other drivers or where drivers come often.
		●		Imagine that you can send a music track to the front car as a gift.
		●		Imagine you are caught in a traffic jam and having nothing to do. But you are invited to someone's personal FM. This time it is initiated by a driver with the topic "The match AJAX vs PSV tonight".
		●	●	Imagine that a car smiles to you, because it is the 10th times you pass each other on the highway. And you can get to know each other
		●	●	Facial expression of car to show the driver's mood: tired, angry
		●	●	Imagine that you can "like" the trendy car on the road.
		●	●	Imagine when you are on the road, the twitter messages of nearby drivers can be displayed.
		●	●	Imagine that you spot a trendy car on the road, you can check its music genre or restaurants history it often visits.
		●	●	You can get informed if a car nearby is from the same city and heading to the same destination as you.
			●	Imagine cars around you display the separation of friends between you and other drivers
			●	Imagine that some drivers can generate colorful "virtual shields" as decoration by augmented reality technology to show their personalities.
			●	Someone can publish the music that he is listening to.

Investigating User Opinions About Social Activities on the Highway Through the Co-constructing Stories Method

The CoConstructing stories method consists of two phases (Figure 4): sensitization and envisioning. The sensitization phase aims to make participants think about their past driving experiences, so that in the elaboration phase they can better envision the future. In the current study, in the sensitization phase pictures of relevant scenarios which were based on real driving experiences (Figure 5, Context Layer) were shown to the participant on the screen. After explaining each scenario, the researcher asked the user whether he recognized the story, and why or why not, engaging in a dialogue with the user and aiming to evoke relevant past experiences. Through questions the researcher encouraged the user to supplement the basic story with real life contents. As a result of this dialogue, user stories revealing past driver experiences were elicited that enriched the researcher's understanding of the current context of driving behaviors.

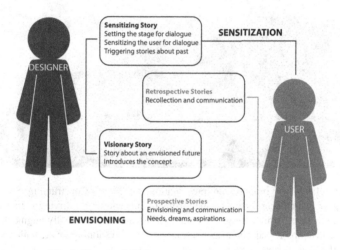

Fig. 4. Phases of CoConstructing Stories interviews

The second phase started with a 20 minute driving video in which 15 ideas were merged. The participants were seated in front of a TV and watched the video showing a driving situation. The video played until an image showing an idea appeared. Then the researcher paused the video, and told the story about this idea with the frame on the screen. Each frame consisted of 3 layers (Figure 5): 1. Context layer, which is an image clipped from the video. 2. Visualized information layer, which shows the social information in a visually augmented way. 3. Envisioning layer, which is the verbal description of each concept. After the explanation of the story, the researcher elicited positive and negative feedbacks about the concept by asking what the user liked and disliked in the story, and why. With these questions, the researcher encouraged the participant to supplement the basic story about the concept with contents representing anticipated future driving experiences, based on his needs, dreams and aspirations. At last, they were asked to fill three 7 points Likert type scales (ranging from -3 to 3), for Useful, Pleasant and Interesting. Additionally, they filled a summary scale for Degree of Liking, expressing the user's overall impression of the concept. The whole session lasted about forty minutes and was audio recorded. 22 participants attended the Co-Constructing stories sessions. They were divided into 2 groups of eleven participants each. One set of fifteen concepts was presented to group one, and the other set of fifteen concepts was presented to group two. All the participants were between 25-30 years old, and had more than 5 years driving experience. An impression of the setup is shown in Figure 6.

Fig. 5. Three layers of information presentation for the CoConstructing Stories method: 1. Context layer, which is an image clipped from a video showing a driving scenario. 2. Visualized information layer, which shows the social information in a visually augmented way (e.g. "Join me!" with icons for discount and restaurant). 3. Envisioning layer, which is the verbal description of each concept.

3   Results and Discussion

3.1   Analysis of Quantitative Data

For each idea, 11 participants gave ratings on four scales, Usefulness, Pleasure, Interest and Degree of Liking.

Correlations
To begin with, inter-scale correlations were calculated to see whether the different scales represented different constructs. Pearson correlations of the 4 dimensional data were found to be all quite high. The correlations between interest and Degree of Liking (0.919), usefulness and Degree of Liking (0.916) were a little higher than between pleasure and Degree of Liking (0.840) (Table 2). This suggests that Degree of Liking is related more to whether a concept is considered useful and interesting than whether it is considered pleasant.

Fig. 6. Setup for CoConstructing Stories method

Inspection of the correlations for the individual categories (Safety, Efficiency, Relatedness and Identity) indicate that the correlations between Degree of Liking and usefulness in the higher levels of hierarchy of needs ("relatedness" and "identity") are lower than in the lower levels of the hierarchy of needs ("safety" and "efficiency"). On the other hand, the correlations between Degree of Liking and pleasure, and Degree of Liking and interest in the higher levels of the hierarchy of needs are higher than those in the lower levels of the hierarchy of needs.

Descriptive Statistics

Figure 7 shows the average Usefulness, Pleasure, Interest and Degree of Liking score, ranging between -3 and +3, of the different concepts grouped by hierarchical need categories: Safety, Efficency, Relatedness, Identity (from left to right). Per category, individual bars represent individual ideas (some concepts belong to two categories and are included in both categories). Almost all concepts in the Safety and Efficiency groups receive positive ratings by the participants. The opinions for the concepts in the Relatedness and Identity categories fluctuate very much.

Table 2. The correlations of 4 dimensional data

		usefulness	pleasure	interest	likeness
usefulness	Pearson Correlation	1	.788**	.881**	.916**
	Sig. (2–tailed)		.000	.000	.000
	N	330	330	330	330
pleasure	Pearson Correlation	.788**	1	.816**	.840**
	Sig. (2–tailed)	.000		.000	.000
	N	330	330	330	330
interest	Pearson Correlation	.881**	.816**	1	.919**
	Sig. (2–tailed)	.000	.000		.000
	N	330	330	330	330
likeness	Pearson Correlation	.916**	.840**	.919**	1
	Sig. (2–tailed)	.000	.000	.000	
	N	330	330	330	330

**. Correlation is significant at the 0.01 level (2–tailed).

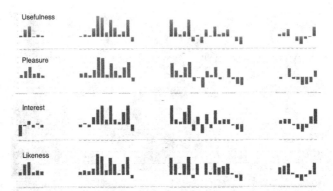

Fig. 7. Average ratings for the individual concepts, grouped by category. From left to right: Safety, Efficiency, Relatedness, Identity. Per category, individual bars represent individual concepts. Ratings range between -3 (minimum) and +3 (maximum). All ratings based on ratings from 11 participants.

Quantitative data provide the general feedback of acceptance of all the concepts from different categories, but what factors influence people to evaluate the concepts? The CoConstructing Stories method elicits in-depth feedback that is specific to the concepts. Some clues emerged from the conversation between the researcher and the participants. There are several main factors that appear to influence participants' feedback of the concepts. For different levels of needs, people pay attention to different aspect of concepts.

3.2   Analysis of Qualitative Data

For Safety concepts, people appear to have little tolerance of others' negative feedback. Receiving negative feedback while driving is considered very frustrating, especially if it comes from other drivers. For instance, if we take concept No.16 ("People can remind other drivers to keep distance"), participants believed they would dislike receiving this feedback from other drivers, but would be open toward being able to send the message themselves. In this category, encouraging people to display certain behavior, appreciating behavior or apologizing for certain behaviour are considered more helpful to enhance the on-road tolerance (Figure 8, concept No.15: "liking the driving behavior") than disliking other drivers' behavior.

For Efficiency concepts, people care very much about the simplicity of the information. They see spending attention on road information as an investment. Only efficient solutions that are properly timed gain acceptance. For example, the concepts No.19 ("People can get "fuel discount" information when their fuel is low") received a high score for Degree of Liking. But some complicated applications, such as concept No. 23 ("The driver can make a travel plan with their friends when driving") obtained less acceptance. Some participants said, "It's not the right place to discuss so complicated issues on the highway."

Fig. 8. Top 6 concepts which gained most acceptance: Concept 26 "Ask for priority"; Concept 19 "Fuel discount"; Concept 24 "Reason of traffic jam"; Concept 15 "Like the driving behavior"; Concept 7 "Volume down"; Concept 12 "Awesome Place".

With regards to the concepts belonging to the Relatedness and Identity categories, the Transparency and the type of Connection between drivers appeared to play a role. Transparency concerns the nature of the information that will be exchanged between drivers: with High Transparency, drivers share personal information like which restaurants they visit and their driving skill, mood or emotion. With Low Transparency, the nature of the information is more impersonal, like which music they like. Usually, the social activity on the highway is a social activity between strangers. Maintaining this social distance is considered very important. Some intermediary like music (Concept No. 24), which prevents leaking personal information but conveys personal identity could be useful to establish a temporary relationship.

With respect to Connection, Existing Connection concerns whether drivers have certain characteristics in common, such as when they work in the same company or whether they have passed each other several times before; it should be noted, though, that the drivers may not be aware of this existing connection. No Existing Connection concerns cases where such common history does not exist. Inspection of the pattern of results indicated that people don't like to interact with people with whom they share no common points. Concept No. 27 ("Twitter message of nearby drivers can be displayed") gains a very low score. " I don't care about the people I don't know" some participants said. But concept No. 2 ("You can get informed if a car nearby is from the same city and heading to the same destination as you") is more accepted by drivers. Also, most participants were not interested in strangers' expression of identity on the highway. They are confused to know the inner feeling of a stranger and they see the decoration of the strangers' car as distraction. On the other hand, for concepts involving the sharing of information between drivers between whom there is an existing connection, for example, if this personal expression is sent by family or friends, participants were more positive about the concept.

4   Conclusions and General Discussion

We investigated which types of concepts for social interaction between drivers are considered useful, pleasant, interesting and liked by drivers. Degree of liking was used as a summary rating. Looking at the Degree of Liking ratings, generally all the concepts belonging to the Safety and Efficiency categories received positive ratings by the participants.

As regards the concepts on the Relatedness and Identity groups, the results were mixed: some concepts were approved while others were clearly rejected. Closer inspection of the pattern of ratings and of the qualitative remarks suggested that for these categories additional factors are at hand. At least two such factors were identified: Transparency and the type of Connection between drivers. It appears that concepts involving the sharing of High Transparency information were liked less because of privacy considerations, and that the absence of an Existing Connection decreases the likelihood of a concept being liked: most participants were not interested to receive information about strangers on the road, especially in the Identity category. Combining the two factors, it appears that concepts which combine Low Transparency and Existing Connection have a high probability of being liked. A decision tree, shown in Figure 9, was created to summarize these results. However, as is clear from the decision tree, the additional factors by no means provide a complete understanding of the pattern of like and dislike, so that further research is needed.

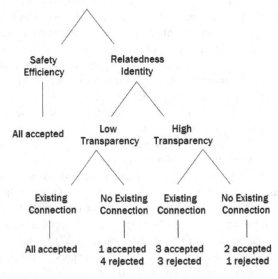

Fig. 9. Decision tree for liking of social car concepts

A set of 30 concepts is a very small sample comparing with the countless applications on the highway in the future. Considering additional concepts may provide clues for additional factors and may help to formulate more precise hypotheses about factors influencing whether concepts will be considered useful and will be liked by drivers. In addition, the scenarios considered were only highway scenarios. Concepts for other contexts such as urban environments will extend the research. Furthermore, the acceptance of applications depends on three distinct perspectives: utility, usability and cost. In this paper, we only considered utility. In future work, new prototypes will be made to investigate contributions of usability and cost, which is related to another important topic of acceptance: How can the information be conveyed to drivers in an appropriate way that balances safety, convenience and joy? Finally, all the efforts are helpful to generate insights about future transportation services for carmakers, governments and researchers.

Acknowledgements. This research has been funded by the Chinese Scholarship Council and facilitated by Eindhoven University of Technology.

References

1. Haglund, M., Åberg, L.: Speed choice in relation to speed limit and influences from other drivers. Transportation Research Part F: Traffic Psychology **3**, 39–51 (2000)
2. Juhlin, O.: Social Media on the Road. Springer Science & Business Media (2010)
3. Rakotonirainy, A., Feller, F., Haworth N. L.: Using in-vehicle avatars to prevent road violence. Centre for Accident Research & Road Safety - Qld (CARRS-Q); Faculty of Health; Institute of Health and Biomedical Innovation; School of Psychology & Counselling (2008)
4. Schroeter, R., Rakotonirainy, A., Foth, M.: The social car: new interactive vehicular applications derived from social media and urban informatics. In: Proceedings of Int'l Conf. on Automotive User Interfaces and Interactive Vehicular Applications 2012, pp. 107–110 (2012)
5. Riener, A.: Driver-vehicle confluence or how to control your car in future? In: Proceedings of Int'l Conf. on Automotive User Interfaces and Interactive Vehicular Applications 2012, pp. 217–224 (2012)
6. Gjoka, M., Butts, C.T., Kurant, M., Markopoulou, A.: Multigraph Sampling of Online Social Networks, arXiv.org, vol. 1008. p. 2565 (August 2010)
7. Waze, S.: Wikipedia.org. Available: http://en.wikipedia.org/wiki/Sachin_Waze (accessed: September 5, 2014)
8. Ozcelik-Buskermolen, D., Terken, J.: Co-constructing stories: a participatory design technique to elicit in-depth user feedback and suggestions about design concepts. In: PDC 2012, pp. 33–36 (August 2012)
9. Maslow, A.H.: A theory of human motivation. Psychological Review **50**(4), 370–396 (1943)

Privacy Classification for Ambient Intelligence

Jasper van de Ven(✉) and Frank Dylla

Cognitive Systems Group, SFB/TR 8 Spatial Cognition,
University of Bremen, Bremen, Germany
{vandeven,dylla}@informatik.uni-bremen.de

Abstract. In the field of ambient intelligence (AmI) privacy is recognized as one of the key factors regarding the acceptance of systems. However, this topic is mostly neglected or only addressed in a simplified form. Our approach is to understand *privacy as a service*, i.e., the AmI restricts its own knowledge rather than only hiding it. Through providing related vocabulary and a basic theory of privacy, we introduce a categorization of privacy related functionality and a classification of privacy affordances an AmI can provide. By investigating and evaluating small prototypical systems we propose a measure to compare different systems with respect to the balance between support provided and privacy.

1 Introduction

As technology and artificial intelligence are increasingly embedded in our everyday life, *ambient intelligence* (AmI)[1] becomes a part of our lives. AmI can support us by controlling our environment, e.g., control lights or heaters, provide desired information, or provide communication possibilities [1,2, e.g.]. The same publications also indicate that the main focus in the related research fields is on (supportive) functionality, design, and creation of systems. Furthermore, privacy is often identified as a key factor regarding the acceptance of AmI. However, due to complexity in most cases it is postponed or addressed only briefly and simplified.

With this work we address a novel approach to support privacy in AmI. The currently dominating common perspective of privacy is on what humans know or can learn about other humans. Furthermore, data available to a system is mostly regarded as save and thus data hiding is regarded as a possibility to provide privacy. However, we see data hiding as not strong and secure enough to guarantee privacy. In contrast, we consider *privacy as a service* preventing a system to contain information that may cause privacy violations. The idea is that if a system does not have information related to privacy violations, it cannot provide this information to other individuals and create privacy violations. Based on this notion, we derive a system classification regarding privacy capabilities. Furthermore, we provide exemplary design patterns to create systems for each category introduced. We investigate differences of these systems by evaluation on a set of simulated scenarios.

---

[1] For reasons of simplicity and generality, we will use the term AmI as synonym for comparable fields of research, e.g., smart environments and media spaces.

© Springer International Publishing Switzerland 2014
E. Aarts et al. (Eds.): AmI 2014, LNCS 8850, pp. 328–343, 2014.
DOI: 10.1007/978-3-319-14112-1_26

In Section 2 we provide definitions of privacy and an overview of AmI systems with a focus on privacy capabilities. Thereafter, we introduce and discuss an alternative definition of privacy focusing on systems rather than humans (Section 3). Based on this definition, a classification of systems is developed and evaluated from the perspective of functionality (Section 4) as well as affordance (Section 5). In order to evaluate systems regarding privacy in a more objective manner, we suggest a measure based on the amount of facts known to the system and the amount of occurring privacy violations (Section 6). We conclude by pointing out next steps to establish design patterns for privacy, applicable in the design and creation of AmI systems.

2   Related Work

Privacy has been acknowledged as an important topic in the field of AmI [2, e.g.]. In the following we will restrict our review of projects to media spaces. We apply this restriction to concentrate on systems consisting of hard- and software and that focus on supporting and connecting humans, i.e., that obviously pose privacy issues.

From our perspective a concrete definition of the concept of privacy within the context of AmI has not been provided so far. This is not surprising when realizing that even today a general understanding of the concept of privacy is not easily available [3–5, e.g.]. Based on this literature, simplified, two major conceptualizations of privacy can be distinguished. On the one hand the concept is defined through a *contextual integrity as a justificatory framework* expressing social norms regarding the access and availability of (personal) information [4, e.g.]. On the other hand it is defined by investigating *privacy problems* and cluster solutions to these problems [3, e.g.]. However, both concepts provide evidence that privacy can in general be understood as a restriction of information availability. Additionally, a common aspect of both approaches is that the concepts of privacy focus on humans. That is, information available to technological systems is only seen as critical if a malicious use occurs (or is possible), i.e., the actual threat are humans accessing information.

Regarding existing, i.e., really built, AmI projects examples include the *Ravenscroft Audio Video Environment* (RAVE) [6] supporting interpersonal communication. The *Family Window* project [7] aimed at providing awareness between separated family members via a video connection. The *ASTRA* project [8] supported awareness through asynchronous communication. A description and introduction of further projects, history, and findings in the field of media spaces are, for example, provided by [1, 2].

In Table 1 we provide a comparison of how privacy is addressed in a selection of existing AmI projects fulfilling our restriction to media spaces. We reviewed whether privacy issues are mentioned at all (*noticed*), a theory of privacy (a statement of how privacy is understood or defined) is provided (*theory*), and whether the implemented system provides a mechanism to handle privacy (*practice*), regardless whether a theoretical foundation is given or not. This comparison indicates, that privacy is acknowledged by most projects and a number of

Table 1. Projects & their consideration of privacy

project	noticed	theory	practice
VideoWindow (1990) [12]	✓		
Portholes (1992) [9]			
RAVE (1992) [6]	✓		o[1]
OfficeWalker (1998) [13]	✓		✓
Oxygen (2001) [14]	✓	o[2]	✓
Ambient Agoras (2002) [15]	✓[3]		
Smart Doorplates (2003) [16]			
Telemurals (2004) [10]	✓		✓
I2HOME (2006) [17]	✓		
ASTRA (2006) [8]	✓		o[4]
IRoom (2008) [18]			
Amigo (2008) [19]	✓	o[2]	
OASIS (2008) [20]	✓		
BAALL (2009) [21]			
Family Window (2010) [7]	✓		o[4]
ATRACO/iSpace[5] (2010) [11]	✓	✓	✓
Family Room (2014) [22]	✓		o[4]

(1) In practice provided by direct access and manipulation possibilities to sensors.

(2) List of issues or effects on a user, but no clear definition of privacy.

(3) Addressed on project website.

(4) Users are expected to negotiate privacy themselves.

(5) ATRACO framework was applied to and evaluated within the *iSpace* environment at the University of Essex.

projects even have some mechanisms to address privacy issues. However, out of 17 reviewed projects only one provides a theory of privacy.

The following three exemplary projects show how different privacy is addressed. The *Portholes* project [9] aimed at mediating awareness by providing regularly updated images of remote locations. This project was created within a controlled scientific environment and it seems that privacy has not been addressed at all. In the *Telemurals* [10] project two university dormitories were connected through an abstracted (distorted) video stream. The project addressed privacy as an issue as it was located at (semi-) public places. They approached the issue by distorting the transmitted video stream in a way, that people were not identifiable. The *Adaptive and TRusted Ambient eCOlogies* (ATRACO) project aimed at task-centered support and was applied to the iSpace smart environment for evaluation [11]. They based their theory of privacy on the notion of *information privacy* (data-hiding) and *territorial privacy* (ensuring specific privacy properties based on a user's location). In addition, they show how this can be implemented by applying a framework realizing so called *activity spheres*. Thus, privacy is added to an existing system, but not as a part of the underlying system design.

Regarding the reviewed projects, we suspect that the extreme difference in the number of projects acknowledging privacy and those handling privacy based on a formulated theory is due to the complexity of the general topic of privacy. Furthermore, the lack of available frameworks or design patterns providing respective functionality adds to this problem.

3 Privacy as a Service

One common aspect of all approaches to privacy we reviewed so far is that they are focused on information available to people. It seems, that technological systems are mostly regarded as trustworthy, at least by their developers. However, as privacy is regarded as a key acceptance factor for ambient intelligence, a system not only needs to ensure privacy, but also to enforce the trust of users that their privacy is addressed. Thus, we aim at an understanding of *privacy as a service* in AmI, i.e., systems that support a theory of privacy and clearly state how the privacy of their users is handled. In order to pursue this aim, first, we need to clarify the terms privacy and privacy policy as well as private and shared information to provide a basis for discussion. Next, we will introduce our privacy service theory, which diverts from previous notions by focusing on knowledge available to a system and not to humans. Furthermore, to illustrate our theory, we introduce a hypothetical system and its fundamental functionality. This system is used later on to illustrate different classes of privacy handling.

Privacy vs privacy policy: We explicitly discriminate between privacy (the theory) and a privacy policy (an instantiation). We separate these two as a policy is a set of restrictions that reflects specific privacy needs. Therefore, a policy can be considered context dependent. However, a sound theory should abstract from contextual aspects. Hence, we propose a *theory of privacy in ambient intelligence based on restrictions of existence, availability, and access to information.* In this context *existence* addresses whether some information is contained in the environment or the AmI, e.g. that an individual exists. *Availability* addresses where a specific information exists. Finally, *access* addresses specific access rights to specific information, e.g., which entity is allowed to access which information in what context. So far, this understanding of privacy is comparable to other existing notions as addressed in Section 2.

Private vs shared information: In general, we can distinguish two kinds of information: *private*, i.e., only available to a single entity, and *shared*, i.e., available to at least two entities. Regarding the exchange of information, two general approaches come to mind: a *centralized* and a *distributed* one. Simplified, in case of a centralized approach entities do not exchange information directly, but via a central entity where information is available to any other entity. In contrast, in the distributed approach entities communicate directly. In both cases information might cause privacy violations the moment it is communicated to some other entity. Additionally, in the centralized approach the central entity is a significant source of privacy violations as it only contains shared information. The major point is that if information is shared, the communicating entity loses control of what is done with the information.

System: In order to transfer the notion of privacy based on keeping information private, i.e., unknown to ambient intelligence, we use the system framework

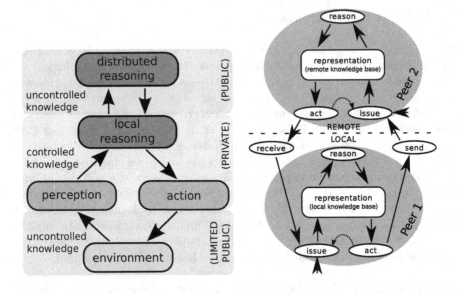

Fig. 1. Ambient intelligence framework

Fig. 2. Representation & reasoning cluster system (RRCS)

provided in [23] as a foundation (cf. Figure 1). It divides a system into three layers regarding functionality: the *environment* layer (orange box), the *interaction* layer (blue boxes), and the *reasoning* layer (brown boxes). We assume that the interaction layer takes care of any kind of transfer between sensors, actuators respectively, and the internal representation, i.e., transforms raw sensor data like video images or laser scans to *abstractions* like objects, numerical values, or relations. The framework also provides an understanding of available information exchange channels. Building on this we introduce a classification regarding the availability of information: *public*, *limited public*, and *private*. Public information addresses information that is stored in a shared location or was propagated and thus, is not under the sole control of the entity where it was created. Limited public information is only available to entities physically present at the location where the information exists. Private information addresses information only available to the entity where it was created. Therefore, we have to distinguish *local reasoning* based on private information and shared information and *distributed reasoning* based on only shared information.

However, the concepts of privacy addressed up to this point are still centered around knowledge available to other entities. Regarding the idea of *privacy as a service* this focus is changed to a system's internal perspective, i.e., centered around knowledge available to the system. The assumption is, that a system cannot violate a user's privacy if it does not posses related information. Thus, privacy as a service means, that an AmI is interested in not possessing any information creating a privacy violation.

In order to introduce and investigate different possibilities to enable such privacy services, we introduce a simple prototypical system. It is based on the AmI framework introduced above (Figure 1) and implements a mostly functional system design pattern. Our exemplary system consists of connected *peers* each created using a number of functions, initially provided parameters, and a knowledge base. In Figure 2 we exemplify our design pattern based on two peers, which we call *representation & reasoning cluster system* (RRCS). Circles denote functions, boxes denote a knowledge representation, i.e., in our case knowledge bases and parameters, and arrows denote the flow of information. In the following, we detail all functions necessary to RRCS by providing a signature and a short description. Within signature descriptions we will use $Time$ (a specific time point t), $Fact$ (a datum f with a time point, e.g., ("x close y", @t)), $Peer$ (a unique peer identifier p), and $Rule$ (an inference rule r, e.g., "if *cond* then f").

- $update : \{Fact\} \times Time \rightarrow \{Fact\}$
  Given a set of facts F, e.g., the current knowledge base available, and a time point t, *update* generates a new set of facts containing all facts contained in F and adds all facts holding at $t - 1$ as also holding at t in the new set of facts.[2]
- $perceive : Time \rightarrow \{Fact\}$
  The *perceive* function aggregates all abstracted sensor readings available at t and provides them as a set of facts.
- $issue : \{Fact\} \times \{Fact\} \times Time \rightarrow \{Fact\}$
  Given two sets of facts (F_1, F_2) and a time point t *issue* returns a set of facts, where all facts from F_2 are added (or removed) to F_1 at t. For example, F_1 represents the current knowledge base available and F_2 contains new knowledge from the sensors, *issue* generates a new aggregated set of facts.[2]
- $receive : \{Peer\} \times Time \rightarrow \{Fact\}$
  Given a set of peers P and a time point t *receive* aggregates any information provided by $p \in P$ at t and returns it as a set of facts.
- $reason : \{Fact\} \times \{Rule\} \times Time \rightarrow \{Fact\}$
  Given F, t and a set of inference rules R, *reason* applies all $r \in R$ based on all facts in F which hold at t. A set of facts containing all facts contained in F combined with the gained facts is returned.[2]
- $propagate : \{Fact\} \times Peer \times Time \rightarrow \{Fact\}$
  Given F, t, and a specific peer p, *propagate* provides a set of facts with all facts from F holding at t to be propagated to p at t.
- $act : \{Fact\} \times \{Rule\} \times Time \rightarrow \emptyset$
  Given F, t, and R, *act* tries to execute actions (given by applying $r \in R$ to F) at t to the environment.
- $send : Peer \times \{Fact\} \times Time \rightarrow \emptyset$
  Given p, F, and t, *send* will transmit F to p at t.

---

[2] We are aware that in most cases it is reasonable to work with consistent sets of facts only. Due to brevity and generality, we neglect this concern here.

Input: kb, rules, actions, peers, time, policy, smodel

```
1  repeat
2  │    kb ← update(kb, time);
3  │    MACRO1
   │    //start perception step
4  │    kb ← issue(kb, (perceive(time) ∪ receive(peers, time)), time);
5  │    MACRO2
   │    //start reasoning step
6  │    kb ← reason(kb, rules, time);
7  │    MACRO3
   │    //start action step
8  │    for peer in peers do
9  │    └    send(peer, propagate(kb, peer, time), time);
10 │    act(kb, rules, time);
11 until TRUE; time ← time + 1;
```

Algorithm 1. Exemplary implementation of the control structure of an RRCS peer

In Algorithm 1 we introduce a prototype of the internal control structure of a peer of an ambient intelligence. It takes an initial knowledge base (kb), i.e., a set of facts, a set of inference rules for reasoning (*rules*), a set of peers being part of the system as well (*peers*), and an initial time point (*t*). Two further parameters are provided, but only used later on while illustrating privacy functionality. These are a privacy policy (*policy*) and a sensor model (*smodel*) providing possible future sensor perceptions. In each iteration first the time of kb is updated. Subsequently, all new information, either provided by sensors or by other peers, is integrated to kb (line 4) and all reasoning rules are applied to this new kb (line 6). Furthermore, information is sent to other peers. Finally, all rules which imply an action to the environment are applied.

We will use this exemplary implementation later (Section 5) to demonstrate strategies to address privacy in ambient intelligence by replacing the macro markers in lines 3, 5, and 7. To achieve this, we will now introduce classifications of privacy from a perspective of functionality as well as affordances.

4   Categories of Privacy Functionality

Privacy functionality addresses methods and processes to handle privacy related tasks in an AmI. We distinguish four different categories of functionality to *detect*, *resolve*, *pretect*, and *shield* from privacy violations. In the following we present a description for each category and give a general signature afterwards.

Violation detection addresses methods and processes allowing a system to detect existing privacy violations. That is, identifying information which creates a conflict within a given knowledge base (KB) regarding a given privacy policy ($Policy$) for a given point in time ($Time$). In case any rule from the policy can be applied, a violation is confirmed and *detect* returns *True*. Otherwise the return value is *False*. This results in the following signature:

$$detect : KB \times Policy \times Time \rightarrow True, False$$

Violation resolution addresses methods and processes to resolve existing privacy violations within a given knowledge base regarding a given privacy policy at a point in time. In case the knowledge base contains a privacy violation wrt. the policy, *resolve* returns a knowledge base not containing any violation, otherwise the original knowledge base is returned:

$$resolve : KB \times Policy \times Time \rightarrow KB$$

A simple but radical example for resolving violations would be to return an empty knowledge base. However, the removal of all information would prevent identification of possibilities to support users. Thus, an additional requirement should be to keep as much information of the original knowledge base as possible.

Violation pretection addresses methods and processes to pretect[3], i.e., predict a privacy violation at a future point in time. As this requires the system to project to the future, a model (*Projections*) predicting future sensor perceptions and information provided by other peers, as well as a set of reasoning rules (*Rules*) have to be provided to the function. If there exist one or more perceptions from the model which cause a privacy violation, it is possible that a privacy violation actually emerges in future. Thus, the function returns *True*. We specifically do not restrict how information can be generated, e.g., by application of inference rules or other reasoning mechanisms. This results in the following signature:

$$pretect : KB \times Projections \times Rules \times Policy \times Time \rightarrow True, False$$

Violation shielding addresses methods and processes to prevent a privacy violation from occurring at all. That is, it shields a knowledge base from adding information (*Input*), i.e., a set of facts, that in combination with a given privacy policy could cause a privacy violation in the future. This requires the system to also check for privacy violations after (possibly) multiple iterations of the internal update and reasoning processes. The knowledge base returned is a combination of the provided knowledge base and additional information, if the new knowledge base does not contain any privacy violation, even after reasoning:

$$shield : KB \times Input \times Rules \times Policy \times Time \rightarrow KB$$

Regarding the provided signatures, these do not necessarily have to have the introduced form for all possibly existing methods and processes of a category. For example, it might be desirable to return a list of existing privacy violations instead of *True* or *False* for the detection or pretection functionality. However, due to simplicity, we assume the introduced signatures for the remainder of this work.

---

[3] Term is derived from prediction and detection

5   Privacy Affordance Classification

Applying combinations of privacy functionality to the general AmI system introduced earlier (see Algorithm 1), we derive six classes of privacy affordance: *privacy oblivious systems* (POS), *privacy aware systems* (PAS), *privacy repairing
systems* (PRS), *privacy projecting systems* (PPS), *privacy conserving systems*
(PCS), and *privacy shielding systems* (PSS). In the following we describe which
privacy functionality has to be applied for each privacy affordance class.

Privacy oblivious systems (POS) neither include any functionality for detecting, resolving, pretecting, nor predicting violations. Thus, these systems do not
handle or address privacy at all. The system design provided in Algorithm 1 is
suitable for a privacy oblivious system, as no privacy functionality is included.

Privacy aware systems (PAS) include functionality for violation detecting only.
Thus, these systems are able to detect existing violations regarding a provided
privacy policy. This information could be used to inform a user that his or
her privacy is being violated. However, a system affording privacy awareness
is not able to address any privacy violation detected as it does not include any
functionality to resolve these conflicts. Furthermore, it is noteworthy that such a
system only detects privacy conflicts that do already exist. To obtain the design
for a privacy aware system, replace the macros (MACRO1, MACRO2, and MACRO3)
in Algorithm 1 with Algorithm 2.

Privacy repairing systems (PRS) include functionality for violation resolution
and most likely, but not necessarily for violation detection. Functionality for violation pretection or prevention is not included. Thus, the system is able to resolve
existing privacy violations. This enables it to traverse from a state with existing
privacy violations to a state without privacy violations. As privacy functionality to resolve violations will in most cases include the functionality of violation
detection, these systems are in most cases also able to detect existing privacy violations. However, regarding the simple *remove all* resolution approach, a detection is not necessary. Nevertheless, such a system would not be very useful as
it will have not left any information to infer support possibilities. It has to be
noted that such a system is not able to prevent the creation of privacy conflicts
and thus, the (short-term) existence of privacy violations. To obtain the design
for a privacy repairing system replace the macros (MACRO1, MACRO2, and MACRO3)
in Algorithm 1 with Algorithm 3. It has to be mentioned that line 1 of Algorithm
3 is not necessary and only limits the calls to the resolve functionality.

```
1 if detect(kb,policy,time) then
      //announce privacy violation
```

Algorithm 2. Privacy addressing for privacy aware systems

```
1  if detect(kb, policy, time) then
2  |  kb ← resolve(kb, policy, time);
```

Algorithm 3. Privacy addressing for privacy repairing systems

Privacy projecting systems (PPS) include functionality for violation pretection (and implied violation detection), but not violation resolution nor violation prevention. Thus, a system is able to predict possible (near-)future privacy violations regarding a provided privacy policy. Using this information a user could be warned about the possibility of having her or his privacy violated. Furthermore, a system might be able to provide information about which action would lead to a privacy violation. This would enable users to protect their privacy. However, the system itself is not able to prevent the creation of a privacy violation or resolve it. To obtain the design for a privacy projecting system replace MACRO1 with Algorithm 4. If additional privacy detection functionality is desired insert Algorithm 2 directly after Algorithm 4 and also replace the macros MACRO2 and MACRO3 with it.

```
1  for perception in smodel do
2  |  if pretect(kb, perception, rules, policy, time) then
   |  |  //address possible privacy violation
```

Algorithm 4. Privacy addressing for privacy projecting systems

Privacy conserving systems (PCS) include functionality for violation pretection (and implied violation detection), violation resolution, but not violation preservation. Thus, the system is able to predict possible (near-)future privacy violations regarding a provided privacy policy and resolve them when they exist. However, the system is not able to prevent violations based on the pretection, but this information could be provided to users to allow them to ensure their own privacy. The system can only resolve violations that already exist. To obtain the design for a privacy conserving system replace macro MACRO1 with Algorithm 4 directly followed by Algorithm 3 and also replace the macros MACRO2 and MACRO3 with Algorithm 3.

Privacy shielding systems (PSS) include functionality for violation prevention. Thus, a system is able to prevent privacy violations from ever occurring. Furthermore, as privacy violations cannot be created, neither detection, resolution, nor pretection is needed. However, a system could comprise this functionality to create the violation shielding functionality. Algorithm 5 provides a design for a privacy aware system.

In Table 2 we provide an overview of the privacy affordance categories introduced above.

Input: kb, rules, actions, peers, time, policy, smodel
1 **repeat**
2   kb ← update(kb, time);
     //start perception step
3   kb ← shield(kb, (perceive(time) ∪ receive(peers, time)), policy, time);
     //start reasoning step
4   kb ← reason(kb, rules, time);
     //start action step
5   **for** *peer in peers* **do**
6   ⌊ send(peer, propagate(kb, peer, time), time);
7   act(kb, actions, time);
8 **until** *TRUE; time ← time + 1*;

Algorithm 5. Privacy shielding system

Table 2. Privacy functionality required for privacy affordances

	detection	resolution	pretection	shielding
privacy oblivious systems (POS)				
privacy aware systems (PAS)	✓			
privacy repairing systems (PRS)	(✓)	✓		
privacy projecting systems (PPS)	(✓)		✓	
privacy conserving systems (PCS)	(✓)	✓	✓	
privacy shielding systems (PSS)	(✓)	(✓)	(✓)	✓

() Implied by other privacy functionality
used or possible, but without impact

6   A Privacy Balance Measure

The question is now how useful or satisfying are systems that are designed based on the concepts introduced above. In order to investigate this issue, we implemented such systems in a prototypical manner. One major question is: "how much does a user benefit from the different designs?". Therefore, we derive a measure, called *privacy balance*, that relates the number of known facts, possible violations, and detected violations. As there will always be a trade-off between service (knowing all facts) and privacy (knowing no fact), the measure should reflect this. In order to approach such a measure we give three small example scenarios (depicted in Figure 3) and calculate the maximum number of informational facts in the knowledge base, existing privacy violations, and reasoning rules fired at each point in time. These numbers are used as the *baseline* for a scenario.

    Each scenario is composed of an environment and a sequence of sensor readings. The environment is a corridor (F) with a connected room (R). Furthermore, several sensors exist (N1, N2) whose sensor ranges separate the corridor

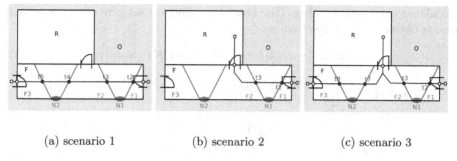

(a) scenario 1   (b) scenario 2   (c) scenario 3

Fig. 3. Scenario depictions

into subregions (N1, N2, F1-F3). R is not covered by a sensor. The blue line in the environment depicts the movement of a person ($P1$) as perceived by a sensor at a specific time point. For reasons of simplicity, time is measured by counting sensor readings. Each blue circle resembles an emitted reading from the sensors. While empty circles denote empty sensor readings, each filled circle represents a sensor reading perceiving person $P1$. Each sensor reading consists of a set of informational facts, where each informational fact consists of a string representing a meaningful symbol and a time stamp. An exemplary sensor reading for time point $t2$ (valid for all scenarios) is provided by the following set of facts:

```
("(P1 in N1)", @t2), ("-(P1 in N2)", @t2), ("-(P1 in F1)", @t2),
("-(P1 in F2)", @t2), ("-(P1 in F3)", @t2), ("(P1 in F1)", @t1),
("-(P1 in F2)", @t1), ("-(P1 in F3)", @t1)
```

The privacy policy contains a single rule: "it must not be known that $P1$ is in R". Furthermore, the system contains reasoning rules implying that if a person lingers in region $F2$ for a certain period of time, then the person is considered to have entered R.

We recorded the number of existing violations and known facts in the knowledge base at three points during the systems main execution loop for each point in time, i.e., violations after update (VAU), before reasoning (VBR), and before action (VBA), and facts after update (FAU), before reasoning (FBR), and before action (FBA). Furthermore, we recored the number of detected violations after update (DAU), after issuing or shielding (DAI), and after reasoning (DAR), as well as the number of pretected violations (DPP). The derivation of values needs to be done for each scenario individually.

These values are used to gain a value indicating the ratio between maximally available numbers in the baseline of the scenario and the recorded number. The privacy balance consists of three independent values: (1) the ratio between available and maximal informational facts in the knowledge base (knowledge available – KA) , (2) the ratio between existing and maximally possible privacy violations (violation protection – VP), and (3) a value relating detected and protected privacy violations (known violations – KV). The equations used to calculate these values are presented in Equations 1 - 4. We denominate the set providing the calculated maximum numbers (the baseline) b and the set providing the actual results obtained using a system e.

$$PB(time) = (KA(time); VP(time); KV(time)) \qquad (1)$$

$$KA(t) = \begin{cases} 1 & \text{if } v_b(t) = 0 \\ \frac{k_e(t)}{k_b(t)} & \text{else} \end{cases}$$

$$VP(t) = \begin{cases} 0 & \text{if } v_b(t) = 0 \\ 1 & \text{if } v_e(t) > v_b(t) \\ 1 - \frac{v_e(t)}{v_b(t)} & \text{else} \end{cases} \qquad (2)$$

$$KV(t) = \begin{cases} 0 & \text{if } v_b(t) = 0 \text{ or } v_e(t) < 0 \\ 1 & \text{if } v_e(t) > v_b(t) \\ 1 - \frac{((2*v_e(t))-(d_e(t)+p_e(t)))}{2*v_b(t)} & \text{else} \end{cases}$$

$$v_{\langle set \rangle}(t) = \sum_{i=0}^{t}((VAU_i^{\langle set \rangle} + VAI_i^{\langle set \rangle} + VAR_i^{\langle set \rangle}) * \frac{i}{time})$$

$$k_{\langle set \rangle}(t) = \sum_{i=0}^{t}(FAU_i^{\langle set \rangle} + FBR_i^{\langle set \rangle} + FBA_i^{\langle set \rangle})$$

$$\qquad (3)$$

$$d_{\langle set \rangle}(t) = \sum_{i=0}^{t}((DAU_i^{\langle set \rangle} + DAI_i^{\langle set \rangle} + DAR_i^{\langle set \rangle}) * \frac{i}{time})$$

$$p_{\langle set \rangle}(t) = \sum_{i=1}^{t}((DPP_{i-1} * pretectfactor_{\langle set \rangle}(i)) * \frac{i}{time})$$

$$pretectfactor_{\langle set \rangle}(t) = fVAU_{\langle set \rangle}(t) + fVAI_{\langle set \rangle}(t) + fVAR_{\langle set \rangle}(t)$$

$$fVAU_{\langle set \rangle}(t) = \begin{cases} 1 & \text{if } DPP_{t-1} \leq VAU_t^{\langle set \rangle} \\ 0 & \text{else} \end{cases}$$

$$fVAI_{\langle set \rangle}(t) = \begin{cases} 1 & \text{if } DPP_{t-1} \leq VAI_t^{\langle set \rangle} \\ 0 & \text{else} \end{cases} \qquad (4)$$

$$fVAR_{\langle set \rangle}(t) = \begin{cases} 1 & \text{if } DPP_{t-1} \leq VAR_t^{\langle set \rangle} \\ 0 & \text{else} \end{cases}$$

The results for scenario 2 and scenario 3 are provided in Figure 4. They indicate the usefulness of the proposed privacy balance measure, as a distinction between systems of different privacy affordance classes is possible. The result of scenario 1 is not presented as it does not contain any privacy violations and only provides the highest possible privacy balance value (1; 1; 1), i.e., all possible information is available and no privacy violations exist at all points in time. This is used as a test case where all systems show the same result.

Figure 4(a) provides the results for scenario 2. Here, a single privacy violation occurs and lasts till the end of the scenario. The results provided by Figure

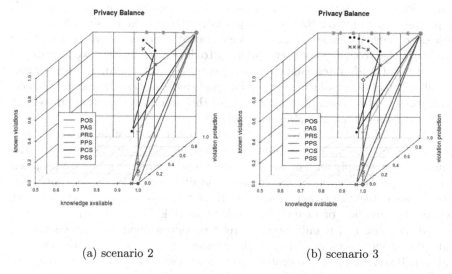

(a) scenario 2   (b) scenario 3

Fig. 4. Evaluation results (abbreviations are explained in section 5)

4(b) address scenario 3 with one temporary privacy violation. They show that the privacy oblivious system (POS) keeps all available information, but does not provide any form of privacy (final privacy balance value of (1; 0; 0)). On the other hand, the privacy shielding system (PSS) loses approximately 50% of the maximally available knowledge, but provides absolute privacy protection (final privacy balance value of (0.576; 1; 1)). As a last example, the result for the privacy conserving system (PCS) clearly shows that a privacy violation happened, but also that it was known beforehand. Furthermore, the repairing part leads to a loss of available knowledge, but smaller than with the PSS. The final privacy balance value is (0.682; 0.909; 1).

These combined results show that it is possible to distinguish between the different privacy affordance classes based on the privacy balance measure introduced. Furthermore, this indicates that the suggested affordance classification is suitable to classify systems in the field of ambient intelligence regarding privacy handling aspects.

However, it has to be noted that the underlying scenario is an important factor regarding the results, i.e., if systems are to be compared they have to be evaluated using the same scenario and the result is not a general factor. In addition, the utilized scenarios are small and based on the same domain, which could have had an influence on the results obtained.

7   Conclusion

Many approaches in AmI are focussed on pragmatic aspects as functionality and design. Although, privacy is recognized as an important issue, it is neglected in most cases. In order to support a more strict integration of privacy in AmI, we propose a perspective change from *privacy as knowledge availability to other entities* to *privacy as a service*, i.e., systems being aware of and restricting their own knowledge to ensure the users' privacy. To illustrate our view, we introduced a prototypical AmI system and extracted four categories regarding privacy functionality: detection, resolution, pretection, and shielding. Furthermore, based on integrating combinations of functionality to this system, we derived six system classes affording different instances of privacy.

The goal of AmI is to provide as much support as possible, which in turn requires to keep as much information as possible. This contradicts with the requirement to comply with privacy in many cases. Therefore, we gave a proposal of a *privacy balance measure* which relates available knowledge, and potential, actual, and detected privacy violations. However, this measure is only a first step in the direction of quantifying privacy, as it is highly dependent on the applied scenario, i.e., it only provides relative values regarding the knowledge and privacy violations available in the scenario given. Furthermore, we used only small scenarios and one prototypical implementation.

Thus, as a next step we will work on larger benchmarks consisting of several large artificial and real world scenarios. Using this benchmark set, we aim at comparing existing systems to gain a better understanding of the current state of implemented privacy handling methods. In addition we aim at implementing a distributed prototype to investigate differences between centralized and distributed AmI regarding privacy as a service. This directly leads to the question of using a single privacy policy vs. multiple different policies.

Acknowledgement. We acknowledge funding by the German Research Foundation (DFG) via the Spatial Cognition Research Center (SFB/TR 8) project R3-[Q-Shape] and the DFG project SOCIAL.

References

1. Dewan, P., Ehrlich, K., Greenberg, S., Johnson, C., Prakash, A., Dourish, P., Ellis, C., Ishii, H., Mackay, W.E., Roseman, M.: Computer supported co-operative work. John Wiley & Sons Ltd (1999)
2. Harrison, S.: Media Space 20 + Years of Mediated Life. Computer Supported Cooperative Work. Springer, London (2009)
3. Solove, D.J.: Understanding Privacy. Harvard University Press (2008)
4. Nissenbaum, H.: Privacy in Context - Technology, Policy, and the Integrity of Social Life. Stanford University Press (2010)
5. Solove, D.J.: Nothing to Hide - The False Tradeoff between Privacy and Security. Yale University Press (2011)
6. Gaver, W., Moran, T., MacLean, A., Lövstrand, L., Dourish, P., Carter, K., Buxton, W.: Realizing a video environment: EuroPARC's RAVE system. In: Proceedings of CHI, ACM. (1992)
7. Judge, T., Neustaedter, C., Kurtz, A.: The family window: the design and evaluation of a domestic media space. In: Proceedings of CHI, ACM (2010)

8. Romero, N., Markopoulos, P., Baren, J., Ruyter, B., IJsselsteijn, W., Farshchian, B.: Connecting the family with awareness systems. Personal and Ubiquitous Computing 11(4) (2006)
9. Dourish, P., Bly, S.: Portholes: supporting awareness in a distributed work group. In: Proceedings of CHI. ACM (1992)
10. Karahalios, K., Donath, J.: Telemurals. In: Proceedings of CHI, USA. ACM (2004)
11. Könings, B., Wiedersheim, B., Weber, M.: Privacy Management and Control in ATRACO. In: de Ruyter, B., Wichert, R., Keyson, D.V., Markopoulos, P., Streitz, N., Divitini, M., Georgantas, N., Mana Gomez, A. (eds.) AmI 2010. LNCS, vol. 6439, pp. 51–60. Springer, Heidelberg (2010)
12. Fish, R.S., Kraut, R.E., Chalfonte, B.L.: The VideoWindow system in informal communication. In: Proceedings of the 1990 ACM Conference on Computer-Supported Cooperative Work. ACM (1990)
13. Obata, A., Sasaki, K.: OfficeWalker: A virtual visiting system based on proxemics. In: Proceedings of the 1998 ACM Conference on Computer Supported Cooperative Work. ACM (1998)
14. Rudolph, L.: Project Oxygen: Pervasive, Human-Centric Computing – An Initial Experience. In: Dittrich, K.R., Geppert, A., Norrie, M. (eds.) CAiSE 2001. LNCS, vol. 2068, pp. 1–12. Springer, Heidelberg (2001)
15. Prante, T., Stenzel, R., Röcker, C., Streitz, N., Magerkurth, C.: Ambient Agoras: InfoRiver, SIAM, Hello. Wall. In: CHI '04 Extended Abstracts on Human Factors in Computing Systems, New York, USA. ACM (2004)
16. Trumler, W., Bagci, F., Petzold, J., Ungerer, T.: Smart doorplate. Personal and Ubiquitous Computing 7(3–4) (2003)
17. Alexandersson, J., Richter, K., Becker, S.: I2HOME: Benutzerzentrierte Entwicklung einer offenen standardbasierten Smart Home -Plattform. In: Proceedings of USEWARE 2006 in German (1946, 2006)
18. Bellik, Y., Jacquet, C.: From the Intelligent Room to Ambient Intelligence 1st Digiteo Annual Forum, Poster (2008)
19. Janse, M.: Amigo-Ambient Intelligence for the Networked Home Environment. Philips Research (August, 2008)
20. Bekiaris, E., Bonfiglio, S.: The OASIS Concept. In: Stephanidis, C. (ed.) Universal Access in HCI, Part I, HCII 2009. LNCS, vol. 5614, pp. 202–209. Springer, Heidelberg (2009)
21. Krieg-Brückner, B., Gersdorf, B., Döhle, M., Schill, K.: Technik für senioren in spe im bremen ambient assisted living lab. Ambient Assisted Living-AAL (2009)
22. Oduor, E., Neustaedter, C.: The Family Room: A Multi-camera, Multi-display Family Media Space. In: Proceedings of the Companion Publication of the 17th ACM Conference on Computer Supported Cooperative Work and Social Computing. CSCW Companion, New York, USA. ACM (2014)
23. Van de Ven, J., Schmid, F., Hesselmann, T., Boll, S.: A Framework for Communication and Interaction in Spatially Distributed Social Groups. In: Proceedings of SISSI, Denmark (2010)

Author Index

Printed in the United States
By Bookmasters